America's
Working
Women

Other works by Rosalyn Baxandall

Picture Windows: Race and Sex in Suburbia

Words on Fire: The Life and Writing of Elizabeth Gurley Flynn

Other works by Linda Gordon

Pitied but Not Entitled: Single Mothers and the History of Welfare

Woman's Body, Woman's Right: A Social History of Birth Control in America (2nd edition)

Heroes of Their Own Lives: The Politics and History of Family Violence

Cossack Rebellions: Social Turmoil in the Sixteenth-Century Ukraine

America's Working Women

Women

A DOCUMENTARY HISTORY

1600 TO THE PRESENT

Edited by

Rosalyn Baxandall
and Linda Gordon

with Susan Reverby

REVISED AND UPDATED

W· W· Norton & Company

New York   London

The text of this book is composed in 10.5/12.5 Electra
with the display set in Bodoni Bold and Helvetica
Composition and manufacturing by The Maple-Vail Book
Manufacturing Group

Library of Congress Cataloging-in-Publication Data

America's working women : a documentary history, 1600 to the
    present / edited by Rosalyn Baxandall and Linda Gordon.—Rev.
    and updated.
        p.   cm.
    Includes bibliographical references.
    1. Women—Employment—United States—History—
    Sources.   2. Women—Employment—United States—
    History.   I. Baxandall, Rosalyn Fraad, 1939–   .   II. Gordon, Linda.
HD6095.A662   1995
331.4'0973—dc20   94-32194

ISBN 0-393-03653-7
ISBN 0-393-31262-3 (pbk)

W. W. Norton & Company, Inc.,
500 Fifth Avenue, New York, N.Y. 10110
W. W. Norton & Company Ltd.
10 Coptic Street, London WC1A 1PU

1 2 3 4 5 6 7 8 9

For all the women, past and present,
who work to make a living and a
life, and to the women's liberation
movement, which inspired our
interest in women's history.

Contents

CONTENTS

CONTENTS

CONTENTS

Illustrations follow pages 80 and 242

Preface to the First Edition

MANY people contributed time, energy and inspiration to this book. Some gave, in addition, ideas, historical materials, and criticisms. For this vital assistance we wish to thank: Carolyn Ashbaugh, Lee and Finney Baxandall, Marlou Belyea, Janet Bertinuson, Dorothy Rose Blumberg and Albert Blumberg, Jeremy Brecher, Susan Porter Benson, Frank Brodhead, Susan Bucknell, Charlotte Bunch, Nancy Cott, Marlyn Dalsimer, Bruce Dancis, Ellen DuBois, Alex Efthim, Mary Ann Ferguson, Luis Nieves Falcon, Harriet, Lewis and Irma Fraad, Jan Gelderman, Martin and Jesse Glaberman, Sherna Gluck, Ann Gordon, Jim Green, Barbara Grief, Florence Howe, Allen Hunter, David Hunt, Oakley Johnson, Liz Kennedy, Gerd Korman, Paul Lauter, Eleanor Leacock, Susan Lee, Jesse Lemisch, Jonathan Levine, Lanayre Liggera, Marsha Love, Alice and Staughton Lynd, Phyllis Lyons, Del Martin, Betita Martinez, Anthony Mazzocchi, John McDermott, David Montgomery, Maurice Neufeld, Tillie Olsen, Susanne Paul, Clary Perez, Elizabeth Pleck, Helen Rodriguez-Trias, Marvin Rogoff, Roberta Salper, Danny Schechter, Howard Schneider, Meredith Schwartz, Susy Scott, Tim Sieber, Ann Snitow, Joseph Starobin, Dorothy Sterling, Temma Kaplan Weiner, Vera Buch Weisbord and Charles Zunser.

The book would not have been possible without the help and aid of librarians and xeroxers in several locations. We would especially like to thank Ernie Lendler and Dorothy Swanson of the Tamiment Institute Library, and the staffs of: West Virginia University Library (in particular Dave and Sara in microfilm and xeroxing respectively); University of Pittsburgh Archives of Industrial Society; Catholic University Archives; the Library of Congress; Wayne State University Archives of Labor History and Urban Affairs; Howard University Archives; Schlesinger Library of the History of Women; Wisconsin Historical Society; the Health Policy Advisory Center; the U.S. Women's Bureau; the Institute for Policy Studies.

Ann Froines edited two sections of the book. Lise Vogel went over our materials on early New England textile workers and made vital suggestions, as did Liz and Stuart Ewen about our sections on housework. Sarah Eisenstein contributed considerably to the conception of the 1890 to 1920 period. Maurine Greenwald gave not only suggestions and support, but inadvertently her automobile to a West Virginia flash flood, in the cause of the book. Evelyn Dershowitz gave generously of her time in xeroxing, typing and doing many other favors too numerous to specify. Annie Chamberlin and Susan Siens not only typed the cumbersome manuscript but, most nobly of all, read it as they went and saved us from numerous mistakes, inconsistencies and nonsensical statements. Toni Morrison, our editor, and Pat Chu, her assistant, and Nancy Inglis of Random House, made this a much better book than we could have done ourselves. Ephraim London helped a great deal with legal advice.

Two of us began this project in teaching courses on women's history. The enthusiasm, imagination and intelligence of our students at New York State College at Old Westbury and the University of Massachusetts at Boston gave us many of the ideas and a sense of purpose for writing the book. Robb Burlage, Keith Dix, Carol Fuller and other friends in the labor movement in West Virginia were of great help and inspiration.

Preface to the Second Edition

WHEN this book finally went out of print after sixteen years and we had to consider revising it, we looked to find what similar books had appeared in this current explosion of women's history. We found some excellent scholarship on aspects of women's work and careers, but there was no other anthology with a focus on working-class women. This seemed to us an indication of the degree to which class has been neglected as a fundamental basis of shared experience.

In revising this book, we rethought everything in it. We reconsidered, for example, the periodization, at first sure that the voluminous new women's history scholarship would convince us to divide the book differently on the basis of questions about changes that were significant for *women*. We were surprised to find, after weeks of discussion, that the old periods still seemed to us the most historically accurate divisions. We of course rethought every selection and have replaced more than half with new material. We have been able to add particularly new materials about the West and about minorities, because women's movements have stimulated more scholarship in those areas. We have rewritten virtually every word of the various introductory essays.

We have also been affected in the last twenty years, of course, by a conservative wave in government and culture and an economic decline in the United States. The second edition expresses our heightened awareness of the possibilities of setbacks and even losses for working women. However, it also reflects the fact that new movements for social change have arisen around unexpected issues and from new identities. For example, the disabled rights movement was not as visible twenty years ago; its recent development has pointed to struggles by and for the disabled in the past. And campaigns against sexual harassment are prominent among working women today while the concept barely existed twenty years ago—although sexual harassment has been suffered and contested by working women for centuries.

In one quite literal sense, every historian who has written about working women contributed to this book, even those who do not know us. Some scholars and activists responded generously to particular requests, and we would like to thank them here: Teresa Amott, Barbara Bair, Ellen Baker, Ava

Baron, Marjorie Bingham, Mary Blewett, Eileen Boris, Geraldine Casey, Elizabeth Clark-Lewis, Blanche Wiesen Cook, Margery Davies, Dennis Deslippe, Sarah Elbert, Elizabeth Ewen, Tess Ewing, Bruce Fehn, Sharla Felt, Lisa M. Fine, Maureen Fitzgerald, Eileen Findlay, Estelle B. Freedman, Jennifer Frost, Donna Gabbacia, Barbara Garson, Evelyn Nakano Glenn, Nancy Gabin, Venus Green, Jacqueline Hall, Kelly Eilis Harris, Darlene Clark Hine, Dolores Janiewski, Robin D. G. Kelley, Linda Kerber, Suzanne Lebsock, Varpu Lindstrom, Maria de Lourdes Lugo-Ortiz, Joan Mark, Leisa Meyer, Joanne Meyerowitz, Ruth Milkman, Maria Miller, Mary Murphy, Peggy Pascoe, Catherine Price, Yolanda Prieto, Malcolm Rohrbough, Vicki Ruiz, Bethel Saler, Leslie Schwalm, Dorothy Sterling, Melvina Young. Susan Reverby began to work with us on this edition, participating in the process of rethinking the overall concepts, periodization, and themes of the book. She also contributed to the first chronological section, and we regret that she could not continue to work with us on this revision.

Rosalyn Baxandall wishes particularly to thank Elizabeth Ewen and Sheila Rowbotham for their suggestions and inspiration and Lisa Maguire and Carol Niles for xeroxing and making life easier. Linda Gordon is especially grateful for the superbly intelligent help of Jennifer Frost and Kelly Eilis Harris.

Introduction

WORK has always been and continues to be an important part of women's identities and strengths. We are today gradually sloughing off the remains of the Victorian cultural ideology that proper women were creatures of leisure rather than labor. In the seventeenth and eighteenth centuries, few would have doubted that women's hard labor was absolutely necessary to maintain daily existence and economic growth. In the twentieth century, the rapid expansion of women's wage labor has further undermined the mythology that work is a male domain. Through labor, women as well as men have participated in the collective human task not only of maintaining society but also of accumulating skills across generations, creating beauty as well as necessity, and elevating the standard of living and the aspirations of humankind.

This anthology seeks to honor the contributions of individual working women as well as the groups they have created. More importantly, it seeks to describe and analyze the conditions of women's work, how they have changed over time, and the sources of these changes.

We focus this anthology on working-class and farm women, including work as diverse as midwifery, child care, domestic service, prostitution, and policing—all but the most elite of occupations. This does not mean that middle-class, professional, and upper-class women have not worked or that their work was not significant. But women who have had the opportunity to do professional work are a minority. In this text, we want to look at the majority. The housekeepers, slaves, factory workers, secretaries, waitresses, and farmers belong in the center of history, not along its edges.

Our choices in this anthology express our view that class matters. We do not believe that existing class categories are always adequate to explain the experience of women or the changes that have occurred in U.S. history. Such explanations require integrating sexual and racial with class dynamics. Nevertheless, we believe that class shaped and continues to shape people's life and work experience.

One prominent example of the inadequacy of traditional class categories is their failure to account for women's unpaid labor. Such labor has been as vital and as demanding as wage labor. The work that we today call "house-work" has often been masked by that title. While raising new generations and preserving the old, women have often run their communities as well as their homes, setting up and maintaining schools, public services, and recreation. On farms, women usually shared in the outside work, tended the animals, planted, picked, weeded, and canned. Yet in the last century, housewives came to be considered "dependents," supported by their husbands or families, their occupations seen as part of the natural functioning of the universe, as instinctive as an animal building a nest, as little noticed as breathing.

Mothers often preferred to work at home because of child care and domestic labor obligations. Even when women did bring in money through their work at home—by taking in boarders, laundry, or children, for example—their efforts often remained invisible, seen as a continuation of routine household chores. Census takers typically ignored these considerable contributions to family incomes, which had the effect of suggesting that working-class families could survive on less money than was really the case.

Until World War II, most women living with husbands took jobs outside their homes only if they were poor or if a hardship befell them—a husband sick or hurt or unemployed. Mothers were expected to remain at home all the time, and if they could not or would not, their absence was normally considered a misfortune or an immorality. For most wives, outside employment meant that their husbands had been inadequate in some respect, and it was therefore a blow to masculine self-esteem. Among African Americans, poverty and employment discrimination meant that men found it harder to get jobs, let alone jobs with decent wages, so that women were far more likely to work outside the home, usually as servants or farm laborers. Most men of all classes and ethnic groups tried with varying degrees of fervor to keep their women at home if they could possibly afford it. Furthermore, most jobs available to women were so oppressive and poorly paid that men honestly hoped to spare their women the hardships of paid employment. Most women themselves preferred full-time housewifery if they could afford it to the alternative—the "double day," or housework plus an outside job.

By contrast, single women, always a substantial minority, have engaged in paid, out-of-home employment in large numbers for centuries. Many of them were also supporting families, contributing large portions of their wages to parents, siblings, and others whether they lived at home or not. Immigrant women often sent significant amounts of money to their relatives in the old country; migrants within the United States, such as African Americans and Hispanics coming to cities, similarly supported relatives in the South and Southwest.

The jobs available to women frequently involved tasks that were an extension of housework—in laundries, canneries, textile and clothing factories, for example. Sometimes being a woman was in itself the qualification and, allegedly, the training needed for this work. These women's jobs were always poorly paid. In the late nineteenth century, women's wages averaged 50 percent of men's. The norm that all women were housewives or housewives-to-be supported a myth that all women were supported by men, lived in families, and needed jobs only for extras, for "pin money." This mythology contributed to keeping women's wages low.

Largely excluded until very recently from both skilled jobs and the opportunity to learn skills, women workers accepted low wages and poor conditions because they had few choices. By offering women only the worst working conditions, employers helped continue a vicious circle: the fact that women's jobs were so unpleasant and poorly paid meant that most working-class women naturally preferred housework, especially since they had to do it anyway after their hours of employment; the fact that women were responsible for housework and children perpetuated their seeing themselves and their being used as marginal workers.

Women continually tried, individually and collectively, to improve their working conditions, but they faced major obstacles. The greatest impediment was employers' determination to keep wages low, to heighten divisions and suspicions within the labor force, and to resist workers' coming together in unions. The kinds of jobs women did also made them difficult to organize: women were more likely to work in isolation, as in domestic service or on farms, for small employers who often could not afford decent wages, or in the service sector where they could not easily win strikes, as in hospitals and schools. In many cases, male workers also discouraged female organizing because they wanted to maintain male domination of paid labor and to reaffirm women's subordination in the home as well as the workplace. Women's responsibility for children added obstacles to their organizing because domestic work limited their time and ability to leave home.

In spite of these obstacles, working women have made significant organizational victories. In male-dominated unions and political organizations, they called attention to the problems of women; in elite-dominated women's organizations, they called attention to the problems of working and poor women. In some industries in some periods, they were able to use strikes to demand better working conditions, and where the situation gave them some leverage—as in the garment and textile industries—they demonstrated extraordinary solidarity and militance. Unfortunately, women's lesser power in relation to employers and to men of their own communities has perpetuated even today an extremely unequal division of labor and wages: women do most of the unpaid household work and are concentrated in the lowest-paying, least desirable jobs.

We hope that this book will prove interesting and useful to a reader new to women's labor history. This goal has determined certain of our choices. For example, we integrate original documents, written or spoken by the working women who are our subjects, with writing about those women by outsiders, including scholars and journalists. In fact there is a fuzzy line between these two categories. For example, we include many pieces by individuals who were both scholars and themselves participants in working women's struggles, such as black leader Fannie Barrier Williams and white social reformer Edith Abbott. In choosing from the vast amount of material now available, because of the growth of women's history scholarship, we have been very selective. We did not want to produce an inventory of women's work in every historical period. Rather, we chose and edited readable and diverse selections to illustrate aspects both of continuity and of change in this history.

We chose selections to illustrate certain major themes in women's labor history. One such theme is the continuity of traditional female occupations. These include housework, care for dependents (children, the elderly, the sick), healing, taking in boarders, laundry, farming, needlework, home work, sex work, and community welfare work. Selections illustrating both the enduring patterns and the changes in this kind of labor can be found throughout this book.

Another continuing theme is the multiplicity of women's work, which creates both benefits and costs for women. It offers women flexibility, variety, and challenges in their family and community labor. In the earliest period, for example, we see the activities of Martha Ballard, who is not only a midwife but also a farmer, home manufacturer, healer who grows her own herbal medicines, and caretaker of her family and community. In the early twentieth century, there is Dr. Suzanne La Flesche Picotte, an Omaha Indian who, in addition to providing medical services, served as a scribe, translator, missionary, teacher, public health advocate and ombudswoman for her people to the U.S. government.

This multiplicity of demands on women has also, however, often created stress and fatigue. It forced many women into working what has come to be called the "double day," laboring both for income and without pay for the maintenance of their households and communities. Slave women had to labor in fields and the "big house" for their masters and then return to cook, clean, sew, and garden for their own families—work that was rewarding because they were doing it for loved ones, but nevertheless exhausting. Home workers did both parts of the "double day" at home, often laboring long hours at finishing garments, for example, interrupting that work occasionally only to cook, clean, and care for their children.

In all periods, working women's responsibility for children formed a major theme. In more traditional societies, children were integrated into the work economy of their families, girls usually working alongside their mothers from early ages while boys were likely to work with their fathers after they grew beyond their "toddler" years. Children's education consisted of an informal apprenticeship with their parents, sometimes followed by a formal apprenticeship. While farm women have been consistently reliant on children's contributions, we also see this dependence on children in a variety of other situations: a Hispanic domestic servant in 1735, immigrant home manufacturing workers in the early twentieth century, a Chinese seamstress in the Depression of the 1930s. Recently, children have often added more than they subtracted from women's workload, although this has done nothing to lessen women's devotion to and gratification from their children.

To the extent that women were employed outside their homes, they faced unique problems—also a continuing theme in the history of women's work. Foremost among these was finding and affording child care that allowed women to feel secure in leaving their children; many women have suffered constant background anxiety about the welfare of their children while they were at work and as a result have been forced into inferior jobs that allowed them more access to or time for their children. Single and elderly women in particular have had to seek collective solutions to their housing needs. Without the help of a male wage-earner, women's low wages have often been insufficient to pay for shelter, and sometimes women workers have tried to get unions, employers, and even the government to provide them with homes. Sexual harassment has been another constant source of misery for working women. Even before women had any legal recourse, they protested and organized against the advances of bosses and fellow workers. Women workers have also traditionally been more concerned than men about their work environments. They have agitated against safety and health hazards, for places and times to rest, for cleaner and more attractive work spaces. The slogan "bread and roses," which arose from the Lawrence, Massachusetts, textile strike of 1912, has come to symbolize this yearning for beauty and leisure, sometimes considered luxuries but actually as vital as bread.

In addition to raising their own particular grievances as workers, women have also displayed certain unique patterns of protest, which are illustrated in virtually every period of this book. Since formal labor organizations have so often excluded or marginalized women, women workers have frequently created their own organizations, which often took characteristically feminine forms. For example, women have created woman-only union locals, clubs, or women's centers instead of unions. Women laundry workers established a cooperative in 1870; reformer Alice Henry discussed women's preference for separate locals in 1915; Chicanas in El Paso, Texas, established a working women's center in the 1980s. They have sought a variety of allies, such as middle- and upper-class feminists, rather than relying exclusively on working-class men, who were often unresponsive. The role of the Women's

Trade Union League, discussed in several selections in the 1890–1920 period, is one example of this pattern. Working women often turned to the government for aid, despite the fact that for most of this history they did not have the full rights of citizenship. Since they could not vote, they found other ways of trying to influence the powerful, through petitioning, lobbying, and demonstrating, for example. Garment workers protested to Secretary of War Stanton in 1864; domestic workers wrote to Eleanor Roosevelt in the 1930s; black WACs in World War II objected to discrimination in letters to the army. Since women have had the responsibility for homemaking, they have been the primary consumers within the working class and therefore understood the connections between the power of workers and of consumers. Consumer activism, notably boycotts, has been a disproportionately female form of protest against high prices, shoddy goods, and discriminatory practices. Selections illustrate a boycott of overpriced kosher meat stores in New York City in 1902 and an African-American boycott in Harlem in 1931 of stores that would not hire blacks.

Other selections illustrate continuing political debates about various aspects of women's work. The most fundamental concerned whether women should ever be employed for wages or outside their homes. We have, for example, Alexander Hamilton's eighteenth-century proposal to exploit women's labor in building U.S. independence from Europe through manufacture; several documents present union and professional men's antagonism toward what they saw as women's encroachment into the male sphere; others present women's arguments for their right and need to earn a living. At other times, this debate focused on the distinction between married and single women—accepting the temporary employment of single women while insisting that married women belonged at home. This argument expressed the widespread although erroneous assumption that men's wages were sufficient to support a family single-handedly, an assumption that has come to be called the family wage system. Other equally important debates took place among women themselves. While some women have emphasized male domination and class and race inequality as the root of their subordinate position as workers, other women have condemned these protests as unwarranted complaints and have argued that women are their own worst enemies, preventing themselves from achieving, and should expect to have to work their way up from the bottom.

We have tried to capture this range of views accurately and respectfully, although we identify with some more than others. We came to write this book because we had identities both as feminists immersed in a social movement of and for women, and as scholars and teachers. Now, twenty years after we began work on the first edition, we retain these multiple connections. Although the movement has changed and we are active in different ways, we have found that our immersion in feminism has enriched our scholarship and that our scholarship has enriched what we can offer to feminism. We see this book not only as a tool for learning and teaching about working women but also as a contribution to advancing their living and working conditions, pride in their history, and the respect that they are accorded.

Before
1820

BEFORE 1820: INTRODUCTION

THE history of North American working women began, of course, thousands of years ago among the many Indian tribes and nations—at least two thousand of them. They had diverse patterns with respect to the sexual division of labor, although it appears that in all groups women contributed skilled and vital labor to their communities. Generally, women did the farming labor and for that reason had higher status and more power in the agricultural societies, such as the Iroquois, Navajo, and Pueblo, as compared to the primarily hunting-and-gathering groups of the Great Plains, such as the Lakota.

Although the European conquest created some trade between Indians and whites, and Indian women were often prominent among the traders, the long-term impact of the conquest was to de-skill and therefore weaken the Indian economies and societies. Although the Europeans' first intentions were to establish colonies, ultimately, in a struggle lasting several centuries, they appropriated virtually all the Indians' lands and damaged their governments and societies. In the Southwest, this conquest required not only sporadic battles with Indians but a full-fledged war with Mexico.

The organization of labor in the European colonies in North America was fundamentally contradictory. Many of the early European immigrants brought with them a critique of feudalism and a commitment to private property and free labor. And in some of the colonies, particularly the northern, small farms and enterprises were the ideal. Yet the colonists' need for labor power led them to impose various forms of servitude in this new world, some of them more oppressive than European serfdom. Among white immigrants, one-half to two-thirds came as indentured servants, or "redemptioners"—having bound themselves to work for masters for periods of up to seven years in order to repay the costs of their sea passage. Others bound themselves out for a year or two at a time when they were in debt. Children and widows were often apprentices; while learning a trade or craft, they too served as unfree laborers for many years. The colonists attempted to enslave Indians. But this slavery never became a stable or a profitable system because of the Indians' resistance. The most lasting form of servitude was, of course, black slavery, which came not only to dominate the southern colonies but to pro-

3

vide as well the basis for southern economic development and a supply of capital for northern commercial and industrial development.

Even among the majority of the population, farmers and artisans who usually owned their land and tools, there was a growing stratification. The U.S. class structure soon became, like the European, a pyramid: at the top were the landed gentry, substantial merchants, and a few early manufacturing capitalists; below were the freeholding farmers, artisans, and shopkeepers; then journeymen, who could look forward to becoming master craftsmen; below them were propertyless laborers; then indentured servants and apprentices; and at the bottom were the slaves and Indians. Women were in all these classes, of course, but when they had to support themselves without aid from husbands and fathers, were usually poorer than men, just as they are today.

The new world offered fresh opportunities to European immigrant women. A shortage of white women, characteristic of the early stages of settlement, gave them some advantages. Even as the shortage diminished, the relative fluidity of a society in formation led to the abandonment of some of the traditional restrictions on women's work. Male settlers looking for wives valued their skills and strength highly. And unlike British women, some American white women could own land in some areas up until the early nineteenth century.

Women derived particular benefit from the system of family production that prevailed in the colonies except on large plantations. Continuing in America their European traditions, the settlers established a division of labor that usually placed men in agriculture and women in manufacture and in some farm tasks that provided both subsistence and marketable products. In this preindustrial society, since most manufacture was done in the home, men, women, and children tended to work together, and as a result the division of labor was less rigid. Men were closer to their children than they would become centuries later, and women understood and assisted in the men's work and were therefore often able to take it over entirely if they were widowed. Men dominated what were defined as the skilled crafts, but women's work was visible and highly valued. While women had second-class status, they were not excluded from the mainstream of production. Women's work—agricultural, manufacturing, child care, healing—was integrated into other forms of production.

Despite the availability of "free" land (which in fact belonged to Indians), despite the greater mobility and absence of patterns of social deference, the American colonies did not have political democracy. White men without property could not, for the most part, vote until the 1820s. Blacks and Indians were deprived of virtually all political rights. So were white women, although in some states women managed to claim and exercise various legal prerogatives.

Resistance to these inequalities grew. Discontent among slaves and servants, male and female, manifested itself most often in individual acts of sabotage and escape. There were some organized slave rebellions, followed by savage repression. The Indians kept up a nearly constant armed resistance, but their weapons were inferior to those of the Europeans and they were often divided by bribery and the colonists' exacerbation of tribal rivalries. In the late eighteenth century, there were several rebellions of small farmers, as well as urban agitation by artisans, laborers, and seamen. These rebels fought regressive taxes and oppressive debt structure, impressment, and other policies imposed by British and colonial rulers.

The largest and most transformative rebellion of all was the American Revolution itself. It expanded representative democracy and instituted a constitutional framework within which struggles for complete democracy could take place legally. It introduced a new nation, conceived on liberal principles, whose rhetoric inspired not only revolutionaries abroad but also its own subjected peoples. Women were, of course, prominent among these, and the revolution stimulated demands for women's advancement and legal rights.

The revolution had an important impact on women. The sense of crisis during the struggle itself broke down some barriers to women's political activism. Even before the outbreak of hostilities, women were organizing boycotts of British goods, since as consumers women felt the injustice of the tax laws most keenly. One of the important new ideas that emerged from the revolutionary period was "republican motherhood," the claim that through their mothering women were transmitting and nurturing crucial democratic principles. This stress on motherhood indicated a de-emphasis on women's identity as producers and the growth of the ideology of domesticity and "separate spheres," which surrendered economic and political primacy to men. Despite women's individual and collective activism during the revolution, this ideology did not give rise to an ongoing women's movement.

Paid and Unpaid Labor

GRINDING CORN

In most of the Native American societies, women dominated agricultural work. Among the Pueblos, however, descendants of the Anasazi and other ancient farming peoples, the cultivation of maize goes back to 3000 B.C. in New Mexico. Women not only farmed but also prepared foods for use and storage. One of the most time-consuming and ancient of these tasks was grinding or milling grain into meal or flour. In the Southwest, tools such as the metate, *a concave bottom stone, and the* mano, *a hand-held grinding instrument, were used for over ten thousand years.*

In the early times when hunting was the major occupation, and wild nuts and seeds were gathered to augment the food supply, each family probably had a crude metate, on which the woman ground the seeds. Any flat rock served her purpose, yet perhaps she might have found a particularly suitable one which she cherished, and took with her as the family followed the game. One metate was enough for her purpose. When she prepared the seeds for the family to eat, she sat down on the ground beside the flat stone, and with a few blows and a circular motion of her mano, held in one hand, reduced the seeds to an edible state.

At a later date, the people began to grow corn, which kept them at home to tend to their crops. Corn became the staple food and more and more was used. Then the woman instead of casually sitting on the ground and grinding with one hand, propped up her lower milling stone on several rocks, kneeled behind it, took a long mano in both hands, set it flat on the metate, and really got down to work. Her metate had a trough so the meal did not spill off on the sides. In her pithouse home, there was not much room and when she could, she worked outside. Her metates had to be portable so that she could carry them in and out, and so that they could easily be put out of the way. She had several metates of varying grades of coarseness, for now the family lived in one place and the heavy grinding stones no longer had to be carried about as perhaps they formerly were.

By and by, the woman, who now had a masonry house with several rooms, thought it would be nice to have one of her metates that she used most often permanently set up. She had plenty of room in her house, and she could easily spare enough space, so she set one of her old troughed metates into the floor at a steeper angle than she had been using it and surrounded it by a slab box, neatly held in place with adobe. This was the first mealing bin. By this time she had discovered that it was easier to grind if she had something to brace her feet against, so the mealing bin was backed up against a wall leaving just enough space for her to kneel in.

The next time she made a bin, she realized it was useless to spend time pecking out the trough in the metate as she had done, because now she had the bin to hold the meal. She used a flat slab of stone to grind on, and found it worked just as well. After this she began to use her mano in a new way so that it had two grinding surfaces. It did not become worn out so soon and the more triangular it became the easier it was to hold, and moreover it saved her the trouble of spreading the meal over the grinding stone as frequently as she had done. As houses increased in size, and rooms were built for storage and other special purposes, there was space enough in the living rooms for several metates to be set up permanently in bins, so that the meal could be lifted from one metate directly to the next as it became ground successively finer and finer. Also several women could grind at the same time and enjoy each other's company.

All this progress in milling stones took many hundreds of years to accomplish, yet each new step made the task easier or quicker or more sociable for the women who were condemned to spend most of their lives grinding corn.

A WHITE WOMAN'S PERSPECTIVE ON INDIAN WOMEN'S LABOR

Some European-American women were captured by Indians in battle, and a few of these remained among the Indians for years, often by choice. Their memoirs, although obviously expressing a European view, offer some correctives to myths about the Indians, such as that concerning the low status and drudgery of Indian women. One such captive was Mary Jemison, born in 1743, captured and adopted by the Seneca Iroquois tribe in 1758. Jemison married a Delaware Indian and, although free to leave, refused to return to white society. This excerpt is from an account she gave to a white minister, who later published it.

Among the Iroquois, the land belonged to women; women controlled the distribution of all food, even that procured by men, and this gave them significant political power in the tribe.

I had then been with the Indians four summers and four winters, and had become so far accustomed to their mode of living, habits and dispositions,

7

that my anxiety to get away, to be set at liberty, and leave them, had almost subsided. With them was my home; my family was there, and there I had many friends to whom I was warmly attached in consideration of the favors, affection and friendship with which they had uniformly treated me, from the time of my adoption. Our labor was not severe; and that of one year was exactly similar, in almost every respect, to that of the others, without that endless variety that is to be observed in the common labor of the white people. Notwithstanding the Indian women have all the fuel and bread to procure, and the cooking to perform, their task is probably not harder than that of white women, who have those articles provided for them: and their cares certainly are not half as numerous, nor as great. In the summer season, we planted, tended and harvested our corn, and generally had all our children with us; but had no master to oversee or drive us, so that we could work as leisurely as we pleased. We had no ploughs on the Ohio; but performed the whole process of planting and hoeing with a small tool that resembled, in some respects, a hoe with a very short handle.

Our cooking consisted in pounding our corn into samp or hommany, boiling the hommany, making now and then a cake and baking it in the ashes, and in boiling or roasting our venison. As our cooking and eating utensils consisted of a hommany block and pestle, a small kettle, a knife or two, and a few vessels of bark or wood, it required but little time to keep them in order for use.

Spinning, weaving, sewing, stocking knitting, and the like, are arts which have never been practised in the Indian tribes generally. After the revolutionary war, I learned to sew, so that I could make my own clothing after a poor fashion; but the other domestic arts I have been wholly ignorant of the application of, since my captivity. In the season of hunting, it was our business, in addition to our cooking, to bring home the game that was taken by the Indians, dress it, and carefully preserve the eatable meat, and prepare or dress the skins.

A MIDWIFE OF MANY TRADES

Historian Laurel Thatcher Ulrich's A Midwife's Tale *brought to life the diary of eighteenth-century midwife Martha Ballard. The diary shows a pattern in women's work that has been continuous for centuries—the multiplicity of women's labor. Ballard not only delivered children; as a midwife, she was also a general healer who grew and processed her own herbal medicines; in addition, she engaged in the variegated domestic labor typical of women householders at this time, in which housekeeping, agriculture, and small manufacturing were indistinguishable. A vital part of Ballard's work involved nurturing her community as well as her family.*

Between August 3 and 24, 1787, Ballard performed four deliveries, answered one obstetrical false alarm, made sixteen medical calls, prepared three bodies for burial, dispensed pills to one neighbor, harvested and prepared herbs for another, and doctored her own husband's sore throat. In twentieth-century terms, she was simultaneously a midwife, nurse, physician, mortician, pharmacist, and attentive wife. Furthermore, in the very act of recording her work, she became a keeper of vital records, a chronicler of the medical history of her town.

AUGUST 1787

3 6* Clear & very hot. I have been pulling flax. . . .

4 7 Clear morn. I pulld flax till noon. . . . Colonel Howard made me a present of 1 gallon white Rhum & 2 lb sugar on acount of my atendance of his family in sickness. Peter Kenny has wounded his Legg & Bled Excesivily.

5 g Clear morn. Mr Hamlin Breakfastd here. Had some pills. I was called at 7 O Clok to Mrs Howards to see James he being very sick with the canker Rash. Tarried all night.

6 2 I am at Mrs Howards watching with her son. Went out about day, discovered our saw mill in flames. The men at the fort went over. Found it consumd together with some plank & Bords. I tarried till Evinng. Left James Exceeding Dangerously ill. My daughter Hannah is 18 years old this day. Mrs Williams here when I came home. Hannah Cool gott Mrs Norths web out at the Loome. Mr Ballard complains of a soar throat this night. . . .

7 3 Clear. I was Calld to Mrs Howards this morning for to see her son. Find him very low. Went from Mrs Howards to see Mrs Williams. Find her very unwell. Hannah Cool is there. From thence to Joseph Fosters to see her sick Children. Find Saray & Daniel very ill. Came home went to the field & got some Cold water root. Then Calld to Mr Kenydays to see Polly. Very ill with the Canker. Gave her some of the root. I gargled her throat which gave her great Ease. Returned home after dark. Mr Ballard been to Cabesy. His throat is very soar. He gargled it with my tincture. Find relief & went to bed comfortably.

---

*The first number indicates the day of the month, the second number the day of the week. Letters indicate Sundays.

9

8 4   Clear. I have been to see Mary Kenida. Find her much as shee was yesterday. Was at Mr McMasters. Their Children two of them very ill. The other 2 recovering. At Mr Williams also. Shee is some better. Hear James Howard is mending. Hannah Cool came home.

9 5   Clear. I workd about house forenoon. Was Calld to Mrs Howards to see James. Found him seemingly Expireing. Mrs Pollard there. We sett up. He revivd.

10 6   At Mrs Howards. Her son very sick. Capt Sewall & Lady sett up till half after 4. Then I rose. The Child seems revivd.

11 7   Calld from Mrs Howard to Mr McMasters to see their son William who is very low. Tarried there this night.

12 g   Loury. At Mr McMasters. Their son very sick. I sett up all night. Mrs Patin with me. The Child very ill indeed.

13 2   William McMaster Expird at 3 O Clock this morn. Mrs Patin & I laid out the Child. Poor mother, how Distressing her
Case, near the hour of Labour and three Children more very sick. I sett out for home. Calld at Mrs Howards. I find her son very Low. At Mr Williams. Shee very ill indeed. Now at home. It is nine O Clok morn. I feel as if I must take some rest. I find Mr Ballard is going to Pittston on Business. Dolly is beginning to weave thee handkerchiefs. Ephraim & I went to see Mrs Williams at Evining. I find her some Better.
death of Wm McMaster*

14 3   Clear & hott. I pikt the safron. Mrs Patten here. Mr Ballard & I & all the girls attended funeral of William McMaster. Their other Children are mending. James Howard very low. I drank Tea at Mr Pollards. Calld at Mr Porters.

15 4   . . . I pulld flax the fornon. . . . I am very much fatagud. Lay on the bed & rested. The two Hannahs washing. Dolly weaving. I was called to Mrs Claton in travil at 11 O Clok Evening.

16 5   At Mr Cowens. Put Mrs Claton to Bed with a son at 3 pm. Came to Mr Kenadays to see his wife who has a sweling under her arm. Polly is mending. I returnd as far as Mr Pollards by water. Calld from there to Winthrop to Jeremy Richards wife in Travil. Arivd about 9 o Clok Evin.
Birth Mrs Clatons son

17 6 At Mr Richards. His wife Delivered of a Daughter at 10 O Clok morn. Returned as far as Mr Pollards at 12. Walked from there. Mrs Coy buryd a dafter yesterday. Mr Stanley has a dafter Dangirous. William Wicher 2 Children also.
Birth Jeremy Richard dafter

18 7 I spun some shoe thread & went to see Mrs Williams. Shee has news her Mother is very sick. Geny Huston had a Child Born the night before last. I was Calld to James Hinkly to see his wife at 11 & 30 Evening. Went as far as Mr Weston by land, from thence by water. Find Mrs Hinkly very unwell.

19 g At Mr Hinkleys. Shee remaind poorly till afternoon then by remedys & other means shee got Easyer. I tarried all night.

20 2 Clear. Mr Hinkly brot me to Mr Westons. I heard there that Mrs Clatons Child departed this life yesterday & that she was thot Expireing. I went back with Mr Hinkly as far as there. Shee departed this Life about 1 pm. I asisted to Lay her out. Her infant Laid in her arms. The first such instance I ever saw & the first woman that died in Child bed which I delivered. I Came home at dusk. Find my family all Comfortable. We hear that three Children Expird in Winthrop last Saterday night. Daniel Stayd at Mr Cowens.

21 3 A rainy day. I have been at home kniting.

22 4 I atended funeral of Mrs Claton & her infant. Am Enformd that Mrs Shaw has Doctor Coney with her. I calld to see James Howard find him low. Mrs North also is sick. . . .

23 5 I sett out to visit Joseph Fosters Children. Met Ephraim Cowen by Brooks' Barn. Calld me to see his Dafters Polly & Nabby who are sick with the rash. Find them very ill. Gave directions. Was then Calld to Mrs Shaw who has been ill some time. Put her safe to Bed with a daughter at 10 O Clok this Evinng. Shee is finely.
Birth Mr Shaws Dafter

24 6 Calld from Shaws to James Hinklys wife in travil. Put her safe to Bed with a son at 7 O Clok this morn. Left her as well as is usual for her. Came to Mr Shaws receivd 6/8. Receivd 6/8 of Mr Hinkly also. Came to Mr Cowens. Find his dafters & Jedy ill. . . . Arivd at home at 5 afternoon. Doctor Coneys wife delivrd of a dafter Last Evening at 10 O Clok.

HOUSEWIVES OF MANY TRADES ─────────────────

Seventeenth-, eighteenth-, and early nineteenth-century Americans took it for granted that housewives would be expert nurses and home manufacturers as well as cooks, cleaners, and gardeners. These traditions of folk technology were passed on orally from generation to generation. When receipts (today spelled recipes) started to be published, it was a sign that the word-of-mouth communication was no longer adequate, which is why these selections are from books published later than this period. They nevertheless contain recipes that were in common use for previous centuries.

In these books, recipes were listed in indiscriminate order. Recipes for food (e.g., how to make catsup, vinegar, cheese, flour), household chemicals (e.g., ink, dyes, hair-curling liquids, priming powder for gun cartridges), and many medicines and curative procedures are intermixed, revealing the breadth of the range of skills women used.

As the field of healing became professionalized and male, physicians began to attack the folk traditions of healing as worthless quackery; an "old wives' tale" came to mean a false superstition instead of good advice. Contemporary reevaluation of the lore of "natural" healing shows that some of these cures were sensible and effective. Notice that two of the recipes—for "preventive lotions"—were for birth control. Women had used birth control techniques since the earliest recorded societies, and many of them were reasonably effective, although of course not as effective as modern techniques.

We are indebted to Kim Brookes for the first part of this selection.

A MODE OF PREPARING PAPER WHICH SHALL RESIST MOISTURE
This process consists in plunging unsized paper once or twice into a clear solution of mastic in oil of turpentine and drying it afterwards by a gentle heat. The paper thus prepared . . . has all the properties of writing paper. . . . When laid out, it is perfectly secure from being injured by mouldiness or mildew, and is not likely to be destroyed by mice or insects.

PLAN FOR PRESERVING THE WALLS OF NEW BUILDINGS FROM DAMPNESS
Spread over the whole thickness of the wall at about two feet from the earth a layer of pit coal, mingled with pitch or rosin and powdered charcoal. . . .

INDIAN CURE FOR HEART-ACHE
Take a piece of the lean of mutton, about the size of a large walnut, put it into the fire and burn it for some time, till it becomes almost reduced to a cinder, then put it into a clean rag and squeeze it until some moisture is expressed, which must be dropped in the ear as hot as the patient can bear.

RINGWORMS
. . . Obtain some blood-root (called also red-root, Indian paint, &c.) . . . slice it in vinegar, and afterwards wash the place affected with the liquid. . . .

HOARSENESS
One drachm of freshly-scraped horseradish root, to be infused with four ounces of water in a close vessel for two hours, and made into a syrup with double its weight in vinegar, is an approved remedy for hoarseness; a teaspoonful has often proved effectual; a few teaspoonfuls, it is said, have never been known to fail in removing hoarseness.

NEW TEST FOR THE DETECTION OF PREGNANCY
. . . Urine must be allowed to stand for from two to six days, when minute opaque bodies are observed to rise from the bottom to the surface of the fluid, where they gradually agglomerate, and form a continuous layer over the surface. This layer is so consistent that it may be almost lifted off by raising it by one of its edges. This is the kisteine. It is whitish, opalescent, slightly granular, and can be compared to nothing better than to the fatty substance which floats on the surface of soups, after they have been allowed to cool. . . . [Its presence indicates pregnancy.]

HANNAY'S PREVENTIVE LOTION
Take pearlash, 1 part; water, 6 parts. Mix and filter. Keep it in close bottles, and use it, with or without soap, immediately after connexion [sexual intercourse].

ABERNETHY'S PREVENTIVE LOTION
Take bichloride of mercury, 25 parts; milk of almonds, 400 parts; alcohol, 100 parts; rose-water, 1000 parts. Immerse the glands in a little of the mixture, as before, and be particular to open the orifice of the urethra so as to admit the contact of the fluid. This may be used as often as convenient, until the orifice of the urethra feels tender on voiding the urine. Infallible, if used in proper time.

VOMITING DURING PREGNANCY
Two or three spoonfuls of the following mixture . . . either occasionally, or when the vomiting and heartburn are more continual, immediately after every meal:—Take calcined magnesia 1 drachm; distilled water 6 ounces; aromatic tincture of rhatany 6 drachms; water of pure ammonia 1 drachm. Mix.

HOME WORK

In preindustrial society, there were no sharp distinctions between "house-work," farming, and manufacturing. Both men and women worked primarily at home, and women typically interspersed house cleaning, child care, and productive labor throughout the day. Nearly all manufacturing was done in the home, some of it under the exclusive jurisdiction of women—such as tex-tiles—and some of it with women assisting their husbands. The presence of skilled manufacture in the home made housewifery a more varied, challeng-ing, and laborious job than it is today and meant that housework often involved the whole family.

The following selections, a description of seventeenth- and eighteenth-cen-tury housewifery, were written by Alice Morse Earle (1851–1911), one of a few pioneering historians of women. She was a prolific writer, producing thir-teen books, but never held an academic job since the universities and colleges of her day did not usually hire women.

The manufacture of the farm-reared wool was not so burdensome and tedious a process as that of flax, but it was far from pleasant. The fleeces of wool had to be opened out and cleaned of all sticks, burrs, leaves, feltings, tar-marks, and the dirt which always remained after months' wear by the sheep; then it had to be sorted out for dyeing, which latter was a most unpleasant process. Layers of the various colors of wools after being dyed were rolled together and carded on coarse wool-cards, again and again, then slightly greased by a disagreeable and tiresome method, then run into rolls. The wool was spun on the great wheel which stood in the kitchen with the reel and swifts, and often by the glowing firelight the mother spun. . . .

For many years after this, housewives had everywhere flax and hemp to spin and weave in their homes, and the preparation of these staples seems to us to-day a monumental labor. On almost every farm might be seen a patch of the pretty flax, ripening for the hard work of pulling, rippling, rotting, breaking, swingling, and combing, which all had to be done before it came to the women's hands for spinning. The seed was sown broadcast, and allowed to grow till the bobs or bolls were ripe. The flax was then pulled and spread neatly in rows to dry. This work could be done by boys. Then men whipped or threshed or rippled out all the seed to use for meal; afterwards the flax stalks were allowed to lie for some time in water until the shives were thoroughly rotten, when they were cleaned and once more thoroughly dried and tied in bundles. Then came work for strong men, to break the flax on the ponderous flaxbreak, to get out the hard "hexe" or "bun," and to swingle it with a swingle knife, which was somewhat like a wooden dagger. Active men could swingle forty pounds a day on the swingling-board. It was then hetchelled or combed or hackled by the housewife, and thus the rough tow was gotten out, when it was straightened and made ready for the spruce distaff, round which it was finally wrapped. The hatchelling was tedious work and irritating to the lungs, for the air was filled with the fluffy particles which penetrated everywhere. The thread was then spun on a "little wheel." It was thought that to spin two double skeins of linen, or four double skeins of tow, or to weave six yards of linen, was a good day's work. For a week's work a girl received fifty cents and "her keep." She thus got less than a cent and a half a yard for weaving. The skeins of linen thread went through many tedious processes of washing and bleaching before being ready for weaving; and after the cloth was woven it was "bucked" in a strong lye, time and time again, and washed out an equal number of times. Then it was "belted" with a maple beetle on a smooth, flat stone; then washed and spread out to bleach in the pure sunlight. Sometimes the thread, after being spun and woven, had been washed and belted a score of times ere it was deemed white and soft enough to use. The little girls could spin the "swingling tow" into coarse twine, and the older ones make "all tow" and "tow and linen" and "harden" stuffs to sell. . . .

The wringing out of this linen yarn was most exhausting, and the rinsing in various waters was no simple matter in those days, for the water did not conveniently run into the houses through pipes and conduits, but had to be laboriously carried in pailfuls from a pump, or more frequently raised in a bucket from a well.

CHANGE WORK AND THE WHANG

Today housework tends to isolate women. But in the preindustrial period, the husbands of poor or middling women were usually farmers, artisans, or small shopkeepers, and in these cases the men did their work at or near home also. Craft or retail shops were usually part of the home, and women often assisted in their husbands' or fathers' work. Furthermore, the closeness of communities made sharing and cooperation feasible and necessary.

It was the custom both among men and women to join forces on a smaller scale and have a little neighborly visiting by what was called 'change-work.' For instance, if two neighbors both were to make soap, or both to make apple-butter, or both to make up a rag carpet, instead of each woman sitting at home alone sewing and fitting the carpet, one would take her thimble and go to spend the day, and the two would sew all day long, finish and lay the carpet at one house. In a few days the visit would be returned, and the second carpet be finished. Sometimes the work was easier when two worked together. One man could load logs and sled them down to the sawmill alone, but two by 'change-work' could accomplish the task much more rapidly and with less strain.

Even those evil days of New England households, the annual house-cleaning, were robbed of some of their dismal terrors by what was known as a 'whang,' a gathering of a few friendly women neighbors to assist one another in that dire time, and thus speed and shorten the hours of misery. . . .

WOMEN IN INDUSTRY ————————————————

The following analysis of women's work in colonial America is from a classic, Edith Abbott's Women in Industry, *published in 1913. Abbott (1876–1957) was one of an extraordinary group of progressive women reformers of the early twentieth century: she worked at Hull-House, a settlement in Chicago begun by Jane Addams, and campaigned for a variety of welfare and protective laws, particularly focused on helping poor and immigrant women. Her sister Grace Abbott, also an active campaigner for social justice, led the U.S. Children's Bureau. Edith Abbott, like Alice Morse Earle, was also an important intellectual and scholar. With Sophonisba Breckinridge (see pp. 131–36), Abbott founded the University of Chicago social work school; she wrote numerous scholarly social work studies as well as journalistic pleas for a decent welfare system; and she pioneered the use of scientific social research as a basis for policy.*

Our primary interests during this early period were agriculture and commerce, and there was very little field for the industrial employment either of men or women. Such manufactures as were carried on in these early industries were chiefly household industries, and the work was necessarily done in the main by women. Indeed, it would not be far wrong to say that, during the colonial period, agriculture was in the hands of men, and manufacturing, for the most part, in the hands of women. . . .

It is of interest to note, too, in this connection that in the case of land allotments in early New England, women who were heads of families received their proportion of planting land; and in Salem, Plymouth, and the Cape Cod towns women could not get enough land. Although spinsters did not fare too well, it is a matter of record that in Salem even unmarried women were at first given a small allotment. The custom of granting "maid's lotts," however, was soon discontinued in order to avoid "all presedents and evil events of graunting lotts unto single maidens not disposed of." . . .

And besides the occupations of a domestic kind, there were, in the seventeenth and eighteenth centuries, various other employments open to them which it may be worth while to notice. . . .

One of the oldest of these was the keeping of taverns and "ordinaries." In 1643, the General Court of Massachusetts granted Goody Armitage permission to "keepe the ordinary, but not to drawe wine," and throughout this century and the next the Boston town records show repeated instances of the granting of such licenses to women. In 1669, for example, "Widdow Snow and Widdow Upshall were 'approved of to sell beere and wine for the yeare ensuinge and keep houses of publique entertainment'," and there are records of the granting of similar permissions to other women on condition that they "have a careful and sufficient man to manage the house." Such licenses were granted most frequently to widows, but occasionally to wives. Thus the wife of Thomas Hawkins was given permission to sell liquors "by retayle" only because of "the selectmen consideringe the necessitie and weake condition of her Husband." . . .

Other kinds of businesses attracted women in this same period. The raising of garden seeds and similar products seems to have been a common occupation. Women were sometimes shrewd traders and, often, particularly in the seaboard towns, venturesome enough to be speculators. . . .

Among the other gainful employments for women in this period which were not industrial might be mentioned keeping a "dame's school" which, though a very unremunerative occupation, was often resorted to. There were, too, many notable nurses and midwives; in Bristol a woman was ringer of the bell and kept a meeting-house, and in New Haven a woman was appointed to "sweepe and dresse the meeting house every weeke and have 1s. a weeke for her pains." The common way, however, for a woman to earn her board and a few pounds a year was by going out to service. But it should be noted that the domestic servant in the seventeenth and eighteenth centuries was employed for a considerable part of her time in processes of manufacture and that, without going far wrong, one might classify this as an industrial occupation. A servant, for example, who was a good spinner or a good tailoress, was valued accordingly, and advertisements in eighteenth-century newspapers frequently mention this as a qualification.

There remain, however, a number of instances in which women were employed in and were even at the head of what might, strictly speaking, be called industrial establishments. A woman, for example, occasionally ran a mill, carried on a distillery, or even worked in a sawmill. The "Plymouth Colony Records" note in 1644 that "Mistress Jenny, upon the presentment against her, promiseth to amend the grinding at the mill, and to keep morters cleane, and baggs of corne from spoyleing and looseing." At Mason's settlement at Piscataqua, "eight Danes and twenty two women" were employed in sawing lumber and making potash. In 1693 a woman appears with two men on the pages of the "Boston Town Records" "desiring leave to build a slaughter house." But all of these seem to have been unusual employments.

There were, however, a great many women printers in the eighteenth century, and these women were both compositors and worked at the press. Several colonial newspapers were published by women and they printed books and pamphlets as well. Women were also employed in the early paper mills, where they were paid something like the equivalent of seventy-five cents a week and board.

Although there is no doubt of the fact that women were gainfully employed away from home at this time, such employment was quite unimportant compared with work which they did in their own homes.

In considering minor industrial occupations within the home we find that a few women were bakers and some were engaged in similar work, such as making and selling of preserves or wine. But the great majority of women in this group were employed in the manufacture of textiles, which in its broadest sense includes knitting, lacemaking, the making of cards for combing cotton and wool, as well as sewing, spinning and weaving.

Some women must have found knitting a profitable by-employment. Knit stockings sold for two shillings a pair, and occasionally for much more. One old account book records that "Ann" sold a "pare of stockens for 16s." Sewing and tailoring were standard occupations and were variously remunerated,— one woman made "shirts for the Indians" at eightpence each, and "men's breeches" for a shilling and sixpence a pair, and in addition to this work of tailoring she taught school, did spinning and weaving for good pay, managed her house, was twice married and had fourteen children.

Spinning and weaving, the processes upon which the making of cloth depended, absorbed a great deal of the time of the women and girls of the period. . . .

In the seventeenth century, the work was household industry; the raw materials were furnished by the household and the finished product was for household use; but so far as any part of it was marketed or exchanged at the village store, the system became closely akin to handicraft. The commodity that was exchanged or sold belonged to the woman as a true craftswoman, the material had been hers and the product, until she disposed of it, was her own capital. When the article was sold directly to the consumer, as frequently happened, even the final characteristic of handicraft, the fact of its being "custom work," was present.

With the expansion of the industry, especially in the latter half of the eighteenth century, a considerable part of the work was done more in the manner of what is known as the commission system. As yarn came to be in great demand, many women were regularly employed spinning at home for purchasers who were really commission merchants. These men sometimes sold the yarn but often they put it out again to be woven and then sold the cloth.

The most important occupations for women, therefore, before the establishment of the factory system, were spinning and weaving. . . .

In concluding this discussion of the employment of women during the colonial period, some reference must be made to the attitude of the public opinion of that day toward their work. The early court orders providing for the employment of women and children were not prompted solely by a desire to promote the manufacture of cloth. There was, in the spirit of them, the Puritan belief in the virtue of industry and the sin of idleness. Industry by compulsion, if not by faith, was the gospel of the seventeenth century, and not only court orders but Puritan ministers warned the women of that day of the dangers of idle living. Summary measures were sometimes taken to punish those who were idle. Thus the "Salem Town Records" show (December 5, 1643) "It is ordered that Margarett Page shall [be sent] to Boston Goale as a lazy, idle, loytering person where she may be sett to work for her liveinge." In 1645 and 1646 different persons were paid "for Margarett Page to keep her at worke." Among the charges against Mary Boutwell in the "Essex Records," 1640, is one "for her exorbitancy not working but liveinge idly."

Perhaps the best expression of the prevailing attitude toward the employment of women at that time is to be found in one of the Providence Laws of Massachusetts Bay for the session of 1692–93. The law ordered that every single person under twenty-one must live "under some orderly family government," but added the proviso that "this act shall not be construed to extend to hinder any single woman of good repute from the exercise of any lawful trade or employment for a livelihood, whereunto she shall have the allowance and approbation of the selectmen . . . any law, usage or custom to the contrary notwithstanding."

It is not, therefore, surprising to find that, in 1695, an act was passed which required single women who were self-supporting to pay a polltax as well as men. That this attitude was preserved during the eighteenth century, the establishment of the spinning schools bears witness. There was, however, the further point that providing employment for poor women and children lessened the poor rates, and the first factories were welcomed because they offered a means of support to the women and children who might otherwise be "useless, if not burdensome, to society."

The colonial attitude toward women's work was in brief one of rigid insistence on their employment. Court orders, laws, and public subscriptions were resorted to in order that poor women might be saved from the sin of idleness and taught to be self-supporting.

WANTED: WOMEN —————————————————————

How did women find paying jobs? Communities were not so closely knit in the New World that people could always count on being provided for by their friends and neighbors, nor could employers necessarily find what they needed by word of mouth. Newspapers served as employment agents, and eighteenth-century advertisements also give us a revealing sampling of the jobs that women did. In a preindustrial society like this, the jobs that women did for pay are pretty much the same as those they did without pay. The use of hired wet nurses was still widespread among the wealthy classes.

Any honest industrious Man, that understands the Management of a Saw-Mill, and Farming, with a wife that understands managing of a Dairy, may be applying to John Moore of New York, be employed on very good Terms; and their having a Child or two, will be no objections.

New-York Post-Boy,
January 23, 1748/9

Wanted. Two White Servant Maids, to serve in a small Family; the one for a Nurse-maid, to take Care of a Child or two; the other to Cook and do the other necessary Work about the House; They must be well recommended and engage to stay a Twelve-Month at least in the Family. Enquire of the Printer.

New York Mercury,
August 27, 1770

Wanted, a Grave, sedate, sober woman, not exceeding thirty years of age, who understands the management of a family, the care of children, and who may be trusted with the keys, such a one by bringing a recommendation, may hear of a good place, by inquiring at the printer's hereof.

New York Mercury,
July 29, 1754

A Woman with good Breast of Milk who is willing to go into a Family is wanted.

New-York Post-Boy, September 7, 1747

A Woman with a young Brest of Milk who is willing to go into a Gentleman's Family.

New York Mercury,
September 19, 1763

Wanted at a Seat about half a day's journey from Philadelphia, on which are good improvements and domestics, A Single Woman of unsullied Reputation, an affable, cheerful, active and amiable Disposition; cleanly, industrious, perfectly qualified to direct and manage the female Concerns of country business, as raising small stock, dairying, marketing, combing, carding, spinning, knitting, sewing, pickling, preserving, etc., and occasionally to instruct two young Ladies in those Branches of Oeconomy, who, with their father, compose the Family. Such a person will be treated with respect and esteem, and meet with every encouragement due to such a character.

Pennsylvania Packet,
September 23, 1780

A FOUNDING FATHER'S VISION OF WOMEN AS FACTORY WORKERS

One major divisive issue among the colonists who broke away from England in the American Revolution was whether the country should remain exclusively agricultural, its citizenry composed of self-sufficient farmers, or whether it needed industrial manufacture in order not to be economically re-colonized by industrializing Europe. The Federalists, such as Alexander Hamilton, believed that an economy balanced between agriculture and industry was necessary. Women were crucial to the Federalist economic vision because the availability of land made men who could own and farm it unwilling to sacrifice their independence and become wage laborers. Hamilton envisaged drawing women into the factories. In this selection from his Report on Manufactures (1791), he tried to convince his readers—who he imagined, of course, to be mainly male—that women's employment would be beneficial to men. In it he enunciated the dubious proposition that women might otherwise be idle, that factory labor would render them more useful. While thousands of young women did begin to work in textile mills over the next decades, they mainly considered their work temporary, expecting to marry and return to farming. It is interesting to speculate whether Hamilton's propaganda could conceivably have produced a system in which men farmed and women regularly worked for wages.

In places where those institutions [factories] prevail, besides the persons regularly engaged in them, they afford occasional and extra employment to industrious individuals and families, who are willing to devote the leisure resulting from the intermissions of their ordinary pursuits to collateral labours, as a resource for multiplying their acquisitions or their enjoyments. The husbandman himself experiences a new source of profit and support from the increased industry of his wife and daughters; invited and stimulated by the demands of the neighboring manufactories.

Besides this advantage of occasional employment to classes having different occupations, there is another, of a nature allied to it, and of a similar tendency. This is—the employment of persons who would otherwise be idle (and in many cases a burthen on the community) either from the bias of temper, habit, infirmity of body, or some other cause, indisposing or disqualifying them for the toils of the Country. It is worthy of particular remark, that, in general, women and Children are rendered more useful, and the latter more early useful by manufacturing establishments, than they would otherwise be. Of the number of persons employed in the Cotton Manufactories of Great Britain, it is computed that four sevenths nearly are women and children; of whom the greatest proportion are children, and many of them of a very tender age.

And thus it appears to be one of the attributes of manufactures, and one of no small consequence, to give occasion to the exertion of a greater quantity of Industry, even by the *same number* of persons, where they happen to prevail, than would exist, if there were no such establishments.

. . . there are circumstances which have been already noticed with another view, that materially diminish, everywhere, the effect of a scarcity of hands. These circumstances are—the great use which can be made of women and children; on which point a very pregnant and instructive fact has been mentioned—the vast extension given by late improvements to the employment of Machines, which substituting the Agency of fire and water, had prodigiously lessened the necessity of manual labour—the employment of persons ordinarily engaged in other occupations, during the seasons, or hours of leisure; which, besides giving occasion to the exertion of a greater quantity of labour by the same number of persons, and thereby increasing the general stock of labour, as has been elsewhere remarked, may also be taken into the calculation, as a resource for obviating the scarcity of hands— lastly the attraction of foreign emigrants. Whoever inspects with a careful eye, the composition of our towns will be made sensible to what an extent this resource may be relied upon. . . .

Servitude

TRICKED INTO SERVITUDE

Many European immigrants to the American colonies were not free. One-half to two-thirds came as indentured servants, or "redemptioners"—having signed a contract to work for a master for periods of up to seven years in order to repay the costs of their sea passage. Others bound themselves out for a year or two at a time when they were in debt. They were poorly paid and often treated rudely and harshly, deprived of decent food, clothing, and privacy. While in service they were not free, and their services could be sold by one master to another. Worse yet, some did not sign indentures willingly. Convicted criminals were sometimes forcibly deported from English and Irish jails to the New World. This popular song tells of a girl who was kidnapped and taken to Virginia.

THE TRAPPAN'D MAIDEN:
OR, THE DISTRESSED DAMSEL
(A POPULAR SONG, MID-SEVENTEENTH CENTURY)

This Girl was cunningly Trappan'd, sent to Virginny from England,
  Where she doth Hardship undergo, there is no Cure it must be so:
But if she lives to cross the Main, she vows she'll ne'r go there again.

Tune of Virginny, or, When that I was weary, weary, O.

Give ear unto a Maid, that lately was betray'd,
  And sent into Virginny, O:
In brief I shall declare, what I have suffer'd there,
  When that I was weary, weary, weary, weary, O.

[Since] that first I came to this Land of Fame,
  Which is called Virginny, O,
The Axe and the Hoe have wrought my overthrow,
  When that I was weary, weary, weary, weary O.

Five years served I, under Master Guy,
  In the land of Virginny, O,
Which made me for to know sorrow, grief and woe.
  When that I was weary, weary, weary, weary O.

When my Dame says 'Go' then I must do so.
  In the land of Virginny, O.
When she sits at Meat, then I have none to eat,
  When that I am weary, weary, weary, weary, O.

The Cloath[e]s that I brought in, they are worn very thin,
  In the land of Virginny, O,
Which makes me for to say, 'Alas, and Well-a-day!
  When that I am weary, weary, weary, weary, O.

Instead of Beds of Ease, to lye down when I please,
  In the Land of Virginny, O;

Upon a bed of straw, I lye down full of woe,
    When that I am weary, weary, weary, weary, O. . . .

So soon as it is day, to work I must away,
    In the Land of Virginny, O;
Then my Dame she knocks, with her tinder-box,
    When that I am weary, weary, weary, weary, O. . . .

If my Dame says 'Go!' I dare not say no,
    In the Land of Virginny, O;
The Water from the Spring, upon my head I bring,
    When that I am weary, weary, weary, weary, O.

When the Mill doth stand, I'm ready at command,
    In the Land of Virginny, O;
The Morter for to make, which makes my heart to ake,
    When that I am weary, weary, weary, weary, O.

When the Child doth cry, I must sing 'By-a-by!'
    In the Land of Virginny, O;
No rest that I can have, whilst I am here a Slave,
    When that I am weary, weary, weary, weary, O. . . .

Then let Maids beware, all by my ill-fare,
    In the Land of Virginny, O;
Be sure to stay at home, for if you do here come,
    You all will be weary, weary, weary, weary, O.

But if it be my chance, Homewards to advance,
    From the Land of Virginny, O;
If that I, once more, land on English Shore,
    I'll no more be weary, weary, weary, weary, O.

RUNAWAY SERVANTS

As the following newspaper notices show, indentured servants frequently sought to escape the difficult conditions of their service.

NANSEMOND, JULY 14, 1737

Ran away some time in June last, from William Pierce of Nansemond County, near Mr. Theophilus Pugh's Merchant: a convict servant woman named Winifred Thomas. She is Welsh woman, short black Hair'd and young; mark'd on the Inside of her Right Arm with Gunpowder W. T. and the Date of the Year underneath. She knits and spins, and is supposed to be gone into North Carolina by the way of Cureatuck and Roanoke Inlet. Whoever brings her to her master shall be paid a Pistole besides what the law allows, paid by

William Pierce

VIRGINIA *GAZETTE*, MARCH 26, 1767

Run away from the subscriber, in Northumberland county, two Irish convict servants named William and Hannah Daylies, tinkers by trade, of which the woman is extremely good; they had a note of leave to go out and work in Richmond county and Hobb's Hole, the money to be paid to Job Thomas, in said county; soon after I heard they were run away. . . . The woman had on an old stuff gown and a light coloured petticoat, and under petticoat of cotton with a blue selvedge at the bottom, a blue striped satin gown, the same with his jacket, two check aprons, and a pair of pale blue calimanco shoes. . . . They had a complete set of tinkers tools. They were seen to have two English guineas and a good deal of silver, and said in Essex county they lived in Agusta, and inquired the road that way. Whoever will apprehend both or either of said servants, and brings them to me, shall have five pounds reward for each, and reasonable travelling charges allowed by

William Taite

SERVANTS' RESISTANCE

The terrible conditions of indenture naturally provoked various kinds of resistance, including appeals to the courts (a right that slaves, of course, did not possess). Living usually in separate families without much chance for contact with others in their position, it was difficult for servants to develop collective forms of protest. Many employed a kind of passive resistance, trying to do as little work as possible and even trying to create difficulties for their masters and mistresses. Of course the masters and mistresses interpreted the servants' recalcitrant behavior as sullenness, laziness, malevolence, and stupidity. One must compensate for that point of view in the following excerpts, written from the masters' perspective, in order to get at what the servants' feelings might have been.

During the colonial period service of every kind was performed by transported convicts, indented white servants or "redemptioners," "free willers," negroes, and Indians.

The first three classes—convicts, redemptioners, and free willers—were of European, at first generally of English, birth. The colonization of the new world gave opportunity for the transportation and subsequent employment in the colonies of large numbers of persons who, as a rule, belonged to a low class in the social scale. . . .

From the very first the advantage to England of this method of disposing of her undesirable population had been urged. . . .

So admirable did the plan seem in time that between the years 1661 and 1668 various proposals were made to the King and Council to constitute an office for transporting to the Plantations all vagrants, rogues, and idle persons that could give no account of themselves, felons who had the benefit of clergy, and such as were convicted of petty larceny—such persons to be transported to the nearest seaport and to serve four years if over twenty years of age, and seven years if under twenty. Virginia and Maryland were the colonies to which the majority of these servants were sent, though they were not unknown elsewhere.

It is impossible to state the proportion of servants belonging to the two classes of transported convicts and redemptioners, but the statement is apparently fair that the redemptioners who sold themselves into service to pay for the cost of their passage constituted by far the larger proportion.

The condition of the redemptioners seems to have been, for the most part, an unenviable one. . . .

The Anglesea Peerage Trial brings out the facts that the redemptioners fared ill, worked hard, lived on a coarse diet, and drank only water sweetened with a little molasses and flavored with ginger. . . .

The wages paid were, as a rule, small, though some complaints are found, especially in New England, of high wages and poor service. More often the wages were a mere pittance. Elizabeth Evans came from Ireland to serve John Wheelwright for three years. Her wages were to be three pounds a year and passage paid. Margery Batman, after five years of service in Charlestown, was to receive a she-goat to help her in starting life. Mary Polly, according to the terms of her indenture, was to serve ten years and then receive "three barrells of corn and one suit of penistone and one suit of good serge with one black hood, two shifts of dowlas and shoes and hose convenient." . . .

Mrs. Mary Winthrop Dudley writes repeatedly in 1636 to her mother, Mrs. Margaret Winthrop, begging her to send her a maid, "one that should be a good lusty servant that hath skille in a dairy." But how unsatisfactory the "lusty servant" proved a later letter of Mrs. Dudley shows:

"I thought it convenient," she writes, "to acquaint you and my father what a great affliction I have met withal by my maide servant, and how I am like through God his mercie to be freed from it; at her first coming me she carried her selfe dutifully as became a servant; but since through mine and my husbands forbearance towards her for small faults, she hath got such a head and is growen soe insolent that her carriage towrds vs, especially myselfe is vnsufferable. If I bid her doe a thinge shee will bid me to doe it my selfe, and she sayes how shee can give content as wel as any servant but shee will not, and sayes if I loue not quietnes I was never so fitted in my life, for shee would make mee haue enough of it. If I should write to you of all the reviling speeches and filthie language shee hath vsed towards me I should but grieue you. My husband hath vsed all meanes for to reforme her, reasons and perswasions, but shee doth professe that her heart and her nature will not suffer her to confesse her faults. If I tell my husband of her behauiour towards me, vpon examination shee will denie all that she hath done or spoken: so that we know not how to proceede against her: but my husband now hath hired another maide and is resolved to put her away the next weeke" . . .

The trials of at least one Connecticut housekeeper are hinted at in an Order of the General Court in 1645, providing that a certain "Susan C., for her rebellious carriage toward her mistress, is to be sent to the house of correction and be kept to hard labor and coarse diet, to be brought forth the next lecture day to be publicly corrected, and so to be corrected weekly, until order be given to the contrary."

SEXUAL EXPLOITATION

Women servants suffered uniquely from the indignities of patriarchal control over their personal lives. The sexual double standard often put them literally in a double bind: powerless to resist advances, and even rapes, by their masters and other men, they were nevertheless given the entire blame for being caught in violation of conventional sexual morality. At the same time, as the following description shows, women servants were frequently kept from respectability because their employment did not allow them marriage.

It was to the master's economic interest to keep his women servants from marriage and to prevent their having illicit sexual relations, very likely to result in childbearing with consequent interruption of work and impairment of health and stamina. As a practical matter the guarding of this interest was most difficult. Work in the fields brought women into intimate contact with the menservants. Household duties exposed them to the advances of members of the master's household, perhaps even the master himself. Poor Richard's advice to his readers in 1736 was doubtless well founded. "Let thy maidservant be faithful, strong, and homely," he cautioned. Children born out of wedlock were an all-too-common occurrence in the servant ranks.

In many of the colonies a servant guilty of bastardy was required to pay the fines and fees usually exacted from free unmarried mothers and, in addition, was obliged to indemnify her master for the loss of services he had suffered through her pregnancy and confinement. Few maidservants had funds of their own or sufficiently prosperous friends or relations to pay these charges. Extra service was the only alternative. While both Maryland and Virginia imposed some measure of responsibility upon the putative father, later Virginia statutes merely required him to give bond for the maintenance of the child, but the obligation of extra service was solely the mother's. Pennsylvania and North Carolina followed Virginia in imposing extra service upon female servants guilty of bastardy. . . . The plentitude of illustrations of extra service imposed upon maidservants for bastardy by the courts from Pennsylvania down to the Carolinas point to the inescapable conclusion that in those areas the master was often enriched far beyond his actual losses. They also demonstrate the direct relationship between illicit unions and the prohibition against the marriages of indentured servants without their masters' consent.

To illustrate the amount of extra service thus imposed, let us consider the case of Ann Hardie, brought into the Ann Arundel court by her master in 1747. She was sentenced to serve six months (for an expenditure of 614 lbs. of tobacco for costs of suit), an additional year (for having a mulatto bastard "to the trouble of his house"), and six months of £3 current for a second child. In addition, the second child's father was required to serve six months or pay £3 currency, and to serve an additional nine months for the child's maintenance. As late as 1780 an extra term of seven years was imposed by the Frederick County court upon Fanny Dreaden for having a "base born child." The bastardy prosecutions of servants Nicholas Millethopp and Mary Barton also illustrate the master's interest in keeping his servants from marrying. The servants pleaded marriage in England, were unable to furnish proof by witness or certificate, and were found by the Virginia county court not to have come into the country as man and wife nor to have declared themselves until some months after their arrival. They had concealed their marriage upon the advice of their importer, who sold them into servitude without revealing their status. They were condemned for fornication and enjoined from living together as man and wife until they had served their terms. "Such presidents [precedents] being allowed," the court concluded, "All whores and Rooges might say the like."

Where the putative father of the illegitimate child happened to be the master, there was a danger that he would brazenly assert his rights at law to extra service from his maidservant. A Virginia statute of 1672 confessed that "late experiments shew that some dissolute masters have gotten their maides with child, and yet claime the benefitt of their service." To prevent such scandalous conduct, the legislature deprived such masters of their legal claims to extra service. Instead, the maidservant was to be sold for the extra term by the church wardens or required to pay 1,000 lbs. of tobacco to the parish. However, the determination of the authorities that the master should gain no extra advantage from his own wrongdoing did not preclude their ordering the maidservant to return to her master and serve out her term. Other than an occasional admonition and the requirement that he post security for the maintenance of the child, no punishment was accorded the master under these acts. One maidservant on a Maryland plantation preferred whipping to marriage with her master, the father of her child, on the ground that "he was a lustful, very lustful man." Under Virginia law, if the unmarried mother happened to have had a criminal record, her master was entitled not only to an extra year of service but to the service of the illegitimate child as well, and it must be borne in mind that the services of a minor between the ages of twelve and eighteen had very considerable economic value on a plantation.

Finally, some of the colonies provided servitude for fornication committed by a servant, male or female, and for miscegenation. A Virginia statute fixed a penalty of a year extra whenever a manservant was convicted of having had illicit relations with a maidservant. A freeman convicted of having relations with a woman servant was liable to serve the master a year. This penalty was later reduced to one-half year extra. The penalty was applied to women servants as well as to men. A Maryland act of 1692 provided that any white woman marrying a Negro would become a servant for seven years; if the Negro were free, he was to become a servant for the remainder of his life.

A SERVANT WOMAN FIGHTS FOR HER SON ———————

Indentured servitude was common in the Spanish as well as the British colonies. In New Spain as in New England, domestic servants were usually and often cruelly treated, but by no means slaves. Indentured servants frequently tried to use the courts to defend their rights, however minimal, sometimes with success. In San Antonio, Texas, in 1735, Anttonía Lusgardia Ernandes gave birth to a child by her patrón (master). (We have no way of knowing whether the child was born out of a mutual relationship or was the result of an assault, to which servants were particularly vulnerable.) When her patrón seized the child, Ernandes appealed to a Spanish court, pleading her economic dependence on her son, and won.

We are grateful to Vicki L. Ruiz for this selection.

Petition of Anttonía Lusgardia Ernandes, August 9, 1735

Mr. Governor and Captain General,

I, Anttonía Lusgardia Ernandes, a free mulatto residing in the presidio, do hereby appear before your Lordship in the best form according to law and my own interests and state that about eight or nine years ago I entered the home of Don Miguel Nuñes, taking a daughter of mine with me. I entered the said home without any salary whatever and while I was working in the said home of Don Miguel Nuñes Morillo I suffered so much from lack of clothing and from mistreatment of my humble person that I left the said house and went to the home of Alberto Lopez, taking two children with me, one of whom I had when I entered the home of the said Don Miguel and another which I gave birth to in his home. Just for this reason, and because his wife baptized the said creature, he, exercising absolute power, snatched away from me my son—the only man I have and the one who I hope will eventually support me. He took him from the house where I live and carried him to his own, I being but a poor, helpless woman whose only protection is a good administration and a good judicial system. Your Lordship will please demand that the said Don Miguel Nuñes, without the least delay, shall proceed to deliver my son to me without making any excuses. I wish to make use of all the laws in my favor, and of Your Lordship, as a father and protector of the poor and helpless, as well as anything else which might be in my favor. I beg and entreat your Lordship, with all due humility and veneration, to be so good as to do as I have requested and thus I shall be benefitted and receive justice and mercy. I swear to this writ in due form and whatever else is necessary.

At the request of Anttonía Lusgardia Ernandes
August 9, 1735

GEORGE WASHINGTON'S SLAVES ————————————

The most exploited working women were the slaves. Slavery was essentially a system of labor used, like indenture, to counter labor shortages and to make possible profitable large-scale agriculture. Slavery was not a peripheral but a central institution in the United States—the basis of the capitalist system. The slave trade and then slave labor on large plantations provided the capital that created, first, an international commerce and, later, a powerful industrial economy.

The brutal treatment of American slaves did not arise simply from the personal sadism of slaveowners but from the owners' desire to maximize the labor they got from their human chattel. European settlers first tried to enslave Native Americans, whom they called Indians. But due to the Indians' effective resistance, strengthened by their familiarity with the land, American Indian slavery never became stable or profitable, and the Europeans turned to an African slave trade. Most southern whites never owned slaves (slightly over a third did at the peak of slavery), and most slaveowners were small famers; the planter aristocracy constituted less than 3 percent of slaveowners by the time of the Civil War. But on these large plantations slaves did all the work, not just the cotton picking that has become a dominant image. Much of this labor was highly skilled and slaves exercised considerable control over how it was done, thereby creating conflicts with their overseers and masters. Slaves also influenced the sexual division of their labor, considering some work fit for men and other work for women.

The following task list from George Washington's plantation, one of the largest in America, dates from 1786 to 1787 and illustrates the variety and division of slave labor.

Tasks on George Washington's Plantations, by Age, Sex, and Season, 1786–1787

Men

Skills

overseer	shoemaker
sawyer	house servant
carpenter	ferryman
miller	carter / wagoner
cooper	brickmaker / bricklayer
blacksmith	gardener

Winter

work on millrace	maul rails
dig ditches	make fences and livestock pens
plow	saw timber
cut rails, posts, and timber	build roads
cut firewood	work in new ground
haul timber and grain	frame barn
kill hogs	make fagots
help fill icehouse	shell corn

BEFORE 1820

Men

Winter

cut straw	beat out hominy
thresh wheat and rye	tend stable
strip tobacco	tan leather
make baskets and horse collars	do odd jobs

Spring / summer

plow	cradle at harvest of wheat and rye
harrow	bind at harvest
roll grain fields	shock wheat and oats
seine fish	gather basket splits and tan bark
sow carrots, cabbage, flax, barley, oats, wheat, and clover	cut and maul fence rails and posts
weed peas	clean swamp
cut straw	fill gullies
cut brush and burn logs	grub fields
tie and heap hemp	dig ditches
thresh wheat and clover seed	make baskets and horse collars
plant potatoes and jerusalem artichokes	cut hay and clover
make corn hills and weed corn	cut corn stalks
plant corn, pumpkins, and peas and replant these	cut firewood
	shell corn

Fall

harvest corn and peas	thresh peas
plow	make livestock pens and feed racks
sow winter grain	
harrow	

Women

Skills

milking	ironing
spinning	cooking
weaving	doing scullery
washing	being house servant

Winter

help at icehouse	clean out stable
cut and gather cornstalks	heap dung
beat out hominy	carry fence rails
hoe new ground	grub swamp, woods, and meadow
thin trees in swamp	husk and shell corn

WOMEN

Winter

burn brush
fill gullies
plow
kill and salt hogs
thresh wheat, rye, and clover seed

strip tobacco
pack fish
strip basket splits
make baskets

Spring / summer

dig post holes
make fences
heap and burn trash
chop plowed ground
harrow
plow
grub meadow
clear new grounds
load dung in carts
gather and spread fish offal
make holes for corn
make pumpkin hills
plant and replant melons
sow carrots
hoe corn ground
bind oats at harvest
stack wheat and rye at harvest
thresh wheat and clover seed
cut sprouts from tree stumps in fields
pile grass tussocks hoed out of weedy
   ground
hoe rough or wet ground plows can't
   touch

prepare meadow for oats and timothy
make hills for sweet potatoes and plant
   them
weed pumpkins (old women and those
   with young children)
care for cattle
pick up apples
level ditches
chop after harrows
grub after plows
clean hedgerows
clean fields
fill gullies in fields
spread dung
hill for peas
plant corn
weed peas
plant cabbages
cut up cornstalks
shell corn

Fall

break and swingle flax
chop in flax
make livestock pens
cut down cornstalks
harvest corn

thresh rye, clover seed, peas, wheat, oats
dig carrots
clean oat and wheat seed
pile cornstalks

BOYS

weed peas
clear trash from fields
carry wheat at harvest
thresh wheat

assist tanners
help in stable
fence (with women's gang)
grub meadow (with women's gang)

BOYS

fill gullies (with women's gang)	gather cornstalks
hoe around stumps	do odd jobs
burn brush	make corn hills (with women's gang)
help with carting	plant corn (with women's gang)
work on road	

GIRLS

make hay	secure grain at harvest (ages 16, 13, and
beat out hominy	12)
burn brush	thresh wheat
help with carting	work on road
make fences	help in stable
bake bread	get water for washing
plow (age 14)	tend sick children
shell corn	

CHILDREN

gather at harvest	carry at harvest

RUNAWAY SLAVES

Although slave women did not flee as often as slave men, due in large part to their obligations for children, they did number among escaping slaves. Escape was a widespread form of resistance. It involved great risks and those caught were severely punished, sometimes even put to death.

ADVERTISEMENT FROM THE VIRGINIA *GAZETTE* (WILLIAMSBURG), MARCH 26, 1767

Run away about the 15th of December last, a small yellow Negro wench named Hannah, about 35 years of age; had on when she went away a green plains petticoat, and sundry other clothes, but what sort I do not know, as she stole many from the other Negroes. She has remarkable long hair, or wool, is much scarified under the throat from one ear to the other, and has many scars on her back, occasioned by whipping. She pretends much to the religion the Negroes of late have practised, and may probably endeavour to pass for a free woman, as I understand she intended when she went away, by the Negroes in the neighbourhood. She is supposed to have made for Carolina. Whoever takes up the said slave, and secures her so that I get her again, shall be rewarded according to their trouble, by

Stephen Dence

ADVERTISEMENT FROM THE *CAROLINA CENTINEL* (NEWBERN, N.C.), JULY 25, 1818

TEN DOLLARS REWARD. Ranaway From the Subscriber living in Jones County, on the 18th. inst. a Negro Woman by the name of Amy, she is tall and stout built, Yellow Complexion, about 40 years of age, with several scars on her cheek and back of her neck, walks with her toes very much out, one of her fore-fingers very crooked near the joint of the thumb, which prevents her from straitening it, and has a very sullen look. The above Negro woman was taken up last winter by Mr. Guilford D. Murphy, up Neuse, where she was harboured. She says she was harboured, by a fellow by the name of Sam, belonging to Gen. Thomas A. Green, she then went to General Simpson's plantation, where she was harboured by his negroes, then crossed over Neuse and was harboured by Mr. Patrick's and William Bryan's Negroes. I will give the above reward for her, delivered to me or secured in Jail so that I get her.

Masters of vessels and all others are forbid harbouring, employing or carrying her away under penalty of the law.

Joseph Hatch
Jones County, July 25th. 1818

1820–1865

1820–1865: INTRODUCTION

In the years 1820 to 1865, a new economic and social force, labelled the "Industrial Revolution," was beginning to transform how Americans worked, lived, and thought about their society. Factories began to produce products that had been customarily made in the home or small shops by hand. Factory production, especially when mechanized, could turn out products at a vastly accelerated rate and with rail transportation deliver them to a national rather than a local marketplace. The factory system required large amounts of capital and both produced and was stimulated by growing urban markets. Industrial production depended on wage labor, long hours, repetitive work, and new forms of labor discipline.

The factory system, still in its infancy, competed with two other forms of labor during this period: plantation slavery, and farm and artisan labor, characterized by small-scale production and skilled craftsmanship. Artisans and farmers were self-employed and sold their products locally. Although it was difficult to compete with industry, which developed first in the East, many artisans and farmers continued to find markets in the developing Midwest and West. Still, the most significant historical change in this period was the growing vitality and power of the industrial way of life.

The rise of industry and growth of cities influenced the development of classes. Between 1820 and 1860, as the per capita income more than doubled, the gap between rich and poor grew, especially in big cities. In the eighteenth century, rich and poor often lived side by side; in the nineteenth, rich and poor became increasingly geographically separated. In the cities, the poor lived in slums, lacking municipal water supplies, sewers, or garbage collection. Disease was rampant; in every American city, there were sanitation-related epidemics, such as yellow fever, cholera, and typhus.

Many small enterprises went out of business. Craftsmen in small shops—for example, tailors and shoemakers—could not compete with large-scale industrial production, and many were forced to become factory workers. Even workers who did not earn wages became increasingly dependent on those that did. Small farmers were similarly affected; those who could not support themselves were forced to give up their farms or to supplement their cash income through seasonal labor.

Industrialization changed life for women as well as for men. At the end of this period, approximately 14 percent of women sixteen and over worked for wages, and about 20 percent of the manufacturing employees were women, of whom 25 percent were under sixteen years old.

In preindustrial society, women's housework was productive, highly skilled, and varied. The removal of labor to factories, and to professionals like doctors and nurses, began a process of reducing women's work to "housework" in its modern definition—cooking, cleaning, and child care. The "housewife" is as much a characteristic and unique industrial worker as the factory operative. This transformation of women from home manufacturers into housewives happened gradually and at different rates in different parts of the country. On farms and in small towns, and among the poor, women's labor still included a great deal of handicrafts and domestic production.

Indeed, in this period the rural white population of the United States was growing in some places while it was shrinking in others, because of westward expansion. The long journey west was rarely undertaken by the very poorest Americans. Nevertheless, the "frontier" influenced all Americans. Not only those who went but even those who stayed were caught up in the reverberations of motion and expansion. Constructing the networks of transportation and communication occupied a large proportion of the country's capital and labor power.

This expansion appeared to most European Americans as the settlement of "virgin lands," but in fact it was mainly the seizure of Indian and Hispanic territory. A variety of methods were used to accomplish this end: war and massacre, annexation, forced removal, broken treaties, and other discriminatory measures. When slavery threatened to follow American expansion westward, however, there was strong resistance, and the controversy over whether slavery could gain new territory heightened the conflicts between the slave and wage labor systems that led to the Civil War.

While economically the Civil War was in some sense a beginning, politically it was a culmination of a powerful wave of political activism. Many reform movements flourished in the 1830s, 1840s, and 1850s. The most important was abolitionism, in which black and white women played a disproportionate role, sometimes working together. Women were active in religious revivals, a popular health movement, labor reform, religious and socialist utopian communities, and a women's rights movement. The first modern labor protest came from female workers at the new cotton textile factories. Most shared not only opposition to slavery but also a favorable attitude toward women's advancement.

An impediment faced by women trying to organize in this period was the ideology of "True Womanhood." This popular myth, disseminated by the clergy and the new women's magazines, expounded the notion that women's rightful place was at home and that women should be delicate, self-sacrificing, and asexual. The ideology stressed that men, buffeted by the stress of business and urban life, were entitled to a home in which they would be served in domestic tranquility by a pious, devoted wife. Although this "ideal" was unattainable for poor, working-class, and farm women, their failure to attain it often made them feel guilty and angry, and their efforts to attain it sometimes made their collective organization as workers more difficult. On the other hand, they also used this ideal of womanhood to help organize as women and to demand better wages and working conditions.

Slaves and Free Blacks

SLAVES FOR SALE

Under the slave system, the master owned your labor as well as your person; human beings were defined as property, bought, sold, and inherited. Under slavery, class relations became race relations.

ADVERTISEMENT FROM THE CHARLESTON (S.C.) *CITY GAZETTE,* FEB. 21, 1825

VALUABLE NEGROES FOR SALE

A Wench, complete cook, washer and ironer, and her 4 Children—a Boy 12, another 9, a Girl 5, that sews; and a Girl about 4 years old.

Another Family—a Wench, complete washer and ironer, and her Daughter, 14 years old, accustomed to the house.

A Wench, a house servant, and two male Children; one three years old, and the other 4 months.

A complete Seamstress and House Servant, with her male Child 7 years old.

Three Young Wenches, 18, 19, 21, all accustomed to house work.

A Mulatto Girl, about 17, a complete Seamstress and Waiting Maid, with her Grandmother.

Two Men, one a complete Coachman, and the other a Waiter. Apply at this Office, or at No. 19 Hasell-street.

Feb 19.

SLAVE WOMEN'S LABOR ───────────────

Slaves lived in two systems, the masters' and their own. Historians debate how well the slaves became socialized to the masters' culture and how much African culture survived but agree that African culture often nourished the slaves and helped them to contest slavery. There was organized, open resistance, like rebellions and running away, alone or in groups, but there was also a great deal of sabotage, passive resistance such as poisoning food, dropping a baby, breaking valuable objects "accidentally," lighting fires, feigning laziness, stealing, or appearing not to understand orders.

Female slaves not only labored for their masters, but after this work was done, they cooked, cleaned, sewed, and tended gardens for their own families. Even though this work was arduous and exhausting, they often enjoyed the chance to work for their families.

During the New Deal, a federally funded writers' project interviewed hundreds of ex-slaves. The women who told their stories were old when interviewed, and their recollections of slavery often dated back to childhood. Most of the interviewers were white, and all memory is problematic. Despite these limitations, their stories reveal much about the work they did, how they were made to do it, and how they managed to survive their difficult lives.

The following are excerpts from the life stories of three women. Many interviewers used a spelling designed to imitate southern black dialect.

ELLEN BETTS, LOUISIANA

I got borned on the Bayou Teche, clost to Opelousas. That in St. Mary's Parish, in Louisiana, and I belonged to Tolas Parsons, what had 'bout five hundred slaves, counting the big ones and the little ones, and he had God know what else. . . . Miss Sidney was Marse's first wife, and he had six boys by her. Then he marry the widow Cornelia, and she give him four boys. With ten children springing up quick like that and all the colored children coming 'long fast as pig'litters, I don't do nothing all my days, but nurse, nurse, nurse. I nurse so many children it done went and stunted my growth, and that's why I ain't nothing but bones to this day. . . .

When the colored women has to cut cane all day till midnight come and after, I has to nurse the babies for them and tend the white children, too. Some them babies so fat and big I had to tote the feet while 'nother gal tote the head. I was such a little one, 'bout seven or eight year old. The big folks leave some toddy for colic and crying and such, and I done drink the toddy and let the children have the milk. I don't know no better. Lawsy me, it a wonder I ain't the biggest drunker in this here country, counting all the toddy I done put in my young belly! . . .

I nurse the sick folks too. Sometimes I dose with blue mass pills, and sometime Dr. Fawcett leave rhubarb and ipecac and calomel and castor oil and such. Two year after the war I git marry and git children of my own and then I turn into the wet nurse. I wet-nursed the white children and black children, like they all the same color. Sometime I have a white one pulling the one side and a black one the other.

I wanted to git the papers for midwifing but, Law, I don't never have no time for larning in slave time. If Marse cotch a paper in you hand he sure whup you. He don't 'low no bright niggers round, he sell 'em quick. He always say, "Book larning don't raise no good sugar cane." The only larning he 'low was when they larn the colored children the Methodist catechism. The only writing a nigger ever get am when he git born or marry or die, then Marse put the name in the big book. . . .

JOANNA DRAPER, MISSISSIPPI

. . . When I is about six year old, they take me into the big house to learn to be a house woman, and they show me how to cook and clean up and take care of babies. That big house wasn't very fine, but it was mighty big and cool, and made out of logs with a big hall, but it didn't have no long gallery like most the houses around there had. . . .

I didn't have to work very hard. Just had to help the cooks and peel the potatoes and pick the guineas and chickens and do things like that. Sometime I had to watch the baby. He was a little boy, and they would bring him into the kitchen for me to watch. I had to git up way before daylight and make the fire in the kitchen fireplace and bring in some fresh water, and go get the milk what been down in the spring all night, and do things like that until breakfast ready. Old Master and Old Mistress come in the big hall to eat in the summer; and I stand behind them and shoo off the flies.

Old Doctor didn't have no spinning and weaving niggers 'cause he say they don't do enough work, and he buy all the cloth he use for everybody's clothes. He can do that 'cause he had lots of money. . . .

One evening 'long come a man and eat supper at the house and stay all night. He was a nice-mannered man, and I like to wait on him. The next morning I hear him ask Old Doctor what is my name, and Old Doctor start in to try to sell me to that man. The man say he can't buy me 'cause Old Doctor say he want a thousand dollars, and then Old Doctor say he will bind me out to him.

I run away from the house and went out to the cabin where my mammy and pappy was, but they tell me to go on back to the big house 'cause maybe I am just scared. But about that time Old Doctor and the man come, and Old Doctor make me go with the man. We go in his buggy a long ways off to the south, and after he stop two or three night at people's houses and put me out to stay with the niggers, he come to his own house. I ask him how far it is back home, and he say about a hundred miles or more, and laugh, and ask me if I know how far that is.

I wants to know if I can go back to my mammy sometime, and he say "Sure, of course you can, some of these times. You don't belong to me, Jo, I's just your boss and not your master."

He live in a big old rottendy house, but he ain't farming none of the land. Just as soon as he git home, he go off again, and sometimes he only come in at night for a little while.

His wife's name was Kate and his name was Mr. John. I was there about a week before I found out they name was Deeson. They had two children, a girl about my size, name Joanna like me, and a little baby boy, name Johnny. One day Mistress Kate tell me I the only nigger they got. I been thinking maybe they had some somewhere on a plantation, but she say they ain't got no plantation and they ain't been at that place very long either.

That little girl Joanna and me kind of take up together, and she was a mighty nice-mannered little girl, too. Her mammy raised her good. Her mammy was mighty sickly all the time, and that's the reason they bind me to do the work. . . .

I sure had a hard row at that house. It was old and rackety, and I had to scrub off the staircase and the floors all the time, and git the breakfast for Mistress Kate and the two children. Then I could have my own breakfast in the kitchen. Mistress Kate always get the supper, though.

Some days she go off with the two children and leave me at the house all day by myself, and I think maybe I run off, but I didn't know where to go. . . .

I stayed at Mr. John's place two more years, and he got so grumpy and his wife got so mean I make up my mind to run off. I bundle up my clothes in a little bundle and hide them, and then I wait until Miss Kate take the children and go off somewhere, and I light out on foot. I had me a piece of that hard money what Master Doctor Alexander had give me one time at Christmas. I had kept it all that time, and nobody knowed I had it, not even Joanna. Old Doctor told me it was fifty dollars, and I thought I could live on it for a while.

I never had been away from the place, not even to another plantation in all the four years I was with the Deesons, and I didn't know which-a-way to go, so I just started west.

I been walking about all evening, it seem like, and I come to a little town with just a few houses. I see a nigger man and ask him where I can git something to eat, and I say I got fifty dollars.

"What you doing with fifty dollars, child? Where you belong at, anyhow?" he ask me, and I tell him I belong to Master John Deeson, but I is running away. I explain that I just bound out to Mr. John, but Dr. Alexander my real master, and then that man tell me the first time I knowed it that I ain't a slave no more!

That man Deeson never did tell me, and his wife never did!

Well, that man asked me about the fifty dollars, and then I found out that it was just fifty cents! . . .

I never will forgive that white man for not telling me I was free, and not helping me to git back to my mammy and pappy! Lots of white people done that. . . .

ELIZA OVERTON, MISSOURI

"Our muthuh; Eliza, was born a slave in 1849, on da farm of her boss; Mr. Madden, in New Tennessee, Ste. Genevieve County, Missouri. Elisa's muthuh wuz also a slave. Muthuh wuz sol' with our grandmuthuh to John Coffman of near Coffman, Missouri, in Ste. Genevieve County. Mr. Coffman had thousands of acres. He had three plantations an' one wuz at Libertyville, Missouri. He had 'bout two hundred slaves. The negroes war tak'n frum one plantashun ta the other, and our grandmuthuh work'd at all three places. 'Ole man Coffman' wuz a mean ol' slave hol'er. He war afraid of his slaves an' had some one else ta do da whippin'. They war rougher on ma aunt; Eleanor, cause she war stubborn. They wud punish da slaves severely fur 'membrance. They whoop'd with a rawhide whop an' trace chains. Wilson Harris wuz whooped at a tree onc't an' when day got thro' he say he wud fight. They whop him some mor' 'til he wus weak an' bleedin'. The other slaves had to grease his shirt ta take it off his back ta koop frum tearin' off de flesh. We can go down thar now and pick out trees whar the slaves war tied an' whipp'd. The trees died on de side whar de slaves war tied. There are three trees on de Coffman farm that I seen dead on one side, an' sum' war in the yard. Thar is one clos' to the Houck Railroad station thar. . . .

"Mr. Coffman had a whole row of slave cabins. Our cabins war small an' we had a corded bed, trundle bed ta slip unda' the big bed ta save room, hoine made split bottom chairs, tin plates, wodd'n boxes, an' a fire-place. John Coffman gave us a 'lowance of food. . . . Many tha time we ran short on food so's one night muthuh went out to wher the hogs war. Mr. Coffman had so many hogs he didn't know how many he had. She had da watershot an' the hogs wer a long ways from Mr. Coffman's house. So she hit a hog in de haad with the ax an' kill'd it. Afta' killin' it she went to the cabin ta get the water an' when she kum' bak one of the other slaves had stole de dead hog. So she hit anuther one in de head an' after fixin' it hid the hog under de puncheon flat of the cab'n. This wus done often. Mr. Coffman use ta kill 'bout one hundred hogs at one time an' den put dem in de smoke-house. My muthuh ud get the key to the smoke-house an' load up an' carry some meat home.

A WHITE MISTRESS ————————————————————

Published in the same year that the slaves were emancipated, the Journal of
a Residence on a Georgia Plantation *enjoyed an intensive wartime fame as a
fierce denunciation of slavery. Written by a well-known British actress,
Fanny Kemble (1809–1893), who was appalled by her American husband's
treatment of slaves on his huge cotton and rice plantations, where she lived
for three and a half months, its purpose was to discourage English intervention and to spur the North to victory. As slaves had no rights or institutions
to appeal to for justice, they sometimes pleaded their cases with the plantation
mistresses, who often, like Fanny Kemble, had little power.*

. . . Yesterday evening I had a visit that made me very sorrowful, if any
thing connected with these poor people can be called more especially sorrowful than their whole condition; but Mr. ———'s declaration that he will
receive no more statements of grievances or petitions for redress through me
makes me as desirous now of shunning the vain appeals of these unfortunates
as I used to be of receiving and listening to them. The imploring cry, "Oh
missis!" that greets me whichever way I turn, makes me long to stop my ears
now; for what can I say or do any more for them? The poor little favors—the
rice, the sugar, the flannel—that they beg for with such eagerness, and
receive with such exuberant gratitude, I can, it is true, supply, and words
and looks of pity, and counsel of patience, and such instruction in womanly
habits of decency and cleanliness as may enable them to better, in some
degree, their own hard lot; but to the entreaty, "Oh, missis, you speak to
massa for us! Oh, missis, you beg massa for us! Oh, missis, you tell massa
for we, he sure do as you say!" I can not now answer as formerly, and I turn
away choking and with eyes full of tears from the poor creatures, not even
daring to promise any more the faithful transmission of their prayers.

The women who visited me yesterday evening were all in the family-way,
and came to entreat of me to have the sentence (what else can I call it?)
modified which condemns them to resume their labor of hoeing in the fields
three weeks after their confinement. They knew, of course, that I can not
interfere with their appointed labor, and therefore their sole entreaty was that
I would use my influence with Mr. ——— to obtain for them a month's
respite from labor in the field after childbearing. Their principal spokes-
woman, a woman with a bright sweet face, called Mary, and a very sweet
voice, which is by no means an uncommon excellence among them,
appealed to my own experience; and while she spoke of my babies, and my
carefully tended, delicately nursed, and tenderly watched confinement and
convalescence, and implored me to have a kind of labor given to them less

exhausting during the month after their confinement, I held the table before me so hard in order not to cry that I think my fingers ought to have left a mark on it. At length I told them that Mr. ——— had forbidden me to bring him any more complaints from them, for that he thought the ease with which I received and believed their stories only tended to make them discontented, and that, therefore, I feared I could not promise to take their petitions to him; but that he would be coming down to "the Point" soon, and that they had better come then some time when I was with him, and say what they had just been saying to me; and with this, and various small bounties, I was forced, with a heavy heart, to dismiss them; and when they were gone, with many exclamations of, "Oh yes, missis, you will, you will speak to massa for we; God bless you, missis, we sure you will!" I had my cry out for them, for myself, for us. All these women had had large families, and *all* of them had lost half their children, and several of them had lost more. How I do ponder upon the strange fate which has brought me here, from so far away, from surroundings so curiously different—how my own people in that blessed England of my birth would marvel if they could suddenly have a vision of me as I sit here, and how sorry some of them would be for me!

. . . Before closing this letter, I have a mind to transcribe to you the entries for to-day recorded in a sort of daybook, where I put down very succinctly the number of people who visit me, their petitions and ailments, and also such special particulars concerning them as seem to me worth recording. You will see how miserable the physical condition of many of these poor creatures is; and their physical condition, it is insisted by those who uphold this evil system, is the only part of it which is prosperous, happy, and compares well with that of Northern laborers. Judge from the details I now send you; and never forget, while reading them, that the people on this plantation are well off, and consider themselves well off, in comparison with the slaves on some of the neighboring estates.

Fanny has had six children; all dead but one. She came to beg to have her work in the field lightened.

Nanny has had three children; two of them are dead. She came to implore that the rule of sending them into the field three weeks after their confinement might be altered.

Leah, Caesar's wife, has had six children; three are dead.

Sophy, Lewis's wife, came to beg for some old linen. She is suffering fearfully; has had ten children; five of them are dead. The principal favor she asked was a piece of meat, which I gave her.

Sally, Scipio's wife, has had two miscarriages and three children born, one of whom is dead. She came complaining of incessant pain and weakness in her back. This woman was a mulatto daughter of a slave called Sophy, by a white man of the name of Walker, who visited the plantation.

Charlotte, Renty's wife, had had two miscarriages, and was with child again. She was almost crippled with rheumatism, and showed me a pair of poor swollen knees that made my heart ache. I have promised her a pair of flannel trowsers, which I must forth with set about making.

Sarah, Stephen's wife—this woman's case and history were alike deplorable. She had had four miscarriages, had brought seven children into the world, five of whom were dead, and was again with child. She complained of dreadful pains in the back, and an internal tumor which swells with the exertion of working in the fields; probably, I think, she is ruptured. She told me she had once been mad and had ran into the woods, where she contrived to elude discovery for some time, but was at last tracked and brought back, when she was tied up by the arms, and heavy logs fastened to her feet, and was severely flogged. After this she contrived to escape again, and lived for some time skulking in the woods, and she supposes mad, for when she was taken again she was entirely naked. She subsequently recovered from this derangement, and seems now just like all the other poor creatures who come to me for help and pity. I suppose her constant childbearing and hard labor in the fields at the same time may have produced the temporary insanity.

Sukey, Bush's wife, only came to pay her respects. She had had four miscarriages; had brought eleven children into the world, five of whom are dead.

Molly, Quambo's wife, also only came to see me. Hers was the best account I have yet received; she had had nine children, and six of them were still alive.

This is only the entry for to-day, in my diary, of the people's complaints and visits. Can you conceive a more wretched picture than that which it exhibits of the conditions under which these women live? Their cases are in no respect singular, and though they come with pitiful entreaties that I will help them with some alleviation of their pressing physical distresses, it seems to me marvelous with what desperate patience (I write it advisedly, patience of utter despair) they endure their sorrow-laden existence. Even the poor wretch who told that miserable story of insanity, and lonely hiding in the swamps, and scourging when she was found, and of her renewed madness and flight, did so in a sort of low, plaintive, monotonous murmur of misery, as if such sufferings were all "in the day's work."

I ask these questions about their children because I think the number they bear as compared with the number they rear a fair gauge of the effect of the system on their own health and that of their offspring. There was hardly one of these women, as you will see by the details I have noted of their ailments, who might not have been a candidate for a bed in a hospital, and they had come to me after working all day in the fields.

HEALING ON THE PLANTATION ————————————

Many older slaves were highly skilled and therefore indispensable to their masters. Some learned these skills, such as rice cultivation, quilt making, and healing, in Africa. The following letters exist because Charles Manigault and his son Louis owned several large rice plantations in South Carolina; they usually stayed in Charleston and had to direct their overseers by mail.

We would like to thank Sharla Felt and Suzanne Lebsock for bringing these letters to our attention.

FROM CHARLES MANIGAULT, C. 1840–43

Hints for Mr. Papot. Be kind in word & deed to all the Negroes for they have always been accustomed to it. Not to meddle too much with any work the Negroes may be doing until he gets more experience in Rice Plantation work as all negroes will be quite satisfied to go wrong if they can put it on any one else—The old Nurse Bina is a woman of the highest character every body has the highest opinion of her Rachel the cook has been on to Charleston in my family She is [illegible] correct & would not wrong you out of a bisquit

Should a Negro come to you & say he is sick you should question him as to what ails him & then tell him to go to the Nurse Bina when you will have time to decide what is best to be given him or her

TO CHARLES MANIGAULT IN PARIS FROM Z[?] HAYNES AT
ARGYLE, 7/1/46

The negroes have been very much effected with Diarroahs & Dysentery which I before mentioned but none have died & the grown negroes have not been attacked with it for some time (though old Harry is now labouring under its effects, I have sent him to the pine land to recruit [recoup?] if pofsible) the children (those at home) are at present considerably effected with it I fear Nancy's child will die. Mom Banah has really managed the disease remarkably well & I am in hopes it may soon subside.

TO CHARLES MANIGAULT FROM LOUIS M. IN GOWRIE, 4/9/53

On Sunday morning about day break Maum Binah died. The last thing she took, was some Tea I sent her on Saturday night. It so happened that I heard on Sunday morning that our Cholera Camp boards were at the Coleraine Landing, so on Monday quite early, I sent off the large flat (with the dead body) and on Tuesday had all the boards safe in the Barn Yard. . . .

FROM CHARLES MANIGAULT AT MARCHLANDS TO LOUIS
MANIGAULT, 4/20/57

Old Mom Bina used every spring to give all the children worm medicine.

We do so at the Farm with great & manifest results. I give what is called the "Dead Shot" which you buy at Savh with instructions how to give it. I wish you to consult Nurse Betty how the Grey Cloth given this winter is linked? & bring me a little pice of the new. . . .

HEALING AS A PROFESSION ———————————

By 1860 there were nearly half a million free blacks in the United States, constituting about 11 percent of the total black population; most (225,000) lived in northern cities, but there were free blacks in the South as well. Free black women often supported themselves and their families, taking in boarders, washing, ironing, sewing, nursing, practicing midwifery, or taking care of children. Phebe Jackson, freed in 1840, became a businesswoman, well known by blacks and whites in Petersburg, Virginia. In an account book, she kept track of the visits and payments. Cupping and leeching were standard medical practices of the day designed to draw out contaminated spirits and blood.

We would like to thank Sharla Felt and Suzanne Lebsock for bringing these selections to our attention.

1843

Aug 10th Mr Jas Dunlop Paid
To Leeching Self $1.50

Aug 8th Mrs. Davis
To Leeching servant at plantation $1.50 Paid

July 31 Mr. Charles Corling Paid
To Attendance [?] $2.50

May 29th Mr. Vaughan
To Cupping Self $1.00

Aug 1st Mr. James [illeg.] Paid
To Leeching and cupping Bob
Davis belonging to Mrs. Robertson $1.50

Aug 10th To Leeching Bob Davis $1.50

Aug 15th To Cupping Bob Davis $1.00

Aug 19th Mrs. H. Davis
To Leeching Self Paid $1.50

Aug 27 Mr. E Williamson Paid
To Cupping Self 1.50
Leeching

Aug 28 Mrs. Rives Paid
To Leeching Self $1.50

Mrs. Lethgo[?]
Jan 14th To Leeching Child 1.50

1844

Mrs. Rives
Jan 15th To Leeching servant Paid 1.50

Mrs. Davis
Jan [illeg.] To Leeching & Cupping Wife 1.50

Mrs. ——— [anon.]
Feb To Leeching servant man, Ben 1.50

Mrs. Moseby To
March 7th Leeching Self 1.50

March 7th For Cupping Colored woman belonging to the Estate of Mr. Cheivis 1.00

The Contested Land

WOMEN ON THE OREGON TRAIL ————————————

Migration within the United States brought its own kind of anguish for women, in which loneliness was combined with great physical hardship and danger. Many women moving slowly westward in their covered wagons kept diaries in which they spoke more openly about these feelings than perhaps their husbands knew. The women may have been expressing fears which their men shared but were conditioned not to express.

The following is excerpted from an unpublished manuscript by Amy Kesselman that is based on many diaries and reminiscences of women on the Oregon Trail.

Today we started across the dreary plains. Sad are the thoughts that steal over the reflecting mind. I am leaving my home, my early friends and associates never to see them again, exchanging the disinterested solicitude of fond friends for the cold and unsympathetic friendship of strangers. Shall we all reach the "El Dorado" of our hopes or shall one of our number be left and our graves be in the dreary wilderness, our bodies uncoffined and unknown remain there in solitude? Hard indeed that heart be that does not drop a tear as these thoughts roll across the mind.

When Elizabeth Goltra, who wrote this diary entry as she was leaving for Oregon from Kansas in 1853, speaks of the sad thoughts that steal over the reflecting mind, she is very specific and detailed. When she speaks of the destination of the travelers she is abstract and even slightly sarcastic. The entry conveys a kind of skeptical distance from the dreams which activated the westward movement. This tone is echoed in many women's trial diaries. It illustrates what Charles Moore, a pioneer of 1852, commented on in his address to the Oregon Pioneer Association in 1904 when he asserted that "For the average woman there was an utter lack of incentive. It was a forced and cheerless march to the promised home on the frontiers of civilization."

As David Potter suggested in his article "American Women and the American Character," the promised land toward which the pioneers were heading was not a land of opportunity for women:

. . . for American women, as individuals, opportunity began pretty much where the frontier left off. For opportunity lay in access to independent employment, and the employments of the frontier were not primarily accessible to women.

Most women were embarking on a journey full of risks and uncertainties, not in the hopes of fulfilling their dreams but, as illustrated by the following letter in the *National Intelligencer* in 1843, as accessories to their husbands:

You of the old states cannot readily conceive the every-day sort of business an 'old settler' makes of selling his improvements, hitching the horses to the big wagon, and with his wife and children, swine and cattle, pots and kettles, and household goods, starting a journey of hundreds of miles to find and make a new home. . . .

> Pull off your coat, roll up your sleeves
> For Jordan is a hard road to travel, I believe.

This song extract, jotted down in the diary of Enoch Conyers, a young man traveling with his relatives, expresses an enthusiasm for the challenges of the trip which is uniformly missing from women's diaries. Instead, we find recurrent anxiety and preoccupation with death. It was women who noticed the graves along the way and consistently reported death and illness on the trains. Sarah Cranstone, a pioneer of 1851, counted every single grave which she passed and recorded them every day. When she doesn't see many graves she explains in her diary that they would probably see more if they weren't traveling on the river bottom. "It makes it seem very gloomy to us to see so many of the emigrants buried on the plains," remarked Cecilia Mc-Millen Adams. Mrs. Lodisa Frizzel, en route to California in 1852, remarked when halfway to her destination that the journey "tires the soul." She went on to say:

> That this journey is tiresome no one will doubt, that it is perilous, the deaths of many will testify, and the heart has a thousand misgivings, and the mind is tortured with anxiety, and often as I passed the freshly made graves, I have glanced at the side boards of the wagon, not knowing how soon it might serve as the coffin for some one of us; but thanks for the kind care of Providence, we were favored more than some others.

A strong element of the sense of apprehension which women's diaries express is the feeling of helplessness. Women felt themselves to be dependent on chance, Providence, and the wisdom of their leaders. As participants in a venture designed and led by men, they had little or no control over the many factors which might determine whether they lived or died. Women's trail diaries illustrate, in an extreme form, a fact of female experience both yesterday and today: powerlessness and uncertainty interact to breed perennial anxiety.

. . . When Maria Belshaw remarked on passing through an attractive part of the countryside, "It's quite pleasant—still give me the home I left in the state of Indiana," it is not Indiana to which she is referring so much as home and community. What community meant for women was primarily the association with other women; the social life centered around church and visiting, in which women shared experience and wisdom. Women attempted to re-create this sense of community on the trail. "During the day," recalled Mrs. Haun,

> We women folk visited from wagon to wagon or congenial friends spent an hour walking ever westward, and talking over our home life 'back in the states' telling of the loved ones left behind; voicing our hopes for the future in the far west and even whispering, a little friendly gossip of pioneer life. High teas were not popular but tatting, knitting, crocheting, exchanging receipts for cooking beans or dried apples or swapping food for the sake of variety kept us in practice of feminine occupations and diversions.

"At night," remembered Mary Warren, "the women would sit around the fire and visit while the men would take the oxen to grass and water. As soon as the fire was big enough to furnish coals all the women would steam up their clay pipes. Everyone smoked then and the tobacco was our own home grown brand."

But while women's reminiscences recall the successful aspects of social life, the diaries more often record the loneliness of women who left close friends behind. In an age without telephones, highways and airplanes, closeness depended on geographical proximity. The relationships which women had developed in the small farming communities from which they came were terminated by the trip west. The finality of separation from friends became more of a reality each day on the trail. In frequent expressions of grief over the friendships they left behind women communicated a profound sense of loss, loneliness and disorientation.

The following poem fragment was the first diary entry written by Agnes Stewart:

To Martha

Oh friend, I am gone forever, I cannot see you now
The damp comes to my brow
Thou wert my first and only friend, the hearts best treasure thou;
Yet in the shades of troubled sleep my mind can see you now,
And many a time I shut my eyes and look into the past.
Ah, then I think how different our fates in life were cast,
I think how oft we sat and played
Upon some mossy stone,
How we would act and do when we were big girls grown
And we would always live so near
That I could always come to you,
And you would come to me, and this we would always do
When sickness came in fevered brow and burning through each vein. . . .

RECOLLECTIONS OF A PIONEER WOMAN ————

When the trip was over, the hardships had just begun. Migrant women were rarely spoiled or idle; most of them had been accustomed to hard work in the European or eastern towns from which they had come. But life on the "frontier," as the whites called it, was more laborious for women because they had to do without even the simplest conveniences. Here Harriet Taylor Upton, a suffragist born in 1853 in Portage County, Ohio, recollects her early education in the oppression of women.

. . . Women had so much to do outdoors that they couldn't bother with things in the house, and women were in great despair over the inconveniences. One sturdy mother became so enraged because her husband pro-crastinated in building an oven, saying that she could no longer bake bread and do all her cooking in one big iron kettle, that she fashioned some bricks of mud and built an oven which was such a success that people travelled out of their way to see it in action. . . . When these early housewives got their ovens to going, they would bake fifty mince pies at a time, put them in a cold room, often "the parlor chamber" as the guest room was called, where they would freeze and would bring them out as occasion required, reheating them by the fire. The woman who made the oven of bricks once had it full of pies when the Indians came along in the night and carried them all off. . . .

Grandfather approved of my energy. I used to follow him around as he worked, sometimes stumbling along behind the plow, hoping he would let me drive. Grandmother always made me remove my dirty shoes on the porch after I had been on one of these plowing expeditions. I drove the hay rake occasionally, but was not a real success at it. I grew so excited under the responsibility that I would forget to release the hay at the proper time. Hours I have sat in the barn with him as he thrashed out the wheat with a hand flail. . . . Then the straw would be forked up, the wheat and the chaff scraped together and later put through a machine called a fanning mill, where the chaff was separated from the grain. I was often allowed to turn the wheel which worked the machine. It was easy to do, but it was a dirty job and my grandmother required me to brush myself and comb my hair before I could go inside the house, and even then bits of straw would remain in my hair for days.

I helped to churn and carried water to the men in the field during harvest time, and fed the chickens and rode into the barn from the field on the hay load. I cut and twisted lamp lighters to be used in the winter to save matches, and sewed carpet rags, and enjoyed doing all these things. I have little respect for the person who invented a do-less Heaven.

Perhaps I like the sugar making time the best of all seasons on the farm. My spring vacations were always spent there. . . . I spent most of my waking hours and some of my sleeping ones in the sugar bush, as the sugar camp was then called. My uncles were patient with me and allowed me to follow them in their work all day. When they drove through the woods gathering up the sap from the buckets hung to the trees and pouring it into casks which were on a sort of sledge with 6-inch boards for runners, I would romp along at their side, falling down at times, drinking out of the full pails at others and riding on the vehicle when I cared to do so. . . .

Just as my grandfather allowed me to run the fanning machine to free the chaff from the wheat, so my grandmother let me reel the yarn she had spun from the spindle to the reeling machine. . . .

Grandmother dried berries, corn, pumpkin; raised her babies, and took into her family anyone unfortunate in the neighborhood. She nursed the sick at their homes when she could leave her own; and when she could not, she brought the well children or the convalescent to her home and cared for them. . . .

After a long hard day, she would gather me in her arms and croon me to sleep, for she could not carry a tune. I thought she was the most beautiful old woman I had ever seen, especially when she wore a cap. Regardless of what she was doing—washing, baking or churning,—she stopped work each morning at ten o'clock, sat down, opened her Bible and read that which her eyes first fell upon. She believed she was led to these verses. Her plain face glowed with love. To be near her was to receive a benediction. She had great sorrows, among them the death of her only daughter, her youngest child, but she never complained. When other women were lamenting about how hard they worked or what troubles they had, she would give a sort of a grunt of disapproval and say, "Oh, shucks!" . . .

WASHDAY IN HISPANIC CALIFORNIA

The Southwest of what is today the United States had been settled by people of Mexican/Indian descent. In the 1830s in California there were large haciendas (mansions) owned by families of Spanish heritage who employed large numbers of servants. In this selection, these servants are collectively washing clothes and taking pride in their skill. Laundry assumed a major proportion of women's household labor.

We watched the women unload the linen and carry it to the upper spring of the group, where the water was best. Then they loosened the horses and let them pasture on the wild oats, while they put home-made soap on the clothes, dipped them in the spring, and rubbed them on the smooth rocks until they were white as snow. Then they were spread out to dry on the tops of the low bushes growing on the warm, windless, southern slopes of the mountain. There was sometimes a great deal of linen to be washed for it was the pride of every Spanish family to own much linen, and the mother and daughters almost always wore white. I have heard strangers speak of the wonderful way in which Spanish ladies of the upper classes in California always appeared in snow-white dresses, and certainly to do so was one of the chief anxieties of every household. When there were no warm springs, the servants of the family repaired to the nearest arroyo and stood knee-deep in it, dipping and rubbing the linen and enjoying the sport.

"COWGIRLS"

The West encouraged women to take on unconventional work as there was a shortage of laborers and less tradition to uphold. Women as well as men worked on the huge Spanish ranches as cowhands.

Well, I washed my clothes, a job I positively hate—I would rather climb a three-thousand-foot mountain—and to make matters more aggravating, as I was in the midst of it, along came two women, one young and quite pretty, who were assisting as vaqueros [cowboys]. A rodeo took place near camp, and several thousand head of cattle were assembled, wild almost as deer. . . . A rodeo is a great event on a ranch, and these women, the wife and daughter of a ranchero, came out to assist in getting in the cattle. Well mounted, they managed their horses superbly, and just as I was up to my elbows in soapsuds, along they came, with a herd of several hundred cattle. . . . I straightened my aching back, drew a long breath and must have blushed . . . and reflected on the doctrine of woman's rights—I, a stout man, washing my shirt, and those ladies practicing the art of vaqueros.

POLYGAMY AND WOMEN'S WORK

Mormons migrated from upstate New York in the 1820s, first to the Midwest and then to Utah, seeking to establish a utopian community, free from moral evils and temptations. They valorized hard work, believing that exertions in the material world directly reflected spiritual standing. Although some Mormons rebelled against it, one of their most controversial practices was polygamy. In this selection, a Mormon woman's diary reveals her positive feeling about it. On the frontier, where conditions were arduous and there were multiple tasks and few resources, the wives shared the work and provided support and companionship for each other.

[1842] We usually bought cloth by the bolt and whoever needed most was served first. In fact we had in our home an almost perfect United Order. No one can tell the advantages of that system until he has lived it. We enjoyed many privileges that single wifery never knew. We did not often all go out together. One always stayed at home and took care of the children and the house. In that way we generally came home with a correct idea of what was given in the sermon.

Whenever one was indisposed she was not obliged to tie up her head and keep serving about the house but she could go to her room and be down knowing that her children and all her share of the work would be attended to. No one was obliged to bend over the wash tub when she was delicate in health or condition. All stepped into the breach and helped each other.

We acted as nurses for each other during confinement. We were too poor to hire nurses. One suit or outfit for new babies and confined mothers did for us all, and when one piece wore it was supplied by another. For many years we lived thus working together cooking over the same large stove with the same great kettles, eating at the same long table without a word of unpleasantness or a jar in our feelings portrayed. The children we bore while we lived together in that poor home love each other more than those that came to us after the raid on polygamists came on and we were obliged to separate and flee in different directions.

To me it is a joy to know that we laid the foundation of a life to come while we lived in that plural marriage that we three who loved each other more than sisters, children of one mother love, will go hand in hand together down through all eternity. That knowledge is worth more to me than gold and more than compensates for all the sorrow I have ever known. . . .

. . . The following Aug. 6th [1850] I gave birth to a still born son, then I nursed Sister Caroline's babe at my breasts six months, which is now br. F[rancis] M. Lyman's wife. [added later] Clara

Sister Bathsheba must take her two children and go and do the work for Father Smith's family, and I must go to br. Calisters and nurs baby as we had no wood, although we had bread stuff & meat groceries &c. Sister Sarah and hannah with their babes went into a little adobie house belonging to br Henry Bigler (as he was away with the Mormon Battalion.) The next June 12.th, 1851. Sister Sarah died leaving her son John Henry who was three years the 18.th, of Sep. following. I was teaching school at that time in the 17.th, ward. I taught 4½ months, I had 56 pupils. Miss Sarah J. Rich was my assistant.

I weaned Clara at the age of 11. months. I then went to stay with sister Hannah, as Father Smith wished me to go and help raise the boys. We colored, hired wove a web of gingham to make ourselves and boys some clothes. When Mr Smith returned from Iron Co. he was appointed to go to Utah Co. to preside. He took me and sister Hannah with the two boys, and settled us in the City of Provo, where I lived, til the boys were Married, being seventeen years. [added later] I think.

. . . We had a very dry warm spring and summer, and we were very destitute of sweet, so the Good Provider sent Honey Dew on to the Cotton-wood and Willow leaves, and so br. Geo. Adair and wife, Sister Hannah and myself took the necessary utencils, went among the bushes, cut bows, washed off the sugar flakes into tubs strained the sap cleansed with milk and eggs then skimmed as it boiled. I understood the prossess nessessary, as I had seen my Mother manufacture sugar from the Maple sap. We four worked two days, made 50. lbs. of nice sugar, besides feasting on Pancakes and Molasses, and making a quantity of candy for the children. Br. Adair carried our Tithing to the Bishop. He said ours was the best of any brought in. He wished to know the reason. Br A told him that he had an old sugar hand along that understood the business.

Before we could raise any fruit, the fields abounded with ground Cherries growing spontaneously, which we appreciated as a great favour from the Giver of all good. I used to take Jonny and Charly long before the Sun peeped over the mountain and go to the field a mile and pick a five galon can full of the precious fruit and go back in time to eat our breakfast, as sister H. would have it ready, and then I would go to my school. Sister H. would fetch her babe sit her on the floor go and pick another can of Cherries. What we did not eat we could sell for a good price as fruit was scarce every where in the Territory.

When things got a little more plenty myself Sister Eliza Terril, Sister Rua Angeline Holden and Sister Hannah Maria Smith took our spinning Wheels and went to a large room in the Seminary and tride our best to see who could reel of the greatest No. of knots from sunrise to sunset. Sister Terril 100,11. knots. Sister Holden not quite so many but better twist on hers. Sister H. M. Smith and I made the best yarn. It was equal for twist but I had a few knots the most but she spun and reeled 80. knots. On the whole we concluded we all beat. We had refreshments four times during the day, indeed, we took solid comfort in our days labour, and our association together.

. . . I was then chosen set apart and blessed to preside over the Relief Society with Sister Rua Angeline Holden for my first, and Sister Nancy Bigler Flemming for my second councelors, Sister Sarah Jane Goff Blackburn Sec'y and Treasurer. We did all we could, with the aid of the good brethren and sisters, to comfort the needy as they came in with Hand-carts late in the Fall. They got their hands and feet badly frosted. Br. Stephen Nixon and wife nursed and took care of them til they were better. We favoured them br. and Sis. N. by quilting a quilt very nicely for them, as our Society was short of funds then we could not do much, but the four Bishops could hardly carry the bedding and other clothing we got together the first time we met. We did not cease our exersions til all were made comfortable. When the Hand Cart Companies arived, the Desks of the Seminary were loaded with provisions for them.

Just at the session of our Oct. Conference news came where these Hand Cart Co's were. President Young and others were excited and anxious for fear those Co's would be caught in the snow in the mountains. They could not go on with the Conference. The Pres't called for men teams clothing, and provisions, and they were soon on the way to meet the Companies with

Pres't Young himself til he got into the Can[y]on. There he took sick and was oblige to turn back. The sisters stripped off their Peticoats stockings and every thing they could spare, right there in the Tabernacle and piled into the wagons to send to the saints in the mountains. [On the Plains] The Snow was fast falling and the saints were just piling down in a heap with the idea that they must all perish when to their great joy they discovered a light at a distance. Then they took new courge and they had everything for their comfort.

I never took more satisfaction and I might say pleasure in any labour I ever performed in my life, such a unimity [unanimity] of feeling prevailed. I only had to go into a store and make my wants known, if it was cloth it was measured off without charge. My councilors and I wallowed through the snow until our clothes were wet a foot high to get things together give out noticeses &c. We peaced blocks carded bats quilted and got together I think 27 Quilts, besides a great amount of other clothing, in one winter for the needy.

What comes next for willing hands to do? The brethren are called to go into the mountains to stand guard to keep the enemy at bay. They want bedding, socks mittens &c. so we sat up nights and knitted all that was needed til we made out a big load with the Quilts and Blankets which we sent out into the mountains to the brethren.

. . . I organized and kept up a Sabbath School for many months before the brethren interfered and reorganized although perfect harmony existed among the teachers and children. The children were so strongly attached to me and took such an interest in their singing and other lessons, that I was appointed to take charge of the female portion and a br. to take charge of the males. Our Choirister visited me and wished me to get up some nice pieces and learn the children to sing preparitory for the celebration on the 24th of July.

"PASSING" AS A MAN

After the 1848 discovery of gold in California, prospecting became a national epidemic. Most of those struck with "gold fever" were single young men, but 5 percent were women and children. California attracted most of the newcomers. On the eve of the gold rush, 1847, the territory had fourteen thousand inhabitants, excluding Indians, who were not counted by the census; a year later the population approached one hundred thousand, and by the end of 1852 it had more than doubled.

In this selection from a memoir, "Mountain Charley's" husband has died. Realizing that there is more money and excitement available to a man, she

assumes male attire. Recently, women's historians have discovered many
instances in which women masqueraded as men to earn a living.

At length, after casting over in my mind everything that presented itself
as a remedy, I determined upon a project, which, improbable as it may
appear to my sex . . . I actually soon after put into execution. It was to dress
myself in male attire, and seek for a living in this disguise among the avenues
which are so religiously closed against my sex.

My first essay at getting employment was fruitless; but after no small number of mortifying rebuffs from various parties to whom I applied for assistance, I was at last rewarded by a comparative success. In my assumed
character, I made the acquaintance of some River men, and among others,
that of the captain of the *Alex. Scott*—a steamer plying between St. Louis
and New Orleans. I made known my desire of obtaining a situation, and he
offered me that of cabin boy, at a salary of $35 per month.

The many rebuffs I had met with in searching for a situation though bitter
at the moment, were in the end of benefit, for they removed to a large extent
that timidity which accompanied my advent as a member of the stronger sex.
I found myself able after a little, to address people without that tell-tale blush
that at first suffused my countenance, and also to receive a rude reply without
that deep mortification which in the beginning assailed me with terrible
force. In short, I found myself able to banish almost wholly, the woman
from my countenance. . . .

The duties of my new position, although menial in their character, were
light. The captain, if he ever suspected my secret, as I have some reason for
believing, respected it and never betrayed me with any degree of harshness,
such as is too frequently to be found in the relations between the head and
inferiors of a Mississippi steamboat. I quietly attended to my own business,
and although never shunning to a marked extent the company and conversation of others, I avoided them when it could be done without exciting
remark. . . .

I remained on the *Alex. Scott* nearly a year, and at the end of that time I
obtained a situation on the *Champion* as second pantryman. At the end of
six months I changed to the *Bay State*, plying between St. Louis and Mem-
phis; and labored in the capacity of second waiter. I did not remain long on
this boat, for an opportunity soon offered itself for me to procure a situation
under my old captain on the *Alex. Scott*, and of this I gladly availed
myself. . . .

My friend the captain died soon after my return, and not caring to remain
under any other, I left the boat and determined to try my fortune on the
land. With this view, I engaged a situation as brakeman, on the Illinois
Central Railroad. This was in the spring of 1854, and I had been on the river
nearly four years. It is needless for me to deny that during this time I heard

and saw much entirely unfit for the ears or eyes of woman, yet whenever tempted to resume my sex, I was invariably met with the thought—what then? I was obliged to pay a certain amount weekly for the education and support of my children; and the chances were but few in case I resumed my other character, that I would be able to command the amount necessary for their support, without at all having reference to my own living. Besides this, as the sensitiveness which greeted my new position wore away, I began to rather like the freedom of my new character. . . .

Just then the California fever had not fully subsided and I was determined to gratify my curiosity by a visit to the Land of Gold. A company was about forming to proceed thither, and I, upon becoming acquainted with some of the men composing the party, determined to form one of them. I invested a portion of my means in an outfit and left St. Louis to go to California by the overland route in the spring of 1855. . . .

I staid . . . till the Pike's Peak fever broke out, when I came back to the States, and spent a few weeks with my children. I then started for Pike's Peak, going by the Santa Fe Mail route, and reached Pike's Peak in the spring of 1859. . . . I immediately went to prospecting for gold, and continued at that for about three months and met with no success. About this time gold was discovered by Gregory in the mountains, and following in the wake of the excitement which the event produced, I went thither and located myself about forty-two miles from Denver City. Finding nothing better to do I opened a Bakery and Saloon. I met with good success, and was making money rapidly, when in the Fall I was taken sick with the mountain fever, and was most unwillingly obliged to give up my business and go back to Denver.

After getting better I rented a saloon known as the "Mountain Boys Saloon," which I kept during the winter. I also took up several claims but never made anything in particular out of them. In the spring of 1859 I grew somewhat tired of the Saloon, and went to Tarry All—a place about one hundred miles from Denver, on the Blue River. I here worked a claim with six hands, and made during that summer about two hundred dollars, clear of all expenses. I then left Tarry All and went to Cache Le Poud, a place on a River of the same name, at the mouth of the Platte. I was there some two months, but meeting with no particular success I determined to leave. I did so, and returned to Denver City and bought my old Saloon and kept it during the winter of 1859.

I continued in my male attire . . . and kept my saloon during the winter of 1859–60. I had a bar-keeper, named H. L. Guerín, whom I married, and in the spring we sold out the saloon and went into the mountains where we opened a boardinghouse and commenced mining. . . .

Factory Life

RULES AND REGULATIONS ————————————————————

Cotton textile manufacturing led in the industrialization of the United States. The South grew cotton, and the North developed factories to process it. Women were quickly drawn into textile production for a number of reasons: because weaving was women's work in the home before it was mechanized; because women could be hired more cheaply than men; because there was a shortage of male labor; and because there was opposition to enterprise that would draw men away from farming, which was still profitable.

During the first half of the nineteenth century, women dominated in the textile industry. In 1831, for example, 18,539 men and 38,927 women worked in the cotton industry. Cotton manufacturing accounted for such a large proportion of the total industrial sector of the economy that as late as 1850 women accounted for 24 percent of the total jobs in manufacturing, although over the next fifty years, the proportion of females dropped to 19 percent.

The first mill operatives in North America were families who were paid in company scrip. However, textile owners in the Northeast also hired the unmarried daughters of farmers, who were often well educated and confident. Most of them worked in the mills only a few years, returning afterward to marriage, the more flexible schedules of domestic work, and, sometimes, school teaching. The good conditions that attracted these women into the mills lasted, at best, two decades. After that, working conditions deteriorated, and textile factory workers were drawn from the poorer classes, often immigrants.

For industry to be profitable, this new work force had to be broken of its old habits of self-directed work. Independent artisans had to be transformed into wage laborers, willing and able to work at the same assignment for long hours and to suppress their own intelligence, inventiveness, and craftsmanship. Workers resisted this transformation both actively and passively. Many textile companies devised detailed regulations of conduct, both in and out of the factory, in efforts to control their workers and thereby increase their productivity. Most of the workers were required to live in boarding houses. They were treated as children because they were young and female. The following is an example of these paternalistic regulations.

POIGNAUD AND PLANT BOARDING HOUSE AT LANCASTER, 1820–30

Rules and Regulations to be attended to and followed by the Young Persons who come to Board in this House:

Rule first: Each one to enter the house without unnecessary noise or confusion, and hang up their bonnet, shawl, coat, etc., etc., in the entry.

Rule second: Each one to have their place at the table during meals, the two which have worked the greatest length of time in the Factory to sit on each side of the head of the table, so that all new hands will of course take their seats lower down, according to the length of time they have been here.

Rule third: It is expected that order and good manners will be preserved at table during meals—and at all other times either upstairs or down.

Rule fourth: There is no unnecessary dirt to be brought into the house by the Boarders, such as apple cores or peels, or nut shells, etc.

Rule fifth: Each boarder is to take her turn in making the bed and sweeping the chamber in which she sleeps.

Rule sixth: Those who have worked the longest in the Factory are to sleep in the North Chamber and the new hands will sleep in the South Chamber.

Rule seventh: As a lamp will be lighted every night upstairs and placed in a lanthern, it is expected that no boarder will take a light into the chambers.

Rule eighth: The doors will be closed at ten o'clock at night, winter and summer, at which time each boarder will be expected to retire to bed.

Rule ninth: Sunday being appointed by our Creator as a Day of Rest and Religious Exercises, it is expected that all boarders will have sufficient discretion as to pay suitable attention to the day, and if they cannot attend to some place of Public Worship they will keep within doors and improve their time in reading, writing, and in other valuable and harmless employment.

SPEED-UPS

By the 1840s, the myth that textile factory work was an opportunity and the "factory girls" a privileged lot had been dispelled, at least among the workers themselves. Declining profits and the depression of 1837 had led the manufacturers to force increases in their workers' productivity through wage cuts and speed-ups. The employers welcomed and even encouraged immigration, particularly of Irish families, into New England, because these newcomers provided laborers more desperate for work than the Yankee girls. But the working conditions declined before the immigrants replaced the native-born workers on a large scale. The first excerpt here is from the Voice of Industry, *a publication of the Lowell mill women; the second from testimony before the Massachusetts House of Representatives hearings on industrial conditions in 1845. Women could not vote, but they did have the right to petition and they used it energetically in their campaign for a ten-hour day.*

It is a subject of comment and general complaint among the operatives that while they tend three or four looms, where they used to tend but two, making nearly twice the number of yards of cloth, the pay is not increased to them, while the increase to the owners is very great.

It is an ingenious scheme which a few capitalists and politicians have invented to blind the eyes of the people—that, because the operatives receive one eighth more pay in the aggregate for accomplishing one third more labor with the same facilities than they did a few years ago, the price of labor has advanced. The price of weaving a yard of cloth has never been lower in this country than at this time. The price for tending, spinning, carding, never lower, nor the wages of those operatives who work by the week. . . .

. . . The first petitioner who testified was Eliza R. Hemingway. She had worked 2 years and 9 months in the Lowell factories; 2 years in the Middlesex, and 9 months in the Hamilton Corporations. Her employment is weaving—works by the piece. . . . She complained of the hours for labor being too many, and the time for meals too limited. In the summer season, the work is commenced at 5 o'clock, a.m., and continued til 7 o'clock, p.m., with half an hour for breakfast and three quarters of an hour for dinner. During eight months of the year but half an hour is allowed for dinner. The air in the room she considered not to be wholesome. There were 293 small lamps and 61 large lamps lighted in the room in which she worked, when evening work is required. These lamps are also lighted sometimes in the morning. About 130 females, 11 men, and 12 children (between the ages of 11 and 14) work in the room with her. She thought the children enjoyed about as good health as children generally do. The children work but 9 months out of 12. The other 3 months they must attend school. Thinks that there is no day when there are less than six of the females out of the mill from sickness. Has known as many as thirty. She herself is out quite often on account of sickness. . . . She thought there was a general desire among the females to work but ten hours, regardless of pay. . . . She knew of one girl who last winter went into the mill at half past four o'clock, a.m., and worked till half past 7 o'clock, p.m. She did so to make more money. She earned from $25 to $30 per month.

MANUFACTURING AND THE DIVISION OF LABOR ——

Industrialization dramatically changed the location of work, the kind of work women did, and the sexual division of labor. Sometimes, as in textiles, women simply followed into the factories work that had been traditionally in the female sphere. At other times, mechanization provided new opportunities for women, because women could be employed for lower wages. The following description of the boot and shoe industry is an example of how technological changes can transform the social patterns of a traditional craft many times over.

This excerpt is from a classic and monumental work, The History of Women in Industry in the United States, *by Helen Sumner. Published in 1910, it was part of a ten-volume work on women and children as wage earners, the first systematic study done in the United States. Helen Sumner (1876–1933) was a reform economist and historian of women and the labor movement. She was the protégé of the widely recognized labor historian and economist John R. Commons and wrote and edited major parts of his* History of an Industrial Society.

It was division of labor which first brought women into the boot and shoe making industry. The introduction of machinery, indeed, later drove large numbers of them out of the business for a time. Types of machinery were soon evolved, however, which made again profitable a division of labor which could utilize the labor of women, and their restoration to the industry followed.

About 1795 or earlier, side by side with the development of the wholesale trade in boots and shoes, shoemakers or cordwainers, as they were called, began to hire their fellows and to gather them into shops where a rough division of labor was practiced. Soon afterwards they began to send the uppers out to women to be stitched and bound. From that time until the introduction of the sewing machine the binding of shoes manufactured for the wholesale market was practically a woman's industry, carried on at home. Localities differed largely, however, in the extent of the employment of women. In Massachusetts the shoe binders appear to have been exclusively women as early as 1810, but in Philadelphia, which was also a large shoe-manufacturing center, the trade remained in the hands of men until much later. A writer in the Philadelphia Mechanics' Free Press in 1829 spoke of the employment of women in shoe making as "derogatory to their sex."

In general, however, by 1830, and in many localities earlier, the manufacture of shoes was divided into two parts—the work of the men in small shops and the work of women in their homes. By 1837 the shoe binders of

Lynn not only bound the edging but did all the inside and lighter kinds of sewing.

There were, however, two more or less roughly marked stages in women's work at shoe binding. In the first stage the family was the industrial unit, the man shoemaker being assisted by his wife and daughters in the part of the work which they could easily perform—the sewing. Even when the shoemaker worked for a "boss," he brought home his materials and turned over the work of binding to the women of the family. Gradually, however, as the business developed, it became customary for the "boss" himself to give out the shoes to be bound directly to the women. The division of labor remained the same, but it was no longer controlled by the shoemaker, but by the "boss." The women, too, instead of having their work and pay lumped with that of the head of the family—instead of being merely helpers without economic standing—now dealt directly with the employer and definitely entered the industrial field. . . .

The introduction of the sewing machine, however, between 1855 and 1865, caused an almost complete transformation in the boot and shoe making industry. Small "stitching shops" equipped with the new machines were at first opened. In Lynn these shops were sometimes small buildings standing by themselves, but more frequently the manufacturers fitted up rooms in the buildings where the men worked. . . .

The women did not, however, after the introduction of the factory system, succeed in retaining their work as completely as they had done in the textile industries. The machines were heavy and difficult to operate, especially the waxed thread sewing machine which was introduced about 1857, and, as a result, were largely operated by men.

The first result of the introduction of machinery in boot and shoe making was, therefore, a decided falling off in the proportion of women employed. In 1850, in the manufacture of boots and shoes, 31.3 per cent of the employees, in 1860 only 23.2 per cent of the employees, and in 1870 only 14.1 per cent of the employees were women. By 1900, however, the proportion of women had risen to 33.0 per cent, higher than in 1850, when all "female hands," regardless of age, were included. In 1905, moreover, the proportion of women was a little over 33 per cent. . . .

It must be borne in mind, moreover, in considering these figures, that before the introduction of the factory system, which immediately followed that of the sewing machine, the women in the industry were home workers and few of them gave their entire time to binding shoes. A larger number, therefore, were required to accomplish a given amount of work than would have been needed under the factory system, even without the aid of machines.

As for the restoration of women to their former position of importance in the industry, it has been occasioned by three factors—improvements in machinery, which have reduced the amount of muscular strength required; the use of water and steam power, which became general between 1860 and 1870; and the further subdivision of labor. Within recent years women have taken the places of men in operating the lighter machines, while children now perform the work that women were doing heretofore. Subdivision of labor, however, as, for example, the splitting up of the process of "heeling" into "nailing," "shaving," "blacking," and "polishing," has tended continually to introduce less skilled labor—first of women and then of children. . . .

In general, it may be said that the boot and shoe industry is the only one of the more important clothing industries in which an industrial cycle has been completed and the women workers have been definitely transferred from the home to the factory. . . .

WOMEN'S STRIKES

Women's collective resistance to degrading working conditions began in the 1820s. Most strikes, or "turn-outs" as the workers called them, sought control over working conditions as much as they sought more money and shorter hours. These strikes show that from the beginning women were at least as militant as men and often fought in solidarity with male workers. Nonetheless, many of these early strikes failed, frequently just fading out as some strikers returned to work and others left for new jobs. Another reason for the failure of both male and female strikes at this time was the lack of permanent organization, which meant there was no way to develop treasuries to support striking workers. Strikes were often spontaneous and leaders were fired. Furthermore, most strikes were local, so coordination with plants located elsewhere was difficult. But despite these failures, workers were amassing power and organizational experience, as this selection, from a 1911 U.S. government history of women workers, illustrates.

In December of the same year (1828), there was a strike of cotton-mill operatives at Dover, N.H., which involved three or four hundred girls and women. This strike, according to one indignant writer in the *Mechanics' Free Press*, "formed the subject of a squib, probably for half the newspapers from Maine to Georgia. The circumstance of three or four hundred girls or women marching out of their factory in a procession and firing off a lot of gunpowder, and the facetious advertisement of the factory agent for two or three hundred better behaved women made, altogether, a comical story quite worth telling."

Another Philadelphia paper said: "The late strike and grand public march of the female operatives in New Hampshire exhibit the Yankee sex in a new and unexpected light. By and by the governor may have to call out the militia to prevent a gynecocracy." Few papers gave the reasons for the turnout, but it is apparent that trouble came on account of an attempt to enforce several new factory regulations. . . .

Inscriptions and placards and even bits of poetry were directed against employers by these early women strikers. One New York paper particularly emphasized this feature in an account stating that "The aggrieved female 'operatives' paraded the town in the received manner, with flags and inscriptions; but, being soon made sensible of their folly, returned, with a few exceptions, to their work." To which another writer, apparently in sympathy with the working women, retorted, with reference to these employers: "What Spartan mothers will their factory girls make who have been trained to sink all the rights of human nature to qualify them to watch a cotton thread." . . .

That the factory girls themselves had no mind for such submission is apparent. They voiced their defiant protests in no uncertain words. When prose seemed unsatisfactory, they did not hesitate to indulge in poetry. "Equally stirring and equally essential in the properly conducted strike of the day," says one writer, "was the verse." That it lent itself most readily to the needs of the hour at the time of the Dover strike is apparent from the question: Who among the Dover girls could—

> Ever bear,
> The shocking fate of slaves to share?

A second strike among the cotton-factory girls of Dover occurred during February and March, 1834. It was caused by a reduction of wages and involved 800 women. The *New York Transcript* asserted that the girls had formed a trade union for mutual support, in spite of the "conditions on which help is hired by the Cocheco Manufacturing Company." This firm on February 28, 1834, advertised for "five hundred females." One condition required applicants to sign an agreement to work for such wages "as the company may see fit to pay and be subject to the fines imposed by the company." Other clauses bound them to accept monthly payments of wages and to forfeit two weeks' pay if they left their employment without first giving a fortnight's notice and securing the permission of an agent of the company.

The most significant requirement, however, was as follows: "We also agree not to be engaged in any combination whereby the work may be impeded or the company's interest in any work injured; if we do, we agree to forfeit to the use of the company the amount of wages that may be due to us at the time." This effort to prevent the spread of trade unionism among the women is the first instance of which we have record where employers forced upon women employees the dreaded "ironclad oath." Its use at this early date indicates that working women had made much greater progress toward organization than has been generally supposed.

To the advertisements of the company announcing employment for "five hundred females" the strikers replied next day as follows:

> GIRLS ON HAND.—There are now five hundred of us in the town of Dover, who are now at work for ourselves, but might possibly answer the wants and wishes of the "Cocheco Manufacturing Company, at Dover, N.H.," excepting that we will not consent to work at the reduced tariff of wages to take place on the 15th of March instant, or even one mill less than the wages lately given. We would just say to our sex in the country that we are not to live here long without plenty of work.

A New York daily trade-union paper, in republishing this manifesto, added:

> We beseech the farmers of our country not to permit their daughters to go into the mills at all, in any place under the present regulations, if they value the life and health of their children.

The Dover factory girls on this occasion, probably chastened by public disapproval of their conduct of five years before, "instead of forming processions and parading the streets, to the amusement of a crowd of gaping idlers, confined themselves for the most part within their respective boarding houses." They did hold in the courthouse, however, probably on March 1, a meeting composed of between 600 and 700 girls, and unanimously adopted a series of strong resolutions. In these resolutions they declared they would never consent to work at the reduced wages, and viewed "with feelings of indignation" the efforts of their employers to place upon those least able to bear it the effect of the "unusual pressure of the time."

They voted to raise a fund to defray the expenses of those who did not have the means to return to their homes, and appointed a committee of 12 to communicate the result of the meeting to the girls employed in the factories at Great Falls, Newmarket, and Lowell. Finally, they arranged to have the proceedings of the meeting published in the *Dover Gazette* and *New Hampshire Globe* "and in all other papers printed in this State whose editors are opposed to the system of slavery attempted to be established in our manufacturing establishments."

IMMIGRANT WOMEN ─────────────────────────────

The increasing number of immigrants in the cities made job competition fierce. Unemployment was common. Even if a man found work, many families could not live on one person's wages. In many cases, there was no man because women, especially the Irish, came to America alone. This excerpt is from a 1949 discussion of immigrant women's work opportunities in New York City in the 1840s and 1850s.

In a city of countless boardinghouses, large hotels, and elegant mansions of the elite, servants were in constant demand. Domestic service, in most instances, required few if any previously gained skills and admirably met the needs of transplanted peasant women and girls. Thus, by 1855, nearly one quarter of all the immigrants in the city were household help, "nurses," laundresses, cooks, and waiters. Barred from American households because of ignorance of the English language, Continental Europeans usually turned to their wealthier compatriots already established in New York. A few from the Caribbean and Latin America lived in the homes of the British, Spanish, and French merchants who employed them. Newcomers from the British Isles, on the other hand, were hired by all but the German-speaking families.

Nearly all the domestic servants who came from Great Britain were born in Ireland. Of the ten thousand to twelve thousand estimated to be in New York City in 1846, between seven thousand and eight thousand were said to be Irish, another two thousand Germans, and the rest French, Americans, and a sprinkling of other nationalities. A decade later nearly 80 per cent of the thirty-five thousand foreign-born servants and waiters living on Manhattan were Irish, while the Germans supplied another 15 per cent. Irish servants formed a quarter of the Irish working population, whereas German servants comprised only one tenth of the German workers. This relative paucity of German domestics resulted from the Teutonic practice of migrating in family groups, an impossibility for the thousands of single Irish girls and women who could barely pay their passage or who reached New York only through the philanthropic efforts of others. Once in the Empire City, Irish women were far better off in wealthier private households than as miserable seamstresses living singly in the slums or as laborers' wives forced to sew in order to make ends meet. German families remained together, often using skills such as tailoring which women and children had shared in Europe. Other immigrant women followed the German pattern: domestic service claimed nearly 15 per cent of the Welsh, 16 per cent of the Swiss, 14.5 per cent of the French, and 10.5 per cent of the Scottish working people living in the city. Among workers born in England, the British provinces of North

America, and Latin America, about one tenth of each group became servants.

An initial handicap of the Catholic Irish servant girls was the prejudice they encountered in America. Potential employers disliked and even feared their religion, shuddered at "Irish impulsiveness" and turbulence, and were disgusted and morally shocked at the Irish propensity for strong drink. While some Americans preferred to hire natives of specific countries, no other immigrant nationality was proscribed as the Catholic Irish were. In congested cities like New York, the presence of a large Irish population sharpened mutual antagonisms, and discrimination against the children of Erin was flaunted in public. The Irish boiled with indignation upon reading the hated words, "No Irish need apply," or their equivalent, as in these advertisements:

> WANTED—An English or American woman, that understands cooking, and to assist in the work generally if wished; also a girl to do chamber work. None need apply without a recommendation from their last place. *IRISH PEOPLE* need not apply, nor any one that will not rise at 6 o'clock, as the work is light and the wages sure. Inquire at 359 Broadway.

> WOMAN WANTED.—To do general housework . . . English, Scotch, Welsh, German, or any country or color except Irish.

All the more obnoxious to the Irish were indications of a preference for the Negro. As the tradition of servitude and the continuing stigma of inferiority prevented most Negroes from pursuing skilled trades, they followed the only course open to them: common labor and the various service occupations. By 1855 some two thousand colored persons were servants, laundresses, cooks, and waiters—over half of all the gainfully employed Negroes. As waiters and coachmen, they were the chief competitors of the Irish, and they sometimes competed with foreigners in menial occupations as whitewashers, carpet shakers, chimney sweeps, and bootblacks. Colored servants were considered more submissive than the Celts, whose reputation for docility under their English rulers was extremely questionable.

Despite the anti-Irish feeling, the great preponderance of Irish housekeepers, nurses, chambermaids, charwomen, laundresses, cooks, and waiters was evidence of a pressing need for them. Good workers usually had no difficulty in getting jobs. Once hired, Irish women found security in the shelter and food provided with such employment, as well as some chance to save money and raise their social status. In the mid-forties wages ranged from $4.00 to $10.00 and averaged $6.00 per month, in addition to free board, lodging, and time for mending and washing. Chambermaids and houseworkers received $5.00 to $6.00 and slop-women $4.00 monthly. Cooks, ladies' maids, nurses, and waiters were better paid, enjoyed more comfortable living quarters, and earned extra compensation if they cared for children.

Although efficient, honest, and virtuous, Irish servant girls astonished even their compatriots by their self-assurance. Poor and uneducated, they reflected in their deportment a newly won status far above the wretchedness of their lot in the Old Country. In New York they often mistook "forwardness if not impertinence" for independence, asserted the *Irish American*, they dressed "too expensively and showily for their calling" and assumed "unbecoming airs." Some forgot themselves "so far as to *hire the employer*, in place of the employer hiring them."

As did the Irish, but in lesser degree, Catholic immigrants from other lands met with religious discrimination in New York. Advertisements for Protestant governesses, cooks, and maids blackballed many French, Germans, and Swiss. Nevertheless, Continental Europeans profited from the vogue of hiring French servants and particularly from the favoritism of an aristocracy of alien merchants.

The employment of women in the Empire City was not limited to domestic service; women were conspicuous in the needle trades. Until the middle of the century, the large majority of seamstresses were American women: wives and widows of mariners, mechanics, and laborers; most of the milliners were also natives, but a sizable proportion was English and French. Dressmakers doing piecework in their homes received $1.00 to $3.00 for each dress, and privately employed seamstresses earned sixty-two and a half cents, seventy-five cents and $1.00 a day. Less independent were the seamstresses in the ready-made clothing industry, who suffered a degradation probably unequaled in any other skilled trade. The competition of country women swarming into the city depressed wages long before the days of immigrant sweatshops. In 1845 the journeymen dressmakers toiled fourteen to sixteen hours a day for the weekly pittance of $1.25 to $1.50. Apprentices worked for six months without wages and frequently paid their employers $10.00 or $15.00 for the privilege of learning the trade.

In the late forties the earlier trickle of foreign women into the sewing trades quickened into a rising flood. The basis of the sweating system had been laid by American employers and American workers, but by mid-century, immigrants not only competed with native labor but contributed as employers to the exploitation of the operatives. Helping to create their own jobs by their demand for cheap dresses, cloaks, and bonnets, the newcomers gradually assumed a dominant role in the sewing trades. By 1855 two thirds of the New York dressmakers, seamstresses, milliners, shirt and collar makers, embroiderers, lace fringe, tassel, and artificial flower makers were foreign-born. Sixty-nine per cent of these immigrants were Irish and 14 per cent German, although in relation to their respective working populations, only 5 per cent of the Irish, English, Scotch, and French and 2 per cent of the Germans (including German Jews) were dressmakers.

The preponderance of Irish seamstresses was a result, not of choice but of necessity. Single Irish women, unable to find positions as servants found the sewing trades the only occupations open to them. Some had become familiar in Ireland with the rudiments of dressmaking. Others mistakenly saw in easily learned needlework the road to independence and advancement. Married women, finding it impossible for their families to subsist on workmen's wages in a decade of rising living costs, tried their hand at the needle. . . .

Controversy about Women's Work

WOMEN PETITION LINCOLN'S SECRETARY OF STATE

The need for rapid production to meet soldier's needs during the Civil War drew 300,000 additional women into wage work, particularly as seamstresses making uniforms. The war, as most wars do, caused inflation and price increases, which made working women's wages worth less. But the war, as wars usually do, also escalated patriotism, which in turn make workers' protests appear more suspect and rendered workers weaker in resisting speed-ups and low wages. With nowhere else to turn, one group of working women appealed directly to the federal government for help.

We would like to thank Marjorie Bingham for bringing this selection to our attention.

TO THE HON. EDWIN M. STANTON, SECRETARY OF WAR.

Sir: Twenty thousand Working Women of Philadelphia, Pennsylvania, respectfully ask your indulgence, while they narrate the causes which compel them to petition for relief at your hands.

At the breaking out of the rebellion that is now deluging our land with blood, and which for a time threatened the destruction of the Nation, the prices paid at the United States Arsenal in this city were barely sufficient to enable the women engaged upon Government work to earn a scanty respectable subsistence. Since the period referred to, board, provisions, and all other articles of female consumption, have advanced to such an extent as to make an average of at least seventy-five per cent,—while woman's labor has been *reduced thirty per cent.* What need of argument? To an intelligent mind, the result must be apparent; and it is perhaps superfluous to say, that it has produced great suffering, privation, and, in many instances, actual hunger. Such, however, is the *truth.*

To alleviate this misery, feed the hungry, clothe the naked, and house the houseless, we appeal to those in authority for a just and reasonable compensation for our labor.

What we need most IS IMMEDIATE AID. You can give it; the power is lodged with you; issue an Order to the Quartermaster-General, authorizing or ordering him to increase the price of female labor until it shall approximate to the price of living.

Let it be done without delay. Send the order at once, and you will have the proud satisfaction of knowing that you have done all in your power to ameliorate the condition of those who have given *their all* to their country; and who now come to that country, not as beggars, asking alms, but as American matrons and daughters, asking an equitable price for their labor. Comply with this, our reasonable request, and hundreds, yea thousands, will rise up and call you blessed.

We also desire to call your attention to the fact, that there are a large number of men in this city who are making immense fortunes off the Government by their contracts; and who, instead of entering into an honorable competition as to who is willing to work for the smallest profit, seem to go upon the principle, who can pay the lowest prices. . . .

TO EDWIN M. STANTON:

July 27, 1864

I know not how much is within the legal power of the government in this case; but it is certainly true in equity, that the laboring women in our employment, should be paid at the least as much as they were at the beginning of the war. Will the Secretary of War please have the case fully examined, and so much relief given as can be consistently with the law and the public service.

A. Lincoln

THE NURSING DEBATE

The increase in women's employment and the debate this engenders is always exacerbated by wars. The extraordinary labors of women in the Civil War were for the most part temporary, and after the peace most returned to their prewar occupations and status. This was not the case, however, in the field of nursing. The Civil War was to American nursing what the Crimean War had been a decade earlier to European nursing: the wartime experiences permanently changed the conventional view of nursing as improper for women to the view that it was a profession not only allowable for women, but one for which they were uniquely suited. This rapid change in ideology, parallel to that of three decades later about clerical work, reveals how malleable are the ideologies about what women are suited for. Where women are needed economically, it may be decided that they are biologically or even spiritually destined.

This selection is an example of the debate about women in nursing early in the Civil War from the point of view of the medical profession.

TO THE EDITOR OF THE *AMERICAN MEDICAL TIMES*

Our women appear to have become almost wild on the subject of hospital nursing. We honor them for their sympathy and humanity. Nevertheless, a man who has had experience with women nurses among male surgical cases, cannot shut his eyes to the fact that they, with the best intentions in the world, are frequently a useless annoyance. Cases are continually occurring in male surgical wards of such a character as require strong arms, and attentions which any reasonable medical man is loath to exact from female nurses. Imagine a delicate refined woman assisting a rough soldier to the close-stool, or supplying him with a bedpan, or adjusting the knots on a T-bandage employed in retaining a catheter in position, or a dozen offices of a like character which one would hesitate long before asking a female nurse to perform, but which are frequently and continually necessary in a military hospital. Besides this, women, as a rule, have not the physical strength necessary. For example—a man having gunshot wounds of grave severity affecting the lower extremities, with perhaps incontinence of urine, or diarrhoea, would not improbably be attacked with bed-sores if not kept scrupulously clean. Should the soft parts of the back begin to ulcerate, local attention becomes doubly necessary. The patient, under these circumstances, requires often to be lifted up carefully, and bodily, so as not to alter the comparative position of his limbs to his body. To do this properly, at least *four* strong men are required, who, stationed two at the shoulders and two at the hips (one hand from each lower assistant steadying the thigh and leg of that side), can thus raise the man steadily and carefully. A fifth would not be out of place in supporting the feet, while the medical attendant washes the excoriated parts, applies the needed dressings, and throws upon the surface of the bed a clean sheet.

Women, in our humble opinion, are utterly and decidedly unfit for such service. They can be used, however, as the regular administrators of the prescribed medicines, and in delicate, soothing attentions which are always so grateful to the sick, and which at the same time none know so well how to give as do noble, sensible, tenderhearted women.

But as hospital nurses for wounded men, they are by nature, education, and strength totally unfitted, i.e. when we consider *all the duties* surgical nurses are called upon to perform. In conclusion, it may be well to state that a surgeon on duty with troops, by showing proper interest in the men, without allowing himself to be humbugged by them, will gain their affection as well as respect.

S.G.

UNION MEN AGAINST WOMEN WORKERS

Male-dominated labor unions often feared the introduction of women into their trades. Not only did they worry that women workers would be used to depress wages and replace men, but they also believed that women's employment would "unsex" women and erode family life. Indeed, some believed that women's employment was a capitalist attack on unions. And printers liked to consider their work a quintessentially "manly art," because it combined intellectual and manly labor. With growing stridency, unions like the National Typographical Union tried to bar women from their trade. Upon occasion journeymen printers walked out on strike when women were hired as typesetters.

But women, who had been printers since the colonial period, resisted exclusion. Although female compositors earned only half what men did, they still earned four to five times as much as typical factory operatives.

We would like to thank Ava Baron for bringing this article to our attention.

TO THE EDITOR OF THE *PHILADELPHIA DAILY NEWS* FROM PRINTERS' UNION, 1854:

. . . The printers of the United States have uniformly opposed the introduction of women into printing offices for the following natural reasons:

1. That females can be employed at rates much lower than we demand and are properly entitled to, and as a consequence employers would use them for the subversion of our national organization.

2. That we do not believe that any benefit can accrue from taking women from the sphere of action God (as is evident from her physical and mental qualities) designed her to occupy. Her faculties are different from those of the male, and any attempt to draw her from her present position in life should be met with that opposition from the American people which would

be exerted against immorality and vice. The purity of woman should be guarded with care, and surely contact with the world in the same method that man finds necessary would have a very pernicious effect upon her morals.

3. That the pretensions made by the press in long and labored articles for the amelioration of the condition of woman are neither more nor less than base hypocrisy, put on to conceal their designs to depress the liberty and reduce the wages of the males.

4. That as wages must fall just in proportion to the increase of printers over demand, the introduction of females into our business at this epoch of our history as a craft would so depreciate the value of our labor as to render it a matter of necessity on the part of both man and wife to labor all the week for about in the aggregate the same compensation that is at present paid to the male for his services; and that as no bettering of the condition of either is effected by such procedure, except to the money-holders, we believe it is contrary to the advanced intelligence of the age, common sense, and justice to sanction such a course of conduct on the part of men who are not printers, but who, through their capital, speculate on the labor of others. . . .

A FEMINIST'S VIEW

The organized women's rights movement in the United States arose in the 1840s from within the anti-slavery movement. Composed primarily of pros- perous Yankee women, the movement's concern with women's work first focused on trying to gain access to higher education and the professions. One such activist was Caroline Dall (1822–1912), who was concerned with poor women, ran a nursery for the children of working women, helped educate free blacks, and believed economic emancipation to be fundamental to women's rights. In this excerpt from her book, Women's Right to Labor *(1859), she argued that prejudices against women's wage labor affected all classes.*

. . . I ask for woman, then, free, untrammelled access to all fields of labor; and I ask it, first, on the ground that she needs to be fed, and that the question which is at this moment before the great body of working women is "death or dishonor:" for lust is a better paymaster than the mill-owner or the tailor, and economy never yet shook hands with crime. . . .

If, in my correspondence with employers last winter, one man told me with pride that he gave from eight to fifty cents for the making of pantaloons, including the heaviest doeskins, he *forgot* to tell me what he charged his customers for the same work. Ah! on those bills, so long unpaid, the eight cents sometimes rises to thirty, and the fifty cents *always* to a dollar or a dollar and twenty-five cents.

The most efficient help this class of workwomen could receive would be the thorough adoption of the cash system, and the establishment of a large workshop in the *hands of women* consenting to moderate profits, and super-intended by those whose position in society would win respect for labor. When I said, six months ago, that ten Beaconstreet women, engaged in honorable work, would do more for this cause than all the female artists, all the speech-making and conventions, in the world, I was entirely in earnest. . . .

I consider the question of intellectual ability settled. The volumes of science, mathematics, general literature, &c., which women have given to the world, without sharing to the full the educational advantages of man, seem to promise that they shall outstrip him here, the moment they have a fair start. But I go farther, and state boldly, that women have, from the beginning, done the hardest and most unwholesome work of the world in all countries, whether civilized or uncivilized; and I am prepared to prove it. I do not mean that rocking the cradle and making bread is as hard work as any, but that women have always been doing man's work, and that all the outcry society makes against work for women is not to protect *women*, but a certain class called *ladies*. . . .

In Ohio, last year, about thirty girls went from farm to farm, hoeing, ploughing, and the like, for sixty-two and a half cents a day. At Media, in Pennsylvania, two girls named Miller carry on a farm of three hundred acres; raising hay and grain, hiring labor, but working mostly themselves. These women are not ignorant: they at one time made meteorological observations for an association auxiliary to the Smithsonian Institute. But labor attracts them, as it would many women if they were not oppressed by public opinion.

"In New York," writes a late correspondent of the "Lily," "I saw women performing the most menial offices,—carrying parcels for grocers, and trunks for steamboats. They often sweep the crossings in muddy weather; and I once saw one carrying brick and mortar for a mason."

Several women last winter, and one or two very young girls, gave evidence of bodily strength by skating from Lowell to Lawrence, with a head wind; and one or two made the ten miles in forty minutes. . . .

I have shown you that a very large number of women are compelled to self-support; that the old idea, that all men support all women, is an absurd fiction. . . .

Plenty of employments are open to them; but all are underpaid. They will never be better paid till women of rank begin to work for money, and so create a respect for woman's labor; and women of rank will never do this till

American men feel what all American men profess,—a proper respect for Labor, as God's own demand upon every human soul,—and so teach American women to feel it. How often have I heard that every woman willing to work may find employment! The terrible reverses of 1837 taught many men in this country that they were "out of luck:" how absurd, then, this statement with regard to women! . . .

Women want work for all the reasons that men want it. When they see this, and begin to do it faithfully, you will respect their work, and pay them for it. . . .

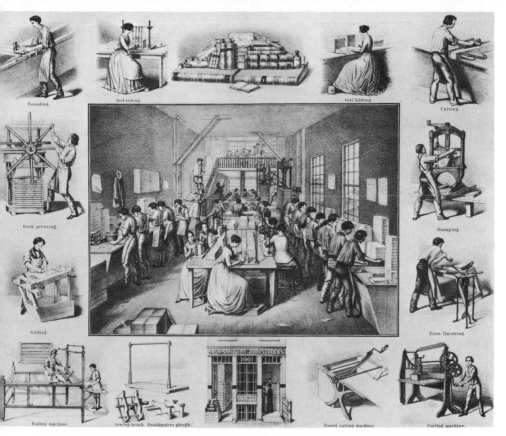

ABOVE. This engraving illustrates the sexual division of labor in nineteenth-century book manufacturing. Such sex segregation was characteristic of almost all work. (*Library of Congress*)

BELOW. Textile production, the cornerstone of American industrialization, relied heavily on women workers, especially after the development of power looms. This 1835 illustration is from one of the Merrimack valley, Massachusetts, factories. (*Museum of American Textile History*)

LEFT. These slaves picking cotton provided wealth for their Southern masters as well as capital for Northern industry. *(Schomburg Center for Research in Black Culture)*

BELOW. Slave women were also responsible for the domestic labor of their households, as we see in this 1864 picture of labor inside a Virginia slave cabin. *(Library of Congress)*

ABOVE. Whole communities often united in support of strikes, and women were frequently in the forefront both as workers and as family members, as in this 1860 Lynn, Massachusetts, shoemakers' strike. *(Library of Congress)* BELOW Wars provided new work opportunities for women, as in the case of these workers filling cartridges at the Watertown, Massachusetts, arsenal, during the Civil War. *(Library of Congress)*

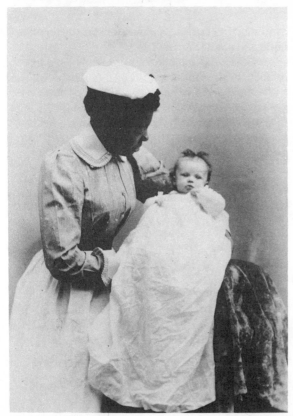

ABOVE. Spurned by male unions, working women often turned to middle-class allies to protect them from dishonest and exploitative employers; this 1874 engraving shows men from the Working Women's Protective Union hearing a complaint. *(Library of Congress)*

LEFT. While most domestic servants in the late-nineteenth-century North were immigrants, blacks were beginning to be able to obtain these jobs, which, given the options, were often desirable. This nanny, in an 1894 New York City photograph, worked for a wealthy family, as is evident from the clothing. *(State Historical Society of Wisconsin, WHi [x3]33476)*

ABOVE. This photograph from a Cheyenne, Wyoming, brothel at the turn of the century resembles a posed family portrait. Most prostitutes, however, worked in less comfortable conditions. (*Front Parlor, Mary Humphrey's, Cheyenne, Wyoming, ca. 1900. Courtesy Amon Carter Museum, Fort Worth, Texas*)

LEFT. Women have often peddled goods on the streets because poverty and/or discrimination kept them from establishing stores. This South Carolina photograph is from the early 1900s. (*Library of Congress*)

LEFT. Through the early twentieth century, most women's work remained agricultural. On a typical farm, in the family division of labor, women did the dairying, vegetable gardening, and caring for animals as this Minnesota photograph illustrates. *(Kenneth M. Wright, Minnesota Historical Society)*

RIGHT. American Indian women of the plains and forest groups usually did all of the farming and much of the manufacturing, as this ca. 1930 photograph of Ojibway women making birchbark containers for maple sap illustrates. *(Kenneth M. Wright, Minnesota Historical Society)*

RIGHT. This Chinese-American immigrant married a white American, becoming a homesteader in Idaho. A respected community leader, Polly Bemis saved lives on several occasions; at her death in 1933, a creek was named in her honor. *(Idaho State Historical Society, 62-44.7)*

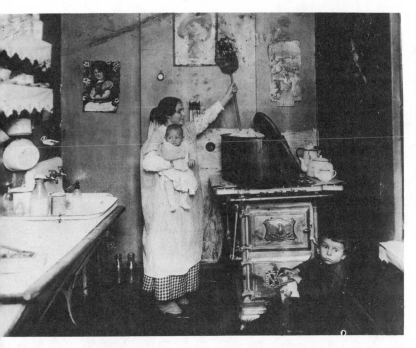

LEFT. Doing the wash was always one of women's most laborious housework tasks, particularly in a small, hot tenement flat as this 1919 photograph from New York City shows. (*National Archives*)

BELOW. In this typical home work scene, documented by the reformer photographer Lewis Hine for the National Child Labor Committee, an immigrant family is making artificial flowers in New York City around 1910. (*Library of Congress*)

Above. This typical sewing room in a garment factory in the first decade of the twentieth century resembles that in which the tragic Triangle fire occurred. The fire hazards are evident. *(Library of Congress)*

Left. New forms of industry, such as canning, drew new groups of women into wage work, such as in this Alaskan fish cannery that hired Indian women. *(Special Collections, University of Washington Libraries, UW 14787)*

LEFT. The government was a major employer of women, as this photograph of women trimming currency in a mint in 1907 shows. *(National Archives)*

BELOW LEFT. At the turn of the century, clerical work rapidly expanded to become a major employer of women. These opportunities were usually limited to high-school-educated white women, but this 1919 photo shows the exception. *(Library of Congress)*

BELOW RIGHT. Despite considerable discrimination against Asian Americans, on some occasions they overcame it, as did Jenny Won, who worked in the Cleveland, Ohio, stock exchange. *(National Archives)*

ABOVE. Black women were increasingly concentrated in domestic service, in part because white women were able to get better jobs. Race uplift institutions, such as Tuskegee Institute, concentrated on preparing women for more skilled jobs, as in this 1920 dress-making class. *(Schomburg Center for Research in Black Culture)*

BELOW. Sharecropping imposed a new form of servitude for Southern agricultural blacks, as this photograph of cotton pickers from the mid-1920s illustrates. *(National Archives)*

1865–1890

1865–1890: INTRODUCTION

THE Union victory in the Civil War strengthened the foundation for a powerful industrial economy. During the war, northern businessmen had been able to obtain windfall profits, in part through graft, favorable legislation, and government subsidies. Afterward, the great capitalists, frequently called "robber barons"—Carnegie, Cooke, Harriman, Morgan, and Rockefeller—forced out their competition to gain monopolies over the nation's resources and labor force. Rockefeller, for example, controlled 90 percent of oil refining by 1879.

Industrialism and railroads transformed the cities and the rural/urban balance of the country. New inland industrial cities arose, like Pittsburgh, no longer needing access to the sea. In 1860 less than one-quarter of Americans lived in a city or town; by the 1890s historian Frederick Jackson Turner declared the frontier a thing of the past. More immediately, industrial growth divided Americans. The experience of the two-thirds to three-quarters of the population who still lived in small settlements diverged considerably from that of the crowded urban industrial and commercial poor. Some families continued to homestead "virgin" land while American Indians were stripped of landownership and confined to reservations. A stream of settlers sought their fortunes in the beautiful western landscape while increasing numbers of slum dwellers rarely saw trees. A steadily increasing proportion of the white population came to depend on free wage labor, while the majority of blacks became ensnared in a new kind of servitude—sharecropping. The South became even more economically "backward" in comparison to the North and Midwest.

Women shared in these regional, class, and race divisions and sometimes experienced them in ways particular to their sex. Class differences in dress, manners, speech, and consumption patterns became more apparent. The gap between a "lady" and a farm woman or urban working-class woman grew.

At the beginning of this period, women's-rights activists were hopeful of rapid gains for women and believed that their movement could speak to and for increasing numbers of women. They dreamed of playing a role in uplifting the freedwomen, and some suffragists went South to teach former slaves.

83

In the 1870s the women's-rights movement deepened its analyses of male dominance and dared to take on such issues as wife beating, birth control, divorce, women's access to jobs and education, and equal pay.

However, despite these good intentions, the growth of class divisions contributed to constricting the women's-rights movement, increasingly orienting it toward Yankee, elite women. In fact, some suffragists began to take anti-black, anti-labor, and antiimmigrant positions. In an example of good intentions gone bad, Susan B. Anthony tried in 1869 to organize a working women's association and to get women trained as typographers by encouraging them to take the jobs of striking male printers. The union, of course, labeled the women scabs (strikebreakers). In addition, the post–Civil War settlement created a bitter division within the old women's-rights/antislavery coalition. Some supported the enfranchisement of black men enacted by the fourteenth and fifteenth amendments (rights that were later abrogated in the South). Others supported universal suffrage, including women, or nothing. Neither side emphasized African-American or working-class causes.

In fact, the respectability of "ladies" rested in part on the labor of other women. "Ladies" relied on maids, seamstresses, laundresses, nannies, and cooks in their domestic lives and on sharecroppers, factory operatives, and working-class housewives for their incomes. In this period, the number of women wage-earners tripled; by 1870 one out of every four nonfarm workers was a woman. But they were restricted to the worst jobs: 70 percent were domestic servants; and of the minority in industry, nearly four-fifths were in the garment trades. Their average age at beginning work was fifteen. Their wages were extremely low, ranging from an average of $4.05 per week in Atlanta to $6.91 in San Francisco. Women's earnings averaged half of men's. Many full-time female workers were malnourished, ill-clothed, ill-housed.

The small but growing proportion of wage-laboring women received little attention or help from the suffrage movement. Instead, they had to look to male and often unresponsive trade unionists for support or, when it was not forthcoming, attempt to organize themselves autonomously. Women workers formed hundreds of local and ephemeral groups in this period: cigarmakers, tailoresses, seamstresses, umbrella sewers, textile workers, printers, laundresses. Although thirty national unions existed, only two craft unions—the printers and the cigarmakers—admitted women.

Industry

RECRUITMENT

Women were so sought after for factory labor that traditional word-of-mouth recruitment could not supply hiring needs. Factories also relied on labor agents who were sent, on a commission basis, into the countryside to recruit women for the mills. Some factories used agents in Europe and recruited immigrants. Sometimes whole families would sign a factory contract; at other times, especially among rural families, a few members would sign up while others remained behind to keep a farm going. The following letters to such agents indicate something of the process. In the first, the wife of the local newspaper publisher tries to help the Langevin family (likely French Canadians) by getting them factory work, and in doing so displays her disdain for workers in general. (We have no way of knowing if Mrs. Langevin wanted to be "helped" in this way.) The second letter, written six months later, tells us something of the very restrictive working conditions that factory labor then involved. The third letter illustrates some of the forms of working-class resistance to control and exploitation by owners and their agents.

Mr. Cumnock [hiring agent for Dwight]: Dear Sir:—I take the liberty of writing a line to you regarding a French family that has recently gone from this place . . . to your town, and are employed by your corporation. The name is Langevin. Mrs. Langevin is as brave and good a woman as she knows how to be, doing her *best* for the great family of eleven children; and as long-continued sickness and ill luck has reduced the family sorely, they certainly need all the encouragement humaneness can give them. Knowing by experience what shiftlessness and utter lack of sense and judgement is generally found among the class you much-tried manufacturers are compelled to employ, I only write to assure you that this family are really above the average of their class; and if any favor by way of good tenement, work, etc. lies in your gift, to assure such favor will not be thrown away in them. They are Protestants, and therefore the Catholic element is not disposed to be over friendly to them; and if Mrs. Langevin should ask for a change of tenement it will be because of this. Pardon my freedom in thus addressing you; and let my deep interest in the family be my excuse. I only wished to commend them to your favorable knowledge, from among the multitude of their class from whom so little is to be expected. The Langevin children are members of Rev. Mr. Best's Sunday school, and their mother writes me that they are much interested in it. It is solid Christianity to help those who are disposed to help themselves. Very respectfully, Mrs. E. C. Stone, wife of the Publisher of the "*Patriot*."

Chicopee May 6 79   Mr. Cumnock   Sir my daughter is said to have gone out of the mill without leave and i beleive it is so i am very sorry she disobeyed so much will you be so kind as to see the overseer and ask him to take her back i hope she will behave better in future if he does not want her himself if he will give her bill so she can get another job for we are poor and need her help i hope he will forgive her this time for my sake yours Mary Langevin

Chicopee, September / 86
Mr. Cumnock
Dear Sir
I would like to let you know about a few french family living on Cabot St one of them Elizabeth Bonvill[sic] No. 23 she is one I brought from Cornwall and she told me that she had five to work in the mills and when she got here she only had two fit to work the oldest was sixteen and she tried to work herself in the cardroom but could not get along and then she left me and went and got a tenement on cabot St No 23 and Kept house for her two children and two of my boarders she took with her, and now five of the ten I brought from Canada lately she coaxed them away to live withe her and she charges them five dollars per month for the use of their rooms and they have to buy their own food and they owe me for their fare from Canada and four more that she helped to runaway from my house at twelve oclock at night and shiped them to Worcester, she is the cause that I loose so much money . . . she says it is good enough for me I have no right to go after so many people it makes them cut the wages down and I think that when the five she has with her now has enough money she will send them to some other place and I will have to loose all they owe me for their fares . . . she is always complaining that she can't make anything in this mill and they go in and out at any time they like after ten . . . Mr. Duplessis No 17 Cabot St he has his house filled with boarders and some of them don't work in the mills and they like it better there because they can come in and out when they like after ten. . . .

CHANGING THE SEX OF JOBS ─────────────

In general, industrial jobs, like preindustrial tasks, tend to be highly sex-segregated and sex-marked: nearly everything is specifically either a male or a female job. But these identifications are not fixed, as this excerpt from the work of labor-history pioneer Edith Abbott shows. (We introduced Abbott in the pre-1820 section; see pp. 16–19.) Her study of cigarmakers shows how women's work history disproves several widely accepted generalizations: first, that women's work moved from the home into the factory; second, that when jobs shift sexes, they always go from male to female because women can be hired for lower wages.

The increased employment of women in cigar-making seems to indicate its tendency to develop into a "women's industry" and furnishes an interesting example of the industrial displacement of men by women. The history of the industry makes it of peculiar interest, because originally the women were displaced by the men, and in these later years, they have only come into their own again.

The manufacture of cigars in this country is an industry of nearly a century's growth, but it has not continuously throughout its history employed a large proportion of women. This is, at first, not easy to understand, for it has always been a trade for which women are seemingly better qualified than men. No part of the making of cigars is heavy work, and skill depends upon manual dexterity—upon delicacy and sensitiveness of touch. . . .

The preliminary process of "stripping," which includes "booking," is the preparation of the leaf for the hands of the cigar-maker. The large mid-rib is stripped out, and, if the tobacco is of the quality for making wrappers, the leaves are also "booked"—smoothed tightly across the knee and rolled into a compact pad ready for the cigar-maker's table. Even in the stripping-room there are different grades of work, all unskilled and all practically monopolized by women and girls.

Division of labor has been slow in making its way into cigar factories. The best cigar is still made by a single workman, and the whole process demands a high degree of skill. Slightly inferior cigars, however, can be made with "molds" by less skilled workmen. . . .

Originally cigar-making was one of the household industries, and in the early years of the [19th] century nearly the whole of the Connecticut tobacco crop was made by the farmers' wives and daughters into cigars known to the trade as "supers," "long mines," and "short sixes." These cigars were sometimes peddled by the women, but more frequently they were bartered at the country stores, where they served as a substitute for currency. All of the groceries and dry goods used by the family during the year were often paid for in this way and represented the exchange value of the "leisure hours" of the farmer's wife. Although these were very inferior cigars, they were sold pretty generally throughout New England. The passing of this early "homestead industry," which existed in Pennsylvania and other tobacco-growing states as well as in Connecticut, was very gradual; for the transition to the factory system did not, in cigar-making, involve the substitution of machine for hand-work, and farmers' wives continued to roll cigars until the imposition of the internal revenue tax—and even after that. Their cigars, however, did not compare favorably with the finer factory-made product, and as Connecticut tobacco grew in favor, it became unprofitable to use it for the cheaper grades of work. Household industry, therefore, furnished a gradually decreasing proportion of the total manufactured product. But, unlike most work that left the home, cigar-making had not finally passed into the factory; for it was to be established as a domestic industry on a much larger scale in the tenements of New York. Two questions are of interest at this point with regard to the history of the employment of women: Did they follow their work from the home to the factory? and, What was their part in the establishment of cigar-making as one of the early tenement industries?

Women undoubtedly worked in the earliest factories. What was possibly the first cigar factory in this country was established at Suffield, Conn., in 1810 and employed only women. In 1832 returns from ten cigar factories in Massachusetts showed 238 women, 48 men, and 9 children employed; but complete statistics for the period are not available. It was estimated that one-third of the persons employed at the trade in Connecticut in 1856 were women, and the census shows that 740 women were employed in 1860. . . .

Cigar-making, as has been pointed out, is a highly skilled trade, and it was early discovered that among our immigrants were men able to make cigars that could compete with those imported from Germany and Spain. These immigrant cigar-makers who proved to have the superior workmanship that was indispensable to the development of the industry, took the places of the American women who had been formerly employed. The Cuban is said to have been the first male cigar-maker employed in this country, and as Spanish tobacco and Spanish-made cigars were in high favor, a large market was found for the Spanish cigars made here by Cuban workmen. Later expert workmen among immigrants from other countries became competitors of the Cuban, and among German immigrants especially were men of exceptional skill and experience in the trade. The woman cigar-maker almost disappeared during this time, and there are men, both cigar-makers and manufacturers, in New York who say that there was "not a woman in the trade," except in the unskilled work of stripping, "back of the seventies"; and a recent report of the commissioner of labor confirms this statement. . . .

The year 1869 begins a new period in the history of the industry. Since then three factors seem to have worked together to bring about a very rapid increase in the employment of women: (1) increased immigration from Bohemia, where women are exclusively employed in cigar factories; (2) the invention of machinery, which has made the skilled workman less necessary; (3) a feeling on the part of employers that women are more docile than men, and that a large proportion of women among the employees would mean fewer strikes.

The immigration of Bohemian women cigar-makers began in 1869, and meant the re-establishment of cigar-making as a household industry—but this time under the domestic rather than the handicraft system. The home-work which occupied the leisure of the Connecticut farmer's thrifty wife is clearly not to be compared with the home-work of the Bohemian immigrant in the New York slums. The New England women were independent producers. They owned their raw material, the homes in which they worked, and the finished product which they disposed of at their own convenience; the tenement women were helplessly dependent upon an employer who furnished the raw material, owned and marketed the product, and frequently charged them exorbitant rentals for the rooms in which they both lived and worked; they were merely hired wage-earners working for a single employer in their own homes instead of in his factory. The explanation of the home-work in both cases is found in the fact that cigar-making is peculiarly adapted for household manufacture, and for this reason it still exists, not only as a domestic industry, but as a lingering survival of handicraft. When the only machine required is a pair of wooden molds, it is possible for the workman to own his own tools and a pair of molds, purchase his tobacco in small quantities, and, by disposing of the product quickly, carry on his trade as his own master and without having any capital.

By 1877, the year of the "great strike" which was meant to abolish it, cigar-making as a tenement industry had become firmly established. It grew rapidly after 1869 and aroused the first determined protest against "unsanitary home-work." Its development was due to Bohemian women who had worked in cigar factories in their own country. It is said that the customary method of Bohemian immigration was for the women to come first, leaving the men at work in the fields. Five or six wives would come over together, work at cigar-making as they did in Bohemia, and send money back for their husbands' passage, and then "the entire united family would take up the manufacture of cigars, emulating the industry of the mother." At this time, too, came the introduction of the team system—a division of labor by which one person prepares the bundles and another rolls them. In Bohemia the men had worked only in the fields, and their wives taught them cigar-making at home after they came over. It was much easier, of course, for these men to learn the relatively unskilled work of "bunch-making" while their wives did the rolling than to learn how to make the whole cigar.

The decade, during which cigar-making established itself as a tenement industry, was also the decade of greatest prosperity in the history of the trade. It was surely a decade of extraordinary exploitation of immigrant labor. Large manufacturers acquired blocks of tenements, for which they charged excessive rentals to their employees, who frequently, too, found themselves obliged to pay high prices for groceries and beer at stores owned by the employer. The expense of maintaining a factory was thus made part of the employees' burden; and the wages of "strippers and bookers" were also saved to the manufacturer, for the tobacco was prepared in the homes by the workers themselves, or more often by their children. The system also proved an effective coercive measure, and the eviction of the tenement strikers by the landlord manufacturers in 1877 was one of the distressing features of the strike. . . .

A majority of the cigars in New York were the product of tenement-house factories, and so large was the proportion of women at work in them that the newspapers and manufacturers referred to the strike, which was directed largely against the home-work system, as an attack on the employment of women and children. In 1882 a circular issued by the union estimated that between 3,500 and 3,750 persons were employed at cigar-making in tenement houses, and it seems reasonable to say that during the decade from 1870 to 1880 between two and three thousand women had engaged in cigar-making in their own homes.

The increased employment of women as a result of the introduction of machinery comes at a later stage in the history of the industry. So many unsuccessful machines were tried from time to time that it is not easy to fix any exact date as the period when machinery was first considered successful enough to be widely adopted. By 1887, however, several of the large factories had begun to use machines, and in 1888 we find machines with women operators taking the places of skilled cigar-makers who were on a strike in Philadelphia. . . . In nine open, or non-union, factories which had more than 4,000 employees, and in all but one of which machinery was used, 73.1 per cent. of the employees were women; while in eight union shops, which used no machinery, and employed only 527 persons, the proportion of women employed was only 36.1 per cent. It is important to note that the machine, the large factory, and the increased employment of women go together. . . .

In discussing further the tendency toward increased employment of women as a means of avoiding or ending strikes, some account may also be given of the relation of the women to the Cigar-Maker's International Union. The union was organized in 1851; and in 1867 the constitution was altered so that women and negroes, heretofore excluded, became eligible to membership. In 1877 women were employed in large numbers to break the strike of that year. Several hundred girls were taught the trade, and employers went so far as to call the strike "a blessing in disguise," since it "offered a new employment for women and secured workers whose services may be depended on at low wages." In this same year, however, the Cincinnati cigar-makers struck successfully for the removal of all women from the work-shops, and in some other cities similar strikes were inaugurated but failed. In 1879 the president of the union announced that one of its aims would be "the regulation of female labor;" and in 1881 he strongly advised the unions, in view of the fact that the employment of women was constantly increasing, "to extend the right hand of brotherhood to them;" and added: "Better to have them with us than against us. . . . They can effect a vast amount of mischief outside of our ranks as tools in the hands of the employer against us." The president of the New York local in 1886 complained that Bohemian women were doing work "that men were formerly employed to do. They have driven the American workmen from our trade altogether. They work for a price that an American could not work for." In 1894 a president of the international union said: "We are confronted with child- and female labor to an alarming extent;" and in 1901, at a meeting of the American Federa-tion of Labor, the cigar-makers asked for the passage of resolutions expressing opposition to the use of machinery in their trade and to the employment of women and children. The hostility of the union to women is not difficult to understand. The women seemed to be lowering a standard wage that the men, through organization, were trying to uphold. They had, moreover, the workingman's belief in the old "lump of labor" fallacy, and for every woman who was employed they saw "a man without a job." The union has, how-ever, stood squarely for the same wage scale for both men and women, while in England the union maintains a woman's scale that is 25 per cent. lower than the men's. As in other industries, a much smaller proportion of the women than of the men in the trade are members of the union, and the women seldom attend the meetings, and take small part in the proceedings when they do.

SWEATSHOPS

The "sweatshop" and the "sweating system" were terms first used in the cloth-ing industry. Later they became synonymous with many low-wage, unsani-tary industries where the work took place in tenements. In this excerpt, Louis Levine, the official historian of the early years of the Ladies Garment Workers Union, describes the origins of the sweatshop.

. . . Already before 1880, there appeared in the women's clothing industry the beginnings of the contracting system. By 1882, when the immigration
of the Jews from Eastern Europe began to assume perceptible proportions,
the distinction between the so-called "inside" and "outside" shop was already
established. The "inside" shops were those which were directly connected
with the selling department of the business firm. In some of these "inside"
shops the garments were cut, made up, bushelled, and examined; in short,
the entire manufacturing process was begun and completed under the same
roof. In other "inside" shops only the cutting and final examining was done,
while the cut garments were sent out to be made up elsewhere, that is in
"outside" shops. The owners of the "inside" shops were the large manufacturers and merchants in whose hands the industry was centered. Those who
operated the "outside" shops became known as contractors. They "contracted" to make up the cut garments for the owners of the "inside" shops at
so much per garment. They were middlemen. Their profit was made by
paying the workers less for making the garment than they received themselves.

The three main features of the sweat-shop have been described as unsani-
tary conditions, excessively long hours, and extremely low wages. The shops
were generally located in tenement houses. As a rule, one of the rooms of
the flat in which the contractor lived was used as a working place. Sometimes
work would be carried on all over the place, in the bedroom as well as in the
kitchen. Even under the best of conditions this would have made for living
and working in grime and dirt. But the conditions were not of the best. . . .
Investigations showed that about one out of every three persons whose living
quarters were examined "slept in unventilated rooms without windows." One
can imagine what happened when these "homes" were also turned into shops
and became home and workshop at the same time.

A writer who made a valiant fight against the evils of the tenement house
and of the sweat-shop, gives a graphic description of the district in New York
City where the sweat-shops were situated.

. . . "Take the Second Avenue Elevated," he writes, "and ride up half a
mile through the sweaters' district. Every open window of the big tenements,
that stand like a continuous brick wall on both sides of the way, give you a
glimpse of one of these shops as the train speeds by. Men and women bend-
ing over their machines or ironing clothes at the window, half-naked. . . .
The road is like a big gangway through an endless workroom where vast
multitudes are forever laboring. Morning, noon, or night, it makes no difference; the scene is always the same." Not only the insides of the tenements
were turned into working places. "It is not unusual," reported the New York
State factory inspector, "when the weather permits to see the balconies of the
fire escapes occupied by from two to four busy workmen. The halls and roofs
are also utilized for workshop purposes very frequently." The same factory

inspector describes one of the many sweat-shops which he visited. This particular one, which was typical of others, was that "of a cloakmaker, who used one room for his shop, while the other three rooms were supposed to be used for domestic purposes only, his family consisting of his wife and seven children. In the room adjoining the shop, used as the kitchen, there was a red-hot stove, two tables, a clothes rack, and several piles of goods. A woman was making bread on a table upon which there was a baby's stocking, scraps of cloth, several old tin cans, and a small pile of unfinished garments. In the next room was an old woman with a diseased face walking the floor with a crying child in her arms."

In the "outside" shops, the working hours were eighty-four per week. But besides "regular" hours, there was "overtime" in both the "inside" and "outside" shops, and in addition many of the workers "took material home and worked until two and three o'clock in the morning." It was quite common to work fifteen and sixteen hours a day, from five in the morning to nine at night, and in the busy season men frequently worked all night. "If you look into the streets any morning," wrote an investigator of conditions in New York City, "at four o'clock you will see them full of people going to work. They rouse themselves up at three o'clock and are often at their machines at four. The latest is sure to be there at five. The general time is five o'clock all year round in good times, winter and summer, and if the boss will give them gaslight, some will go even earlier than three o'clock." Old-timers in the industry are fond of telling to-day about the over-zealous workers of those days, cloak pressers and operators, who saved time and rent by sleeping on "bundles" in the shop between working. It was a current saying that one could always do a little more work by "borrowing a couple of hours from the following day." No wonder the industry, and especially the cloakmaking trade, early acquired the sad distinction of being the "worst-driven trade in the matter of hours in the season." . . .

The spread of the contracting system tended to keep wages at a low level. In New York City, where the effects of the sweat-shop system were most keenly felt, wages were from $15 a week in 1883 to $6 and $7 in 1885. The New York State Bureau of Labor Statistics reported that the "very best" workers were "getting $10 a week, while the women employed in the industry were earning from $3 to $6 a week." According to the report, "some even with the aid of their families and working fourteen hours a day could earn only $12 and $15 a week. Others could only make $4 by working ten hours a day." Towards the end of the decade wages in New York City rose a little, the average wage of cloakmakers in 1888 being about $12 a week.

The investigators of the sweat-shop denounced it as a "system of making clothes under filthy and inhuman conditions" and as a "process of grinding the faces of the poor." Some of these investigators were especially aroused by conditions in the cloak trade. "This trade," we read in one of the official reports, "is one of those which have justified the complaints against the hardships and underpay of labor" and against "the shocking conditions under which work is done in a Christian community where we have so much charitable sentiment and a sanitary administration." In explaining these conditions, the investigators generally took the view that the sweat-shop was the result of the inferior standards introduced by the immigrants. Some even declared the sweatshop a special Jewish institution explicable by the "racial" and "national" characteristics of the Jewish workers. An official of the State of Pennsylvania wrote that the Russian Jews "evidently prefer filth to cleanliness," while another investigator of the problem concluded that the "factory system with its discipline and regular hours" was "distasteful to the Jew's individualism" and that the Jewish worker preferred "the sweat-shop with its going and coming."

The bias involved in such explanations is evident. Sweating in the United States existed in the men's clothing trades long before the coming of Jewish and Italian immigrants. It has existed in various industries in other countries. Sidney and Beatrice Webb pointed out many years ago that in England "all the evils of sweating exist where neither Jews nor foreigners have as yet penetrated . . . or where their competition is but little felt." In other words, sweating is primarily an industrial problem, a phase of the general problem of cheap and exploited labor. The Jewish, and later also the Italian, garment workers worked in sweat-shops because they had no other entry into American industry.

SHALL MARRIED WOMEN WORK?

In preindustrial societies, and among farm people even in modern society, everyone worked; making a living was a family project to which men, women, and children all contributed. As employers sought workers who would sell their labor for wages, a new ideal developed—the family wage. This was supposed to be a system in which men became the only breadwinners while their wives and children remained domestic, women doing housework and child care only. In fact it never worked. The family wage has always been a myth. Only a minority of men have ever been able to earn enough single-handedly to support a family. Most families depended on wives' and children's earnings also.

However, the effects of the family-wage ideology were powerful nonetheless. It made men feel that their wives' earning reflected poorly on their adequacy as providers, possibly threatening their masculinity. It made working wives feel guilty and transient in their work, and thus made it harder for them to struggle for better jobs and pay. It divided workers, even working women, perpetuating the false belief that married women worked only for "pin money," for "extras," not out of necessity, and that they held jobs that might otherwise be available to those who really "needed" them.

In the following letters to a newspaper from workers in shoe factories, we see this conflict.

We thank Mary Blewett for this selection.

FEBRUARY 1, 1879
Mr. Editor,—In last week's *Record*, . . . I noticed this: "Working women, why don't you organize?" . . . I grew more and more indignant and resolved to write the *Record* a letter giving some of the reasons why the D.O.S.C.'s [Daughters of Saint Crispin, the female shoe workers union] membership fails to increase. . . . Why my blood fairly boils and I get righteously angry when I think of some of the causes which have brought down the price of our labor! But let me tell you: In the first place, the shops are thronged with married women, the greater portion of whom (and these are the ones I censure) have good, comfortable homes, and girls whose fathers are amply able to provide them with all the necessaries and comforts of life, but their inordinate love of dress, and a desire to vie in personal adornments with their more wealthy sisters, takes them into the workrooms. . . . Ask *them* to join the order, and they are horrified at the thought! They don't want any better wages: they have a home, no board to pay, and so long as they can get enough for pin money, they are content. . . .

Our brother workmen can organize, and redress their wrongs; but for us there is no hope, and the bosses know it just as well as we; so they snap their fingers at us, and as each returning season comes round, they give us an extra cutdown in lieu of cutting down the men, knowing full well there are plenty of married women, with well-to-do husbands, and half supported girls who stand ready to work the few short weeks in which work is given out, at any price they can get. . . . Organize! Would that we might, so that our number might become a power to be feared. I could almost weep tears of blood when I think upon our wrongs.

A Stitcher

FEBRUARY 8, 1879.
Mr. Editor,— . . . I cannot quite agree with "A Stitcher" in thinking that "married women" and "half-supported girls" are the stumbling blocks in the way of organization. The great majority of our girls are not "half supported," neither are the majority of married women employed in our shops blessed with "comfortable homes" and "well to do husbands": if there are a few of this class, they are *very* few compared with the many who are obliged to work

for their daily bread. . . . married women have been well represented in the D.O.S.C. organization, and . . . they have always proved zealous and ardent supporters of that order. . . . There are not many women inside our shoe shops today who are not obliged to work. . . .

Americus

FEBRUARY 22, 1879

Mr. Editor,— . . . Ah! my dear Stitcher. . . . You say: "So long as there are a surplus of laborers, with a scarcity of work," I shall protest against the married women question." And I reply:—So long as there are "a surplus of laborers with a scarcity of work" so long will your protest be of no avail. So long as there are "a surplus of laborers with a scarcity of work" so long will many married men find it impossible to support their families, and when the husband and father cannot provide for his wife and children, it is perfectly natural that the wife and mother should desire to work for her husband and her little ones, and we have no right to deny her that privilege. . . .

My dear child, don't blame married women if the land of the free has become a land of slavery and oppression. Women are not to blame. . . .

Americus

MARCH 1, 1879

Mr. Editor,— . . . For years I have been homeless, thrown here and there by circumstances, but have kept my eyes and ears open to all that has been going on around me; and many times I have been deeply pained at the utter selfishness manifested by a certain class of married women in the shops, till I have been thoroughly disgusted with them all. . . .

. . . from statistical reports there is found to be sixty odd thousand more females than males in the state of Massachusetts, and it is safe to say three-fourths of them have to earn their own support. Now these can never have homes of their own unless they make them. No strong arm on which to lean can ever rightfully be theirs. In the face and eyes of this, can it be fair for them to have to compete with married women who have protectors, in the struggle for bread, besides all the other obstacles in their way?

. . . It is no use, "Americus"; since the days of Mother Eve women have been at the bottom of nearly every trouble: and . . . I think a foolish extravagance in dress and love of display on the part of women, has caused many a once honest man to turn thief, and has helped, if did not wholly, bring about this fearful crisis of distress and want. . . .

A Stitcher

STOOL PIGEONS AND BLACKLISTS ————————————

Among the problems facing labor organizers were stool pigeons, *people who spy on other workers and report on their activities to management, and* blacklisting, *circulating names of labor activists among employers who then refuse to hire them. These letters from the files of a textile factory—the first from a spy, the second from a labor agent—illustrate both these problems.*

Malvina Fourtune and her brother Henry Fourtune it was them who started the strike and they go from house to house and tells the people to keep up the strike and any how all the Fourtunes were a nucience to the Corporation since them around the town and Frank White also and Faufite Parenti No 11 Cabot St most live in Cabot St and the Dufriesne related to the Fourtunes they are as bad as them and others that is like them is the Samsons they live on Dwight St and the Greenwoods and Odile Roy they are all of the head strikers and even since these people are in the mills they have made trouble and they have seen living here for many years most of them worked in Chicopee falls in summer and come and work here in winter and make trouble and when I bring some stranger they are the first to discourage them and tell them they won't make nothing and the Desilla and Samsons of Cabot St they are all alike and they all think they are going to win the strike this is what I hird from some who newe it well

Lyman Mills

Holyoke, Mass. June 21st 1882

J. M. Cumnock, Agent.
Dear Sir.
We note the names Victoria Lenroy and Justine Nadeau and will "black list" them.

Yours truly
Theop. Parsons, Agent

BUILDING A COOPERATIVE ————————————

When trade union activity did not prove successful, many working people, women as well as men, tried to form producer cooperatives as a way to gain independence from "wage slavery." The Troy, New York, Laundry Union went that route. Established sometime in the 1860s, it became one of the *most militant women's unions in the country. We get a glimpse of their spirit and class consciousness from the fact that they contributed large amounts of money—once $1000, once $500—to striking male unions. Their leader, Kate Mullany, became a national organizer of women for the National Labor Union, the first such appointment in U.S. history.*

When the union lost a bitter strike in 1869, its members formed a collar manufacturing cooperative and, encouraged by activists in the women's rights movement, sought investments from wealthy supporters, as the following appeal, published in a woman suffrage journal in 1870, shows. Unfortunately the cooperative failed, as it has always been difficult for enterprises which pay workers well to compete with those that underpay.

A private letter from Kate Mullany, President of the "Laundry Union and Co-operative Collar Co.," of Troy, New York, says:

> I wrote to know what the ladies are doing in the way of taking the stock for our company. We are getting started now. We have enough subscribed to begin with, and we are starting up with a good prospect of getting a quick sale for our goods as soon as we have got them ready for the market. Of course, we depend altogether on the working people of the country, and on the people who are able and willing to help working girls and wish to see them get along.
> Yours, KATE MULLANY,
> President Collar Laundry Union

The stock is five dollars per share, and is only an investment, which will directly benefit working girls, not a charity. The interest will be regularly paid, and the stock bought in by the girls themselves as soon as possible. Any person wishing to subscribe for one share or more can address a note to Kate Mullany, President of the Troy Laundry Union.

UNION ORGANIZING

The first large-scale national labor federation in the United States was the Knights of Labor, established in 1869. The union began to organize women in 1881 and at its peak included over one hundred all-women locals or assemblies. These locals had as members all kinds of workers—not just industrial wage laborers but housekeepers and farmers—and black as well as white women participated. By 1886 the Knights of Labor women were strong enough (relatively, that is; there were still only sixteen women delegates out of six hundred) to win a department of women's work with a full-time organizer.

The job went to Leonora Barry, a hosiery worker, who became the country's first woman professional union organizer. Born in Ireland in 1849, brought to upstate New York as a young child, Barry became a young widow who went into a factory to support her children. By 1886 she had become a "Master Workman" (or president) of a Knights of Labor assembly of nearly one thousand women. A tall, commanding woman, Barry developed a humorous and charismatic speaking style and soon became widely sought after as a lecturer. For the next four years, she traveled extensively for the Knights, organizing women's and men's locals, lecturing on women's issues, and lobbying for protective labor legislation. On the road so much she virtually had no home, she had to send one child to a convent and another to her sister-in-law. She established not only union locals but also some cooperative factories and a working women's benefit fund and was a leader in the successful campaign for Pennsylvania's factory inspection act of 1889.

The following selections from Barry's reports from the field show the difficult conditions for working women, the obstacles to organizing them presented by employers and male trade unionists, the feminist consciousness she found among some women workers, and her own changing perspective on labor organizing. Although Barry found that women workers appeared to be happier in separate locals, she herself believed this to be a mistaken approach and ended her organizing career recommending that the Knights' separate Woman's Department be abolished.

1887

Having no legal authority I have been unable to make as thorough an investigation in many places as I would like, and, after the discharge of Sister Annie Conboy from the silk mill in Auburn, in February last, for having taken me through the mill, I was obliged to refrain from going through establishments where the owners were opposed to our Order lest some of our members be victimized; consequently the facts stated in my report are not all from actual observation but from authority which I have every reason to believe truthful and reliable.

Upon the strength of my observation and experience I would ask of officers and members of this Order that more consideration be given, and more thorough educational measures be adopted on behalf of the working-women of our land, the majority of whom are entirely ignorant of the economic and industrial question which is to them of such vital importance; and they must ever remain so while the selfishness of their brothers in toil is carried to such an extent as I find it to be among those who have sworn to demand equal pay for equal work. Thus far in the history of our Order that part of our platform has been but a mockery of the principles intended.

Went to Auburn, N.Y., Feb. 20. I found the working-women of this city in a deplorable state, there being none of them organized. There were long hours, poor wages and the usual results consequent upon such a condition.

Not among male employers alone in this city, but a woman in whose heart we would expect to find a little pity and compassion for the suffering of her own sex. To the contrary, on this occasion, however, I found one who, for cruelty and harshness toward employees, has not an equal on the pages of labor's history—one who owns and conducts an establishment in which is manufactured women's and children's wear. Upon accepting a position in her factory an employee is compelled to purchase a sewing machine from the proprietress, who is agent for the S.M. Co. This must be paid for in weekly payments of 50 cents, provided the operative makes $3. Should she make $4 the weekly payment is 75 cents. At any time before the machine is paid for, through a reduction of the already meager wages, or the enforcement of some petty tyrranical rule—sickness, anger or any cause, [if] the operative leaves her employ, she forfeits the machine and all the money paid upon it, and to the next applicant the machine is resold. She must also purchase the thread for doing the work, as she [the employer] is an agent for a thread company. It takes four spools of thread at 50 cents a spool to do $5 worth of work, and when $2 is paid for thread, and 50 cents for the machine, the unfortunate victim has $2.50 wherewith to board, clothe and care for herself generally; and it is only experts who can make even this. Many other equally unjust systems are resorted to of which lack of space forbids mention.

I succeeded in organizing two Local Assemblies in this city, one of wood-workers, and one women's Local Assembly, numbering 107 members, which has grown rapidly and is now one of the most flourishing Local Assemblies in the State. Here it was that Sister Annie Conboy was discharged from the silk mill for having taken me through the mill, although she had received permission from her foreman to take a friend through, yet, when the proprietor found out I was a Knight of Labor she was discharged without a moment's warning. . . .

May 12 returned to complete the work mapped out for me in D.A. [District Assembly] 99. Summing the State of Rhode Island up, on the whole, the condition of its wage-workers is truly a pitiful one—its industries being for the most part in the control of soulless corporations, who know not what humanity means—poor pay, long hours, yearly increase of labor on the individual, and usually a decrease of their wages, the employment of children, in some cases, who are mere infants. The following is a fair sample of the contemptible, mean trickery resorted to by some of the kings of the cotton industry. A law in this State prohibits the compulsory labor of women over ten hours per day. Upon one occasion women weavers were asked to work overtime. They refused. The foreman went to the men weavers, asked them to work overtime, saying it would be money in their pockets, a favor to their employer, and would make the women jealous of their larger months' wages. Then they would consent to work overtime, too. This is only one instance of how the wage-workers are made the instruments of injury to one another.

The years of cruel oppression and injustice which those people have endured has so sapped the milk of human kindness from their hearts that the same system of selfishness applied to them by their employers they in turn practice toward each other; and to this and no other reason can be traced the falling off in the jurisdiction of D.A. 99, as well as in many others. . . .

1888

On March 25 to April 1 I represented women in the Knights of Labor at the Women's Congress at Washington, D.C. The good results of that meeting have been widespread. As to all countries represented there by delegates, a more satisfactory knowledge of the aims and objects of Knighthood were obtained than could have been disseminated by any other method; also in a number of cities and towns of our own land. Women who heretofore ignored the cause of workingwomen now work earnestly and faithfully for their welfare. . . .

Rockford, Ill. . . . July 4 was celebrated here under the name of our "Foremothers' Day." It has been celebrated of "Our Forefathers" for so many years that the women of Rockford conceived the idea of resurrecting our good old foremothers for a change. It was a glorious success, notwithstanding the pressure of political effort to make it a failure. Over 3,000 people listened to my address on the need and benefit of organization. . . .

Closed a meeting August 27 at Norristown, Pa. A few of both sexes comprise the Local, and even those stand in terror of losing their positions if it were known they were organized, as one firm had offered a reward of $25 for information of a Knight of Labor in their employ. . . .

From September 19 to October 4 I visited the jurisdiction of D.A. 95, in Danbury, Conn. The principal industry is hatmaking; very many married women are employed, owing largely to the idle time men have in this industry. The women do the binding, banding, putting in the tips and sweatbands, also making tips; wages are fairly good, conditions very good, as this industry is thoroughly organized.

It has been intimated that the Woman's Department was started on sentiment. Well, if so, it has turned out to be one of the most thoroughly practical departments in the Order. Without egotism I can safely say it has done as much effective work in cheering, encouraging, educating and instructing the women of this Order in the short year of its existence as was done by the organization in the whole time of women's connection with it previous to its establishment. . . .

I have made many unsuccessful attempts to found a manufactory of women's and children's underwear so that I could have some positive proof to offer against the slop-shop [sweat shop] or contract made work. I have been partially successful, as a plant is being established in Elizabeth, N.J., and the girls of the Solidarity Co-operative Shirt Company of New York have commenced the production of these garments, so that now we will have something to offer the public, as being well made and well paid for instead of the garments manufactured by men who sacrifice human happiness, life and immortal souls on the altar of selfish greed and low, sordid, groveling ambition. . . .

1889

My work has not been confined solely to women and children, but to all of earth's toilers, as I am of the opinion that the time when we could separate the interests of the toiling masses on sex lines is past. If it were possible, I wish that it were not necessary for women to learn any trade but that of domestic duties, as I believe it was intended that man should be the bread-winner. But as that is impossible under present conditions, I believe women should have every opportunity to become proficient in whatever vocation they choose or find themselves best fitted for.

A few words about the Woman's Department. When I took a position at its head I fondly hoped to weld together in organization such a number of women as would be a power for good in the present, and a monument to their honor in the relief it would establish for the women of the future. I was too sanguine, and I am forced to acknowledge that to fulfill my best hopes is a matter of impossibility; and I believe now we should, instead of supporting a Woman's Department, put more women in the field as Lecturers to tell women why they should organize as a part of the industrial hive, rather than because they are women. There can be no separation or distinction of wage-workers on account of sex, and separate departments for their interests is a direct contradiction of this, and also of that part of our declaration which says "we know no sex in the laws of Knighthood." Therefore, I recommend the abolition of the Woman's Department, believing, as I now do, that women should be Knights of Labor without distinction, and should have all the benefits that can be given to men—no more, no less—thereby making it incumbent upon all to work more earnestly for the general good, rather than for sex, Assembly or trade.

A FATE WORSE THAN DEATH

Like many feminists and labor activists of the time, Leonora Barry believed that married women should work outside their homes only in cases of dire economic necessity. So when in 1890 she married another Knight, she immediately quit her job (although she was to remain a political activist and public speaker until her death in 1930). It is revealing that her boss, Terrence V.

Powderly, leader of the Knights of Labor, used the metaphor of death in this letter to describe her marriage. The only woman delegate at the 1890 Knights convention declined to take Barry's job, and the Woman's Department was dissolved. By then, the Knights were losing strength, although some vigorous local assemblies continued active into the twentieth century.

. . . The request for the services of Sister Barry comes from other localities but she can not comply, in fact, Sister Barry's days are numbered. You will never, in all probability, rest eyes on her again. I know you will unite with me in sorrowing over this, for us, unhappy event, but the fates are against us and soon the name of Sister Barry will exist only in the fond remembrance of the members of our Order and her many friends outside of it. She has not yet been called across the dark river but she will soon be buried in the bosom of a Lake that shall wash away all claim that we may have to her, and the papers will chronicle the event in this way: On April 17th, at St. Louis, Mrs. L. M. Barry of Amsterdam, N.Y. to O. R. Lake of St. Louis, Mo., the Rev. Mr. ———— officiating. The bride was dressed in a ————. Brother Glocking, words fail and you will have to describe the bridal outfit yourself. . . .

Coping with New Conditions

SITTING BULL MOURNS FOR INDIAN WOMEN ————

The European-American project of "civilizing" Indians included getting them to take up agriculture and branding their hunting-and-gathering lifestyle as inferior. Coincidentally, European settlers had a self-interest in steering the Indians toward agriculture because it required less land and would allow whites to take over more of the traditional Indian hunting lands.

Gendered interests also figured importantly in this "civilizing" project. Most European Americans believed that men should be the primary, even the exclusive, breadwinners. In farming families, this opinion is reflected in the common usage that describes men as farmers and women as farmers' wives, although the women's work was as essential to agricultural production as the men's. But among many American Indians, women were the farmers, often owning the land and tools. Nevertheless, missionaries, reformers who tried to help Indians, and the federal government worked to impose a "proper" sexual division of labor upon the Indians, which required divesting Indian women of their traditional labor and base of power. In the selection below, Omaha chief Sitting Bull, speaking in 1881, expresses his concern about what this white norm would mean for Indian women.

Sitting Bull was interviewed while in captivity at Fort Randall, in South Dakota territory, by Alice Fletcher (1838–1923), a pioneering ethnologist, Indian welfare reformer, and women's-rights activist. Had she been a man, Fletcher would likely have become an academic but, deprived of that option, she read archaeology and ethnology independently. Inspired by a meeting with Omaha Indian Susette La Flesche, an Indian activist (and sister of Dr. Suzanne La Flesche Picotte; see pp. 143–47), Fletcher went to live with the Omahas, observed their great sufferings, and spent the rest of her life agitating for Indian land rights and welfare.

We are grateful to Fletcher's biographer, Joan Mark, for this selection, and to Linda Kerber for bringing it to our attention.

When I was visiting Sitting Bull at Fort Randall, where he is held as a prisoner of war [in 1881], he talked to me of the future. He said that the old life was gone. The game had been killed and driven away by the white man. . . . The skill of the hunter was now of no use, nor was the valor of the warrior; man's avocation was gone. . . . As he talked, his wife entered the tent bearing wood in her arms. She laid the sticks on the fire, and threw herself down beside it resting on her elbow, and leaning her head on her hand. The light from the kindling fire lit up her handsome face and sparkled on her brass bangles. . . . Sitting Bull looked at her silently for a few moments, and then turned to me, saying: "You are a woman, take pity on my women, for they have no future. The young men can be like the white men, till the soil, supply the food and clothing, they will take the work out of the hands of the women, and the women, to whom we have owed every thing in the past, will be stripped of all which gave them power and position among the people."

FREEDWOMEN STRUGGLE FOR RESPECT

The most dramatic change in women's working conditions came with the emancipation of the slaves and the North's victory in the Civil War. But the history of emancipation has often presented the ex-slaves as passive beneficiaries, freed by Lincoln and the Union army. In fact, the freedmen and freedwomen took an active part in the war and the destruction of slavery and to a large extent freed themselves and forced the government to grant them citizenship. They also struggled for decent working conditions afterward. Many former slaveowners did not accept the conditions of a free labor market, but tried to retain their work force in nearly enslaved conditions, refusing to honor agreements about hours of work and job description, attempting to beat workers and bar them from leaving. At the close of the war, the federal government established the Freedmen's Bureau to help former slaves by supplying provision, schools, and medical aid. The bureau also attempted to provide a counterweight to southern authorities, trying to insure fair treatment of former slaves by landowners, employers, and the state. African Americans used the bureau to defend their rights and economic entitlements against southern state governments and powerful white citizens. Unfortunately, the Freedman's Bureau was abolished and the northern troops withdrawn, and despite the efforts of freed people, the southern states reestablished segregation and the economic and political subordination of blacks.

The following report from an agent of the Freedman's Bureau resulted from a complaint initiated by a freedwoman insistent on being treated with respect, as a worker and as a citizen.

We are grateful to Leslie Schwalm for this selection.

> Office of Agent of Bureau of
> Refugees Freed men &c
> Combahee Ferry So. Car.
> October 10th 1865.

To
  Maj Gen'l R. Saxton,
    Asst Commissioner

Sir: I respectfully beg leave to call your attention to the following case which was reported to me; as the alleged offense took place a place several miles beyond my reach,—within 8 miles of Walterboro—, and I think that if the offense can be proven the offender should be punished. The facts as reported are as follows. Hagar Barnwell, living on the plantation of Clark Sanders, Colleton District S.C. states that her former master—for whom she is now at work under a contract—Mr. Clark Sanders ordered her to go into the Kitchen & go to work, which she refused to do, as she had contracted to work in the field, and had a crop which needed her attention, & for other reasons. Upon her refusal he (Sanders) after abusing her, by cursing &c, told her she must either go to cooking or leave the plantation. She Hagar chose the latter alternative, and began to get ready to leave when he (Sanders) called her again, and after threatening her life, holding a "Pestle" over her head, saying that "if it was not for her crop he would kill her before she was many days older," took her to a shed near by & "tied her up" by the thumbs, in such a manner that her feet barely touched the ground, keeping her in that position at least one hour, when he released her telling her to go to work in the field. While "tied up" she was seen by the plantation people (Freedmen) also by two white men viz: Jack Carter & Benny King. Hagar states that she went immediately to Walterboro & reported the case to Capt. Armstrong, who commands the Post, who referred her to a Major Burbridge, who told her to go to the Court House & wait until Court opened when her case would be attended to. She did as directed, and after waiting until Court opened & closed again without being called upon, she came back to the plantation, and afterward came to me to obtain redress. As this is if proven, clearly a case of illegal punishment, coming within the provisions of Gen'l Order No. 1, Hd Qrts Asst. Commr Beaufort S. C. June 20th 1865, should it not be investigated & if the offender is found guilty, should he not be punished as provided? As the locality is some 20 miles distant from this place, I cannot attend to it personally, but think that the matter should be fully investigated by someone in the vicinity who has authority.

I am Sir Very Respectfully
Your Obd't Servt
G. G. Batchelder

A WIFE BEGINS EARNING

The myth of the family wage affected families personally and emotionally, even when it was evidently impossible to achieve. It often made women feel timid and helpless, never more so than on the frontier, far from kinfolk and friends. It made husbands think it improper for women to earn and made women fear their husbands' responses to their own efforts on behalf of their families. Such was the case of Amy Green, wife of a Colorado prospector, in 1871. But it did not take her long to assert herself and to demonstrate considerable adaptiveness in her determination to bring in some income.

. . . About the middle of March, in the same year, my husband, with several other men, engaged in prospecting for coal; the distance being about five miles from Greeley. I was compelled to live alone with my two little children. Oh, what a fearful undertaking it was for me, who had never passed a night without a protector, in the way of father, brother or husband! My husband knew how timid I was, and it caused him great sorrow to absent himself from home, a place more dear than any other on this earth, to a true and loving husband. But what could he do; we had then been living ten months out of pocket, and the prospects for the future were not at all flattering; hence it behooved us to sacrifice the happiness of which he had never before been deprived. . . . It was now dark and I was afraid to so much as look outside of the door. It was then that I realized, for the first time, that I occupied the responsible position of the head of a family. . . . All of a sudden, I was brought to my feet by the sound of approaching footsteps, which halted at the door. . . . For a moment my tongue seemed palsied; but realizing that it would not better the matter to remain silent, I ventured to enquire who the intruder was, and also the nature of his business. Not receiving an immediate answer I repeated my demand. Horror of horrors! he wanted shelter for the night. I told him I was not prepared to entertain strangers, but if he would remain where he was a few moments, I would consult my husband, pretending that he (my husband) had just stepped into a neighbors. This he consented to do. I then took my two little charges and slipped out at my back door, flying in haste to the Greeley Hotel. I acquainted the proprietor of the affair, who soon went and informed the tramp that there was room for him at the hotel. After being assured that my unwelcome visitor was safely lodged, I returned home accompanied by one of the hotel girls, who remained with me through the night, but I did not indulge in sleep. I kept watch until the light of day dawned. . . .

I was then aroused by a rap at my door, which at first startled me, but after reflecting a moment I answered, then proceeded to arrange my toilet in haste and soon ascertained that my visitor was in search of bread. I directed him to the bakery, but he informed me that it was home made bread he was in search of. I told him I would bake bread for sale if I was sure I would have customers enough to make it pay. With this he appeared much delighted and assured me six to begin with. When I showed him one of my loaves he declared it was as large again as the baker's, besides he did not like their bread. After wishing my early visitor good morning, I proceeded to arrange matters as to engage in the capacity of a baker, and 'ere the sun sank behind the western horizon I had ten applicants for bread. When I finished the first sack of flour, I found that my profits amounted to four dollars, besides, I had gained the reputation of giving larger loaves than any other person engaged in the business in town. The only thing which I had to contend with was the anticipated disapproval of my husband in regard to my new enterprise, having heard him express himself in reference to my attempting to take boarders. I much feared the result would be a veto in this case. I therefore resolved to keep the secret from him as long as I could. The week passed by more rapidly than usual; every day brought new customers. I had baked the last of three sacks when Saturday came. This day was to bring my husband home, and O how glad I was yet, how I feared that my secret would be divulged. I did not expect him until Saturday night and I knew he would only remain until Sabbath evening, or Monday morning, so I set myself to work to devise a plan to keep my customers away during his visit. I sent my two children to deliver the bread to each customer, requesting them not to come for more until Monday. . . .

"There comes papa! There comes papa!" cried the two children, "Let us run and meet him." . . . "O papa," said the younger. "Mind what mamma told you Frank," said his little sister endeavoring to put the child on his guard. "No I isn't going to tell papa not at all," said he. "Come children," said I, "you are monopolizing all of the time; mamma wants to talk." My husband, not being of suspicious disposition, took no notice of my embarrassment. Supper now being ready we all gathered around the table. I had not finished my first cup of tea, when a loud rap sounded at my front door. I instantly sprang up and hastened to receive my visitor. After bidding him good evening, I paused to learn his business. "I would like a couple of loaves of bread, ma'am, if you please," said he. "I have only bread enough, sir," said I, "to last me through the Sabbath;" and I turned to leave the stranger but, he was not to be put off in this way. "Madam," said he, "perhaps I am not at the right place. Is this where Mrs. Green lives?" "It is," said I; "but there are more than one family of the Green's." "Is there, indeed, ma'am. Sure then I'm wrong, and I'll be after seeking them." I shut the door and returned to finish my supper. "Who was that and what did he want?" asked my husband. "O, a man hunting bread," said I, carelessly. "What brought him here hunting bread," said he, "does he not know where the bakery is? Strange," he continued, "that he should call at a private house?" I treated the affair with indifference and turned the subject to that of prospecting for coal. Everything went on in my favor until my little folks grew tired and sleepy and wished to go to bed. When the kiss good-night had been repeated, my little boy, wishing to assure me of his faithfulness, whispered in my ear loud enough to be heard across the room: "Mamma, I didn't tell papa, not at all." At this papa laughed heartily, for he well knew that he had a good joke on me. He did not ask the little fellow to divulge, as he feared it might teach him to break his promise, but he said to me: " 'Murder will out,' won't it?" This compelled me to reveal the secret. When I had concluded he sighed, and then said: "Well if you think it best I have nothing to say." My heart sank within me and perhaps a tear glistened in my eye, as I brushed it away, saying: "You believe in 'Woman's Rights,' and I deem that it is my right and also my duty to aid you when I can, without interfering with my household affairs." He let me do the rest of the talking and I flattered myself that I convinced him. . . .

Monday came, and my husband took his leave for the coalshaft. After relieving my lonely heart by indulging in a good cry, I bathed my head and eyes and then repaired to my daily task. While my bread was baking the thought occurred to me that I could use the fire for another purpose, at the same time, and, with coal at twelve dollars per ton, it was necessary to economize, and I determined to apply to the washer woman for ironing. This I did, and was quite successful.

A SALESWOMAN

Among the realities masked by family-wage ideology was that some husbands did not earn anything at all. Such was the case for Mrs. J. W. Likins of San Francisco. In 1871, she plunged into a most untraditional occupation for a woman: she became a traveling saleswoman.

Now begins the one great struggle of my life. I scarcely know where to turn or what to do. . . . Bidding my dear ones keep up courage, I start out. Never before did I know the meaning of the word poverty. Now I felt it in all its keenest pangs—everything looked dark and cloudy. I started for the Post-office. Not being able to pay car hire, I went on foot. On my way I passed the book-store of H. H. Bancroft, then on the corner of Montgomery and Merchant streets. In the window I noticed a card, with the words "Agents Wanted" on it. Stepping into the store a gentleman advanced to meet me. I asked him "Do you employ lady agents?" "Yes," he replied, "allow me to take you to the Subscription Department." There I was shown to the gentleman in charge. I found him to be a frank kind-hearted gentleman.

. . . After talking for a few moments, he showed me an engraving of [President] Grant and his Family, in upright form; told me his terms, what to sell it for, and how much commission I would get. . . . We made a bargain; he giving me a book to take orders in, and two of the pictures, told me to go on Montgomery street. . . .

Taking them on my arm, order-book in my hand, I started up Montgomery street, calling on one and all, up stairs and down, in every room.

Some looked at me curiously, others with pity, and *some few* with contempt, while I endeavored, in my embarrassment, and in an awkward way, to show the picture.

I worked on faithfully until three o'clock in the afternoon, when I returned to my miserable room; but it contained those dear to me, where I found them very anxious about me. They soon cheered up, as I told them the events of the day.

Tuesday morning I again resumed my work; for five days I canvassed steadily, nothing of importance occurring.

In this time I made many dollars, which I put to good use, buying comforts for myself and family, and preparing my little girl for school again.

Eight o'clock every morning would find me in the street-car on my way to the business part of the city. I had one of the pictures mounted on canvass and rollers, that I used as a sample copy, taking orders, to be delivered in two or three weeks, and sometimes as far as two months.

It was now just before Grant's election, and great excitement concerning it prevailed. The Democrats arguing in favor of *their* candidate, and the Republicans in favor of *theirs*.

In almost *every* room, in front of every store or business house, and on every street corner, I would find gentlemen in groups, whispering or conversing in low tones; I suppose plotting and planning for the coming campaign; while others were loud and boisterous in expressing their opinions.

It was a great trial for me to know just how to approach them, for the one almost frightened me, and the others so grave and solemn, still I did not pass any of them; with a heavy heart I would step up, unroll the picture, saying, "Gentlemen, I have a fine engraving of General Grant and his family."

After they had looked at it, which they very seldom failed to do, I would present my order-book, take them in rotation, and insist upon one and all to subscribe, and was generally very successful. They would treat me kindly, and were very polite, with the exception of some few ruffians who seemed to have forgotten "their mother was a woman," would hurt my feelings, in many ways, with regards to Grant's life and character, on this coast, before the war; as though *I* was accountable for the way he had acted. . . .

An old man was standing in the door-way of his shop; I spoke to him, unrolled the picture and asked him to subscribe. He was a strong Democrat and was not long in letting me know it.

"You d—— women think you will rule the country. There is a clique of you who go prowling around, having secret meetings, lecturing all over the country on women's rights; *here you* are roaming around with that d—— picture of that loafer Grant. There was one of your *clique* in here the other day, lecturing on temperance. I told her in plain English to leave my shop; I would have no women's rights around me."

I replied, "Thank you for your hint; I am not in your shop, nor do not intend crossing your door-way, for fear I might become polluted, for you certainly are the most profane ruffian I ever met."

At this he became very angry, and I *think* He would have struck me, *had he* dared. . . .

That evening . . . I went to Mrs. T.'s room. . . . After telling her how well I was succeeding, I tried to persuade her to take Sacramento, and some of the upper counties. . . .

She finally consented to try and canvass Sacramento; for she, like myself, was very tired of the restaurant, and was willing to do anything that was honorable and honest to get away from it.

She went in company with me to the store, where I introduced her to Mr. S.; at first, she was somewhat embarrassed, but his kind and easy manners soon reassured her.

I told him I did not wish the whole Coast. That Mrs. T. could have Sacramento, Marysville and Grass Valley. The bargain was closed.

I now selected out of the remaining territory what I desired, which were San Francisco, Santa Clara and San Joaquin counties. . . . I had made up my mind to go to San José to canvass and take orders, during the Fair in that place, which was to commence in a few days.

. . . I went to the hall where the Fair was to be held, to try and secure some space where I might put a small table and a chair, but there wasn't any vacancy. The agent for the Florence Sewing Machine, who had a large space, kindly offered me room in one corner. Mrs. M—— the landlady, loaned me a table and a chair. After they were conveyed to the hall, I arranged my pictures on the table and took my seat behind them, feeling more like a culprit than anything else.

Although it was a short time since I had commenced to canvass, and knew it was an honorable and legitimate business, still it *seemed* to me very much like begging. As ladies and gentlemen would pass me, I would try in many ways to gain their attention, but I acted so awkward and out of place that I did not succeed very well.

Some would stop for a moment and admire the engraving; few ladies would insist upon their husbands buying, but I scarcely took any orders.

I soon found it was not the place for me; if I wish to sell anything I must get out among the crowd.

Standing close to the entrance, I tackled every one I would see, something after the fashion of a little news-boy.

"Ladies and gentlemen, here's a fine engraving of General Grant and family," insisting upon one and all, who stopped to look at it for a moment, to subscribe. In the afternoon as I was going around among the machinery, I overheard an old man, who had a patent wash-boiler, and I suppose feeling very important, say to one of the superintendents of the Fair, as he passed by him, "Why do you allow that woman around here with that picture, trying to get everyone's attention; why, a minute ago, while a gentleman was look-ing at the boiler; she had the impudence to ask him to patronize her."

He answered, "This is a free country, and as she don't seem to be doing any harm, she has as much right in here as any one else." . . .

PROSTITUTION

*One of the worst jobs for women in the nineteenth century was being a prosti-
tute. Patronized by men of all classes, prostitution was stratified, and while
the working conditions were far worse in poor neighborhoods, all prostitutes
risked disease, assault, robbery, and death.*

*Sexual conservatives tended to view prostitution as a necessary social evil,
a "sewer" that could drain the poison from the rest of society and preserve the
appearance of monogamous marriage. This ideology sentenced thousands of
poor women to be sacrificed to men's presumably irrepressible sexual lust in
order to maintain the "purity" of privileged women. The extensiveness of prostitution showed the seamy side of Victorian sexual ideology, which held that
respectable women had little if any sex drive, submitting to their husbands'
desires only out of obedience and the desire to reproduce, while the male sex
drive was strong and uncontrollable.*

*Liberal reformers, such as William Sanger, challenged that Victorian mor-
alism to some degree. He insisted on presenting prostitution as a job, not a
sin. Sanger was resident physician at the Blackwell's Island Women's Prison
in New York City, where he interviewed a sample of two thousand prostitute
inmates. In his presentation of data in this 1858 report, he showed that prostitution's chief recruiting agent was poverty.*

New York	1	prostitute	to	every	57	men.
Buffalo	1	"	"	"	57	"
Louisville	1	"	"	"	56	"
New Haven	1	"	"	"	76	"
Norfolk	1	"	"	"	26	"
Savannah	1	"	"	"	39	"
and the mean of the whole is	1	"	"	"	52	"

This mean may be fairly assumed as the proportion existing in all the
large cities of the Union, and the farther assumption that the men who visit
houses of prostitution form one fourth of the total population will give a basis
upon which the total number of the Prostitutes in the United States may be
estimated with some accuracy. The calculation can not, of course, be
claimed as absolutely correct, as that would be an impossibility, but is submitted as a probability on which the reader can form his own conclusion. . . .

QUESTION. What was the cause of your becoming a prostitute? . . .

First in order stands the reply "Inclination," which can only be understood
as meaning a voluntary resort to prostitution in order to gratify the sexual
passions. Five hundred and thirteen women, more than one fourth of the

gross number, give this as their reason. If their representations were borne out by facts, it would make the task of grappling with the vice a most arduous one, and afford very slight grounds to hope for any amelioration; but it is imagined that the circumstances which induced the ruin of most of those who gave the answer will prove that, if a positive inclination to vice was the proximate cause of the fall, it was but the result of other and controlling influences. . . .

But it must be repeated, and most decidedly, that without these or some other equally stimulating cause, the full force of sexual desire is seldom known to a virtuous woman. . . .

Destitution is assigned as a reason in five hundred and twenty-five cases. In many of these it is unquestionably true that positive, actual want, the apparent and dreaded approach of starvation, was the real cause of degradation. The following instances of this imperative necessity will appeal to the understanding and the heart more forcibly than any arguments that could be used. As in all the selections already made, or that may be made hereafter, these cases are taken indiscriminately from the replies received, and might be indefinitely extended. . . .

M. M., a widow with one child, earned $1.50 per week as a tailoress. J. Y., a servant, was taken sick while in a situation, spent all her money, and could get no employment when she recovered." . . .

M. S., also a servant, received *one dollar a month wages*. A. B. landed in Baltimore from Germany, and was robbed of all her money the very day she reached the shore. M. F., a shirt-maker, earned one dollar a week. E. M. G.: the captain of police in the district where this woman resides says, "This girl struggled hard with the world before she became a prostitute, sleeping in station-houses at night, and living on bread and water during the day." He adds: "In my experience of three years, I have known *over fifty cases* whose history would be similar to hers, and who are now prostitutes." . . .

"Seduced and abandoned." Two hundred and fifty-eight women make this reply. These numbers give but a faint idea of the actual total that should be recorded under the designation, as many who are included in other classes should doubtless have been returned in this. It has already been shown that under the answer "Inclination" are comprised the responses of many who were the victims of seduction before such inclination existed, and there can be no question that among those who assign "Drink, and the desire to drink" as the cause of their becoming prostitutes, may be found many whose first departure from the rules of sobriety was actuated by a desire to drive from their memories all recollections of their seducers' falsehoods. . . .

The probabilities of a decrease in the crime of seduction are very slight, so long as the present public sentiment prevails; while the seducer is allowed to go unpunished, and the full measure of retribution is directed against his victim; while the offender escapes, but the offended is condemned. Unprincipled men, ready to take advantage of woman's trustful nature, abound, and they pursue their diabolical course unmolested. Legal enactments can scarcely ever reach them, although sometimes a poor man without friends or money is indicated and convicted. The remedy must be left to the world at large. When our domestic relations are such that a man known to be guilty of this crime can obtain no admission into the family circle; when the virtuous and respectable members of the community agree that no such man shall be welcomed to their society; when worth and honor assert their supremacy over wealth and boldness, there may be hopes of a reformation, but not till then. . . .

. . . the man whose conduct to his wife is such as to lead her to vicious practices. . . .

C.C. "My husband deserted me and four children. I had no means to live." . . .

J.S. "My husband committed adultery. I caught him with another woman, and then he left me." . . .

A.G. "My husband eloped with another woman. I support the child." . . .

A.B. "My husband accused me of infidelity, which was not true. I only lived with him five months. I was pregnant by him, and after my child was born I went on the town to support it." . . .

C.H. "My husband was a drunkard, and beat me." . . .

P.T. "My husband was intemperate, and turned out to be a thief. He was sent to prison."

QUESTION. What trade or calling did you follow before you became a prostitute?

Occupations	Numbers	Occupations	Numbers
Artist	1	Shoe-binders	16
Nurse in Bellevue Hospital, N.Y.	1	Vest-makers	21
School-teachers	3	Cap-makers	24
Fruit-hawkers	4	Book-folders	27
Paper-box-makers	5	Factory girls	37
Tobacco-packers	7	Housekeepers	39
Attended stores or bars	8	Milliners	41
Attended school	8	Seamstresses	59
Embroiderers	8	Tailoresses	105
Fur-sewers	8	Dress-makers	121
Hat-trimmers	8	Servants	933
Umbrella-makers	8	Lived with parents or friends	499
Flower-makers	9	Total	2000

Before leaving the question of employment, the effects of different branches of female occupation, as inducing or favoring immorality, must be noticed. Apart from the low rate of wages paid to women, thus causing destitution which forces them to vice, the associations of most of the few trades they are in the habit of pursuing are prejudicial to virtue. The trade of tailoress or seamstress may be cited as a case in point. One mode in which this business is conducted between employer and employed is as follows: The woman leaves either a cash deposit or the guarantee of some responsible person at the store, and receives a certain amount of materials to be made up by a specified time: when she returns the manufactured goods she is paid, and has more work given her to make up. This may seem a very simple course, and so it is, but one feature in it gives rather a sinister aspect. The person who delivers the materials, receives the work, and pronounces on its execution, is almost invariably a man, and upon his decision rests the question whether the operative shall be paid her full wages, or whether any portion of her miserable earnings shall be deducted because the work is not done to his satisfaction. In many cases he wields a power the determinations of which amount to this: "Shall I have any food to-day, or shall I starve?" . . .

"WHITE SLAVERY"

In the late nineteenth century, the possibilities of profiteering from prostitution outstripped the supply of "willing" women. Pimps and organized criminals responded by developing coercive recruitment techniques, using force or deception to entrap women into prostitution. This brutal "white slave trade" spurred reformers into action; their pressure intensified police repression of pimps and madams and eventually helped pass the federal Mann Act in 1910 in an effort to control interstate vice commerce.

The outcry about this "white slave trade" was somewhat exaggerated, in part because most reformers, especially feminists, found it uncomfortable to admit that many women found prostitution a rational choice given the wretched alternative jobs available to poor women. Moreover, the alarm about the "white slave trade" captured anxieties about young women entering large cities in search of work and the possibilities of a sex life unsupervised by family and community. But some women did become prostitutes as a result of rape, violence, and threats. Once thus "recruited," many women feared to flee because they believed that losing their virginity ruined them forever, that even their own families might reject them.

"White slave trade" was an apt phrase because it revealed the racial as well as sexual fears involved. That is, coercive prostitution became objectionable mainly when it began to take in European Americans. When it victimized black or immigrant women, it was usually noticed by government and white

reformers only as part of a condemnation of whole racial groups. In San Francisco, for example, because Chinese women were not allowed entry into the United States, many thousands of Chinese women were smuggled in and forced into prostitution and a slavery far more literal than "white slavery." But when this was discovered, it led to a campaign to end Chinese immigration, not to protect Chinese women. The following is an excerpt from testimony on this matter before a California state senate committee investigating Chinese immigration in 1876.

San Francisco, April 12, 1876. Rev. Otis Gibson sworn.

Q. What is your profession?

A. A clergyman. . . I was a missionary to the Chinese of the Methodist Episcopal Church. . . .

Q. Do you know upon what terms the Chinese are imported into this country?

A. They come free. I think all Chinamen come free, except the women. . . .

Q. Is it not a well-settled matter that a great many people are held in slavery here—bought and sold?

A. Only the women. I don't think there is a man so held. The women as a general thing are held as slaves. They are bought or stolen in China and brought here. They have a sort of agreement, to cover up the slavery business, but it is all a sham. That paper makes the girl say that she owes you four hundred dollars or so, passage money and outfit from China, and has nothing to pay. I being the girl, this man comes up and offers to lend me the money to pay you if I will agree to serve him, to prostitute my body at his pleasure, wherever he shall put me, for four, five, or six years. For that promise of mine, made on the paper, he hands him the four hundred dollars, and I pay the debt I owe you according to contract. It is also put in the contract that if I am sick fifteen days no account shall be taken of that, but if I am sick more than that I shall make up double. If I am found to be pregnant within a month, you shall return the money and take me again.

Q. Then, so far as the women are concerned, they are in slavery? . . .

A. Yes, sir. And even after the term of prostitution service is up, the owners so manage as to have the women in debt more than ever, so that their slavery becomes life-long. There is no release from it.

Q. When these people become sick and helpless, what becomes of them?

A. They are left to die.

Q. No care taken of them?

A. Sometimes, where the women have friends.

Q. Don't the companies take care of them?

A. Not frequently.

Q. Is it not a frequent thing that they are put out on the sidewalk to die, or in some room without water or food?

A. I have heard of such things; I don't know. . . . Sometimes the women take opium to kill themselves. They do not know they have any rights, but think they must keep their contracts, and believe themselves under obligations to serve in prostitution.

Q. What is their treatment? Is it harsh?

A. They have come to the asylum all bruises. They are beaten and punished cruelly if they fail to make money. When they become worn out and unable to make any more money, they are turned out to die.

The Rev. A. W. Loomis, a Presbyterian clergyman, at the head of the Chinese Mission established by his church in San Francisco, says,

These Chinawomen that you see on the streets here were brought for the accommodation of white people, not for the accommodation of Chinese; and if you pass along the streets where they are to be found, you will see that they are visited not so much by Chinese as by others—sailors and low people. The women are in a condition of servitude. Some of them are inveigled away from home under promise of marriage to men here, and some to be secondary wives, while some are stolen. They are sold here. Many women are taken from the Chinese owners, and are living as wives and as secondary wives. Some have children, and these children are legitimate.

Q. These women engaged in prostitution are nothing more than slaves to them?

A. Yes, sir; and every one would go home to-day if she were free and had her passage paid.

Q. They are not allowed to release themselves from that situation, are they?

A. I think they are under the surveillance of men and women, so that they cannot get away. They would fear being caught and sold again, and carried off to a condition even worse than now.

Q. Are not the laws here used to restrain them from getting away—are they not arrested for crime?

A. Oh, yes. They will trump up a case, have the woman arrested and bring people to swear what they want. In this way they manage to get possession of her again. . . .

Mr. Alfred Clark, for nineteen years past connected with the police force of San Francisco, and for the last eight years Clerk of the Chief of Police, testifies as follows, "In regard to the vice of prostitution, I have here a bill of sale of a Chinawoman, and a translation of the same." Witness submits a paper written in Chinese characters, and reads the translation, as follows:

An agreement to assist the woman Ah Ho, because coming from China to San Francisco she became indebted to her mistress for passage. Ah Ho herself asks Mr. Yee Kwan to advance her six hundred and thirty dollars, for which Ah Ho distinctly agrees to give her body to Mr. Yee for service of prostitution for a term of four years. There shall be no interest on the money. Ah Ho shall receive no wages. At the expiration of four years Ah Ho shall be her own master. Mr. Yee Kwan shall not hinder or trouble her. If Ah Ho runs away before her time is out, her mistress shall find her and return her, and whatever expense is incurred in finding and returning her Ah Ho shall pay. On this day of agreement Ah Ho, with her own hands, has received from Mr. Yee Kwan six hundred and thirty dollars. If Ah Ho shall be sick at any time for more than ten days, she shall make up by an extra month of service for every ten days sickness. Now, this agreement has proof—this paper received by Ah Ho is witness.

Tung Chee

Twelfth year, ninth month, and fourteenth day (about middle of October, eighteen hundred and seventy-three).

An Agreement to Assist A Young Girl Named Loi Yau.

Because she became indebted to her mistress for passage, food, etc., and has nothing to pay, she makes her body over to the woman, Sep Sam, to serve as a prostitute to make out the sum of five hundred and three dollars. The money shall draw no interest, and Loi Yau shall serve four and one-half years. On this day of agreement, Loi Yau receives the sum of five hundred and three dollars in her own hands. When the time is out, Loi Yau may be her own master, and no man shall trouble her. If she runs away before the time is out, and any expense is incurred in catching her, then Loi Yau must pay the expense. If she is sick fifteen days or more, she shall make up one month for every fifteen days. If Sep Sam shall go back to China, then Loi Yau shall serve another party till her time is out; if, in such service, she should be sick one hundred days or more, and cannot be cured, she may return to Sep Sam's place. For a proof of this agreement, this paper.

Dated second, sixth month of the present year.

Loi Yau.

SELF-HELP OR PROTEST? ————————————————————

Despite the controversies about married women's employment, the majority of working women remained single and young, often having come alone to large cities in search of jobs, leaving their families in small towns or abroad. Though they received low pay, which continued to be justified by the myth that women had men to support them and did not need a living wage, they were divided about how to improve their lot. Some insisted on forbearance and self-help, convinced that a woman who worked hard and did not complain would make it. Others believed such an approach constituted blaming the victim and considered it more effective to organize and protest collectively, as the following 1873 letters from working women to a Chicago newspaper illustrate.

We are grateful to Joanne Meyerowitz for this selection.

SEPTEMBER 4, 1873

The good people in their bright and happy homes know not what a rough and flowerless path the feet of the homeless girls tread, even in the brightest season of their experience; worried by long hours of toil; worried in mind by the thought that our earnings are not enough to pay daily expenses, and provide for a few days of lost time through sickness or lack of work, the former often borne while the eyes watch the movement of the fingers plying the needle, and longing—God only knows how longing—for the simple boon to close the weary lids, and forget in sleep's life troubles, at least while pain lasts, if not forever. . . . There are many homeless sewing girls in Chicago, poor like myself, who were born in happy homes, but now alone are struggling for an existence. . . . Providing cheerful homes for us at prices we could afford to pay, [would] thus relieve our minds of the ever worrying thought: How are we to live on our earnings?

Josephine

OCTOBER 26, 1873

I have found the world generous as well as just. Six years ago I came to Chicago on borrowed money, and I have fought my way from the bottom to the top. I could tell as sad a story as any one, if I chose, of toil and hardship. Onward and upward was my motto. I *would not* fail, and did not. To-day my debts are all paid; I have a handsome wardrobe, all the comforts and many of the luxuries of life, a neat bank-account of $2000; and live easily and happily. All the result of my own labor. What one has done, any girl with good health and ordinary abilities can do. There is no pity in my heart for the thousand weeping sisters. Oh, shame on their stupidity! When they glory in being half-clothed and half-fed, they glory in their own degradation. The world is wide, and any girl with health, who can't support herself, deserves sound scolding instead of pages of pity. Stop fuming, and simply *act*. If you want help, first help yourselves. If you work for $5 or $6 a week, and never advance you may be sure the fault is nearer home than you seem to think.

Experience

NOVEMBER 2, 1873

I am nearly boiling with indignation when I read a letter of opposition. It is my private opinion that the lady who signed herself "Experience" in last Sunday's Tribune, was a gentleman. . . . I'm an orphan, but have been brought up by relatives as respectable as anyone, or, in other words, am a lady. I have cared for myself for three years, and can tell of many hardships. I move we have a meeting. Let all the working-girls come, and leading men of the city, and everybody else if they can. Let me hear from someone else. Never mind if it is hard to do and makes you nervous. Take courage as I did.

American Girl

NOVEMBER 9, 1873

What women want is not charity, but justice. Let them be thoroughly educated and follow any vocation they please, without being thought masculine for it, or out of their appropriate sphere. Almost all working-women have to support one or more persons. . . . How many centuries will it take to raise woman to her proper place? Let us go on. How we do advance! She may yet be thought equal to her Lord and Master that now is.

Working-Girl

PETITION FOR A WORKING WOMEN'S HOME ———

Another result of the family-wage myth—the idea that women could rely on men to support them—was inadequate housing for working women, the majority of whom were single. Few earned wages high enough to pay for decent apartments. And they had no wives to help them make a dark, damp basement flat into a home. Yet their dreams of domestic comfort were no less vivid than those of married women. The desire for a home was notable in the grievances of women workers, who sometimes came up with imaginative, radical, and strikingly modern proposals to address the issue. In this case, a group petitioned the Massachusetts legislature for state aid for housing. Their demands are being discussed at a joint meeting of working women and some middle-class women allies in Boston in 1869. This report is from the Working-man's Advocate, *one of the most influential labor papers of the period.*

A convention of Boston work women was held in that city on the 21st ult. at which some extraordinary developments were made. We append some of the discussions:

Miss Phelps said: . . . We do not think the men of Massachusetts know how the women live. We do not think if they did they would allow such a state of things to exist. Some of us who signed the petition have had to work for less than twenty-five cents a day, and we know that many others have had to do the same. True, many get good wages comparatively for women. There are girls that get from $1 to $1.50 per day, either because they are superior laborers or have had unusual opportunities. . . . [But] there are before me now women who I know to be working at the present time for less than twenty-five cents a day. Some of the work they do at these rates from the charitable institutions of the city. These institutions give out work to the women with the professed object of helping them, at which they can scarcely earn enough to keep them from starving; work at which two persons, with their utmost exertions cannot earn more than forty-five cents a day. These things, I repeat, should be known to the public. They do not know how the daughters of their soldiers fare. I do. They have a little aid, to be sure, from the State, but it is only a little and they have to-day to live in miserable garrets without fire, and during the cold winters, with scanty food and insufficient clothing, they go out daily to labor-along these beautiful streets. Do not you think that they feel the difference between their condition and that of rich, well-dressed ladies who pass them? If they did not they would be less than human. But they work on bravely and uncomplainingly, venturing all things for the hope of the life that is to come. We know that there is wealth enough in this state and in this city to remedy this state of things, and that it only needs to be brought before the people to be done.

. . . There are lands close to the city of Boston, which can be bought at prices ranging from 50 to 75 an acre, near enough to the city for working women to come to their work there or take it home. And these homes can be made cheaply. It can be done at a less cost than these poor women now occasion in the shape of public charities. . . . How much better to have these girls independent, earning their own living, enjoying their own homes than, that they should be compelled to go to station-houses for soup.

The people have wondered how these girls live. Can you imagine how you should live upon 20 cents a day. Rent is one or two dollars at the lowest and there is your clothes and your food. Count it up. Where does it come from? There is often no resource in health but the charities, or in sickness but the hospital. As for the hospitals, the poor girls that have been there have told me that they would almost sooner lie down and die than go again. But we think the women could sustain themselves under the plan we propose, even at the small wages they get. It seems like a good deal to do, but day by day the pennies will count up, and after a time the homes be secured.

And then, again, these girls working and living in these garrets and cellars, damp, unwholesome places, are not well. They cannot go into kitchens and do housework as their mothers did. Men often ask me why these working women do not go into housework. One sufficient reason is that there are not houses enough for them all nor any large proportion of them. But if there were they are not skilled in housework, and mistresses would not have them. Another reason is that their strength is not sufficient. They have not been so brought up and thus . . . labor they have been employed at has so weakened their whole system, bodily and mental, that they cannot do the work.

They are said to be improvident and shiftless. I grant it. Who would not be in their condition? Make their condition better and they will not resort to the streets after dark. Make their condition better and you will see them educate themselves for skilled labor and become what our grandmothers were, good wives and good mothers. . . . Give these women little homes and they will not be obliged to take work at such rates.

Many of these women sent their husbands, their brothers, their sons to the battlefield. They were alone, listening to every echo, and expecting by every mail news of loved ones' deaths. And the torture of that suspense who can tell? It is far, far worse than the strife of the war itself. And then when the little homes we ask for them will save them from starvation, I ask, have not soldiers widowes, have not soldiers daughters, a right to have them. Have they not earned it? I know the State will help them. I know it. We do not want to blame any one. We do not feel that individuals were to blame. It is the fault of the system which makes women homeless. . . .

Only help us to earn a home that we can attach ourselves to, that will make us feel that we have a country. It has been said that we can go anywhere and be at home. Women cannot. It is because they have no homes. They have a husband's or a father's home, none of their own. And to those poor working women they have no husband or Brother, only think what a boon a home of their own would be. . . . We ask in this petition that these homes should pass to our female heirs, if we should have any; that then should be kept in the hands of women. We do not want that by trick and chicanery they should pass into the hands of speculators. . . .

I am met often with the objection that these women can go to California or Nevada. But our mothers live here. We know not these distant places. We cannot get work where we are acquainted; how can we be certain to get it where we are not acquainted? This is the invariable feeling of these girls. Why do they not go into the country and work in a farmhouse? Girls love independence, girls love society, just as much as men do. A woman must have some intellectual society or she goes down. I am no speechmaker— only a worker. . . .

Mrs. Warner said she had learned that the pay of the paper-box makers and tailoresses had been raised that day for fear they would attend this meeting. These paper-box makers get from $2.50 to $3 per week. How can they live on that? Where do they get their dresses? I say to you ladies that every costly dress you wear makes three prostitutes. Some girls in the city of Boston got out of employment last winter. They went to a firm on Winter street, and asked for employment. They were told that they could not be given enough to support them, but if they had gentlemen friends to dress them, they would be hired.

1890–1920

1890–1920: INTRODUCTION

Between 1890 and 1920, the United States became the most powerful nation in the world. The engine for this power was unprecedented industrial development, which drew an increasing proportion of the population into wage labor. While women remained a small proportion of this new working class—20 percent in 1920—their rate of entry into wage labor was escalating dramatically.

Large corporations exercised great influence over almost all aspects of government and society. For example, U.S. Steel and Standard Oil had assets and employees greater than those of large state governments. Corporate expansion abroad was supported by U.S. military and diplomatic interventions into the Philippines, Central America, the Caribbean, and China. The United States became an imperial power. "Dollar diplomacy," dedicated to protecting U.S. investments abroad, further stimulated industrial growth in the United States.

Meeting the new demand for labor, massive immigration in this period transformed the working class. The immigrants were no longer mainly from western and northern Europe, but from Russia and eastern and southern Europe. Their appearance, language, and religion often distinguished them sharply from many earlier Americans. The migration of blacks to the northern and midwestern cities also increased. Unfamiliar urban environments combined with low wages, poor housing, and substandard working conditions created ghetto slums. Employers exploited ethnic differences, placing workers from diverse groups side by side to make communication more difficult in an attempt to prevent workers' solidarity.

The poverty of many new immigrants combined with the rapidly increasing demand for labor drew more women into the wage labor force. As the United States became more ethnically and racially diverse, women's jobs became more ethnically and racially segregated. Although white collar jobs for women grew, they went almost exclusively to white, English-speaking high school graduates. Immigrant women, by contrast, were likely to work in factories. Although the great majority of women remained rural and worked not for wages but on farms or in households, it was in the cities that population was growing quickest and poverty was most visible and it was the new urban working-class women who attracted the attention of a growing reform movement.

Indeed, this period was richer in radical and reform movements than any in U.S. history. Many of these movements included struggles to improve the lives of working women. Women were active, for example, in populism, a mass political and economic movement of farmers that emerged in the 1880s and 1890s, strongest in the South and Midwest. Populist women also often considered themselves suffragists, socialists, and temperance advocates; and in some sections of the country, there were black populist women who sought racial advancement and equality.

In the cities, middle-class and elite activists, also including many women, mobilized against corruption and attempted to prevent social disorder through political and economic reforms. Their movement was so effective that this entire period has become known as the Progressive Era, a label taken from the third party on whose ticket ex-president Theodore Roosevelt ran for the presidency in 1912. Progressive women revitalized not only the woman suffrage movement, finally victorious in 1919, but also a variety of other reform causes aimed particularly at helping the poor. They pushed through laws regulating the safety of food, drugs, and housing; struggled unsuccessfully to ban child labor; and won the first public welfare program in the United States, a system of state aid to single mothers. While the Progressives were in some ways democratic, campaigning for civil service and honesty in government and against the political machines, in other ways they were elitist, working toward the consolidation of local political control in the hands of the educated business and professional classes—even disenfranchising many poor and working-class voters.

In the South, most Progressives supported the imposition of Jim Crow, i.e., segregation, laws. Racial segregation in the South spread and intensified in the late nineteenth century, serving to maintain the power of southern planters and industrialists who relied on a racially divided, low-wage labor force. While Progressives preferred to enforce this system legally, they rarely spoke out against the use of terror against blacks, such as lynchings and organized threats from groups like the Ku Klux Klan.

Responding both to these southern conditions and to discrimination in the North, African Americans organized the first modern civil rights movement in this period. Women played a prominent role in this movement, active in anti-lynching, uplift, and anti-discrimination causes; in the 1890s they organized the National Association of Colored Women, the first national black organization in the United States, and in many locations women were the backbone of the National Association for the Advancement of Colored People, established in 1909.

The labor movement, like Progressivism, had both progressive and conservative aspects. The most important trade union organization at this time was the American Federation of Labor (AFL), which was devoted to protecting the interests of skilled workers while neglecting and even deliberately excluding the largest parts of the working class: immigrant, minority male, and virtually all female workers. The AFL was a craft union, organizing workers in specific occupations. The increasing numbers of unskilled workers needed industry-wide organizations in order to defend their interests. One such was the Industrial Workers of the World (IWW). Because of its concern for unskilled, mass-production workers, and because of its inclusiveness in organizing—taking in blacks, Chinese, the unemployed, agricultural workers, even hobos—the IWW supplied important leadership in several great strikes, in which women were sometimes the majority.

Working-class militancy contributed to a powerful socialist movement that peaked in this period. The U.S. native socialist tradition combined with European Marxism to build a Socialist Party, which brought together radical intellectuals, big-city immigrant workers, western miners and farmers, migrant workers, and many other socialists. The Socialist Party attracted not only many working women but also many Progressive social feminist reformers.

After 1917 the United States experienced a rapid shift to the right. This shift was a reaction to the strength of these various progressive movements, intersected by the patriotic and xenophobic response that World War I—like all wars—engendered. The Bolshevik Revolution in Russia in 1917 inspired some Americans but also frightened many others, including those in power, who fought back with repressive measures directed at a wide variety of progressive movements. As a result, many were hounded, arrested, jailed, and deported.

The progressive political alliances of this period hinted at a potential for a mass women's movement greater than in any previous period. But a mass women's movement was not born, largely because women still lacked some of the conditions necessary for autonomous political activism—such as economic independence, education, and access to birth control.

Migrants and Immigrants

BLACK MIGRANTS ─────────────────────

From 1916 to 1919, more than half a million African Americans left the South for the industrial cities of the North and Midwest, and nearly one million more were to follow in the 1920s. In the South, floods and the recurrence of the boll weevil had devastated cotton crops. The passage of "Jim Crow" segregation laws in the '90s and the increase in lynchings and violence were making life in the South increasingly miserable and dangerous for blacks. In addition, a rising level of black education created expectations which the Southern economy and conditions could not meet.

In the North, World War I had cut off European migration and taken many thousands out of the labor force. Northern factories sent labor agents to the South to encourage the migration of black workers, offering to pay rail fares to the cities. Black newspapers like the Chicago Defender *also encouraged the migration by painting rosy pictures of working and living conditions in the cities. Southern blacks also learned about life up north from personal letters, just as foreign immigrants had.*

The result was overwhelming: between 1910 and 1920 the black population of Chicago increased by 65,000 people, or 148.2 percent; in Detroit, by 611.3 percent. Many whole families migrated together; others sent one member to earn enough to bring up the rest of the family, often a woman. The pattern was not unlike that of many other immigrant people who came to the cities hoping to better their way of life.

This selection is from letters sent to the Chicago Defender *by black people in the South inquiring about jobs in Chicago.*

Jacksonville, Fla., May 22, 1917.

Chicago Defender:

I wish to go North haven got money enuff to come I can do any kind of housework laundress nurse good cook has cook for northern people I am 27 years of age just my self would you kindly inderseed for me a job with some rich white people who would send me a ticket and I pay them back please help me. I am brown skin just meaden size.

Biloxi, Miss., April 27, 1917.

Dear Sir:

I would like to get in touch with you a pece of advise I am unable to under go hard work as I have a fracture ancle but in the mene time I am able to help my selft a great dele. I am a good cook and can give good recmendation can serve in small famly that has light work, if I could get something in that line I could work my daughters a long with me. She is 21 years and I have a husban all so and he is a fireman and want a positions and too small boy need to be in school now if you all see where there is some open for me that I may be able too better my condission anser at once and we will com as we are in a land of starvaten.

From a willen workin woman. I hope that you will healp ne as I want to get out of this land of sufring I no there is som thing that I can do here there is nothing for me to do I may be able to get in some furm where I dont have to stand on my feet all day I dont no just whah but I hope the Lord will find a place now let me here from you all at once.

Jacksonville, Fla., April 29, 1917.

My dear Sir:

I take grate pleazer in writing you. as I found in your Chicago Defender this morning where you are secure job for men as I realey diden no if you can get a good job for me as am a woman and a widowe with two girls and would like to no if you can get one for me and the girls. We will do any kind of work and I would like to hear from you at once not any of us has any husbands.

ADJUSTING TO THE CITY

Between 1890 and 1920, approximately 12 million people immigrated perma-nently to the United States, many from southern and eastern Europe. (About 18 million immigrated, but about one-third of them returned to their native lands.) They differed sharply from earlier European migrants: they were pri-marily Catholic, Orthodox, and Jewish; they were not English-speaking; they were sometimes darker in complexion and seemed more alien to the northern Europeans who dominated the United States. They entered a rapidly urbanizing society now deeply divided by class. The white Protestant elite, accustomed to controlling the country, felt its political and economic domi-nance threatened by these new immigrants. While some elite groups responded by trying to put into place discriminatory quotas and restrictive legislation, other groups, associated with charity and social work, devised programs to assimilate and "Americanize" these newcomers. They lobbied for compulsory education. They set up institutions, such as settlement houses, in immigrant neighborhoods. Their efforts included progressive reforms, such as public health measures, tenement regulation, water and sewage disposal systems, regulation of food and drug purity, and the beginnings of state and local welfare provision. However, their reform agenda also reflected ignorance and disregard for the cultures of the immigrants and an assumption that their Anglo-American middle-class culture was superior in every way.

Some Progressive reformers were more reflective, open to respecting and even learning from immigrants and their culture. Sophonisba Breckinridge (1866–1948) was one of the greatest and most democratic of these reformers, unusually thoughtful and responsive to the needs of others. A national social work leader, she pioneered the use of social research in support of child labor laws, factory health and safety regulation, wages and hours laws, civil rights and women's rights. In this selection from a 1921 publication, Breckinridge shows us, in a typically sensitive yet tough analysis, that methods of housework that were efficient in the old country were not necessarily beneficial in the new urban industrial environment.

The work that the housewife must do in the care of the house is the maintenance of such standards of cleanliness and order as are to prevail. It includes the daily routine tasks of bedmaking, cooking, sweeping, dusting, dishwashing, disposing of waste, and the heavier work of washing, ironing, and periodic cleanings.

The foreign-born housewife finds this work particularly difficult for many reasons. In the first place, housekeeping in the country from which she came was done under such different conditions that it here becomes almost a new problem in which her experience in the old country may prove of little use. . . .

Mrs. P., a Polish woman from Posen, for example, said that:

Houses in the village in which she lived were made of clay, with thatched roofs, clay floors, and about ten feet high. They were made in rows, for four families or two families, with one outer door opening from a hall into which the doors from all the dwellings opened. Each dwelling had one small window, and a fireplace. Water was out of doors. In the four-family house there were two chimneys. The outside door did not open into the road.

The floors were covered with sand, and new sand was put on when the room was cleaned. The fireplace had a hook from which hung the kettle, and in one corner was the oven, a little place set off by a board covered with clay. Walls were whitewashed. Mrs. P. said that the housework is much more difficult in this country, with the cleaning of woodwork, washing windows, care of curtains, carpets, and dishes, and more elaborate cooking. In the old country the family washing was done only once a month, except in cases where there were small children. Then it was done weekly; and if the family lacked sufficient clothing, the washing had to be done oftener. There the meal was one dish, from which the entire family ate; here there is a variety of food and each person has his own plate and eating utensils, so that even the dishwashing is a greater task. In coming to this country many women do not see that the windows need washing or that the woodwork should be cleaned, etc.

The beds were made of boards covered with straw, not as a straw mattress. Sheets were laid over the straw to make it softer. Each person had two pillows, very large and full, so that they sleep in a "half sitting" position. Feather beds are used for warmth, and no quilts or blankets were known in the old country.

Lithuanian women, likewise, have pointed out that at home most of the women worked in the fields, and that what housekeeping was done was of the simplest kind. The peasant house consisted of two rooms, one of which was used only on state occasions, a visit from the priest, a wedding, christening, or a funeral. In summer no one sleeps in the house, but all sleep out of doors in the hay; in winter, women with small children sleep inside, but the others sleep in the granary. Feather beds are, in these circumstances, a real necessity. Thus the bed that is found in this country is unknown in Lithuania, and the women naturally do not know how to care for one. They not only do not realize the need of airing it, turning the mattress, and changing the bedding, but do not even know how to make it up properly.

Other processes of housekeeping—dishwashing, scrubbing, and washing—prove equally difficult, and it is said that most of the women do things in the hardest possible way, chiefly because the processes are different here and they lack the technique to do their work in the easier way. Naturally, too, when work in the fields has occupied most of their time, they lack also habits of order and routine in their household tasks. . . .

The experience in doing the family washing is said to typify the change. In Italy washing is done once a month, or at most, once a fortnight, in the poorer families. Clothes are placed in a great vat or tub of cold water, covered with a cloth on which is sprinkled wood ashes, and allowed to stand overnight. In the morning they are taken to a stream or fountain, and washed in running water. They are dried on trees and bushes in the bright, Italian sunlight. Such methods of laundry work do not teach the women anything about washing in this country, and they are said to make difficult work of it in many cases. They learn that clothes are boiled here, but they do not know which clothes to boil and which to wash without boiling; and as a result they often boil all sorts of clothing, colored and white, together. In Italy washing is a social function; here it is a task for each individual woman.

Cooking in this country varies in difficulty in the different national groups. In the case of the Lithuanians and Poles, for example, the old-country cooking is simple and easily done. Among others it is a fine art, requiring much time and skill. The Italian cooking, of course, is well known, as is also the Hungarian. Among the Bohemians and Croatians, too, the housewives are proverbially good cooks and spend long hours over the preparation of food. Croatian women in this country are said to regard American cookery with scorn. They say that Croatian women do not expect to get a meal in less than two or three hours, while here all the emphasis is on foods that can be prepared in twenty or thirty minutes.

It is not always easy to transplant this art of cookery, even if the women had time to practice it here as they did at home. The materials can usually be obtained, although often at a considerable expense, but the equipment with which they cook and the stoves on which they cook are entirely different. The Italian women, for example, cannot bake their bread in the ovens of the stoves that they use here. Tomato paste, for example, is used in great quantities by Italian families, and is made at home by drying the tomatoes in the open air. When an attempt is made to do this in almost any large city the tomatoes get not only the sunshine, but the soot and dirt of the city. The more particular Italians here will not make tomato paste outdoors, but large numbers of Italian families continue to make it, as can be seen by a walk through any Italian district in late August or early September.

. . . If the housewife wishes to reduce her work in this country, she finds that some of the ingredients which make our cooking simpler are unknown to her. The Bohemians, for example, do not know how to use baking powder, and the same is true of the women in Lithuanian, Polish, and Russian groups, where the art of cooking is less developed. . . .

. . . Cleanliness of house, clothing, and even of person is extremely difficult in a modern industrial community, without an adequate supply of hot and cold water within the dwelling. We are, however, very far from realizing this condition. . . . The United States Immigration Commission, for example, found that 1,413 households out of 8,651 foreign-born households studied in seven large cities, shared their water supply with other families. . . .

Cleanliness is also dependent, in part, upon the facilities for the disposition of human waste, the convenient and accessible toilet connected with a sewer system. These facilities are lacking in many immigrant neighborhoods, as has been repeatedly shown in various housing investigations. For example, in a Slovak district in the Twentieth Ward, Chicago, 80 per cent of the families were using toilets located in the cellar, yard, or under the sidewalk, and in many cases sharing such toilets with other families. One yard toilet was used by five families, consisting of twenty-eight persons. The danger to health, and the lack of privacy, that such toilet accommodations mean have been often emphasized. In addition, it enormously increases the work of the housewife and makes cleanliness difficult, if not impossible.

. . . The fact should always be kept in mind that, to the extent to which the foreign born are from rural districts, they have the difficulty experienced by all who are forced to adjust themselves to an economy built on money, as distinguished from an economy built on kind. In the country where things are grown, there is little opportunity for acquiring a sense of money values.

It is then peculiarly difficult to value in terms of the new measure those articles with which one has been especially familiar under the old economy. For example, when vegetables and fruits have been enjoyed without estimating their value, it is difficult to judge their value in money. While meat was before thought out of reach, it may be purchased at exorbitant rates under the new circumstances, because one has no idea of how much it should cost. Evidence as to this kind of difficulty is found among all groups. It takes the form, sometimes, of apparent parsimony, sometimes of reckless and wasteful buying.

The Lithuanians seem, for example, to experience difficulties of this kind everywhere. The small farmer in Lithuania was accustomed to an irregular cash income at harvest time. Sometimes it carried over from one year to another, while young stock was growing. He had little need of money except for extraordinary expenses, such as those for farm machinery, or building. The local store, which was usually co-operative, carried only such imported articles as salt, sugar, spices, tea, and coffee. All other foods were produced at home or secured through neighborly exchange. All the clothing for the family was of home manufacture, even to the cloth. . . .

The immigrant housewife is restricted by her ignorance of places and methods of marketing, and so feels the necessity of buying in the immigrant neighborhood. Among the 90 Chicago families from whom schedules were obtained, representing Bohemian, Croatian, Italian, Polish, Russian, Serbian, Slovak, Slovenian, and Ukrainian groups, 72 purchased all their food in the neighborhood stores, 2 kept their own stores, and only 16 were seeking bargains in other localities. . . .

The 72 families who were marketing exclusively in their own neighborhoods were patronizing for the most part stores owned by foreign-speaking people or those employing foreign-born salesmen to attract the housewives of particular groups. A Croatian woman says that when she tries to do her marketing downtown she sees many new things and would like to ask what they are used for, but she does not know how to ask. In her neighborhood store the grocer can easily explain to her. . . .

The difficulty with the language, however, extends beyond merely talking in the store. A Ukrainian mother, who admits being afraid to go beyond her own neighborhood, is perhaps typical of many foreign-born mothers to whom a trip to the central shopping district is a strange and terrifying adventure.

There is also the question of the means with which to buy. An Italian mother says that she buys at the chain store when she has the cash, and at other times in the Italian stores where, although the prices are higher, she can run a charge account. The system of buying on credit at the local store is spoken of as practically universal in all the foreign-born groups. The purchaser carries a small blank book, in which the merchant enters in large figures merely the sum charged, with no indication of what was bought or the amount. The account is settled on pay day by the man of the family. There is, of course, every chance for inaccurate entry. . . .

Even the skilled housekeepers have little experience in buying. At home they were used to storing vegetables in quantities; potatoes in caves, beets and cabbage by a process of fermentation, other vegetables and fruits by drying. In the United States this sort of thing is not done. There is, in the first place, no place for storage, and the initial cost of vegetables is high and quality poor, and the women know nothing of modern processes of canning [which leads to] the consequent necessity of buying very little at one time. . . . It must never be forgotten that among the lower-income groups, to have more in the house is to have more eaten, and that cannot be afforded.

Besides the high prices, one of the other limitations of the foreign-born neighborhood store is the low quality of the food. This may be illustrated by a description of the markets in one Lithuanian neighborhood back of the stockyards. . . . Stock in all these stores is the same; there is a great deal of fresh meat, apparently the poorer cuts, scraps, etc.; shelves are filled with canned fruits, canned vegetables, canned soups, and condensed milk; there is much of the bakers' "Lithuanian rye bread," and quantities of such cakes as are sold by the National Biscuit Company. No fresh vegetables are to be seen in any of these stores. . . .

Rural Labor

FAMILY FARMING: NORTH DAKOTA

The ideal of the family farm, representing independence in the Jeffersonian tradition, was a powerful molder of American culture, and it has been presented in the history books only as white. But, in fact, women worked on many kinds of family farms. The Hidatsa Indians lived in North Dakota, where at least half of their livelihood came from farming, done exclusively by women on land owned by women. The following description of some of their agricultural labor was recorded by an early-twentieth-century anthropologist from the recollections of Buffalo Bird Woman, an elderly Hidatsa woman.

My grandmother was one of the last women of my tribe to cling to old-fashioned implements. Two other women, I remember, owned bone hoes when I was a little girl; but Turtle, I think, was the very last one in the tribe who actually worked in her garden with one.

As I grew up, I learned to work in the garden, as every Hidatsa woman was expected to learn; but iron axes and hoes, bought of the traders, were now used by everybody, and the work of clearing and breaking a new field was less difficult than it had been in our grandfathers' times. . . .

I was about nineteen years old, I think, when my mothers determined to clear ground for a second field, west of the village. We chose a place down in the bottoms, overgrown with willows; and with our axes we cut the willows close to the ground, letting them lie as they fell.

The next spring my father, his two wives, my sister and I went out and burned the felled willows and brush which the spring sun had dried. We would go out after breakfast, burn until tired of the work, and come home.

We sought to burn over the whole field, for we knew that this left a good, loose soil. We did not pile the willows in heaps, but loosened them from the ground or scattered them loosely but evenly over the soil. In some places the ground was quite bare of willows; but we collected dry grass and weeds and dead willows, and strewed them over these bare places, so that the fire would run over the whole area of the field. It took us about four days to burn over the field.

We Hidatsa women were early risers in the planting season; it was my habit to be up before sunrise, while the air was cool, for we thought this the best time for garden work. Having arrived at the field I would begin one hill, preparing it, as I have said, with my hoe; and so for ten rows each as long as from this spot to yonder fence—about thirty yards; the rows were about four feet apart, and the hills stood about the same distance apart in the row.

The hills all prepared, I went back and planted them, patting down each with my palms. Planting corn thus by hand was slow work; but by ten o'clock the morning's work was done, and I was tired and ready to go home for my breakfast and rest; we did not eat before going into the field. The ten rows making the morning's planting contained about two hundred and twenty-five hills.

I usually went to the field every morning in the planting season, if the weather was fine. Sometimes I went out again a little before sunset and planted; but this was not usual.

It was usual for the women of a household to do their own planting; but if a woman was sick, or for some reason was unable to attend to her planting, she sometimes cooked a feast, to which she invited the members of her age society and asked them to plant her field for her.

The size of a garden was determined chiefly by the industry of the family that owned it, and by the number of mouths that must be fed. . . .

Corn and weeds alike grew rapidly, and we women of the household were out with our hoes daily, to keep ahead of the weeds. We worked as in planting season, in the early morning hours. We hoed but once, not very many weeds coming up to bother us afterward. In my girlhood we were not troubled with mustard and thistles; these weeds have come in with white men.

A platform, or stage, was often built in a garden, where the girls and young women of the household came to sit and sing as they watched that crows and other thieves did not destroy the ripening crop. We cared for our corn in those days as we would care for a child; for we Indian People loved our gardens, just as a mother loves her children; and we thought that our growing corn liked to hear us sing, just as children like to hear their mother sing to them. Also, we did not want the birds to come and steal our corn. Horses, too, might break in and crop the plants, or boys might steal the green ears and go off and roast them.

Girls began to go on the watchers' stage to watch the corn and sing when they were about ten or twelve years of age. They continued the custom even after they had grown up and married; and old women, working in the garden and stopping to rest, often went on the stage and sang.

The watchers sometimes rose and stood upon the stage as they looked to see if any boys or horses were in the field, stealing corn. Older girls and young married women, and even old women, often worked at porcupine embroidery as they watched. Very young girls did not embroider. . . .

In my father's family, one of my mothers and I usually attended to the actual picking. It was her habit to get up early in the morning, go to the field and pluck the squashes from the vines, piling them up in one place in the garden. She returned then to the lodge; and after the morning meal, the rest of us women of the household went out and fetched the squashes home in our baskets.

The baskets, as they were brought in, were borne up on the drying stage, and the squashes emptied out on the floor for slicing and drying; squashes not cooked and eaten fresh were sliced and dried for winter, excepting those saved for seed.

When the squashes, emptied from the baskets, made a great heap on the floor of the drying stage, the women of the family made a feast, cooking much food for the purpose; some old women were then invited to come and cut up the squashes with knives, into slices to dry. We regarded these old women as hired; and I remember that in my father's family we hired sometimes eight, sometimes ten, sometimes only six. I think that at the time I was a young woman, when my mothers made such a feast, about ten old women came.

These old women ascended the drying stage and sat, five on either side of the pile of squashes. Each of the old women had a squash knife in her hand, made of the thin part of the shoulder bone of a buffalo, if it was an old-fashioned one; butcher knives of steel are now used.

All the better slices, the ones to be retained by the family that hired the old women workers, were spitted on willow rods to dry. . . .

Bean planting followed immediately after squash planting. Beans, however, were very commonly planted not in open ground, but between our rows of corn.

Threshing was in the fall, after the beans had ripened and the pods were dead and dried. When the vines were dry, I took out into the field half of an old tent cover and laid it on the ground in an open space made by clearing away the corn stalks. This tent cover, so laid, was to be my threshing floor. I took up some of the dry vines and laid them on the tent cover in a heap, about three feet high. I got upon this heap with my moccasined feet and smartly trampled it, now and then standing on one foot, while I shuffled and scraped the other over the dry vines; this was done to shake the beans loose from their pods. . . .

We stored our corn, beans, sunflower seed, and dried squash in cache pits for the winter, much as white people keep vegetables in their cellars. A cache pit was shaped somewhat like a jug, with a narrow neck at the top.

Descent into big cache pits was made with a ladder. In smaller pits, when standing on the floor within, my eyes just cleared the level of the ground above, so that I could look around. When such a pit was half full of corn, I could descend and come out again, without the help of a ladder. At other times I had to be helped out; I would hold up my hands, and my mother, or some one else, would come and give me a lift. Usually, two women worked together thus in a cache pit, one helping the other out, or taking things from her hands. One of my mothers was usually my helper.

The digging and storing of a cache pit was women's work. For digging the pit, a short-handled hoe was used: of iron, in my day; of bone, I have heard, in olden times.

When the cache pit was all dug, it had next to be lined with grass. The grass used for this purpose, and for closing the mouth of the cache pit, was the long bluish kind that grows near springs and water courses on this reservation; it grows about three feet high. In the fall, this kind of grass becomes dry at the top, but is still green down near the roots; and we then cut it with hoes and packed it in bundles, to the village.

I remember, one time I went out with my mother to cut grass. I took a pony along to pack our loads home. I loaded the pony with four bundles of grass, two on each side, bound to the saddle. A bundle was about four feet long and from two and a half to three feet thick, pressed tight together. One bundle made a load for a woman. Besides the four bundles loaded on my pony, my mother packed one bundle back to the village, and three or four dogs dragged each a bundle on a travois.

We reckoned that three of these bundles would be needed to line and close a large cache pit; and two and a half bundles, for a smaller pit. A hundred such bundles were needed to cover the roof of an earth lodge. Long-established use made us able to make the bundles about alike in weight, though of course we had no scales to weigh them in those days.

We were careful to spread the grass lining evenly over the walls; and we were especially careful not to let the root ends get matted together, as they were very apt to do.

The cache pit was now ready to be stored. My mother and I—and by "my mother" I mean always one of my two mothers, for my mother that bore me was dead—fetched an old tent cover from the earth lodge and laid it by the cache pit so that one end of the cover hung down the pit's mouth. Upon this tent cover we emptied a big pile of shelled ripe corn, fetched in baskets from the bull boats in which it had been temporarily stored inside the lodge. We also fetched many strings of braided corn and laid them on one side of the tent cover. Lastly, we fetched some strings of dried squash and laid them on the tent cover.

Leaning over the pit, I handed my mother the braided strings that now lay in a heap on the tent cover. My mother took the string of corn, folded it once over, and laid it snugly against the wall of the cache pit. My mother continued thus all around the bottom of the pit, until she had surrounded it with a row of braided corn laid against the wall, two ears deep; for the strings, being doubled, lay therefore two ears deep. When this series was completed, the bottom of the cache pit was surrounded by strings of braided corn, which, because doubled, now lay four ears deep.

My mother now called to me that she was ready for the shelled, or loose, corn. I pushed the shelled corn that lay on the tent cover into the cache pit, until the floor of the pit was filled up level. I next passed down a string of dried squash, seven fathoms long. The object of our putting the squash in the center of the shelled corn was to protect it from dampness. The shelled ripe corn did not spoil very easily, but dried squash did. We were careful, therefore, to store the strings of squash in the very center of the cache pit and surround them on every side with the loose corn; this protected the squash and kept it dry.

We continued working, my mother and I, until the cache pit was filled. In an average-sized cache pit, we would usually store four seven-fathom strings of dried squash, coiled each in a heap in the center of the cache and hidden as described, in the loose corn; and as I recollect it, I think it took about thirty or more strings of braided corn to lie around the wall of an average-sized pit; but my memory here is a little uncertain, and this estimate may not be quite accurate.

FAMILY FARMING: ARIZONA

Although the family in this excerpt from an oral history had migrated from Mexico to Arizona in the late nineteenth century, in doing so they were joining other Hispanic peoples who were not migrants but had lived there for centuries. The Salazar family ran a typical farm. They produced a variety of goods—fruit, vegetables, cattle, chickens, pigs—and everyone in the family worked. Sexual division of labor structured even the children's work, but it is evident in this selection that even the girls did skilled, necessary, and at times heavy labor.

My name is Rosalía Salazar Whelan. I was born on February 4, 1904, at my parents' home in Aravaipa Canyon. My father's name was Epimenio Salazar. He was born in Oposura, Sonora, Mexico. He was a full-blooded Opata Indian. . . .

My mother's name was Crespina López de Salazar. She was born at Estación Llano, Sonora, Mexico, in about 1873. She and one of her sisters—my Tía Carmen—came with their grandmother Refugia—Doña Cuca—to Arizona when they were very young children. . . .

After my father and mother were married they went and lived in Aravaipa Canyon. . . . [My father] had gone to Aravaipa Canyon looking for work. He worked as a cowboy there with a man named John Dunlap. . . . I think that is when he claimed his land there. [Family sources set the date of Epimenio's arrival in Aravaipa Canyon as 1865.] . . .

My father was one of the first people to settle in Aravaipa Canyon, but later there were other families too, mostly Mexicanos, old families that had been there for a long time. . . . There were some Americanos too, but just a few. . . .

My father had a cattle ranch in El Cañón and a farm. He had a lot of land there. He kept most of his cattle in another place down below the canyon, towards the mountains. They called it "El Campo de Caballos." Later the Anglos named it Horse Camp. In those days the land was not fenced; it was all open range. All the rancheros and vaqueros in the area would gather the cattle during roundup and there would be thousands of cattle together in one place. Then they would drive the cattle to Willcox and ship them from there. It took them four days to drive the cattle that far.

My brother Guadalupe used to take care of my father's cattle at El Campo de los Caballos. From the time he was very small my father taught him how to ride a horse. . . . All of us girls also learned to saddle and ride a horse at a very early age. But in those days one didn't wear pants; we wore skirts and rode sidesaddle. We called the sidesaddle "el albordón."

We had quite a few horses as well as the cattle. We had quarter horses for working the cattle and another kind of horse for the *tiros*—the teams that pulled the wagons. My father had four teams of horses that he used for the wagons for the farm to haul wood, the harvest to the barn, the grain and hay for the animals, and to carry provisions from Willcox: I, and sometimes my sister Lucía, used to go with my father once a year to get supplies—the staples that we did not grow ourselves. It took two days to get to Safford and three days to get to Willcox. *Toditito el día en el sol.* (All the long day in the sun.) We camped by the side of the road. . . .

It may be true that my sisters and I worked harder than the daughters of our neighbors. My parents only had one son, and as my brother Guadalupe got married very young, we had to fill in and do the work of men. . . .

Sometimes when I am sitting around and talking about those days to my friends that are my age, they say they don't believe me, that it is not possible that women did such work! I tell them, "It is true! When you have to, you have to! What you're taught, you learn!" But sometimes I stop to think and remember, and I say to myself, "How did we do it?" I remember nights when we would go to bed, and I didn't know whether or not I'd be able to sleep from weariness.

From the time we were very young we had our chores—there is always so much work on a farm. When we were small, one of our jobs was to bring in kindling at night for the morning fire. We had to get up at 4:30 or 5:00, and who at that hour is going to go outside and gather kindling? We had to milk the cows before we went to school, and then we walked to school. It was a couple miles from our house over there by the T-Rail Ranch. We had a clock—do you know what that clock was? We'd hear my father make a sound—hrrumph, hrrumph, hrrumph. And we knew it was time to get up, because we had to take him his coffee to bed before we went outside to start on our chores. He was the boss all right. . . .

As we got older we had other jobs as well. We washed. We ironed. We worked in the milpa. We picked fruit and vegetables. . . .

My mother worked very hard. It was enough work just with the large family that she had. She was always tending to the kitchen, not only to cook for our family but for the men that came to help my father. . . .

My mother made her tortillas medium sized. ¡Y *muy parejitas, muy parejitas!* (Smooth and even!) She used to say, "You girls never learned to make tortillas the right way. Except for your oldest sister, Pastora. She makes them like I do." Sometimes she even made tortillas from the wheat we grew on the farm. We'd grind the flour ourselves on the metate.

You know, I get to thinking. I say to myself, "Todo se acaba." ("Everything comes to an end.") When you get older you don't do things the way you used to when you were young. My sisters and I used to make lots of tortillas, piles of them, because when you go out to work in the fields you don't have time to come in and make them at midday.

My mother sewed for us. She mended. She patched. She made us our underwear from manta cloth. And our blouses and skirts and housedresses. She had a treadle machine, and she ordered material from a catalog. She even bought our shoes that way. Every once in a great while she bought us a ready-made dress. When we needed a little better dress, Tía Carmen made it for us, but don't think for a minute that we had many clothes.

My father had a *dicho* (proverb). *Acuérdense que no es pecado ser pobre, pero ser dejados, ¡Ay Chivarras!* (Remember, it is not a sin to be poor, but to be dirty, heaven forbid!) My sisters and I had the chore of the washing and ironing. It was a lot with that big family. We washed twice a week. And all on the washboard. We gathered wood and made a big fire and hauled water. We boiled the clothes and then added more hot water and rinsed everything twice. There were so many clothes to hang that we even had to drape it over the branches of the mesquites. And then we used those heavy irons made out of cast iron. We'd put them on the wood stove to heat. My mother helped with folding and ironing the dish towels. We'd also wash and iron for some of the Americanas—wives of the ranchers who lived in El Cañón—to earn a little extra spending money. There were times when I would iron from seven o'clock in the morning until five o'clock in the afternoon. When it was cold, we'd find a spot of sun to warm our backs; and when it was hot, we'd look for a bit of shade to cool us.

A DOCTOR OF ALL TRADES

Suzanne La Flesche Picotte (1865–1915) was the daughter of a prominent Omaha Indian leader. Educated at the Hampton Institute of Virginia, a school for blacks and Indians, and at the Women's Medical College of Pennsylvania, where she graduated first in her class, she returned to her tribe as a physician and Presbyterian missionary at age twenty-five. Married and then widowed, she raised two sons alone. She remained working on the reservation for the rest of her life and became a tribal leader, a most unusual position for an Omaha woman.

Dr. Picotte's contributions to her people had both helping and controlling aspects, like Sophonisba Breckinridge's. It was estimated that in her twenty-five years as a physician she treated every member of the Omaha tribe and saved the lives of many. At the same time, she believed that enforcing European Christian norms, including temperance and women's devotion to their husbands, was one of her most important responsibilities. In addition to serving as doctor and missionary, she took on a wide variety of other tasks, serving as scribe, translator, teacher, public health advocate, ombudswoman for her people to the Bureau of Indian Affairs, and personal counselor. The fact that women healers often took on a multiplicity of jobs for their communities, as we have also seen in the case of Martha Ballard (in Before 1820, pp. 8–11), was a characteristic theme of women's work. The following are some typical daily entries in her diary.

We are grateful to Peggy Pascoe for this selection.

SEPT. 20, 1910

Was called a little after seven by Mrs. Grant who said she wanted me to come down right away to see Willie who was suffering intensely. He had appendicitis and abcess had ruptured into bowel. Called Ream [another physician] who had been attending him. Sent him to [hospital] in S.C. [Sioux City] on 11 A.M. train. Went to Train to see him off. Mary Pilcher—asked after baby—of Geo. Woodhull—I told her the particulars & she sent message by me. Advised Dora Cox how to feed the baby. . . . Elsie P. Harlan asked me to help her about her trust funds some mistake about it. Wrote Kneale, also for Theresa M. to have trust funds for oldest girl for early treatment. Found out financial arrangements . . . Nellie Sprinter wants to find out her heirship interests. Was called to Mrs. Guy Stabler's at 9 P.M. to see girl with tonsillitis. Gave her alcohol sponge. Called to Hospital to see Mrs. J. and baby—called to MCM to see baby—reached home at 11 P.M.

SEPT. 26, 1910

W. Reese Harlan came early to ask me to get her rents for her. . . . Had a long talk with W. and R. about settlement of their difficulties. Yellow Fox came to tell me Nettie was objecting to the will—the old woman came also to tell me—I told them not to worry as Nettie would be only injuring herself to persist. Uriah came for me to write a letter for him. . . . Nettie Solomon came in, in afternoon to see about will business. She want away satisfied & found it was best for her. W. came in to ask me what I tho't of her plans in regard to her difficulties with R. I told her what I tho't it was best for her to do. Had letter from K & M. Want me to hurry Chase up about the work they want him to do Phoned to Pender to Chase. Wm Harlan came in to see about his leg and heirship interests, Geo. Webster came to get crutches for his wife I had ordered. John Sheridan's wife and 3 daughters came to stay all night with me, for John was drunk and they were afraid of him.

SEPT. 27, 1910

Mrs. Sheridan & 3 girls had breakfast with me. Wanted me to talk to John and see if he wouldn't do better, Promised her I would do so. . . .

SEPT. 28, 1910

Went out to . . . at 6:30 this A.M. A white family as Hart & Ream were out of town. Indigestion but child in bad condition with mucous colitis passing puss and blood. Prescribed diet and treatment & told them to send for Ream if necessary for I could not spare the time. . . . Heard Little Turkey's wife died after a few hours illness. Arthur Ramsey's wife yesterday A. M. and Geo. Field's baby buried today. . . . Went out in auto in afternoon to Mrs. Little Turkey's. Found Jennie Lovejoy Smith and Henry Lovejoy and Milton Smith and Grant families there. I told them to bury her as soon as possible. Said they would. . . .

SEPT. 30, 1910

. . . Geo. Woodhull, nurse, and Mrs. Woodhull & baby came down at 9:20 from Sioux City. They are going to stay a few days at my house so the baby can get well. Nurse seems to be alright.

OCT. 1, 1910

. . . Jos. Menick asked me to get authority to repair & have house painted and bills paid & to draw money himself so he could spend as he wanted to. Helped him out. Phoned Small for Gertrude about her transportation— meals and sleeper. . . . Chase came in to call & tell me he had called council & wanted me present on Tuesday. Soloman Woodhull said he had eaten mescal and what the bean-eaters [Mexicans, Chicanos] said was true. Wanted to find out about his taxes. Yellow Fox wanted me to be Gov't interpreter.

OCT. 4, 1910

. . . Had a council in P.M. . . . Present: H. Chase Little Cook Simeon Hallowell Nebraska Hallowell White Horse John Springer Rabbit Silas Wood Little Soldier Teokaha in order to talk about claims of tribe against Gov't. . . . Don Lyon asked me to see his wife with a view of bringing about a reconciliation—she said she did not want to live with him any more so she aplied for a divorce. . . .

OCT. 10, 1910

. . . Have been sick all week—Susan Webster came on Monday and staid for several days as she was having trouble with Thomas. . . .

ELECTION DAY NOV. 8, 1910

Have been electioneering all morning against Dahlman. Have been successful with all I saw. Attended to Arthur Ramsey about mortgaged property.
. . . Mrs. Lawrence Duval brought her baby in for me to see—it was colicky
& I gave her directions how to care for it. In the P.M. went to Macy to see
the Omahas vote . . . None voted for Dahlman. . . .

NOV. 11, 1910

Looked after erysipelas case first thing. Mrs. Dan Grant sent for me and
asked me to get 6 chairs for them from the hotel man—he refused to let
them have anything. Neither had he cleaned up as Board of Health directed
him to—so I served notice on him by Marshal. In P.M. went to Council at
Macy—the Omahas did not want to pay taxes on restricted lands and blamed
the Gov't for everything thing. They felt hard toward Abbot and roasted him
and white people who were present. . . .

DEC. 19, 1910

William Sherman came to tell me that his baby was dead. . . . I took up a
little white dress & ribbon for the baby. I also took up a disinfectant. I had a
talk with the poor little mother about God's love for the little ones and the
Home he had prepared for them. Noah & Susan Lovejoy came for medicine
for Dick's baby. I told Susan how to feed him and how to give the medicine
& to let me know how he gets along. Paul's baby & Ed Kemp both died
yesterday. Amos Mitchell's baby is to be buried today. Marguerite [Margue-
rite LaFlesche Farley, her sister] & Nettie went to funeral at Macy. Geo.
Fox came to ask me to write a letter for him, also to read 3 letters to him and
to look up back annuity money for Jas.—there is evidently a mistake somewhere so I wrote Mr. Small. . . .

DEC. 20, 1910

. . . Me-pe Walker came & asked me to phone to Govt Of[fice] for her and
get her $50.00. They said she could have it. Nettie S. phoned early & asked
me to get $20.00 for her from G[overment] O[ffice] for Bertha. Mr. Small
said he would send it. I examined Grace F. and gave her directions how to
take care of herself. Arthur Ramsey came in to have me tell him of Geo.'s
condition and to advise him on other matters. He looked so lonely and pitiful
I invited him to dinner. Mr. Beith came in to talk over the church windows
with Mr. Anfin & I, and we concluded the price of $129.99 was very reason-
able. Daisy Mitchell Walker insisted on my interpreting for her, her mother,
sister, and Arthur about their heirship lands and explaining everything about
the papers they had to sign before they signed them. . . . Cyrus Phillips
came in to have me write a prescription for medicine for Jefferson's 3 yr. old
child. Also to advise him about his daughter's trouble with her husband, and

asked me to do what I could to help her. He also said he was going to Washington with Chase to get the patents in fee to his wife's heirship lands.

Mrs. Jewett said the old lady was very low and she did not think she would live long. She had made an application for a patent in fee and wanted to know what reply had been made. This afternoon I want with Mr. Beith to collect money for the repairs of the Church at Macy as we have a deficit of $600. We went around all afternoon and got $180.00 in cash and about $70 more promised. We are not near thro' but it was getting dark so we stopped. Miss Agnes called me in to see Parrish Saunsoci's baby so I went in. It is very sick and has pemphigus—temp. 106—ordered water frequently per [illegible] and tepid pack—whiskey 15 [mg?] as necessary & ointment to sores. Went up to Mrs. Keefe's in evening and took up a branch of mistletoe Miss Agnes had given me.

DEC. 21, 1910

This morning worked on data of cases, number and kinds of sickness so we can forward them to Mother Gertrude so she can help us to raise money for the hospital. Y. Fox came in for me to write a letter—and also Little Soldier. Caroline Tyndall came in for me to see about Margaret's affair with Paul. Also about her own kinship interests.

Ida Miller gave me $5.00 for the Xmas tree at Macy. The boys & I ordered a box of apples to give the Indian children at the tree.

I did some shopping for the Mahaffey, King and Coates children—white children who are very poor. The boys and I are going to send them some things to eat and toys. I refused a call to Beckner's white people because I have to save myself for Indian work. . . .

DISCONTENT ON THE FARM

Until 1920 the majority of Americans lived in the countryside or in towns with fewer than twenty-five hundred inhabitants. Farm work was still the most common form of women's labor.

A romantic image of rural life had been influential in the settling of America. But when the U.S. Department of Agriculture sent out a mass questionnaire to farm wives in 1914, the women expressed a great deal of discontent, including some rather frank criticisms of their husbands.

TEXAS

The condition of the farm women of the South is most deplorable. Her liege lord is availing himself of labor-saving appliances such as reaper, binder, thresher, riding plow, gas engines, etc., while the woman's labor-saving help consists of her sewing and washing machines. The routine work of the southern farm woman is about as follows: at this time of the year she is up at 5 A.M. preparing the breakfast, often building her own fire; milks the cows, cares for the milk—churns the cream by hand. Puts the house in order, gets the dinner, eats with the family at noon; leaves the house in disorder, goes to the cotton field and picks cotton all the afternoon, often dragging a weight of 60 pounds along the ground. At about sundown she goes to the farmhouse, puts the house in order, washes the dishes left over from the noon meal, prepares the supper—most of the time too tired to eat; gets the children to bed, and falls asleep herself—and so it goes on from day to day. Somehow she finds the time to do the washing and ironing, mending, knitting, and darning between times. If she is under 45 years of age, while all this is going on she is either enceinte [pregnant] or she is nursing a baby. The result is she is weak and frail as a rule. There are a few well-to-do farmers in whose homes we find better conditions, but the above description of conditions applies to negroes, to white tenants and to the young farmers who are trying to build their homes. Get statistics of the sale of farm implements and the sales of nostrums for the cure of the ills of women and you will ascertain the relative condition of the farmers and their wives in the South. . . .

COLORADO

. . . As a farmer's wealth increases he buys more land and stock, requiring more help; builds larger houses, which take more labor to keep in order; sends his sons and daughters away to school; hires extra help in the sons' places, and deprives his wife of the help of her daughters. . . .

Serving hot, substantial meals at 6 o'clock A.M., 12 o'clock noon, and 6 o'clock P.M., and clearing up the dishes, I leave the reader to figure out how much time a woman has to leisurely enjoy church, afternoon clubs, or social visiting, even with an automobile on the farm. The remedy for all the trouble is simple. Every wife should flatly refuse to labor for any one outside of the family. That much is a duty, more is an imposition, considered all right by farmers because it has become customary. As I say, the remedy is simple. Each wife can "strike. . . ."

Some may argue that the daughters of the house share the work of the mother, or a hired girl lends her assistance. This may be true in some parts of the country. Most girls in the Rocky Mountain tier of States marry before they are 20. The unmarried daughter in the house is the exception to the rule. Hired girls are scarce for the same reason and do not care to work on farms.

OREGON

The farmer may aid a great deal by sticking to the 10-hour labor system, which will lighten the labor of the woman on the farm. I know a great many farmers who will be in the field by 6 A.M. plowing, and they plow 13 hours. Of course the mother of the family must arise very early in order to prepare breakfast. The husband doesn't mind the long hours of labor because he thinks when he harvests the crop he will get his pay. The hired man gets paid for his work, but the tired housewife on the farm merely gets her board and clothing, the same as the farmer's work animals.

OKLAHOMA

The main cause of it all in my opinion is because the majority of us are landless people, renters and homeless, therefore, a dissatisfied, discontented and enslaved people. Now, if you really wish to do something to help the farmers' wives you must work to get the Government to lend money direct to the farmers and their wives (not through the bankers or any one else) with which to buy themselves homes. . . .

The Government ought to tax the land held for speculation purposes to the limit and let the use and occupancy of land constitute title to land, and then the renters everywhere could get little homes and be prosperous people. Putting $50,000 in the banks to help the farmers is of no benefit to them, as they can not pay the high rate of interest to the bankers.

The farmer gets only about one-half what the spinner pays for the cotton, and this causes the women and children to kill themselves from exposure and hard work to pay the bills. The banks of this country usually charge from 24 to 40 percent on money. If you borrow $100 March 1, they make your note payable October 1 for $124, with interest from maturity, to avoid the usury law. This causes these women to work and pay all grafts—those I have spoken of are the worse—and our children are going uneducated and dying from exposure and women dying from consumption, where, if we had our just rights, we could live and let live. . . .

TEXAS

Many farm women don't get off their own premises more than a dozen times a year. The fathers get so accustomed to the mothers' staying at home, they seem to forget that they might enjoy a little rest and recreation and really feel that she must stay at home "to keep the ranch going," as I have heard them express it. And the mother gets so accustomed to it, she, too, seems to forget she is human. The more intelligent and broader-minded men become, the more they appreciate woman and understand that she is equal in all things. But the men in the country realize this far less than the men in town. . . .

CARETAKING

Women in the United States today spend, on average, more time caring for elderly and/or ailing relatives than for children, in part because people are living longer. Although in the past, child care may have been more demanding because women had more children, nevertheless caring for kinfolk, neighbors, and community members has constituted a substantial part of women's labor (and comparatively little of men's). This caretaking requires not only kindness, patience, and sensitivity, but also a wide variety of hard labor—bathing, lifting, cooking, cleaning, doing laundry, running errands, just being there—and taking responsibility. But this care was also often communal and mutual. More recently caretaking has become more solitary and also more bureaucratized, involving the time-consuming and often frustrating labor of obtaining services and benefits from various agencies for the needy person. In addition, many of the caretakers are also holding down jobs.

A diary written by Nannie Stillwell Jackson in 1890 and 1891 portrays women's supportive relationships in unusually rich detail. The wife of a small farmer in Arkansas, Nannie saw her close friend Fannie Morgan as often as four times a day. Nannie's entry for June 19, 1890, reveals their close interdependence: "I went up and washed the dishes for Fannie & helped her so as she could get an early start to washing for she had such a big washing. . . . I baked some chicken bread for Fannie & some for my self, & she gave me some dried apples & I baked 2 pies she gave me one & she took the other I made starch for her & me too." Nannie also relied on Fannie for emotional support. Nannie wrote that she liked to tell Fannie "my troubles because it seems to help me to bear it better when she knows about it." When Nannie feared that she would die in childbirth, she asked Fannie to care for her two daughters. In addition, Nannie frequently exchanged goods and services with at least twenty other women, both white and African-American. Care for the sick and the dying was embedded in this collective female life.

"I have had a heap of company this week," wrote Nannie a week after giving birth. Her visitors included Miss Joe, Miss Ruth, Mrs. Chandler, and Fannie, who "stayed with me 4 nights." When Mrs. Dyer "was terribly afflicted with boils," Nannie, along with several other women, visited her. Fannie gave pills to Nannie's daughter, and Nannie visited Fannie when the latter was "sick taking pills." Both women spent time at the home of Mrs. Caulk when her baby was ill. When Nannie herself fell ill, Fannie cooked breakfast for her; Mrs. Gifford and Bettie Newby came by in the evening. After Mrs. Hornbuckle's son died, Nannie and her husband stayed with her at night; the following day, Nannie returned to the Hornbuckle house, got material for the coffin, and went to the home of Fannie, who helped make "the pillow and face cover."

Sickness at the Archdale house required a range of services from several women. On March 22, 1891, Nannie "set a while" with Mrs. Archdale's sons Bill and Lee, both of whom had pneumonia; she continued to visit the house regularly over the next few days, reporting on March 28 that the sons were better but that the daughter had fallen ill. On April 8, Mrs. Archdale herself became ill and sent for Nannie; the latter, in turn, summoned Fannie, and together they gave Mrs. Archdale "a dose of oil & turpentine & some gum camphor." Various other women spent the next few nights with the patient. Mrs. Archdale's son Lee came to the Jacksons' house for dinner, and he took food to Fannie, who also was not well. On April 11, all members of Mrs. Archdale's family appeared to be recovering. Nannie "cleaned up the dishes & stratened things about there some"; she also gave Lee Archdale two of his meals. The following day, Nannie had time to visit three women in addition to Mrs. Archdale. Then, on April 13, Mrs. Archdale took a turn for the worse; Nannie visited her "5 or 6 times," and she and Fannie spent the night. On April 14, Mrs. Archdale died: "Mrs. Morgan [Fannie], Mrs. Newby & I Mr. Jackson Kate McNiel & Fannie Totten all set up . . . & we dressed her and laid her out." Although a flood prevented the women from attending the burial, Nannie "fixed things about in Mrs. Archdale's house."

When Nannie was too busy to engage in caregiving activities herself, she relied on her 12-year-old daughter Lizzie and her 9-year-old daughter Sue to fulfill her responsibilities; in this way, she was able to extend the range of her neighborly services. Thus, when Fannie had to spend the night with her sick mother, Lizzie "churned" for Fannie, ate supper at her house, and then accompanied Fannie to her mother's. Nannie also sent both Lizzie and Sue to stay with Fannie when the latter was sick, and the two women who might have been expected to tend her had gone to spend the night at the home of a boy who had just died. The following day, Fannie took Lizzie with her to visit the bereaved mother.

Nannie was intensely aware of sickness in her friends' homes, even when she was not directly involved in rendering care. She noted when Fannie's stepson Asher "took pills" and when he had a "chill." On July 9, 1890, she listed the women who visited Mrs. Hunley's "very sick" baby. On January 5, 1891, she wrote that Fannie and Nellie Smithee "went down to set up with Mrs. Hunley." A few days later, Nannie "lent Nellie Smithee my shawl & Lizzie's bonnet for she & Fannie had to go down to sit up with Mrs. Maggie Stroud & Bettie Hunley they are both sick." Fannie and Nellie returned to Nannie's house in the morning to report how the patients were faring.

In short, care for the sick and the dying was part of the continual flow of services among Nannie Jackson's friends. . . .

Industrial Labor

TAKING IN BOARDERS

Taking in boarders has traditionally been one of the most common forms of women's labor, and so it was for poor, urban, immigrant women in this period, because it allowed them to work at home. Boarding places were needed because many foreign immigrants and migrants from the rural United States left their families behind when they came to the cities. A 1907 survey of working-class families in New York City found that half the households had boarders. The rent paid by the boarders, earned by the washing, cooking, and cleaning labor of the woman householder, was frequently essential to the economic survival of her family. Yet this work was usually ignored by censustakers and those who counted "working women." Today, boarding is again increasing as a way of making ends meet in a constricting economy. This account by a middle-class woman reformer of 1910 reveals both her subjects' hard work and her own inability to understand their living conditions.

Family life in Homestead depends for its support almost entirely upon the men's earnings; women and children rarely work outside the home since the steel plant and machine works cannot use them and there are no other industries in the town. . . .

Among the immigrant families, however, and among all those in which the man's earnings fell within the day labor rate, our budget studies disclosed that another and exceptional source of support was resorted to; namely, payment from lodgers. It is upon the women of the household that this burden falls. In families where the man's wage was normally less than $12 a week, more than half found it necessary to increase their slender income in this way. . . .

Against many of these deaths was the physician's entry "malnutrition due to poor food and overcrowding"; that is, the mother too poor, too busy, and too ignorant to prepare food properly, rooms over-tenanted, and courts too confined to give the fresh air essential for the physical development of children. A priest told me he believed that the taking of lodgers caused the appalling death rate among the babies in his parish. Neither preaching nor pointing out to women personally the folly of the economy had sufficed to check the habit.

Not only is the mother too busy to give much time to her babies, but she also suffers from overwork during pregnancy and from lack of proper care afterward. Housework must be done, boarders must be fed, and most women work until the day of confinement. In accordance with their home customs, almost all of them employ midwives and call a doctor only in an emergency. I was told by a local physician that nearly half of the births in Homestead, the large proportion of them among the Slavic people, were attended by midwives. . . .

The women have few opportunities for relaxation. Sometimes they gossip around the pump or at the butcher's, but washing, ironing, cleaning, sewing and cooking for the boarders leave little time for visiting. The young people perhaps suffer most from the lack of home festivities. A two-room house has no place for games or "parties," or even for courting; there is not even space enough, to say nothing of privacy. So young folks are driven to the streets for their gayety. Almost the only time when the house is really the scene of festivity is when those primal events, birth, and marriage, and death, brings together both the old-time friends and the new neighbors. . . .

The men are inclined to trust all financial matters to their wives. It is the custom in Homestead for the workman to turn over his wages to his wife on pay day and to ask no questions as to what it goes for. He reserves a share for spending money; otherwise his part of the family problem is to earn and hers to spend. When the man was at home and I suggested to him that they keep accounts for this investigation he usually referred the matter genially to the wife, saying, "Oh, she's the one that knows where the money goes. If she wants to help you out she can."

Though the men show in general a frank appreciation of home comforts, they do not always realize all the work behind them. One wife said, "The only time 'the mister' notices anything about the house is when I wash the curtains." But many chance remarks showed that the women realizes the importance of keeping the home attractive. One woman compared her husband, who stayed at home evenings unless they went to "the show" together, with the man next door who was always going off to Pittsburgh "on a lark." Her explanation of the difference was simply, "I always put on a clean dress and do my hair before he comes home, and have the kitchen tidy so he will enjoy staying. But she never tidies up a bit." Her kitchen was spotless, with a bright geranium in the window; that of her neighbor was hot and mussy and the children were noisy. No wonder the husband did not care to stay at home; but in a small house with washing and cooking to do, with babies to look out for, it is often hard for the housekeeper to have time or energy, after the children are home from school and the dinner cooked, to stop and make herself presentable. That so many women do this is a proof of their energy and genuine ability.

Supper time in Homestead will always be associated in my mind with one family whom I knew. When the men began to come from the mill in the evening the mother with a fresh apron on and the two children in clean dresses came out on the front porch. The children sat on the lowest step until the father was in sight, and long before I could recognize him were off down the street, the older one to carry his bucket, the little one to take possession of his hand. After supper he smoked contentedly with a child on each knee and talked with his wife of the day's doings. That hour of rest was bought at the price of a busy day for her; she swept off porch and walk, she washed almost daily to keep the dresses clean, she had dinner all cooked before he came. A woman must be a good manager and have the courage to appear cheerful when tired, if she is to make the evening at home happy.

The thoughtful women are especially conscious that part of the responsibility for keeping the men away from the saloons belongs to them. The heat and thirst due to mill work, combined with the lack of other amusements, make the brightness and festivity of bar-rooms very appealing, and intemperance is consequently a serious evil in the town. The wives feel that they must help to overcome this temptation. One woman told me that she had been brought up to consider it wrong to play cards. She feared, however, that if she refused to have them in the house, her husband who was fond of playing would be tempted to go to the back rooms of the saloons for his entertainment. So, putting aside her scruples, she planned informal gatherings to play in the evenings. To her the drink evil was the more serious. There are many, however, to whom these real homes are not possible. . . .

THE NIGHT SHIFT

Women with children have often worked night shifts because they have to care for their families during the day. Theirs is a particularly burdensome double day, as they return from working all night to children who are just waking up. Often they have difficulty getting any sleep. In the last few decades, shift work has again expanded (see pp. 312–14).

This excerpt comes from Life and Labor *(December 1914), the monthly newspaper of the Women's Trade Union League, an active women's reform group composed of working women and their middle-class allies.*

One of the worst abuses coming in the train of modern industry is the night work that falls to the lot of women, especially married women with children. The effects on the health of the worker herself from overwork and want of sleep and the necessary neglect of the children telling on their health are all brought out in the pathetic account given of the women night workers in a cordage works in Auburn, N.Y. . . .

The wretched life that a poor woman leads who, because of poverty is induced to take employment in a factory at night, and who is at the same time compelled to do her housework and take care of her children during the day can be gathered from the evidence.

The twine made is used for agricultural machines. The night shift employs more than 130 women, and half as many men. Very few speak English. Poles are predominant, Italians next. A *large proportion of the women are married*.

The night force work from 7 P.M. to midnight, when they have half-an-hour for supper; and from 12:30 A.M. to 5:30 A.M., five nights a week, making fifty hours weekly. No men under 18 nor women under 21 are on the night shift.

The investigators state that men workers are scarce, and the mill cannot get enough men to work at night, but also that *it would be impossible to engage men at the same rates that are paid women and get the same efficiency*.

The management bring forward reasons so hoary with age that it is time they became extinct.

1. If night work were prohibited in this state the company would be compelled to transfer the night work from this plant to plants in other states.

2. If night work of women were prohibited throughout the United States, the company would be compelled to enlarge its buildings and equipment. . . .

It was impossible to strike any average of the wages earned, which are on a piece-work basis. One woman earned $12; the lowest listed group of 11 from $6 to $7, and a group of twenty-three earned such varying sums below $6 that no definite wage could be named.

One of the saddest features in the life of these working women is found in the paradox that the employers do not seem to have been brutal; obeyed the State laws; followed without protests suggestions made by the Commission as to ventilation, the removal of dust from the air of workrooms by a specially installed plant; did not inflict the heaviest work upon women; reported all accidents to the proper authorities; and employed a physician and two matrons to take care of the health and comfort of the women. And yet, what a life it is these married workers lead. . . .

M. R.—I am strong and healthy and I am glad to work and take care of my children. Else what would become of them? Don't stop the night work with troubling the foreman. They might shut down and then (pointing to the little girl) she will have nothing to eat and nothing to wear. I don't want to have to work days, as then my children are alone. The boss had warned the girls that their wages are going to be cut if they talk to the investigators.

Mrs. M. N.—You can't feed and clothe a lot of children on what a man makes any more. (She changed from night to day work because it took all her strength to stay up all day beside. Now working days, she gets up and dresses and cares for all the children before she goes to work. Children were ragged and tattered and sickly.)

N. M.—I would rather work days if I could leave my baby with some one. I burn up my pay envelopes, my pay is so small I am ashamed.

Y. Z.—I want to work nights so I can take care of my children in the day. Why ain't men's pay more so women wouldn't have to work? I spent lots of money on my eyes; the dust makes them so sore. It's hard to work nights, but you got to live. . . .

All the women with families did their own housework; they prepared three meals a day, including breakfast, after a night's work. They also did the washing for the family. They averaged about 4½ hours sleep a day. The time of sleep varied with the individual. Some slept an hour or two in the morning and for a time in the afternoon; others slept at intervals of about an hour each during the day. They all slept in bedrooms which had been occupied during the night by husband and children. When the mother works at night the little ones learn to keep quiet out of doors while she is sleeping in the day time.

HOME WORK

"Home work" in the early twentieth century referred to manufacturing labor done in the home. Through a system of subcontracting, employers distributed batches of work to families to complete in their homes. Although one family member was nominally the employee, it often took an entire family's labor to earn enough to survive. Industries that operated on the piecework system (that is, where workers were paid by the item rather than by the hour) most often used this kind of labor. Employers often preferred home work because they saved the overhead costs of maintaining a factory. And home work drove down wages in general by undercutting the slightly better paid factory or sweat-shop workers.

In preindustrial times, families had also worked together in their homes, and worked very hard, but they defined their own tasks and set their own pace. In the industrial period, piece rates were set so low that workers were pressured to labor long hours at a killing speed. Surveys showed that home work presented more health and safety hazards than factory work. Furthermore, the work was usually seasonal, and the workers were unemployed for large parts of the year. The home-work system turned city tenements into factories. For the family there was no longer a home to which they could escape from the monotony and constant pressure of repetitive hand labor.

In recent decades, there has been a resurgence of home work (see pp. 306–8).

This selection is from an investigation by Mary Van Kleeck of the circumstances of Italian artificial flower makers. Home work was particularly common among Italian families because many Italian husbands forbade their wives to work outside their homes. Van Kleeck (1883–1972) was a distinguished and radical progressive-era reformer, first director of the U.S. Women's Bureau, founder of the Russell Sage Foundation's social research programs, and in the 1930s a leftist social work leader.

Four large questions are pertinent. Who are the workers making flowers at home? How much do they earn? In what type of family are they found? Is the system good for the workers, the trade, and the community?

These questions were answered for the flower trade by interviewing family after family. . . .

In a tenement on Macdougal Street lives a family of seven—grandmother, father, mother, and four children aged four years, three years, two years and one month respectively. All excepting the father and the two babies make violets. The three-year-old girl picks apart the petals; her sister, aged four years, separates the stems, dipping an end of each into paste spread on a piece of board on the kitchen table and the mother and grandmother slip the petals up the stems.

"We all must work if we want to earn anything," said the mother. They are paid 10 cents for a gross, 144 flowers, and if they work steadily from 8 or 9 o'clock in the morning until 7 or 8 at night, they may make 12 gross, $1.20. In the busy season their combined earnings are usually $7.00 a week. During five months, from April to October, they have no work. They live in three rooms for which they pay $10 a month. The kitchen, which is used as a workroom, is lighted only by a window into an adjoining room. The father is a porter. Both he and his wife were born in Italy but came to New York when they were children. The wife when a child, before she was able to work in a factory, made flowers at home. Later she worked in a candy factory. "That's better than making flowers," she said, "but we can't go out to work after we're married." . . .

When visited, she was working on yellow muslin roses for which she was paid 25 cents a gross. There were five petals of different shapes, and each must be put into its right place. The first one was twisted around the "pep" to make the bud. Then paste was smeared upon another petal which was slipped up the wire stem. Two others were pasted on and then the tube stem slipped over the wire, and the flower hung on a line above the kitchen table to dry. . . .

In another tenement nearby is a young married woman who, working alone at home, can earn the exceptional wage of from $8.00 to $12 in a week. She is a skilled brancher and represents the experienced worker who has learned the trade in the shop, an unusual type among home workers. She had made flowers for fifteen years before her marriage. Her wages from home work usually equal those of her husband, who is a porter in a saloon. Her mother-in-law does the housework and takes care of the eleven-months-old baby, thus leaving the mother free to work without interruption. The flowers given her are made abroad and branched or bunched here. Manufacturers usually do not give out such work unless they are sure that they can trust the worker's skill. In a day she can branch about two gross of the kind upon which she was engaged at the date of our visit. "But it's all according to the work," she said. "Sometimes I can make $1.50 and sometimes $3.00 a day. You can't count home work by the day, for a day is really two days sometimes, because people often work half the night. When the boss asks me how many flowers I can make in a day I say I cannot tell, but I know how many I can do in an hour. Some girls are so foolish. I've heard them praising themselves and telling the boss that they did the work in a day. They're ashamed to say they worked in the night too. But they only hurt themselves, for the boss says if they earn that much in a day he can cut the price." In the summer this woman works on feathers, which her employers give her in order not to lose track of so skilled a home worker during the dull season of the flower trade. . . .

INDUSTRIAL HEALTH

Occupational diseases were a common part of workers' daily existence. Some occupations had their own particular diseases. "Wrist drop" (an inability to hold one's hand up straight) afflicted painters, caused by the lead in paint. The Mad Hatter of Alice in Wonderland *was patterned after the hatters who often became mad from the mercury used in the manufacture of felt. In the nineteenth century and before, little attention was paid to these diseases; they were an expected part of working-class life.*

As more women became industrial workers, women social reformers and some public health officials became worried about the effects of industrial work on women's reproductive capacity and thus on future generations. Reformers used the women-as-weaker-sex argument to promote protective legislation for women. The most progressive also hoped that, since so many women were integrated into a factory work force, if an employer was forced to reduce working hours for women employees, he would have to reduce the hours for all employees in a plant. Some of the outcry, however, was based on questionable medical evidence that women were weaker and more subject to illness than men.

The women's movement of recent decades has renewed concern with the health hazards of many jobs, from the chemicals used in making computer chips to the dangers to the eyes, muscles, and reproductive system of working at computers themselves (see pp. 330–32).

Sadie is an intelligent, neat, clean girl, who has worked from the time she got her working papers in embroidery factories. She was a stamper and for several years before she was poisoned, earned $10 a week. In her work she was accustomed to use a white powder (chalk or talcum was usual) which was brushed over the perforated designs and thus transferred to the cloth. The design was easily brushed off when made of chalk or of talcum, if the embroiderers were not careful. Her last employer therefore commenced using white lead powder, mixed with rosin, which cheapened the work as the powder could not be rubbed off and necessitate restamping.

None of the girls knew of the change in powder, nor of the danger in its use. The workroom was crowded and hot, the stampers' tables were farthest from the windows and the constant use of the powder caused them to breathe it continually and their hands were always covered with it.

Sadie had been a very strong, healthy girl, good appetite and color; she began to be unable to eat, had terrible colic, but continued to go to work in spite of the fact that she felt miserable. Her hands and feet swelled, she lost the use of one hand, her teeth and gums were blue. When she finally had to stop work, after being treated for months, for stomach trouble, her physician advised her to go to a hospital. There the examination revealed the fact that she had lead poisoning—which was unaccountable as no one knew that her work had involved the use of lead until some one who had been on the job also recalled hearing the manager send a messenger out with money several times to buy a white lead powder.

Sadie was sick in the hospital for six months (losing $10 per week). She said her employer bought off several of her witnesses, but before the case came to trial two years later several of them also became ill and consequently decided to testify for her. The employer appealed to the girl's feelings and induced her, on the day of the trial, to accept $150. He said that he had had business reverses and consequently would be unable to pay in case she won.

Her lawyer was suing for $10,000. At the present time the girl is 23 years old and though she has apparently good health, she is no longer strong and is very susceptible to disease.

The Tradition of Struggle

POPULIST WOMEN'S PERSPECTIVE ————————————

In the 1890s, a massive rural-based reform movement—populism—struggled against the power of big capital, particularly banks and railroads, to squeeze small farmers. At its peak, populist third-party candidates were quite successful, polling over a million votes in 1892. Populist women enunciated a distinctive approach to issues of women's work. They insisted on recognition of and respect for the exhausting labor of farm women while also sharply criticizing farm men, in some ways more militantly than did urban women in radical movements. They particularly resented the uneven distribution of the benefits of technology—men's work becoming mechanized while women's remained preindustrial. These articles by Frances Garside are from the Farmer's Wife, *published in Kansas, which was a stronghold of women's populist, socialist, suffrage, temperance, and peace activism.*

We are grateful to Ellen Baker for this selection.

SEPTEMBER 1891:

With the beginning of harvest comes the hardest time of the whole year for women folks on the farm. When the heads of wheat begin to turn brown, the housewives bestir themselves to lay in large stores of supplies to cook for harvest hands, and to try to secure help in the kitchen during the busy season.

Improved machinery for reaping grain lessens the number of hands required for harvesting, and the steam thresher increases the amount required at threshing time, but compensates somewhat by shortening the time of their stay. Threshers are looked upon as a sort of plague, or necessary evil and the common enemy of woman kind. They drop in unexpectedly before breakfast or just after supper, and always at dinner. The unsuspecting family may be taking a quiet breakfast when eight or ten men will walk in, wash their faces and sit down to the table. The horrified housekeeper knows full well that this means twenty men for dinner and for every meal until the great wheat stacks are exhausted which takes sometimes two or three weeks.

New machinery has done much to lighten and lessen the work of men on the farm—riding plows, patent drills, self binders, headers and steam threshers all tend to do this; but machinery has as yet wrought but little benefit to farmers' wives. Dishwashing, cooking, scrubbing and ironing, like perpetual motion, seem to be beyond the skill of inventors. Women's work on the farm is constant, unceasing toil—a never-ending, recurring round of duties, "world without end." All the hard work consequent upon the harvest, which is mostly cooking, has to be done in hot weather, the hardest time of the whole year to do this kind if work, and also at a time when it is next to impossible to obtain help for the kitchen. Many a farmer's wife with a babe lying in the crib and two or three small children to be cared for, patiently gets through the herculean task all alone, except such help as the men folks can give morning and evening. The farmers' wives are not merely "help-meets" in subduing the wilds of this western country, but have done their full share of solid, hard work as *equal partners*; and if there is a credit balance on either side, it is in favor of the women.

The women on the farms are intelligent as a class. They work, and read and think. They devote what leisure time they have to reading, instead of fashionable dress and society calls. Consequently they are well informed on the leading topics of the day; and many a woman now living on a Kansas farm, in her girlhood attended the best schools in the east. Yet these women are disfranchised. The legislature of Kansas passed a law called the "Municipal Suffrage Law," which granted to women living in cities the right to vote for municipal offices, but neglected to provide any privileges for this great army of women who reside in the country; and if in the campaign of 1890 the farmer women massed their strength and energy to elect the candidates on the People's ticket, no one can blame them. It spoke well for their political sagacity and excellent knowledge of "ways and means."

JANUARY 1893:

The women who live in cities can form no estimate of the work done day after day by the farmer's wife on the frontier. . . .

Nowhere is a man so completely lord and master as on the farm. His mother was a farmer's wife and lighted the fires, his wife shall do the same. While the kettle is boiling she does the milking. . . . The milk is carried into the cellar in great heavy pails that would try a man's strength, and she returns to the work of getting breakfast. During the process of the meal she cannot sit back and eat and rest, as many do, but is kept jumping up and down waiting on the men folks and children. It is often a question . . . if she ever gets a chance to eat at all. Then the children are to be started off to school, and though the credit of their education falls to the father it is the mother who does extra work that they may go, and who pulls them out of bed and starts them off in time every morning.

[A detailed description of the rest of the day's work follows.]

It is seldom that a farmer feels that he can afford to hire help in the kitchen. To brighten the dreariness of her life [the farmer's wife] has close to the seldom opened front door a bed of half starved looking flowers—old

fashioned coxcomb, four-o'clocks, grass pinks and a few other cheerful looking plants that will thrive under neglect. She makes everything that her family wears except hats and shoes. She has no time to think of rest or self.

It is in most cases her lot to welcome a new baby every other year, and
the only time when help is employed to assist her is for a period of two or
three weeks when the little stranger arrives. The births of the babies are about
all that vary the monotony of her life. Occasionally death calls and takes
from her tired arms a little life and leaves in its place an added pain in her
heart. She is old and tired out at thirty.

When her daughters reach the age at which they could assist her the
dreary prospect of a frontier life appalls them, and they seek employment in
town. . . . Late at night, when all the members of the family are in bed, a
light will shine out across the prairie from the family living room. It is by
this light the farmer's wife is doing her mending and sewing, and it will shine
out long after the occasional travel that way has stopped and no one but
the one that blows it out knows at what hour the patient burden bearer's
labors cease.

THE AFL VIEW

*The leadership of the unions making up the American Federation of Labor
believed that women should stay at home. The AFL's newspaper continually
condemned the employment of women in industry. Most AFL unions prohibited women members. As one leader summed up their position: "Keep women
out of the trade, and if not, out of the union."*

*Under pressure from women, the AFL appointed Mary E. Kenny as an
organizer in 1892, but when her term expired she was not rehired or replaced.
Between 1903 and 1923, a period of great expansion in women's employment,
the AFL hired only thirty women organizers, most of them for very brief periods of time.*

*The following views of Edward O'Donnell, the secretary of the Boston Cen-
tral Labor Union, are typical of the AFL hostility to working women. It is
interesting to note that he uses Victorian arguments and language identical
with those employed by elite conservatives in the nineteenth century—referring to women's "nature" and the sanctity of the home.*

The invasion of the crafts by women has been developing for years amid
irritation and injury to the workman. The right of the woman to win honest
bread is accorded on all sides, but with craftsmen it is an open question
whether this manifestation is of a healthy social growth or not.

The rapid displacement of men by women in the factory and workshop has to be met sooner or later, and the question is forcing itself upon the leaders and thinkers among the labor organizations of the land.

Is it a pleasing indication of progress to see the father, the brother and the son displaced as the bread winner by the mother, sister and daughter?

Is not this evolutionary backslide, which certainly modernizes the present wage system in vogue, a menace to prosperity—a foe to our civilized pretensions? . . .

The growing demand for female labor is not founded upon philanthropy, as those who encourage it would have sentimentalists believe; it does not spring from the milk of human kindness. It is an insidious assault upon the home; it is the knife of the assassin, aimed at the family circle—the divine injunction. It debars the man through financial embarrassment from family responsibility, and physically, mentally and socially excludes the woman equally from nature's dearest impulse. Is this the demand of civilized progress; is it the desire of Christian dogma? . . .

Capital thrives not upon the peaceful, united, contented family circle; rather are its palaces, pleasures and vices fostered and increased upon the disruption, ruin or abolition of the home, because with its decay and ever glaring privation, manhood loses its dignity, its backbone, its aspirations. . . .

To combat these impertinent inclinations, dangerous to the few, the old and well-tried policy of divide and conquer is invoked, and to our own shame, it must be said, one too often renders blind aid to capital in its warfare upon us. The employer in the magnanimity of his generosity will give employment to the daughter, while her two brothers are weary because of their daily tramp in quest of work. The father, who has a fair, steady job, sees not the infamous policy back of the flattering propositions. Somebody else's daughter is called in in the same manner, by and by, and very soon the shop or factory are full of women, while their fathers have the option of working for the same wages or a few cents more, or take their places in the large army of unemployed. . . .

College professors and graduates tell us that this is the natural sequence of industrial development, an integral part of economic claim.

Never was a greater fallacy uttered of more poisonous import. It is false and wholly illogical. The great demand for women and their preference over men does not spring from a desire to elevate humanity; at any rate that is not its trend.

The wholesale employment of women in the various handicrafts must gradually unsex them, as it most assuredly is demoralizing them, or stripping them of that modest demeanor that lends a charm to their kind, while it numerically strengthens the multitudinous army of loafers, paupers, tramps and policemen, for no man who desires honest employment, and can secure it, cares to throw his life away upon such a wretched occupation as the latter.

The employment of women in the mechanical departments is encouraged because of its cheapness and easy manipulation, regardless of the consequent perils; and for no other reason. The generous sentiment enveloping this inducement is of criminal design, since it comes from a thirst to build riches upon the dismemberment of the family or the hearthstone cruelly dishonored. . . .

But somebody will say, would you have women pursue lives of shame rather than work? Certainly not; it is to the alarming introduction of women into the mechanical industries, hitherto enjoyed by the sterner sex, at a wage uncommandable by them, that leads so many into that deplorable pursuit. . . .

THE TRADE UNION WOMEN'S PERSPECTIVE

The Women's Trade Union League, organized in 1903 and influential throughout this period, brought together working-class and more privileged women to fight for better conditions for working women and to train working-class women for leadership. In the process, WTUL women came to understand better the obstacles preventing women from organizing and assuming leadership. Alice Henry (1857–1943), an Australian journalist who came to the United States in 1906, was influenced by a stop at Hull-House and became the editor of the WTUL journal Life and Labor *(from which "The Night Shift" and "A Union Home for Working Women" in this section were taken). She returned to Australia off and on, where she participated in campaigns for civil rights for aboriginal peoples.*

The commonest complaint of all is that women members of a trade union do not attend their meetings. It is indeed a very serious difficulty to cope with, and the reasons for this poor attendance and want of interest in union affairs have to be fairly faced.

At first glance it seems curious that the meetings of a mixed local composed of both men and girls, should have for the girls even less attraction than meetings of their own sex only. But so it is. A business meeting of a local affords none of the lively social intercourse of a gathering for pleasure or even of a class for instruction. The men, mostly the older men, run the meeting and often are the meeting. Their influence may be out of all proportion to their numbers. It is they who decide the place where the local shall meet and the hour at which members shall assemble. The place is therefore often over a saloon, to which many girls naturally and rightly object. Sometimes it is even in a disreputable district. The girls may prefer that the meeting should begin shortly after closing time so that they do not need to go home and return, or have to loiter about for two or three hours. They like meetings to be over early. The men mostly name eight o'clock as the time of beginning, but business very often will not start much before nine. Then, too, the men feel that they have come together to talk, and talk they do while they allow the real business to drag. Of course, the girls are not interested in long discussions on matters they do not understand and in which they have no part and naturally they stay away, and so make matters worse, for the men feel they are doing their best for the interests of the union, resent the women's indifference, and are more sure than ever that women do not make good unionists.

Among the remedies proposed for this unsatisfactory state of affairs is compulsory attendance at a certain number of meetings per year under penalty of a fine or even losing of the card. (A very drastic measure this last and risky, unless the trade has the closed shop.)

Where the conditions of the trade permit it by far the best plan is to have the women organized in separate locals. The meetings of women and girls only draw better attendances, give far more opportunity for all the members to take part in the business, and beyond all question form the finest training ground for the women leaders who in considerable numbers are needed so badly in the woman's side of the trade-union movement today.

Those trade-union women who advocate mixed locals for every trade which embraces both men and women are of two types. Some are mature, perhaps elderly women, who have been trade unionists all their lives, who have grown up in the same locals with men, who have in the long years passed through and left behind their period of probation and training, and to whose presence and active cooperation the men have become accustomed. These women are able to express their views in public, can put or discuss a motion or take the chair as readily as their brothers. The other type is represented by those individual women or girls in whom exceptional ability takes the place of experience, and who appreciate the educational advantages of working along with experienced trade-union leaders. I have in my mind at this moment one girl over whose face comes all the rapture of the keen student as she explains how much she has learnt from working with men in their meetings. She ardently advocates mixed locals for all. For the born captain the plea is sound. Always she is quick enough to profit by the men's experience, by their ways of managing conferences and balancing advantages and losses. . . .

But with the average girl today the plan does not work. The mixed local does not, as a general rule, offer the best training-class for new girl recruits, in which they may obtain their training in collective bargaining or cooperative effort. . . . Many of the discussions that go on are quite above the girls' heads. And even when a young girl has something to say and wishes to say it, want of practice and timidity often keep her silent. It is to be regretted, too, that some trade-union men are far from realizing either the girls' ends in their daily work or their difficulties in meetings, and lecture, reprove or bully, where they ought to listen and persuade.

The girls, as a rule, are not only happier in their own women's local, but they have the interest of running the meetings themselves. They choose their own hall and fix their own time of meeting. Their officers are of their own selecting and taken from among themselves. The rank and file, too, get the splendid training that is conferred when persons actually and not merely nominally work together for a common end. Their introduction to the great problems of labor is through their practical understanding and handling of those problems as they encounter them in the everyday difficulties of the shop and the factory and as dealt with when they come up before the union meeting or have to be settled in bargaining with an employer.

DOMESTIC SERVICE AS UPLIFT

Two civil rights strategies competed among black activists in this period, a dominant one associated with Booker T. Washington and a dissident perspective associated with W. E. B. Du Bois. Washington promoted self-help, vocational education, and perseverance in southern agriculture and handicrafts, thereby hoping that blacks would prove to whites that they were ready for political rights and would not threaten white power. Du Bois, in contrast, advocated integration, higher aspirations, and political and social confrontation with the white establishment. Among black women activists, these divisions were less sharp, partly because black women leaders were struggling against sexism as well as racism. Many women simultaneously promoted "uplift," self-help among their people, and protests against segregation and discrimination—for example, in education, housing, and employment. In this speech, Fannie Barrier Williams (1855–1944), a Chicago social welfare activist, believed that mere realism required black women to excel at domestic service, given their exclusion from other paid jobs, but on other occasions she pushed women to overcome these restrictions.

When domestic service becomes a profession, as it surely will, by the proper training of those who follow it, what will be the condition of colored girls who would participate in its benefits? It is now time to prepare ourselves to answer this question. In my opinion, the training for this new profession should be elevated to the dignity and importance of the training in mathematics and grammar and other academic studies. Our girls must be made to feel that there is no stepping down when they become professional house-keepers. The relative dignity, respectability, and honor of this profession should first be taught in our schools. As it is now, the young woman in school or college knows that if she enters domestic service, she loses the relationships that she has formed. But schools of domestic science cannot do it all. The everyday man and woman who make society must change their foolish notions as to what is the polite thing for a young woman do. The kind of stupidity that calls industrial education drudgery is the same kind of stupidity that looks upon the kitchen as a place for drudges. We must learn that the girl who cooks our meals and keeps our houses sweet and beautiful deserves just as high a place in our social economy as the girl who makes our gowns and hats, or the one who teaches our children. In what I have said on this particular phase of our industrial life, I do not wish to be understood as advocating the restriction of colored girls to house service, even when that service is elevated to the rank of a profession. My only plea is that we shall protect and respect our girls who honestly and intelligently enter this service, either from preference or necessity. . . .

There is still another consideration which suggests the importance to the colored people of taking the lead in helping to improve and elevate this service. Race prejudice is kept up and increased in thousands of instances by the incompetent and characterless women who are engaged in this work. While there are thousands of worthy and really noble women in domestic service who enjoy the confidence and affection of their employers, there is a large percentage of colored women who, by their general unworthiness, help to give the Negro race a bad name, for white people North and South are very apt to estimate the entire race from the standpoint of their own servant girls. When intelligence takes the place of ignorance, and good manners, efficiency, and self-respect take the place of shiftlessness and irresponsibility in American homes, one of the chief causes of race prejudice will be removed.

It should also be borne in mind that the colored girl who is trained in the arts of housekeeping is also better qualified for the high duties of wifehood and motherhood.

Let me say by the way of summary that I have dwelt mostly upon the opportunities of domestic service for the following reasons:—

1. It is the one field in which colored women meet with almost no opposition. It is ours almost by birthright.

2. The compensation for this service, in Northern communities at least, is higher than that paid for average clerkships in stores and offices.

3. The service is susceptible of almost unlimited improvement and elevation.

4. The nature of the work is largely what we make it.

5. White women of courage and large intelligence are lifting domestic service to a point where it will have the dignity of a profession, and colored women are in danger, through lack of foresight, of being relegated to the positions of scrub women and dishwashers.

6. The colored girl who has no taste or talent for school teaching, dressmaking, or manicuring is in danger of being wasted in idleness, unless we can make domestic service worthy of her ambition and pride.

7. There can be no feature of our race problem more important than the saving of our young women; we can perhaps excuse their vanities, but idleness is the mildew on the garment of character.

8. Education has no value to human society unless it can add importance and respectability to the things we find to do.

9. Though all the factories and offices close their doors at our approach, this will be no calamity if we are strong enough to so transform the work we must do that it shall become an object of envy and emulation to those who now deny us their industrial fellowship.

BOYCOTTS

Riots as a form of protest have been used repeatedly by poor people to obtain economic or political goals, and bread riots were a particularly female form. While rioters have often been viewed as an unorganized, irrational rabble, riots frequently had an internal logic and principled objective. Preindustrial people, not accustomed to inflation, had a strong sense of the "just price" of basic commodities and considered those who charged more to be criminals. Thus one of the functions of food riots was to mete out justice and punishment, not to loot.

Some such riots were actually an organized boycott, a premodern form of community pressure made more powerful when people worked and lived in close-knit neighborhoods. In 1902 Jewish immigrant women, led by a woman butcher, organized a boycott of kosher meat butchers who, they believed, were overcharging. The boycott, described here in newspaper articles, began on the Lower East Side of New York City and spread to Brooklyn, Newark, and Boston. The women punished the butchers by closing down their shops and destroying their meat by dousing it with kerosene; they demanded the setting of a reasonable price by a rabbi, their chosen arbitrator.

BROOKLYN MOB LOOTS
BUTCHER SHOPS

Rioters, Led by Women, Wreck a Dozen Stores Dance Around Bonfires of Oil-Drenched Meat Piled in the Street—Fierce Fight with the Police.

A mob of 1,000 people, with women in the lead, marched through the Jewish quarter of Williamsburg last evening, and wrecked half a dozen butcher shops. Men and women who were seen coming out of the shops with meat and chickens in their hands were attacked. In the throng of women leaders of the mob there were many who carried bottles of kerosene oil. . . .

During the march the crowd attacked the butcher stores, carried the meat they found there into the street, poured oil upon the heap, and set fire to it, while the men and women yelled their approval and danced about the bonfire. . . .

Butchers Appeal to Police for Protection

Practically all of the kosher butchers on the east side served notice yesterday on the Captains of the various police precincts that they intended to open their shops today and asked that the police protect them against any attacks that may be made by the women rioters who have been attacking the shops for selling meat, and the customers for buying meat, when a boycott was on against the prevailing high prices. . . .

During the day, however, a circular, printed in both Yiddish and English, was distributed, showing that the matter is by no means settled. The circular, signed by four of the association leaders, representing the committee of fifty, is as follows:

"Women, victory is near. Order and persistence will win the struggle against the butchers. Do not buy any meat. All the organizations fighting against the Jewish meat trust have now united under the name of the Allied Conference for Cheap Kosher Meat. Brave and honest men are now aiding the women. The conference has decided to help those butchers who will sell cheap kosher meat under the supervision of the rabbis and the conference. The trust must be downed. For the present do not by (sic) any meat. Patience will win the battle. Seek the sympathy for your cause of old and young. Respectfully, Dr. D. Blaustein, the Rev. I. Zinster, the Rev. P. Joches, Mrs. Shatzburg, and the committee of fifty. . . ."

"It is conservatively estimated that 50,000 Jewish families have been abstaining from the use of meat for over two weeks. The people feel very justly that they are being ground down, not only by the Beef Trust of the country, but also by the Jewish Beef Trust of the City, which has now as its ally the Retail Butchers' Association. The people realize the seriousness of the situation and are ready to fight the trust for months if necessary. . . ."

THE SHIRTWAIST UPRISING

The rapidly growing ready-to-wear garment industry was one of the largest employers of women in the United States in the period from 1890 to 1920; many worked in manufacturing blouses, then known as shirtwaists. The shirtwaist strikes of New York and Philadelphia during the winter of 1909–10 were the first large-scale women's strikes: 80 percent of the twenty to thirty thousand workers who participated were women. The strikes were long and bitter, with mass arrests and police brutality against picketers. Strikers received massive support from outsiders, particularly women organized by the Women's Trade Union League and the Socialist Party. WTUL support was especially crucial to the strike, organizing relief stations, providing bail and other legal services, arranging publicity and fund-raising.

The workers failed to win their key demand—union recognition. One of the worst problems in the strikes, and one of the main reasons for their failure, was that the male union leaders refused to support the women workers in their determination to hold out for all their demands. Many reformers also withdrew their support when the union leadership did, leaving the strikers alone. Another problem was a leadership dominated by Russian Jews, who were often scornful of the Italians and native-born Americans for what they believed was a lesser militancy.

Despite defeat on the union recognition demand, the strikes won important gains for working women and created a basis for the continuing struggle for unionization. The strikes were training grounds for many women who went on to become organizers and served as powerful proof that women could organize and fight effectively.

Helen Marot (1865–1940), author of this selection, was secretary of the Women's Trade Union League, a socialist, and a leader both in social research and in labor and educational reform.

. . . The shirtwaist-makers' "general strike" as it is called, followed an eleven years' attempt to organize the trade. The union had been unable during this time to affect to any appreciable extent the conditions of work. In its efforts during 1908–9 to maintain the union in the various shops and to prevent the discharge of members who were active union workers, it lost heavily. The effort resolved itself in 1909 into the establishment of the right to organize. The strike in the Triangle Waist Company turned on this issue. . . .

The company had undertaken to organize its employes into a club, with benefits attached. The good faith of the company as well as the working-out of the benefit was questioned by the workers. The scheme failed and the workers joined the waist-makers' union. One day without warning a few weeks later one hundred and fifty of the employes were dropped, the explanation being given by the employers that there was no work. The following day the company advertised for workers. In telling the story later they said that they had received an unexpected order, but admitted their refusal to re-employ the workers discharged the day previous. The union then declared a strike, or acknowledged a lockout, and picketing began.

The strike or lockout occurred out of the busy season, with a large supply at hand of workers unorganized and unemployed. Practical trade unionists believed that the manufacturers felt certain of success on account of their ability to draw to an unlimited extent from an unorganized labor market and to employ a guard sufficiently strong to prevent the strikers from reaching the workers with their appeals to join them. But the ninety girls and sixty men strikers were not practical; they were Russian Jews who saw in the lockout an attempt at oppression. . . . The men strikers were intimidated and lost heart, but the women carried on the picketing, suffering arrest and abuse from the police and the guards employed by the manufacturers. At the end of the third week they appealed to the women's trade union league to protect them, if they could, against false arrest. . . .

A brief inspection by the league of the action of the pickets, the police, the strike breakers and the workers in the factory showed that the pickets had been intimidated, that the attitude of the police was aggressive and that the guards employed by the firm were insolent. The league acted as complainant at police headquarters and cross-examined the arrested strikers; it served as witness for the strikers in the magistrates' court and became convinced of official prejudice in the police department against the strikers and a strong partisan attitude in favor of the manufacturers. The activity and interest of women, some of whom were plainly women of leisure, was curiously disconcerting to the manufacturers and every effort was used to divert them. At last a young woman prominent in public affairs in New York and a member of the [Women's Trade Union] league, was arrested while acting as volunteer picket. Here at last was "copy" for the press.

During the five weeks of the strike, previous to the publicity, the forty thousand waist makers employed in the several hundred shops in New York were with a few exceptions here and there unconscious of the struggle of their fellow workers in the Triangle. There was no means of communication among them, as the labor press reached comparatively few. . . .

The arrests of sympathizers aroused sufficient public interest for the press to continue the story for ten days, including in the reports the treatment of the strikers. This furnished the union its opportunity. It knew the temper of the workers and pushed the story still further through shop propaganda. After three weeks of newspaper publicity and shop propaganda the reports came back to the union that the workers were aroused. It was alarming to the friends of the union to see the confidence of the union officers before issuing the call to strike. Trade unionists reminded the officers that the history of general strikes in unorganized trades was the history of failure. They invariably answered with a smile of assurance, "Wait and see."

The call was issued Monday night, November 22nd, at a great mass meeting in Cooper Union addressed by the president of the American Federation of Labor. "I did not go to bed Monday night," said the secretary of the union; "our Executive Board was in session from midnight until six a.m. I left the meeting and went out to Broadway near Bleecker street. I shall never again see such a sight. Out of every shirtwaist factory, in answer to the call, the workers poured and the halls which had been engaged for them were quickly filled." In some of these halls the girls were buoyant, confident; in others there were girls who were frightened at what they had done. . . .

As nearly as can be estimated, thirty thousand workers answered the call, or seventy-five per cent of the trade. Of these six thousand were Russian men; two thousand Italian women; possibly one thousand American women and about twenty or twenty-one thousand Russian Jewish girls. The Italians throughout the strike were a constantly appearing and disappearing factor but the part played by the American girls was clearly defined.

The American girls who struck came out in sympathy for the "foreigners" who struck for a principle, but the former were not in sympathy with the principle; they did not want a union; they imagined that the conditions in the factories where the Russian and Italian girls worked were worse than their own. They are in the habit of thinking that the employers treat foreign girls with less consideration, and they are sorry for them. In striking they were self-conscious philanthropists. They were honestly disinterested and as genuinely sympathetic as were the women of leisure who later took an active part in helping the strike. They acknowledged no interests in common with the others, but if necessary they were prepared to sacrifice a week or two of work. Unfortunately the sacrifice required of them was greater than they had counted on. The "foreigners" regarded them as just fellow workers and insisted on their joining the union, in spite of their constant protestation, "We have no grievance; we only struck in sympathy." But the Russians failed to be grateful, took for granted a common cause and demanded that all shirtwaist makers, regardless of race or creed, continue the strike until they were recognized by the employers as a part of the union. This difference in attitude and understanding was a heavy strain on the generosity of the American girls. It is believed, however, that the latter would have been equal to what their fellow workers expected, if their meetings had been left to the guidance of American men and women who understood their prejudices. But the Russian men trusted no one entirely to impart the enthusiasm necessary for the cause. It was the daily, almost hourly, tutelage which the Russian men insisted on the American girls' accepting, rather than the prolongation of the strike beyond the time they had expected, that sent the American girls back as "scabs." There were several signs that the two or three weeks' experience as strikers was having its effect on them, and that with proper care this difficult group of workers might have been organized. For instance, "scab" had become an opprobrious term to them during their short strike period, and on returning to work they accepted the epithet from their fellow workers with great reluctance and even protestation. Their sense of superiority also had received a severe shock; they could never again be quite so confident that they did not in the nature of things belong to the labor group. . . .

The feature of the strike which was as noteworthy as the response of thirty thousand unorganized workers, was the unyielding and uncompromising temper of the strikers. This was due not to the influence of nationality, but to the dominant sex. The same temper displayed in the shirtwaist strike is found in other strikes of women, until we have now a trade-union truism, that "women make the best strikers." . . . Working women have been less ready than men to make the initial sacrifice that trade-union membership calls for, but when they reach the point of striking they give themselves as fully and as instinctively to the cause as they give themselves in their personal relationships. It is important, therefore, in following the action of the shirtwaist makers, to remember that eighty per cent were women, and women without trade-union experience.

When the shirtwaist strikers were gathered in separate groups, according to their factories, in almost every available hall on the East Side, the great majority of them received their first instruction in the principles of unionism and learned the necessity of organization in their own trade. The quick response of women to the new doctrine gave to the meetings a spirit of revival. Like new converts they accepted the new doctrine in its entirety and insisted to the last on the "closed shop." But it was not only the enthusiasm of the new converts which made them refuse to accept anything short of the closed shop. In embracing the idea of solidarity they realized their own weakness as individual bargainers. "How long," the one-week or two-weeks-old union girls said, "do you think we could keep what the employer says he will give us without the union? Just as soon as the busy season is over it would be the same as before." . . .

Important as were the specific demands, they were lightly regarded in comparison with the issue of a union shop.

Nothing can illustrate this better than the strikers' treatment of the arbitration proposal which was the outcome of a conference between their representatives and the employers. In December word came to the union secretary that the manufacturers would probably consider arbitration if the union was ready to submit its differences to a board. The officers made reply in the affirmative and communicated their action at once to the strikers. Many of the strikers had no idea what arbitration meant, but as it became clear to them they asked, some of them menacingly, "Do you mean to arbitrate the recognition of the union?" It took courage to answer these inexperienced unionists and uncompromising girls that arbitration would include the question of the union as well as other matters. The proposition was met with a storm of opposition. When the strikers at last discovered that all their representatives counseled arbitration, with great reluctance they gave way, but at no time was the body of strikers in favor of it. A few days later, when the arbitrators who represented them reported that the manufacturers on their side refused to arbitrate the question of the union, they resumed their strike with an apparent feeling of security and relief. Again later they showed the same uncompromising attitude when their representatives in the conference reported back that the manufacturers would concede important points in regard to wage and factory conditions, but would not recognize the union. The recommendations of the conference were rejected without reservation by the whole body.

The strikers at this time lost some of their sympathizers. . . .

It was after the new year that the endurance of the girls was put to the test. During the thirteen weeks benefits were paid out averaging less than $2 for each striker. Many of them refused to accept benefits, so that the married men could be paid more. The complaints of hardships came almost without exception from the men. Occasionally it was discovered that a girl was having one meal a day and even at times none at all.

In spite of being underfed and often thinly clad, the girls took upon themselves the duty of picketing, believing that the men would be more severely handled. Picketing is a physical and nervous strain under the best conditions, but it is the spirit of martyrdom that sends young girls of their own volition, often insufficiently clad and fed, to patrol the streets in mid-winter with the temperature low and with snow on the ground, some days freezing and some days melting. After two or three hours of such exposure, often ill from cold, they returned to headquarters, which were held for the majority in rooms dark and unheated, to await further orders.

It takes uncommon courage to endure such physical exposure, but these striking girls underwent as well the nervous strain of imminent arrest, the harsh treatment of the police, insults, threats and even actual assaults from the rough men who stood around the factory doors. During the thirteen weeks over six hundred girls were arrested; thirteen were sentenced to five days in the workhouse and several were detained a week or ten days in the Tombs.

The pickets, with strangely few exceptions, during the first few weeks showed remarkable self-control. They had been cautioned from the first hour of the strike to insist on their legal rights as pickets, but to give no excuse for arrest. Like all other instructions, they accepted this literally. They desired to be good soldiers and every nerve was strained to obey orders. But for many the provocations were too great and retaliation began after the fifth week. It occurred around the factories where the strikers were losing, where peaceful methods were failing and where the passivity of the pickets was taunted as cowardice. . . .

Before the strike every shop was "open" and in most of them there was not a union worker. In thirteen short weeks three hundred and twelve shops had been converted into "closed" or full union contract shops.

But the significance of the strike is not in the actual gain to the shirtwaist makers of three hundred union shops, for there was great weakness in the ranks of the opposition. Trade-union gains, moreover, are measured by what an organization can hold rather than by what it can immediately gain. The shirt-waist makers' strike was characteristic of all strikes in which women play an active part. It was marked by complete self-surrender to a cause, emotional endurance, fearlessness and entire willingness to face danger and suffering. The strike at times seemed to be an expression of the woman's movement rather than the labor movement. This phase was emphasized by the wide expression of sympathy which it drew from women outside the ranks of labor.

It was fortunate for strike purposes but otherwise unfortunate that the press, in publishing accounts of the strike, treated the active public expression of interest of a large body of women sympathizers with sensational snobbery. It was a matter of wide public comment that women of wealth should contribute sums of money to the strike, that they should admit factory girls to exclusive club rooms, and should hold mass meetings in their behalf. If, as was charged, any of the women who entered the strike did so from sensational or personal motives, they were disarmed when they came into contact with the strikers. Their earnestness of purpose, their complete abandon to their cause, their simple acceptance of outside interest and sympathy as though their cause were the cause of all, was a bid for kinship that broke down all barriers. Women who came to act as witnesses of the arrests around the factories ended by picketing side by side with the strikers. These volunteer pickets accepted, moreover, whatever rough treatment was offered, and when arrested, asked for no favors that were not given the strikers themselves.

The strike brought about adjustments in values as well as in relationships.

Before the strike was over federations of professional women and women of leisure were endorsing organization for working women, and individually these women were acknowledging the truth of such observations as that made by one of the strikers on her return from a visit to a private school where she had been invited to tell about the strike. Her story of the strike led to questions in regard to trade unions. On her return her comment was, "Oh they are lovely girls, they are so kind—but I didn't believe any girls could be so ignorant." . . .

LIFE IS CHEAP, PROPERTY IS SACRED

The working-class tradition encompasses defeats as well as victories. One tragic memory was that of the Triangle Shirtwaist Company fire in which 146 women (some estimates say 143, some 147) died on March 25, 1911. The fire was not an unforeseeable accident, but the result of criminal negligence on the part of the company. Triangle was an exceptionally antiunion firm, notorious for its terrible working conditions. The women and girls could not escape because the company had locked the doors to the stairs from the outside to prevent employee theft or escape; there were no fire extinguishers, and there was only one fire escape. It would have taken three hours to empty the building. The women were all dead within twenty minutes. Most of the bodies could never be identified, but were buried in numbered coffins.

The excerpt that follows comes from a speech by Rose Schneiderman (1882–1972), a socialist, feminist labor organizer, and social reformer who later worked for Franklin Roosevelt's New Deal. A working-class Jewish immigrant, she had been a working women since age thirteen. Here she is speaking at a meeting two months after the fire, called to demand better safety regulation. The meeting, held at the Metropolitan Opera House, attracted many upper- and middle-class reformers; and by the time Schneiderman rose to speak, she was irritated and exhausted by the platitudes mouthed by those who did not share the experience of working-class people.

I would be a traitor to these poor burned bodies if I came here to talk good fellowship. We have tried you good people of the public and we have found you wanting. The old Inquisition had its rack and its thumbscrews and its instruments of torture with iron teeth. We know what these things are today: the iron teeth are our necessities, the thumbscrews the high-powered and swift machinery close to which we must work, and the rack is here in the "fire-proof" structures that will destroy us the minute they catch on fire.

This is not the first time girls have been burned alive in the city. Each week I must learn of the untimely death of one of my sister workers. Every year thousands of us are maimed. The life of men and women is so cheap and property is so sacred. There are so many of us for one job it matters little if 143 of us are burned to death.

We tried you, citizens; we are trying you now, and you have a couple of dollars for the sorrowing mothers and daughters and sisters by way of a charity gift. But every time the workers come out in the only way they know to protest against conditions which are unbearable, the strong hand of the law is allowed to press down heavily upon us.

Public officials have only words of warning to us—warning that we must be intensely orderly and must be intensely peaceable, and they have the workhouse just back of all their warnings. The strong hand of the law beats us back when we rise into the conditions that make life bearable.

I can't talk fellowship to you who are gathered here. Too much blood has been spilled. I know from my experience it is up to the working people to save themselves. The only way they can save themselves is by a strong working-class movement.

ETHNIC UNITY

In 1912 Lawrence, Massachusetts, became the site of one of the most militant and massive strikes in U.S. history. A town of woolen mills employing thirty thousand, Lawrence was located in the center of New England's textile industry. The strike was of national significance to the labor and women's movements in several respects: first, it proved that unskilled workers of many different nationalities could unite; second, it developed the tactics of mass picketing; third, in an industry in which 50 percent of the workers were women, it showed that women could offer militance and leadership even when working alongside men. The strike popularized the song "Bread and Roses," which communicated the workers' desires for beauty and leisure as well as necessities.

The strike not only won the major demands of the workers but also set off a wave of strikes throughout the New England textile region. It was not a permanent victory, however. During the next year, employers launched a campaign to defeat the organization, using spies and immigrant scabs from Quebec, blacklisting the strike leaders, and propagandizing against the union through a "God and country" campaign with the help of a right-wing priest. Ultimately, the employers began to close down some of their mills.

This description of the Lawrence strike is from a manuscript written in 1954 by Elizabeth Gurley Flynn (1890–1964), an Irish-American labor orga-

nizer famed for her charismatic speaking, a founder of the American Civil Liberties Union who later became chairwoman of the Communist Party. Flynn was imprisoned several times for her radical principles. She was sent to Lawrence in 1912 by the Industrial Workers of the World, a revolutionary industrial union that opposed the conservative, craft-unionist AFL.

The strike broke with dramatic suddenness on January 11, 1912, the first payday of the year. A law reducing the hours of women and children under 18 from 56 hours a week to 54 had been passed by the Massachusetts legislature. It affected the majority of the employees. The employers had strongly resisted the passage of this law. Now they cut the pay proportionately in the first pay envelope. Wages were *already* at the starvation point. The highest paid weavers received $10.50 weekly. Spinners, carders, spoolers and others averaged $6 to $7 weekly. Whole families worked in the mills to eke out a bare existence. Pregnant women worked at the machines until a few hours before their babies were born. Sometimes a baby came right there in the mill, between the looms. The small pittance taken from the workers by the rich corporations, which were protected by a high tariff from foreign competition, was the spark that ignited the general strike. "Better to starve fighting than to starve working!" became their battle-cry. It spread from mill to mill. In a few hours of that cold, snowy day in January, 14,000 workers poured out of the mills. In a few days the mills were empty and still—and remained so for nearly three months.

It was estimated that there were at least 25 different nationalities in Lawrence. The largest groups among the strikers were: Italians, 7,000; Germans, 6,000; French Canadians, 5,000; all English speaking, 5,000; Poles, 2,500; Lithuanians, 2,000; Franco-Belgians, 1,100; Syrians, 1,000—with a sprinkling of Russians, Jews, Greeks, Letts and Turks. The local IWW became the organizing core of the strike. They were overwhelmed by the magnitude of the job they had on their hands and sent a telegram for help to Ettor in New York City. He and his friend, Arturo Giovannitti, responded to the call on the promise of Haywood, James P. Thompson, myself and others to come as soon as possible, which we did. Ettor and Giovannitti . . . organized mass meetings in various localities of the different language groups and had them elect a strike committee of men and women which represented every mill, every department and every nationality. They held meetings of all the strikers together on the Lawrence Common (New England's term for park or square), so that the workers could realize their oneness and strength. . . . There were 1,400 state militiamen in Lawrence, which was like an armed camp. Clashes occurred daily between the strikers and the police and state troopers.

The period of activity for Ettor and Giovannitti was cut short by their arrest on January 30, 1912. A tragedy on the picket line gave the authorities the excuse to get rid of Ettor and Giovannitti. In a fracas between police and pickets, a woman striker, Anna La Pizza, was killed. The two strike leaders, along with a striker, Joseph Caruso, were lodged in the county jail. Caruso, who had been on the picket line, was charged with murder, and the strike leaders were charged with being accessory to murder because of their speeches advocating picketing. It was the same theory of constructive conspiracy which had sent speakers at the Haymarket protest meeting in Chicago to their deaths on the gallows 25 years before. . . .

The militiamen were mostly native-born "white-collar" workers and professionals from other parts of the state who openly showed their contempt for the foreign-born strikers. Colonel Sweetzer, their commander, banned a mass funeral for Anna La Pizza. He ordered the militia *not* to salute the American flag when it was carried by strikers. His orders were "Shoot to kill. We are not looking for peace now." Many acts of brutal violence were committed by these arrogant youths on horseback, such as riding into crowds and clubbing the people on foot. When they marched afoot, they carried rifles with long bayonets. On the same day Ettor and Giovannitti were arrested, an 18 year-old Syrian boy striker, John Rami, was bayonetted through the lung, from the back, and died. In the course of the strike several persons were injured with bayonets. The orders were to strike the women on the arms and breasts and the men on the head. This was actually reported in a Boston paper. . . .

When Haywood came to Lawrence in February 1912 to assume the leadership of the textile strike it created a national sensation. . . . Haywood had been tried for murder five years before, due to his labor activities. . . . But the more he was attacked the more the strikers loved "Big Bill." The strike committee elected him its chairman in place of Ettor. . . .

Haywood introduced special meetings of women and children. It was amazing how this native-born American, who had worked primarily among English-speaking men, quickly adapted his way of speaking to the foreign-born, to the women and to the children. They all understood his down-to-earth language, which was a lesson to all of us. I was then 21 years old and I learned how to speak to workers from Bill Haywood in Lawrence, to use short words and short sentences, to repeat the same thought in different words if I saw that the audience did not understand. I learned never to reach for a three-syllable word if one or two would do. This is not vulgarizing. Words are tools and not everybody has access to a whole tool chest. The foreign-born usually learned English from their children who finished school after the lower grades. Many workers began to learn English during these strike meetings. . . . I have met many American workers who are highly intelligent, better thinkers by far than the average Congressman, but they are handicapped by their meager vocabularies from communicating their thoughts to others in speech and are even more limited in writing. . . .

Wherever Bill Haywood went, the workers followed him with glad greetings. They roared with laughter and applause when he said: "The AFL organizes like this!"—separating his fingers, as far apart as they would go, and naming them—"Weavers, loom-fixers, dyers, spinners." Then he would say: "The IWW organizes like this!"—tightly clenching his big fist, shaking it at the bosses. . . .

We held special meetings for the women at which Haywood and I spoke. The women worked in the mills for lower pay and in addition had all the housework and care of the children. The old-world attitude of man as the "lord and master" was strong. At the end of the day's work—or, now, of strike duty—the man went home and sat at ease while his wife did all the work preparing the meal, cleaning the house, etc. There was considerable male opposition to women going to meetings and marching on the picket line. We resolutely set out to combat these notions. The women wanted to picket. They were strikers as well as wives and were valiant fighters. We knew that to leave them at home alone, isolated from the strike activity, a prey to worry, affected by the complaints of tradespeople, landlords, priests and ministers, was dangerous to the strike. We brought several Socialist women in as speakers, and a girl organizer, Pearl McGill, who had helped organize the button workers of Muscatine, Iowa. The AFL revoked her credentials for coming to Lawrence. We did not attack their religious ideas in any way, but we said boldly that priests and ministers should stick to their religion and not interfere in a workers' struggle for better conditions, unless they wanted to help. We pointed out that if the workers had more money they would spend it in Lawrence—even put more in the church collections. The women laughed and told it to the priests and ministers the next Sunday.

We talked especially to the women about the high cost of living here— how they had been fooled when they first came here when they figured the dollars in their home money. They thought they were rich till they had to pay rent, buy groceries, clothes and shoes. Then they knew they were poor. We pointed out that the mill owners did not live in Lawrence. They did not spend their money in the local stores. All that the businessmen received came from the workers. If the workers get more, they will get more. The women conveyed these ideas to the small shopkeepers with emphasis and we heard no more protest from them about the strike after that. . . .

The IWW was held up to scorn by John Golden, head of the United Textile Workers of America, because "it had only 287 members there" when the strike began. He had made no attempt to organize and defend the foreign workers against the wage cut of January 11, 1912. In fact, he had ordered the skilled workers to stay at work. . . . But Golden had not been able to hold the highly skilled weavers and loom-fixers in the mills. . . . They could not work alone even if they had wanted to, and they did not want to do so.

We talked to the strikers about One Big Union, regardless of skill or lack of it, foreign-born or native-born, color, religion or sex. We showed how all differences are used by the bosses to keep workers divided and pitted against each other. . . . This was more than a union. It was a crusade for a united people—for "Bread and Roses." . . .

Our concepts as to how socialism would come about, were syndicalist to the core. There would be a general strike, the workers would lock out the bosses, take possession of the industries and declare the abolition of the capitalist system. It sounded very simple. Our attitude toward the state was sort of Thoreau-like—the right to ignore the state, civil disobedience to a bosses' state. For instance, Bill Haywood threatened to burn the books of the strike committee rather than turn them over to an investigation committee. He was arrested for contempt of court. However much or little the workers absorbed our syndicalist philosophy, they cheered Bill's defiance to the skies. . . .

We spoke of their power, as workers, as the producers of all wealth, as the creators of profit. Here they could see it in Lawrence. Down tools, fold arms, stop the machinery, and production is dead—profits no longer flow. We ridiculed the police and militia in this situation. "Can they weave cloth with soldiers' bayonets or policemen's clubs?" we asked. "No," replied the confident workers. "Did they dig coal with bayonets in the miners' strikes or make steel or run trains with bayonets?" Again the crowds roared "No." We talked Marxism as we understood it—the class struggle, the exploitation of labor, the use of the state and armed forces of government against the workers. It was all there in Lawrence before our eyes. We did not need to go far for the lessons. . . .

The children's meetings, at which Haywood and I spoke, showed us mainly that there were two groups of workers' children in Lawrence, those who went to school and those who worked in the mills. The efforts of the church and schools were directed to driving a wedge between the school children and their striking parents. Often children in such towns become ashamed of their foreign-born foreign-speaking parents, their old-country ways, their accents, their foreign newspapers, and even their strike and mass picketing. The up-to-date, well-dressed native-born teachers set a pattern. The working-class women were shabbily dressed, though they made the finest of woolen fabrics. . . . Some teachers called the strikers lazy, said they should go back to work or "back where they came from." We attempted to counteract all this at our children's meetings. . . . The parents were pathetically grateful to us as their children began to show real respect for them and their struggles. . . .

Suffering increased among the strikers. They had no financial reserves. They needed fuel and food. Their houses, dilapidated woodframe barracks, were hard to heat. Committees of strikers went to other cities to appeal for support. Labor unions, Socialist locals, and workers in Boston, Manchester,

Nashua, Haverhill and other places responded generously. Eleven soup kitchens were opened. The workers of Lowell, a nearby textile town, led a cow garlanded with leaves, to the strikers of Lawrence. I felt sorry for her with her festive appearance and her mild eyes. But she had to be slaughtered to feed hungry children. Her head was mounted and hung up in the Franco-Belgian Hall. . . .

A proposal was made by some of the strikers that we adopt a method used successfully in Europe—to send the children out of Lawrence to be cared for in other cities. The parents accepted the idea and the children were wild to go. On February 17, 1912, the first group of 150 children were taken to New York City. A small group also left for Barre, Vermont. A New York committee, headed by Mrs. Margaret Sanger, then a trained nurse and chairman of the Women's Committee of the Socialist Party, came to Lawrence to escort them. . . . Five thousand people met them at Grand Central Station.

On February 24, 1912, a group of 40 strikers' children were to go from Lawrence to Philadelphia. . . . At the railroad station in Lawrence, where the children were assembled accompanied by their fathers and mothers, just as they were ready to board the train they were surrounded by police. Troopers surrounded the station outside to keep others out. Children were clubbed and torn away from their parents and a wild scene of brutal disorder took place. Thirty-five frantic women and children were arrested, thrown screaming and fighting into patrol wagons. They were beaten into submission and taken to the police station. There the women were charged with "neglect" and improper guardianship and ten frightened children were taken to the Lawrence Poor Farm. The police station was besieged by enraged strikers. Members of the Philadelphia committee were arrested and fined. It was a day without parallel in American labor history. A reign of terror prevailed in Lawrence, which literally shook America. . . . Famous newspaper reporters and writers flocked to Lawrence. . . .

At the insistent demand of Socialist Congressman Victor Berger of Milwaukee the House Rules Committee held a hearing in Washington, D.C. in March 1912. . . . More than 50 striker witnesses came from Lawrence to tell their stories and show their pay envelopes. The cause of the strike, extent of their poverty, the conditions of their lives, the violence of the authorities, were all revealed by them to the American people in this Congressional hearing. . . . There was no more interference with the children leaving Lawrence after that. . . .

On March 1, 1912, the American Woolen Company announced a 7.5 per cent [wage] increase in 33 cities. On March 6, 125,000 workers in cotton and woolen mills of six states were raised 5 to 7 per cent. On March 14, the Lawrence strike was settled with the American Woolen Company, the Atlantic Mill and other main mills. Twenty thousand workers assembled on the Common to hear the report of their committee. It was the first time in six weeks they were allowed to use the Common. Haywood presided at the meeting and introduced the delegates of all the nationalities. The demands which they had won secured an increase in wages from five to 20 per cent; increased compensation for overtime; the reduction of the premium period from four weeks to two weeks and no discrimination against any worker who had taken part in the strike. . . . The Arbitration Committee promised to help get Ettor and Giovannitti speedily released. The workers pledged to strike again if they were not freed. They had wrested millions from their employers. Yet their leaders, Ettor and Giovannitti, were still in danger of death, so they did not go back to work happy.

A UNION HOME FOR WORKING WOMEN ————————

Unions are usually associated with demands for more money and shorter hours. But this has not always been true, especially for women, who have frequently fought for "roses" as well as "bread." In this selection, waitresses have succeeded in fulfilling their dream of a women's home. This priority—in a direct line with the petition for a working women's home in 1869 (see pp. 120–23)—shows the fallacy of assuming that all women live in families and illustrates the continuity of women's responsibility for caretaking. Moreover, finding a decent and safe place to live was one of the major problems facing single working women who migrated into the cities leaving families behind in small towns or the countryside.

Out in one of the fine residence districts of Seattle, with a magnificent view of lake and mountains, stands a handsome house that has the distinction of being the only Waitresses' Recreation Home in the United States.

It is the property of Waitresses' Union Local 240 of Seattle, and what it means to the girls of the union, only they can really know. The story of its acquisition is almost like a fairy tale.

The Union was organized March 23, 1900.

"It was the first of its kind to form as a girls' local," says Miss Alice M. Lord, secretary-treasurer of the union. "A good many people thought an organization run by girls would not last long. But you see, the girls belong to a race whose forefathers fought for the liberty of humanity in 1861–65, and they are fighters too,—this time for the liberty of the wage-earner.

At the time of the organization we were working eleven and twelve hours a day, seven days a week, for five dollars. One or two of the restaurants paid seven dollars a week. The first step forward was to shorten our hours of labor and increase our salary. We asked and got a ten-hour day, with a salary of eight dollars and a half a week. Some of the proprietors paid nine dollars. The union waitresses in Seattle had secured a ten-hour day a year before the state law went into effect. But we still had to work seven days a week while other workers enjoyed one day of rest out of the seven. The next thing we did was to change this, so that by furnishing a substitute we can have one day of rest and recreation.

It wasn't long before the thought occurred to us, 'Why should women be compelled to work longer hours than the state says its employees shall work?' And it was then that the idea was conceived of asking the legislature to grant an eight-hour day to women workers. It was the Waitresses' Union that started the ball rolling and kept it rolling until its size fairly scared our law-makers; and the women got their eight-hour day. The law, after failing in three successive legislatures, was passed at the fourth attempt, in 1911, and has since been upheld by the Supreme Court. . . .

But as to the home. For four years it has been the dream of the girls to have a home of their own, where sick sisters, not in such a condition as to need hospital care, could recover in comfort, where vacations could be spent, and where the social and home life that girls must have if they are to remain mentally, morally or physically healthy, could center.

For four years they worked and saved and gave dances and entertainments with this vision before them. A lot was bought, and their exertions were redoubled, to earn the money for the house. . . .

It was on April 8, 1913, that the deed was presented. . . . Not the least of the pleasure they have had out of it has been the furnishing. They had the money they had earned to build with, and with this and the kindly gifts of friends and comrades of other unions, who seemed only to have been waiting for a signal to join in seeing how much they could do to help. . . . It is comfortably filled all the time. Ailing girls are taken care of there, restful "days off" are spent there, modest little luncheons and parties are given there and from its homelike atmosphere the girls go back to their work with fresh strength and courage.

WAGES FOR HOUSEWORK

In this period, many working-class organizations and individuals became socialist. In fact, the Socialist Party was a significant third party during these years, commanding support from many middle-class as well as working-class progressives, running in national and local elections, and winning control of a number of big-city governments, such as Milwaukee, Schenectady, Toledo, and Dayton. In 1912 the Socialist Party candidate for president, Eugene

Debs, drew 6 percent of the vote. Most socialist leaders, like those of all the other parties, were male and did not consider women's issues important— although the socialists were the first major party to endorse woman suffrage.

Nevertheless, a strong socialist-feminist theory and practice developed. Women struggled in many Socialist Party locals for such issues as birth control, access to jobs and education, and women's equality in the workplace, the union, and the political arena. One of their more radical ideas, revived in the women's movement of the 1970s, was wages for housework—a campaign to respect and compensate women for their unpaid domestic labor. This wages-for-housework statement was written in 1913 by Josephine Conger-Kaneko from Missouri, a columnist in a socialist newspaper; with the help of her husband, prominent Japanese socialist Kiichi Kaneko, she founded the socialist women's paper (called first Socialist Woman *and later* Progressive Woman*), from which this selection is taken.*

Does a woman support her husband's employer?

Has anybody ever thought about a woman's part in her husband's contract for his wages?

Has anybody ever thought that when a man gets married he DOESN'T RECEIVE A PENNY MORE FOR HIS WORK THAN WHEN HE WAS SINGLE, AND THAT THEN HE GOT BARELY ENOUGH TO BOARD AND CLOTHE HIMSELF?

Evidently nobody has thought much about these things. And least of all the woman herself. So, let us see about it.

And you, madam, must see about it with us. It means something to you. It might mean that you are to have a new voile dress next spring, instead of making over that old thing again that you were married in ten years ago.

For that is just what it amounts to—your husband's employer getting the dimes and dollars that should be yours for a new dress and the other things you need so much to lead a normal, happy life.

Here is the situation. Your husband works eight or ten hours a day, and receives a cash return for his work. You work twelve or fifteen hours a day, AND NEVER SEE A CASH RETURN FOR YOUR WORK.

Your husband works to produce saleable goods for the man who employs him. YOU WORK TO KEEP A HOME AND FEED YOUR HUSBAND SO THAT HE CAN KEEP ON WORKING TO PRODUCE SALEABLE GOODS FOR THE MAN WHO EMPLOYS HIM.

Your husband, working for his employer, produces in a year, say $2,500 (the U.S. census statistics say the average worker produces this much in a year) and he gets back in wages $500 (census statistics also say that a man's average wage a year is $500).

Now, YOU make a home for your husband, cook his meals, wash his clothes and mend them; in fact, you keep him in trim and working order so he can produce $2,500 a year for his employer. Your husband gets back from what he makes $500.

WHAT DO YOU GET?

If you hired out to families to do the washing alone, you would get $2 a day and your car fare and lunch. If you went from family to family six days in the week, washing for them, you would get six free lunches and $12.

Working this way, your work is from 8 in the morning till 5 in the afternoon. After you are through with your work you have the evening to yourself, and $2 in your pocket.

When you work to keep your husband in good order for his employer you don't get through at 5 o'clock, and you don't have your evening for yourself. Nor do you have $2 in your purse at the end of the day.

No. Not exactly.

You work ALL HOURS, at BOARD WAGES. That is, you get a part of the food you cook, and live in the house you keep, and you can have a dress occasionally that you make, FOR WORKING ENDLESS HOURS THAT YOUR HUSBAND MAY BE AN EFFICIENT WORKER FOR HIS EMPLOYER.

And what does your husband's employer get out of it? Taking the U.S. census as a guide, he gets on the average $2,000 out of your husband's work. The employer gets $2,000, your husband gets $500, and YOU GET SOME OF THE FOOD YOU COOK, AND THE RIGHT TO LIVE IN THE HOUSE YOU KEEP.

It is a very nice arrangement—for the employer. Not so very nice for the husband, AND A SLAVE'S LIFE FOR YOU.

But a man needn't get married, some one says. The employer doesn't demand that he be married.

Oh, yes, workingmen have to get married. Not the individual man here and there, perhaps. But the masses of them. That is an undisputable fact, and we would not drag it into this except that some very short-sighted person will raise the question, and think he has shattered to star-dust our contention that a woman supports her husband's employer, by saying that A WORKINGMAN NEEDN'T GET MARRIED.

If he DOESN'T MARRY, whose children are going to do the world's work in the future? Not the employer's children. On the contrary, the employer WANTS his employes to marry, and raise up children to work for his heirs when THEY are grown.

So it is an indisputable fact that the workingman must get married. BUT IS IT AN ABSOLUTELY ESSENTIAL FACT THAT THE WOMAN MUST BE THE GOAT AND BEAR THE HARDEST, TOUGHEST, MOST SLAVISH END OF THE DEAL?

THAT IS WHAT SHE IS DOING TODAY!

When a man gets married, does he go to his employer and say: Now, Mr.

Employer, I am going to take a partner to help me live as a decent man should live, and so increase my efficiency for my work with you. For her part in our three-cornered deal I think you had better allow me so-and-so.

Does Mr. Young-Man-About-to-Be-Married say that? No, he doesn't. If the boss hears that he is to be married he may unbend his dignity enough to say: "Well, Bill, old man, I hear you are going to hook up with a mighty nice girl. That's right. Every honest fellow should settle down and raise a family." And Bill—well, he just grins. That's all. It's real pathetic, that grin of Bill's. It stands so often for inefficiency. He just don't know what else to do. So when the boss unbends enough to "congratulate" him on the greatest event of his life he grins and feels that a great favor has been bestowed upon him.

But the new little wife! Heaven help her. Bill's grin won't coin into dollars; won't buy new dresses; won't buy baby clothes; won't pay the doctor's bill; won't hire any of the back-breaking work of the house done. The little wife has somehow got to manage to attend to all of these things herself, or go without. And keep Bill going besides, so he can produce saleable goods for the boss.

It's pathetic, but the wives have got to get at the problem themselves. The Bills DON'T KNOW HOW. Their ignorance and stupidity in some things is appalling.

So, next time your husband comes home with $10 in his pocket when he should have $20, ask him where YOUR share is. And don't be put off with the silly answer that you are getting your room and board out of HIS $10 for your share. Tell him you can go out and work by the week and bring home $12, AND YOU WANT TO KNOW WHAT IS GOING TO BE YOUR END OF THE DEAL BETWEEN HIM AND HIS EMPLOYER.

Time was when a man gave his slave men their board and clothes, AND GAVE THE WIVES OF THE SLAVE MEN THEIR BOARD AND CLOTHES ALSO. Today a wage slave gets the equivalent of HIS board and clothes in wages—and the wife of the wage slave gets nothing.

The employer thus gets off a whole lot easier than he did when he owned slaves and was responsible for the physical welfare of the whole family.

THE UNPAID AND GROSSLY EXPLOITED LABOR OF MARRIED WOMEN IN THEIR HOMES MAKES IT POSSIBLE FOR THE EMPLOYER TO PILE-UP IMMENSE PROFITS OUT OF HIS BUSINESS, WHICH, OF COURSE, IS HIGHLY SATISFACTORY TO HIM.

But is it to you, O Woman, who must pay the price?

BIRTH CONTROL

Margaret Sanger, the woman whose name is most associated with birth con-
trol, began her work as a nurse among poor immigrants. She wrote on birth
control, venereal disease, and other women's health problems for the New
York Call, *a socialist paper, until her articles were censored for being*
"obscene." She saw birth control as a means of self-determination particularly
important to the poor. In the years 1914 to 1919, birth control leagues sprang
up throughout the United States, supported primarily by radical women.
These selections come from letters to Sanger from women asking for birth con-
trol information.

Please tell me what to do to keep from having any more babies. I am only
twenty-six years old and the mother of five children the oldest eight years
and the others six, four and two, and I have four living. The last time I had
a six month's miscarriage and I have been weak ever since. It happened this
past August. My husband is gone to try to find work and I have to support
my children myself. I have to work so hard until I feel like it would kill me
to give birth to another. I am nervous. My back and side give me a lot of
trouble. I am not able to give my children the attention that I desire. I take
in washing to support my children, I suffered this last time from the time I
got that way until I lost it and am yet weak in my back. Please! for my sake
tell me what to do to keep from having another. I don't want another child.
Five is enough for me.

I don't care to bear any more children for the man I got he is most all the
time drunk and not working and gone for days and nights and leave me alone
most of the time. I'm sewing for support me and my baby that is two years
old and one dead born so I know you don't blame me for not wanting any
more children and he is always talking about leaving me he might as well
for what he is doing but I am worried that I may get in wrong.

I was married when I was seventeen and seven months. After nine months
married I had a miscarriage eight months. After fourteen months I had a
baby boy and he is living and is now seven years old. After three years I had
another boy. He was born with consumption in the bones and would shake
his head one side and another, but doctors did not know what that was. Now
I have them nervous spells myself. All through my marriage life I have been
working in factories. I took my children to the day nursery. Two months
before the birth of my last child my husband deserted me with my children.

He had left home eleven times before that but always came back, but that night his mother gave him money to go out of town. I was then married five years to him. After four years I could not get no trace of him I got the divorce. I had to work hard to keep my furniture and pay the rent as I did not want to go boarding. Now as I was twenty-six and as I had no one to depend on I married again. He is a good young man of twenty-five and he is not a lazy gambler like the other, but even with that I fear having any more children as they will not be healthy. We were married a few months ago and neither of us had any money and he is only a laborer and makes twenty-five dollars a week, so you see I have struggled with the first husband and I wish I will not struggle with this one, so please if you can help me.

WORKING WOMEN FOR SUFFRAGE

The woman suffrage movement was led by educated, prosperous women. But pro-suffrage views were widespread among working-class and poor women, and in the 1910s, Wage Earners Suffrage Leagues began to appear. A woman garment worker gave the following speech at a 1912 mass meeting criticizing antisuffrage legislators.

Mollie Schepps, Shirt Waist Maker, answers the New York Senator who says:

"Now there is nobody to whom I yield in respect and admiration and devotion to the sex."

We want man's admiration, but we do not think that is all there is to live for. Since economic conditions force us to fight our battle side by side with man in the industrial field we do not see why we should not have the same privileges in the political field in order to better the conditions under which we must work. . . . We demand a voice as to how politics shall be conducted. Yes, we want man's admiration, but not the kind that looks well on paper or sounds good when you say it. (Applause.) What we want men to do is to practice, to stop talking of the great comforts that they have provided for us; we know in most of the cases we are the providers; we also want them to know that in these days they will have to try to win our admiration. . . .

Don't you gentlemen worry, our minds are already made up as to what we are going to do with our vote when we get it. Another reason is given against woman suffrage; it is said that equal say will enable the women to get equal pay, and equal pay is dangerous. Why? Because it would keep the women from getting married. Well, then, if long, miserable hours and starvation wages are the only means man can find to encourage marriage it is a very poor compliment to themselves. In the name of a purer marriage we must have equal voice in making the laws for we have found out from experience that it is not only men who have to get married.

There are a few facts from the shirtwaist strike I would like to call to your attention. . . . When the bosses hired thugs to break our ranks and create riots, the police arrested the girls; when the girls were brought before the judge, he showed his *devotion* by sending a sixteen-year-old girl, Rose Perr, to the workhouse for six days. And for what crime, on what evidence? Simply that a thug accused her of violating the law while picketing. The word of the thug was taken in preference every time to the innocent girl's. Again when we sent a committee to Mayor McClellan to speak for protection for 30,000 women on strike in the shirt-waist industry, and to protest against the brutality of the police, what answer did the Mayor give the committee? This. He could not be bothered with any striking shirt-waist makers. Had that same committee represented 30,000 men, men who would have a vote at the next election, you can bet that the committee would have received a different answer, for it would mean 30,000 votes at the next election. This is the kind of respect, admiration and devotion we receive from our admirers the politicians when we fight for a better condition and a decent wage.

One year later, when we had the terrible disaster of the Triangle Shirtwaist factory, where our bodies were burned by the wholesale and many jumped from the tenth floor and smashed their poor bodies rather than be roasted. Then again those very same gentlemen, that a year ago tried to break our ranks when we fought for a safer place to work in, shed tears over the bodies on the sidewalk crushed to pieces. . . . we can not, and must not, wait until our sisters that live in comforts get the votes for us. We know that they have everything that their heart desires in order to make life worth while. That is no reason why they should not have the ballot, but working women must use the ballot in order to bring about conditions where all may be able to live and grow because they work. The ballot used as we mean to use it will abolish the burning and crushing of our bodies for the profit of a very few.

1920–1940

1920–1940: INTRODUCTION

REFORMERS concerned with the status of women had high hopes for the changes women voters would create, particularly with respect to the problems of workers. They expected to see better workplace health, safety, hours, and wages enforced by law; public health insurance; government aid to the poor; an end to political corruption; and many other reforms at local, state, and federal levels. Eventually, they were disappointed. Some reformers had viewed suffrage as the end rather than the means, and they retired from activism with a sigh of relief (and exhaustion) after the amendment finally passed. Others were intimidated by the massive anti-"Red" scare that followed World War I, a period of repression that stigmatized many progressive causes by associating them with Bolshevism. Few anticipated the massive resistance that conservative and corporate groups would mobilize against progressive reforms.

Because of the frustration of these expectations, historians of women have usually regarded this time period as one of losses or at best a standstill for women, the beginning of the long hiatus between the first and second waves of feminism. This judgment remains accurate, but it requires some important modification. Several important developments changed the situation for working women during these twenty years.

First, the numbers and proportions of employed women continued to grow in new kinds of jobs. Clerical work became steadily more common, at least among white women, as an occupation for women. New kinds of service work—more often commercial and public as opposed to domestic service—drew in women, such as waitressing, saleswork, and operating telephones.

Second, the incorporation of married women into the labor force increased rapidly. In 1920, married women constituted 23 percent of employed women; by 1940, thanks in part to the Depression, they made up 36 percent—but this proportion never dropped, even as prosperity returned. Married women's employment, which had long been common among the poor and especially minorities, not only changed the shape of many families but also changed the nature of the labor force.

Third, U.S. manufacturers faced a need to open up new markets, especially if they were to head off a recession after World War I, so they sought new ways to stimulate domestic consumption. The 1920s stand out as a period of rapid increase in advertising and the sale of consumer goods, particularly to women—from electric appliances and new cleaning products to clothes and makeup. Equally important was the increased sale of prepared foods—from commercial bread to canned fruit. For women who could afford these products, housework changed considerably. These developments did not necessarily reduce the amount of time spent in housework, however, because, as if to compensate, standards of cleanliness and child care increased.

In the middle of this period, the United States (and virtually the whole world) was hit by the greatest economic depression in history. The crash produced great suffering; economic need was no longer hidden among the long-term, minority, and rural poor but was now affecting the once-prosperous middle and working class. The breadth and depth of the problems produced massive protest and organizing; when Franklin Roosevelt assumed the presidency in 1933, he responded with a wide array of emergency relief and reform measures.

The New Deal, as Roosevelt's programs were called, had mixed effects on women. Emergency relief programs kept many from starving, and federal control gave some relief to many who were almost entirely excluded from local programs, such as African Americans in the South and Latinos in the Southwest. There was discrimination against women and minority men, however, in the distribution of federal relief, especially jobs, and in the permanent economic security programs such as Social Security; the largest permanent program for women, Aid to Dependent Children, for mothers without a male income to help them raise children, was tiny and very stingy in its stipends. But many other women gained from federal provision for their male breadwinners.

Another important long-term product of the Depression was the legalization of union organizing and the CIO's massive unionizing drives. While the CIO's efforts were mainly directed at male industries, and the main areas of women's employment remained nonunionized, women benefited not only through their male family members but also through the more positive, even dignified image of the working class (although that image was still primarily male). Perhaps for the first time in U.S. history, this working class was now understood, by the big unions, to include minorities as well as whites, in part because the several million African Americans who had migrated north in search of industrial jobs were proving themselves to be reliable and active unionists. The greatly increased influence and status of the Left further strengthened a political culture that viewed working women with greater respect. Both communist and socialist parties gained members and legitimacy. Left-wing organizations were the only white-dominated national groups to support black demands for an end to lynching—a position the white women's groups were unwilling to take in this period.

So while women's rights organizations declined in this period, women's activism did not. Women were disproportionately represented in the Left, in agitation for relief and welfare, in community and civil rights organizing. And these mobilized women came from a broad spectrum of the society, laying the basis for the eventual re-emergence of a women's movement which would represent not only the elite but also the more diverse majority.

Nonindustrial Work

CHANGES IN HOUSEWORK

By the early twentieth century, mechanization had not only transferred the production of most goods to factories but also transformed household labor. In the early nineteenth century, men who were industrial wage earners still had wives who made household goods by hand. A century later those housewives did more shopping and much less home manufacture.

Industrial growth required expanding markets; and by the early twentieth century, a major new market area was private consumption. Between 1920 and 1940, the advertising industry developed powerful techniques to stimulate buying. By the end of the 1920s, two-thirds of the national income was spent in retail stores. Shopping replaced home production in a housewife's work. Women became the objects and victims of ad campaigns that used women's fears and insecurities, already intensified by the disintegration of traditional roles, to encourage them to seek fulfillment through purchases. The decline of home production also dissolved some cooperative work (for example, the "change-work" described on pp. 15–16). Housewifery became more isolated, which increased women's vulnerability to the pressures of advertisement.

These changes were felt unevenly in different classes and regions, occurring first in the great industrial cities and last in the rural areas. Somewhere in between was Muncie, Indiana, the subject of Robert and Helen Lynd's famous Middletown, *published in 1929. Its population had shot up from six thousand in 1885 to thirty-five thousand in 1920; 2 percent of its people were foreign-born and 6 percent black.*

The Lynds' work is of methodological as well as substantive interest. They used statistical data about social practices and opinions to show us a process of change. The factors they discuss illuminate the larger changes in the whole society: the decline in traditional notions of sexual division of labor, so that men are "helping with the housework" more; the impact of the advertising industry on women particularly; the decline in servants and home production and the replacement of homemade goods by store-bought commodities.

. . . The providing of clothing for individual members of the family is traditionally an activity of the home, but since the nineties it has tended to be less a hand-skill activity of the wife in the home and more a part of the husband's money-earning. One of the housewives interviewed lived in 1890 on a farm just south of town, where wool was clipped from sheep and practically all the family clothing spun by the women of the family. The common practice a generation ago, however, was to buy "goods" and make the garments at home. As late as 1910 there was practically no advertising of women's dresses in the local newspapers, and goods by the yard were prominently featured. Today the demand for piece goods is, according to the head of the piece goods department of Middletown's largest department store, "only a fraction of that in 1890." This store conducted a sale in 1924 at which two bolts of the featured material were sold, "but in 1890 we'd have sold ten bolts the first day." . . .

At no point can one approach the home life of Middletown without becoming aware of the shift taking place in the traditional activities of male and female. This is especially marked in the complex of activities known as "housework," which have always been almost exclusively performed by the wife, with more or less help from her daughters. In the growing number of working class families in which the wife helps to earn the family living, the husband is beginning to share directly in housework. Even in families of the business class the manual activities of the wife in making a home are being more and more replaced by goods and services produced or performed by other agencies in return for a money price, thus throwing ever greater emphasis upon the money-getting activities of the husband. This is simply another instance of the shuffling about of "men's ways" and "women's ways" observable among all peoples, for "it is partly a matter of accident as to how culture is adjusted to the two parts of the group."

As noted . . . the rhythm of the day's activities varies according to whether a family is of the working or business class, most of the former starting the day at six or earlier and the latter somewhat later. . . . Of the ninety-one working class wives who gave data on the amount of time their mothers spent on housework as compared with themselves, sixty-six (nearly three-fourths) said that their mothers spent more time, ten approximately the same, and fifteen less time. Of the thirty-seven wives of the business group interviewed who gave similar data, seventeen said that their mothers spent more time, eight about the same, and twelve less time.

The fact that the difference between the women of this business group and their mothers is less marked than that between the working class women and their mothers is traceable in part to the decrease in the amount of paid help in the homes of the business class. It is apparently about half as frequent for Middletown housewives to hire full-time servant girls to do their house-work today as in 1890. The thirty-nine wives of the business group answering on this point reported almost precisely half as many full-time servants as their mothers in 1890, and this ratio is supported by Federal Census figures. . . .

"Every one has the same problem today," said one thoughtful mother. "It is easy to get good girls by the hour but very difficult to get any one good to stay all the time. Then, too, the best type of girl, with whom I feel safe to leave the children, wants to eat with the family." The result is a fortification of the tendency to spend time on the children and transfer other things to service agencies outside the home. A common substitute for a full-time ser-vant today is the woman who "comes in" one or two days a week. A single day's labor of this sort today costs approximately what the housewife's mother paid for a week's work.

Smaller houses, easier to "keep up," labor-saving devices, canned goods, baker's bread, less heavy meals, and ready-made clothing are among the places where the lack of servants is being compensated for and time saved today. Working class housewives repeatedly speak, also, of the use of running water, the shift from wood to coal fires, and the use of linoleum on floors as time-savers. Wives of the business class stress certain non-material changes as well. "I am not as particular as my mother," said many of these housewives, or, "I sometimes leave my supper dishes until morning, which my mother would never have thought of doing. She used to do a much more elaborate fall and spring cleaning, which lasted a week or two. I consider time for reading and clubs and my children more important than such care-ful housework and I just don't do it." These women, on the other hand, mention numerous factors making their work harder than their mothers'. "The constant soot and cinders in this soft-coal city and the hard, alkaline water make up for all you save by new conveniences." A number feel that while the actual physical labor of housework is less and one is less particular about many details, rising standards in other respects use up the saved time. "People are more particular about diet today. They care more about having things nicely served and dressing for dinner. So many things our mothers didn't know about we feel that we ought to do for our children."

Most important among these various factors affecting women's work is the increased use of labor-saving devices. . . .

It is in part by compelling advertising couched in terms of certain of women's greatest values that use of these material tools is being so widely diffused: "Isn't Bobby more important than his clothes?" demands an advertisement of the "Power Laundries" in a Middletown paper.

The advertisement of an electrical company reads, "This is the test of a successful mother—she puts first things first. She does not give to sweeping the time that belongs to her children. . . . Men are judged successful according to their power to delegate work. Similarly the wise woman delegates to electricity all that electricity can do. She cannot delegate the one task most important. Human lives are in her keeping; their future is molded by her hands and heart."

Another laundry advertisement beckons: "Time for sale! Will you buy? Where can you buy back a single yesterday? Nowhere, of course. Yet, right in your city, you can purchase tomorrows. Time for youth and beauty! Time for club work, for church and community activities. Time for books and plays and concerts. Time for home and children." . . .

The rapid and uncontrolled spread of such new devices as labor-saving machinery under a system of free competition makes the housekeeping of Middletown present a crazy-quilt appearance. A single home may be operated in the twentieth century when it comes to ownership of automobile and vacuum cleaner, while its lack of a bathtub may throw it back into another era and its lack of sewer connection and custom of pumping drinking-water from a well in the same back yard with the family "privy" put it on a par with life in the Middle Ages. Side by side in the same block one observes families using in one case a broom, in another a carpet sweeper, and in a third a vacuum cleaner for an identical use, or such widely varying methods of getting clothes clean as using a scrub board, a hand washing machine, an electric machine, having a woman come to the house to wash, sending the clothes out to a woman, or sending them to a laundry for any one of six kinds of laundry service. . . .

New cultural demands pressing upon this earlier compact home and family are altering its form: geographical vicinage and permanence of abode apparently play a weaker part in family life; there are fewer children and other dependents in the home to hold husband and wife together; activities adapted to the age, sex, and temperament of its members are replacing many whole-family activities; with the growth of these extra-home activities involving money expenditure comes an increased emphasis upon the money nexus between members of the family; the impetus toward higher education, sending an increasing proportion of boys into lines of work not shared by their fathers, is likewise tending to widen the gap between the generations in standards of living and habits of thought; such new tools as the telephone and the automobile, while helping to keep members of the family in touch with each other, are also serving to make separate activities easier. . . .

SHARECROPPING

Sharecropping replaced slavery as the dominant form of labor for African Americans after the Civil War. At the end of the nineteenth century, 90 percent of blacks lived in the South, 80 percent of those in rural areas; of these, 90 percent were sharecroppers, also called tenant farmers. (There were also plenty of white sharecroppers, often equally poor.) Most blacks were prevented from becoming landowners and had to farm by "renting" white land in return for a share of the crop. The conditions of sharecropping were not really "free labor"; like the conditions against which Hagar Barnwell struggled (see pp. 104–6), the system often involved violence and threats of violence against croppers to enforce labor requirements and the setting of rents so as to keep these farmworkers perpetually in debt and thus unable to accumulate enough money to buy land of their own. Lynching was disproportionately directed against those blacks who sought upward mobility through business or landownership. Since blacks had been deprived of political rights by the end of the nineteenth century, they also had no access to legal appeals.

So it is hardly surprising that sharecroppers struggled against this system in a variety of ways. Already in the late nineteenth century, they had formed unions in several places, attempting to bargain collectively with landowners. The Depression of the 1930s stimulated intensified activism, and tenant farmers formed further unions that succeeded in bringing their terrible conditions to national attention. Some of these unions were racially integrated, which made them particularly threatening to southern white power. Unfortunately, the mainstream northern industrial unions, both AFL and CIO, rebuffed the sharecroppers. Women were sharecroppers as well as men, and active in the unions, although they have been neglected by historians. The following brief reminiscence is by Naomi Williams, sharecropper, teacher, and a member of a tenant farmers' union in Arkansas.

During the Depression I had a crop of my own. And if I had a little leisure time to get off, I'd go over there to the boss's place and pick cotton. And that was for 35 cents a hundred. I was a good cotton picker; and I picked 300 pounds in one day to get me a dollar and a nickel. I'd go out there in the early morning just so you could see a row of cotton. It was hard, but I made it. I tried to keep my own account at the commissary store. But now where the cheating came in was on this stuff you put on the cotton, fertilizer and all that kind of stuff, and in the seeds. When they sell the cotton, they wouldn't give me what the cotton was worth. They put it there and I had to pay it all. I was renting but I wasn't supposed to pay it all. But I had all that to pay. Yes, I owed them at that store everything. I gathered crops so much.

And then when I'd get enough crop gathered, then I'd pay him. I had got all my groceries and that would leave me with nothing.

I usually made forty and forty-five bales, more sometimes, and I had enough money to run me through the winter, to buy new children's clothes for school and to buy groceries to last till the next time they start to furnish over in the spring. They didn't never give us nothing until the first of April. But I was wise. I'd buy enough of what I couldn't raise to last till April or May. I was raising hogs, had cows, and made my own garden and put up dry food, beans and peas and all that. I done worked myself to death.

And another thing, they didn't allow no colored children to even go to school but seven months, and they made them stay in the field and the white kids was going to school all kind of every way. I wouldn't stick for that now. I taught school until I got so many children I couldn't get nobody to take care of them and it took all I made. But I taught before I had the three little children. And when I got the fourth one I had to quit and take care of them. You know, in them days you had to know how to teach everything, from the first to the eighth grade. But I wasn't getting nothing but $35 a month. They raised it to $45 about a month after I quit. But I had to pay somebody to keep my babies. And them people charged me $2, $3 each kid a month. That's $10. And then I had to feed them and go get them, bring them home, had to do this and do that, and when I'd get finished with all that I wouldn't have $10. And I just quit teaching. My husband say, "Go 'head and quit teaching and sit down and maybe you'll get some peas and okra."

DOMESTIC SERVICE

Domestic service remained the most common occupation for women through 1940. It is the most traditional of women's wage work—with examples in nearly every period of this book—but it changed its form and meaning dramatically over time. In rural communities, many farm families hired occasional help during particularly busy periods—the men more likely to work on planting or harvesting, women on other agricultural chores such as canning, buttermaking, or grain processing. In these close-knit communities, there was no stigma attached to being a domestic; those hired were often the daughters of neighbors, were equal in social status to their employers, and often shared bedrooms and even beds with members of the family for whom they worked. As class differences developed, however, domestic service became a distinctly inferior job, usually performed by members of low-status racial/ethnic groups (blacks in the Southeast, Hispanics in the Southwest, immigrants elsewhere). These live-in servants were excluded from family rooms, required to wear uniforms, and expected to work at any hour with very little time off.

In the twentieth century, new work opportunities for women allowed domestic servants to bargain for better conditions. In some places, domestics began refusing to wear uniforms. One of their main victories was in shifting to day work, setting definite hours and going home to their own families at night. That was the situation of Mrs. Taniguchi (pseudonym) who immigrated to San Francisco from Japan in 1923. This interview, conducted in Japanese in 1975 when she was an old woman, shows the place of domestic service in the overall context of a woman's life; it also challenges some stereotypes about domestic service and shows that women might take pride in it despite the drudgery involved. *

We are grateful to Evelyn Nakano Glenn, who conducted this interview.

I and most of my friends do housecleaning, including those who attend my church. Since we don't know how to do anything else, we do housework and sewing. The *issei* women working in San Francisco are usually in laundry, housecleaning, and sewing for dry cleaners. The elderly often baby sit. Those who know how to sew are sometimes engaged in sewing jobs. They alter clothes to make them shorter or longer, and often do this sort of work at home. These are the types of jobs we have.

[Before the war] I was running a laundry shop in Berkeley, a small shop. I didn't do the washing in my own place, but would send the wash to that big union place in Oakland. They would do the washing and I would iron and fold these before returning them to the customers. I was getting the commission for doing that. And the war started, so I couldn't continue my business.

So I began housework after the war. When I first started working, since I hadn't had much chance to enter Caucasian homes, I was a little frightened. But after I got used to it, it became very easy. And I concluded after working for a while that the most important thing in this type of job is to think of and be able to predict the feelings of the lady of the house. She would teach me how to do certain things in the beginning, but after a month or two, I gradually came to learn that person's likes and tastes and ideas. So I try to fulfill her wishes—this is only my way of doing it, of course. For example, I'll change the water in the vase when it's dirty or rearrange wilting flowers while I'm cleaning the house. In that way I can become more intimate with the lady of the house in a natural way and the job itself also becomes more interesting. I work there almost as if it were my own home. Sometimes I plant flowers in the large garden without being asked when I discover there aren't many growing there. So then I'll start to feel affection even for that garden. Since I sometimes replant my own flowers in the garden where I

---

* Interview conducted in Japanese in 1975. A pseudonym is used to ensure confidentiality.

work, I become even closer to that home. I feel almost as if I own two houses. After working a long time, I can go to a new house and be able to understand the preferences of the lady of the house. So rather than the payment I get, it's the work itself that I enjoy.

I was born in 1907. My father and mother were farmers. I had two brothers and four sisters. I used to be spoiled since I was the youngest, but when I acted up my mother always set me straight. My father was a very strict person. He'd get mad even if I entered the room in an improper fashion. I was a lively child, so when I came home from school, I would sometimes forget to arrange my shoes neatly after entering the house. My father would get after me right away for doing things like that. So even now, I pay attention to details and think that I should keep my shoes in the closet arranged neatly. My parents taught me to keep my home clean, although of course, it's hard to keep it immaculate.

I didn't get much education: eight years. In those days there were no kindergartens, only elementary, higher elementary, and women's high school. I was 16 years 11 months old (Japanese system; 15 years 11 months western system) when I came to this country. Very young. So I didn't have time to study.

My husband came here when he was 16. [For a while] he was a farmer in Concord. But he felt he needed to get some education, so he went to San Francisco and became a "school boy." He attended night school. He knew about the immigration bill which would be enacted in 1924, so he returned to Japan in 1923, got married and brought me here.

We worked together at the Hayashi laundry. I first learned to iron clothes. There was a large machine called a mangle for ironing flat things, like sheets and pillow cases. Well, I learned to operate that machine too. The machine kept me busy. I'd have to feed it continuously with clothes and linen. On the other end I'd have to fold the sheets and so forth, so it was a rather busy job. I did think it was a little hard. Women worked that machine, but the job of arranging the linen was handled by men. The job of arranging the linen was hard work. So it wasn't hard work for the women, but since it kept us so busy it seemed like hard work. Especially since I had just come from Japan and had never even seen a machine.

Wages were low then. I can't say how many hours we worked. There were rooms there that we stayed in. And the cook there prepared breakfast, lunch and dinner for us. So it was very convenient. We wouldn't have to ride a bus or anything. After deducting for all those things, our wages ended up pretty low. Together, I think we earned about $40 a month.

We were married in 1923 and our first child was born one year later. I worked while he was still a baby. We were living at the Hayashis at the time. Since our room was right next to the work site, I would set time aside at regular intervals for feeding my child and changing his diapers. When my second child came, we were living in an apartment, and my husband was ill. My father-in-law took my [oldest] child to Japan, and I went back to Hayashi's laundry to work. [Later] I went back to Japan with my [four] children, left two of them there and returned to the U.S. The older daughter was growing up, so my father-in-law insisted that she return to Japan to receive a Japanese education. By doing so, he thought we would all go back to Japan, but it didn't work out that way.

After the war, our family's farm in Japan was taken over by others as a result of the occupation period reforms. So we decided not to go back to Japan and were thinking of calling my father-in-law to the U.S. (My mother-in-law had passed away previously.) But that seemed difficult too. My eldest daughter stayed in Japan. We called our other children back to the U.S.

(Do you like housework?)

Yes I like it. Because I can really get into the place I'm working at and feel part of it. Even if I were offered a laundry job again, I wouldn't take it. It's too hard. [One has] to do the same thing over and over again. House cleaning, though, involves doing all sorts of different things in different rooms, so four hours pass by very quickly. And I can do it as if I'm cleaning my own rooms. Because it's filled with variety. Laundry work is monotonous and tiring. And the places I work now aren't even dirty. Of course I wouldn't like to clean up places that are filthy, but the houses I go to now are all clean.

(What kind of person do you like to work for?)

Of course I prefer people who aren't too picky. People who let me do it the way I want to. Everyone who does house cleaning feels that way, I think. We prefer to be left to clean the house our own way. We don't like those who say, "There's some garbage over there, so be sure to clean it up."

(Did you ever have someone you didn't like?)

In some places I work while the family members are out of the house. In those cases, when the Mrs. returns home she usually says "hi" and greets me, letting me know she's come home. But in this one house the Mrs. would come in very very quietly without any warning, so it made me feel as if she was spying on me to make sure I wasn't doing anything wrong. I disliked that a great deal. Japanese people don't sit down and watch the television just because the owner isn't home. So I felt insulted then, thinking she suspected me.

A "GOLDDIGGER"

Just as "traditional" as domestic service has been women's use of sex to earn a living. Today feminists refer to the general category "sex work," which can *include everything from suggestive phone talk to stripping to prostitution. It is widespread because women lack access to good jobs, because sex work requires no formal training, and because men will pay a great deal for it. Most sex work is dangerous and unhealthy, and certainly the women who do it are usually victimized by individual men and by lack of opportunity in general. But this does not mean that all sex workers are duped or passive; some have been manipulative, active, even successful at achieving some upward mobility. This 1926 account of golddigging comes from a sixteen-year-old who worked as a taxi dancer in a dance hall in Chicago. She came from rural Wisconsin, where she worked from the age of nine as a domestic servant, seasonal farm laborer, and waitress. When she was around fourteen, her father died. She quit school, and her mother went on welfare and became a prostitute. Her mother tried to induce her to prostitute, but she had "different ideals." She was married briefly and had a child whom she left with her husband when he fell in love with another woman. She came to Chicago "with $1.50 in my purse and no friends in the city." As a taxi dancer, she made about thirty dollars a week.*

We are grateful to Joanne Meyerowitz for contributing this selection.

It doesn't pay to go straight. The girl who goes crooked gets all she wants. Now look at me, if I had gone crooked I could have more silk stockings and a new dress right now, when I'm wearing my room-mate's dress. . . . I don't go to the [dance] hall to make friends. I go there to make money. . . .

The first impression a girl has to make is that she is a good girl under hard circumstances. Then when a fellow asks for a date she tells him how hard up she is and she would like to go out but that she needs the money and has to come to the [dance] hall and work every night. Then [I] get the idea across to him that I'll go with him, if he'll pay me what I'd make if I stayed in the hall that night. When he asked how much that is, I make it seven or eight dollars rather than four dollars which it usually is. I always insist on getting that money before I go out, then they take me to a cafe and after I've gotten a good meal off of him, I invent some way of getting away. One way is to ask to be excused, having meant either to telephone or go to a rest room and then I go out another door and ditch him, but if there is only one door and the fellow can see me leaving I call up an older girl where I live to come right down to where I am to walk in and claim me as her niece and to threaten to make a scene and so I go off with her. I always pay her taxi fare and split on a fifty-fifty basis on the rake-off. Of course, I can only work that a few times but there's one born every minute and a lot of these come up to these [dance] halls.

A WOMAN CRITICIZES OTHER WOMEN ————————

World War I brought some new job opportunities for women as men joined the armed forces. In the federal civil service, in the chemical, automobile, iron, and steel industries, and in banking and even the stock market, women got, temporarily, a crack at new jobs. But when the war ended, women lost almost all the ground they had gained.

The best new opportunities, and those most likely to become permanently available to women, were in office work. These opportunities in turn created an incentive for women to complete high school and, among the most privileged, even college. (In 1920, 280,000 women attended college, or 7.6 percent of all U.S. women.) Many of these college women, who often remained single by choice in these years, made their way into professional and managerial jobs, especially into social work, nursing, and teaching. Class differences among women, once arising mainly from the position of their fathers or husbands, now emerged from women's own positions, along with a division between "career women" and other women who considered themselves employed only temporarily, until they married. These differences were reflected in debates—which we have seen in previous periods too—about the degree to which women were themselves responsible for their disadvantaged position in the labor market. Augusta Bratton, successful in a banking career, had strong opinions on the subject, convinced that women as a group displayed inefficiency on the job and had only themselves to blame for not being promoted as much as men.

We are grateful to Angela Kwolek-Folland for this selection.

Women have never had such a wonderful opportunity to prove their fitness as now. This opportunity was thrust upon us just at a time when we were beginning to realize that brains were given us to use, and that there was room in the business world for both masculine and feminine brains, provided they were well trained. Before the war, there were only certain lines open to us. Now we find ourselves face to face with necessity, not choice, and it has become not only a personal affair but virtually our patriotic duty to keep things running smoothly while the men are away.

The question most interesting to both employer and employee just now is, Are women as efficient as men? The officers say, "No; it takes three women to do the work of two men." I tried to find the reason. . . . I was convinced that our women clerks brought just as much intelligence to their work as the majority of men. They turned out nearly as much work—when they worked. There is the keynote of the whole situation—*when they work!* I find that women as a class are not so reliable as men. They cannot be depended upon to be always at their posts. . . .

I want to impress upon you all . . . that I am speaking now of women as a class—not of the few individuals who are at their desks regularly, attending strictly to business and remaining there even when sick until they have to be forcibly pried away. To those women it is second nature to be faithful. If by chance they are ever absent, you know it was necessary. . . .

But there are many who give in to trivial ailments when it is not absolutely necessary. Would they relinquish a pleasure excursion with the same readiness with which they give up office work? Would they absent themselves so often if a certain amount per day were deducted from their salary? . . .

Lack of systematic business training has much to do with the difference between the work of men and women. A boy's education is planned to fit him for a business career. He knows that if he gets a living he will have to work for it; and, whether he likes it or not, he usually buckles down. . . . A girl generally goes into business as a sort of temporary proposition, as a means of meeting expenses until some one comes along to meet them for her. . . .

There is another reason why women fall short of maximum efficiency. They are still taking advantage of their sex to usurp privileges which would never occur to men to take. They are not really willing to accept the bad with the good in the work, but instinctively take the lighter end of the burden as their right. I don't mean that women should cease to expect the little courtesies of life from the men they work with. These courtesies hurt no one. They are beneficial to both men and women and help to keep the line drawn between the two. But when it comes to the work, there should be no sex. . . . If we want to hasten the day when we will be worth the same wage as the men, we must actually demonstrate that we are physically able to accomplish it. When that day comes there will be no more argument. . . .

A man seems to have a stronger sense of duty than a woman. The office is an integral part of his life. To most women, the office is the place where they must be kept in for a certain number of hours, for a certain compensation. The women who have overcome this attitude of mind and have made the work a part of themselves are the ones who are going to step into the men's places and make good. They are the very few in this office of whom the officials say, "They are as good as men." At the present time that is the highest compliment a man thinks he can pay a woman. . . . I wonder if the time will ever come when the position will be reversed, and the women will be able to say, "Why, he's nearly as good as a woman!"

NEW TECHNOLOGY: TYPISTS

As the size and centralization of business and government increased, the need for clerical labor increased exponentially. A new piece of technology—the typewriter—was both a result of this new requirement for efficient record-keeping and a facilitation of women's employment, as sociologist Margery Davies explains.

In the last few decades of the nineteenth century, American corporations underwent a period of rapid growth and consolidation. As business operations became more complex, there was a large increase in correspondence, record-keeping and office work in general. This expansion of record-keeping and the proliferation of communications both within and between firms created a demand for an expanded clerical labor force. In 1880 there were 504,454 office workers who constituted three percent of the labor force; by 1890 there were 750,150 office workers. The number of office workers has been increasing ever since. In order to fill the need for clerical workers, employers turned to the large pool of educated female labor. . . . In 1880, 13,029 women graduated from high school in the United States, as compared to only 10,605 men. The figures for 1900 show an even greater disparity: 56,808 female high school graduates and 38,075 male. . . . Excluded from most of the professions, these women were readily available for the clerical jobs that started to proliferate at the end of the nineteenth century. . . .

Prior to the Civil War there were no women employed in substantial numbers in any offices, although there were a few women scattered here and there who worked as bookkeepers or as copyists in lawyers' offices. During the Civil War, however, the reduction of the male labor force due to the draft moved General Francis Elias Spinner, the U.S. Treasurer, to introduce female clerical workers into government offices. At first women were given the job of trimming paper money in the Treasury Department, but they gradually moved into other areas of clerical work. The experiment proved successful and was continued after the end of the war. Commenting upon this innovation in 1869, Spinner declared "upon his word" that it had been a complete success: "Some of the females [are] doing more and better work for $900 per annum than many male clerks who were paid double that amount." . . .

Although women started to work in government offices during the Civil War, it was not until the 1880's that women began to pour into the clerical work force. In 1880, the proportion of women in the clerical labor force was 4 percent; in 1890 it had jumped to 21 percent. By 1920, women made up half of the clerical workers: 50 percent of all low-level office workers (including stenographers, typists, secretaries, shipping and receiving clerks, office machine operators, and clerical and kindred workers not elsewhere classified) were women. In 1960, 72 percent of them were. This tremendous increase in the number of women office workers has changed the composition of the female labor force. While in 1870 less than 0.05 percent of the women in the labor force were office workers, by 1890 1.1 percent of them were. In 1960, 29.1 percent of all women in the labor force were office workers. . . .

A second factor which eased women's entrance into the office was the invention of the typewriter. By the 1890's the typewriter had gained widespread acceptance as a practical office machine. . . .

It seems fairly clear that it was not until businesses began to expand very rapidly that employers saw the usefulness of a mechanical writing machine. Changes in the structure of capitalist enterprises brought about changes in technology: no one was interested in making the typewriter a workable or manufacturable machine until the utility of having such a machine became clear. But the typewriter no doubt also gave rise to changes in office procedure. Writing was faster on a typewriter. The increase in correspondence and record-keeping was caused in part by the existence of the machine. . . .

The typewriter also facilitated the entrance of women into the clerical labor force. Typing was "sex-neutral" because it was a new occupation. Since typing had not been identified as a masculine job, women who were employed as typists did not encounter the criticism that they were taking over "men's work." In fact, it did not take long for typing to become "women's work": in 1890, 63.8 percent of the 33,418 clerical workers classified as stenographers and typists were women; by 1900, that proportion had risen to 76.7 percent. . . .

Clerical work attracted women because it paid better than did most other jobs that women could get. In northeastern American cities at the end of the nineteenth century clerical wages were relatively high: domestic servants were paid $2 to $5 a week; factory operatives, $1.50 to $8 a week; department store salesgirls, $1.50 to $8 a week; whereas typists and stenographers could get $6 to $15 a week. Also, clerical work enjoyed a relatively high status. A woman from a middle-income home with a high school education was much more likely to look for clerical work than for work as a house servant or as a factory girl making paper boxes, pickles or shoes. . . .

However, despite the fact that women were pouring into offices at the end of the nineteenth century, they still met with disapproval. An engraving of 1875 shows a shocked male government official opening the door on an office that has been "taken over by the ladies." The women are preening themselves before a mirror, fixing each other's hair, reading *Harper's Bazaar*, spilling ink on the floor—in short, doing everything but working. The engraving makes women working in an office seem ludicrous: women are seen as frivolous creatures incapable of doing an honest day's work. . . . A decent girl was risking her morality if she invaded the male preserve of the office. . . . The office was a dangerous place for a woman of virtue. Even in 1900, some people counseled women to leave the office and return to their homes, where they rightfully belonged. . . . In 1900, the *Ladies' Home Journal* warned women that they could not stand the physical strain of working in a fast-paced business office, that business girls and women were apt to suffer a nervous collapse.

But by 1916 the *Journal* was comparing the faithful female secretary to some heavenly body who "radiated the office with sunshine and sympathetic interest." It had not taken very long for the ideology to shift and for people to accept the presence of women in offices. Bok [editor of the *Ladies Home Journal*] had argued in 1900 that women, by virtue of their "nature," were unsuited to the office. But only a few years later, the *Journal* came close to arguing that the "natural" temperament of women made them good stenographers. And by 1935, *Fortune* had concocted a full-fledged historical justification for the assertion that "woman's place was at the typewriter." . . .

The image of the secretary as the competent mother-wife who sees to her employer's every need and desire was a description which most fitted a personal secretary. Here certain "feminine" characteristics ascribed to the job of personal secretary—sympathy, adaptability, courtesy—made women seem the natural candidate for the job.

Not all clerical workers were personal secretaries. For the large proportion of clerical workers who were stenographers, typists, file clerks and the like, another ideological strain developed, emphasizing the supposed greater dexterity of women. These workers were seldom assigned to one particular boss, but instead constituted a pool from which any executive could draw as he wished. In the case of these low-level clerical workers, personal characteristics such as sympathy and courtesy seemed less important. . . . People started to argue that women seemed to be especially suited as typists and switchboard operators because they were tolerant of routine, careful, and manually dextrous. . . . Differentiating office workers by sex is not the same as dividing them into groups distinguished, say, by eye color. The sexual division of labor in the office—where men hold the majority of managerial positions and women fill the majority of low-level clerical jobs—is a division which is strengthened by the positions which men and women hold outside the office. . . . Patriarchal relations between men and women . . . were carried over into the office. These patriarchal social relations meshed very conveniently with office bureaucracies, where the means by which the workers were told what to do was often an extremely personalized one. For although the number of clerical workers was large, they were often divided into small enough groups so that five or six typists, stenographers or file clerks would be directly accountable to one supervisor. And if that supervisor was a man (as was generally the case in the early twentieth century) and those clerical workers were women, it is easy to see how patriarchal patterns of male-female relations would reinforce the office hierarchy.

The segmentation of the office work force by sex thus promoted a situation where a docile mass of clerical workers would follow without rebellion the directives of a relatively small group of managers. The ideology that women, by virtue of their "feminine docility," were naturally suited to fill the low-level clerical jobs, can be seen as an important buttress of the stability of the hierarchical office structure.

The Depression

FAMILY LIFE

Unemployment and the Depression deeply affected family relations. Some men, like Mr. Raparka in the excerpt below, found that their loss of breadwinner status undermined their accustomed position of power and authority in the home. Women, often forced to work harder than ever to keep their homes together, sometimes became more resistant to male domination and sought to renegotiate family relationships on a more egalitarian basis. Depression experiences demonstrated the extent to which women's subordination in families often arises from men's control of money.

The impact of unemployment did not destroy the Raparka family, but the adjustments made necessary did lead to a complete reorganization of the structure of family relationships. When Mr. Raparka lost his job in the fall of 1933 he dominated the family. Two years later it was Mrs. Raparka who was the center of authority. . . .

Mr. Raparka as the chief breadwinner dominated this situation. His rule was stern and strict. He was not above putting down any dissension from his decisions, either on the part of the children or his wife, by force. On one occasion ten years previously his wife had left him for five days when he knocked her downstairs during an argument. The children received frequent whippings which only he was permitted to administer. All requests for money were made to him. He never told his wife how much he earned or how much he saved. She knew only that on payday she would receive her weekly allowance for household expenses, that he gave her and the children money for clothes and extras when he agreed that their requests were reasonable. . . .

Apparently the evenings at home involved a mutual sharing of individual activities and interests. All members were regular at religious service and church activities. The weekly family party at the movies was the chief form of recreation. All were interested and nearly equally concerned about the welfare of the baby and shared a pride in every sign of his development. Polish was spoken in the home, and even when schoolmates were present the shame at the parents' language handicap, so frequent in the children of immigrants, did not appear on the surface. The children spoke freely to their parents in Polish. The division of labor within the home provided for a sharing of duties between mother and daughter only, but father and sons were proud of the immaculate and well-kept home and contributed occasionally small items of home decoration from their earnings.

How thoroughly this institutional structure depended on the father continuing his function as the chief breadwinner, however, became evident within two weeks after he lost his job. Earnings of $15 a week had provided no margin of safety, no savings. At best the plane of living had been supported in a hand-to-mouth fashion. The unemployment coincided with the need for new clothes for school. The food for the baby could not wait. A change from fresh to canned milk resulted in convulsions which alarmed the whole family. Mrs. Raparka's pains in the back, present since the birth of the child, suddenly became worse. Her husband, with no money to pay for a doctor, refused to call one either for the mother or child for two weeks. This decision was resented by the whole family. Finally he borrowed money from an aunt without telling his wife. She discovered the loan when the aunt, having suffered an accident, asked for the money back to meet her own expenses. He cashed his insurance policy to pay the aunt, again without telling his wife. He had exhausted his available resources and one day pawned his overcoat. Hunting for work in an early snowstorm, he caught a cold which rapidly developed into a serious illness.

At this point Mrs. Raparka took the initiative. She went to the Catholic Social Service Bureau and asked for help. She received medical attention for her husband and milk for her baby. From this moment the shift in family organization began. When Mr. Raparka regained his feet in about ten days he was furious at this move. He sullenly told his wife to mind her own business when she suggested that he go to the Department of Public Charities where the Catholic society had suggested there might be additional aid. He undertook a desperate search for work and finished a two weeks' job hunt a thoroughly beaten man. The change wrought in him by this experience is evidenced by the fact that for the first time in his life he submitted to his wife's insistence that he help with scrubbing the floors and doing the washing (though he still refused to hang out clothes, in which activity "he would be seen"). The notes of our visitor who arrived several times while he was engaged in domestic duties indicates his sullen resentment at this change in status. The notes also indicate that the wife was gaining a new position of authority in her supervision of her husband's efforts. On several occasions she insisted he do over again what he had not done well. His response to this request made in the presence of the visitor was to grab his coat from the hook and flee from the house, slamming the door behind him. At this juncture Mrs. Raparka would remark, "He'll be back. He say he look for work. But then why not find? He no look. He can help here." Then she would go into a long criticism of her husband. She could not understand why he couldn't find work; he always had before. He must be getting lazy. Maybe if she made him work at home he would find a job in self-defense.

We do not know the course this readjustment would have taken had it not been for two facts. The first was that Mrs. Raparka decided to look for a job herself. After a futile search of ten days, she learned that jobs cannot be had for the asking. The stories her husband told of "No Help Wanted" signs, company police who wouldn't even let one apply, blunt refusals, and vague promises were true. She declared she was filled with shame at making her husband work at home.

At about the same time Mr. Raparka got a job on C.W.A. (Civilian Works Administration), and later under F.E.R.A. (Federal Emergency Relief Administration), for the same wages he had formerly received as a molder's helper—$15 a week. Once more the normal pattern of family affairs was on the way to being reestablished. It was noticed, however, that children and wife did not recognize his authority with the same passive submission as before. Possibly an adolescent assertion of independence was overdue. In any case the two older children argued frequently with their father when his decisions crossed their own desires. Mrs. Raparka also insisted that he turn over his work relief wages to her in full. This he refused to do, but his refusal had to be repeatedly made. Nor did he close the issue once and for all as he would have done a year before. He was less belligerent in the enforcement of his authority, and the renewal of the former pattern of relationships appears to have been the result of restored habits rather than of any dogmatic assertion of his own position as head of the family. This situation continued until the fall of 1934. The elder son, now graduated from trade school, obtained work as a mechanic and was soon earning $25 a week. The importance of this change lies in two facts. In the first place, since the F.E.R.A. wages were based on a budgetary deficiency estimate, added family resources of $25 a week automatically cut Mr. Raparka off work relief. Once more he became "unemployed," and a noncontributor to the support of the family. His status, dependent on his economic contribution, was once more under attack. In the second place, the earnings of the children in foreign-American families are customarily handed over to the mother. The son followed this procedure. Mrs. Raparka now had in her possession $10 a week more than the family resources had amounted to for some time, and *she* controlled the purse strings. It was her husband's turn now to ask her for money for his personal needs. She did not give him an allowance. Each request was judged on its own merits. She now decided how much would go for current expenses and how much would go to pay back bills, what clothes she and the children would have, whether the dentist would be consulted, and whether the daughter could go to the high-school ball. To this shift in roles the husband could offer no objection outside of sullen resentment, since his privilege in the control of expenditures depended on his provision of the income. He was not even called on to share in such decisions. The mother and the older son talked over the matter and shared that responsibility. When the daughter graduated from high school two years later and began earning, she also was taken into the family councils. When the younger son finished the eighth grade, the mother and older son disagreed as to whether he should go to trade school or to Hillhouse [college preparatory high school]. The son, in true paternal fashion, insisted that his younger brother should have the opportunity he had missed. But the mother eventually carried the day, by the use of identical arguments the father had used to send the elder son to trade school.

The consolidation of the mother's position was aided for a four-month period during which the father took a job on a farm as laborer for $20 a month and his keep. This occurred in the summer of 1935. With him absent from home, the organization of family life around the mother's authority proceeded without interruption even from Mr. Raparka's sullen dissent. When he returned to the family circle it was as a beneficiary not as a partner. One day while our visitor was present he went out saying he thought he could commit suicide. Mrs. Raparka remarked, "He won't, you know. But if he did, maybe I could get widow's aid and my boy, he could get married."

In the summer of 1938, Mr. Raparka asked for money to go to New York in search of a job. He has not been heard of since. But his departure caused little change in the routine or structure of family life. He long since had ceased to be an integral part of the major business of family activities. . . .

LEANING ON CHILDREN

In virtually all farm families and in many early industrial families, children's labor was essential. Girls did housework; both boys and girls did farm and factory labor. Before this century, most Americans considered it far more appropriate for children than for mothers to be employed outside their homes. Just as the Depression, paradoxically, sometimes had a liberating effect on wives, it also in some cases liberated children, because unemployment freed adults to do more of the housework! After decades of a campaign against child labor and for compulsory education, the first federal law against child labor was passed, part of the Fair Labor Standards Act of 1938, partly as an effort to stop child workers from "stealing" jobs from adults. But the antichild labor law was in effect biased in gender terms: it did not regulate girls' unpaid domestic labor.

Girls' household labor was by no means always oppressive, however. This Chinese-American girl worked very hard, but her home labor was also an apprenticeship and a cultural expectation.

Jade Snow was barely eleven in this depression year of 1933.

Some of their relatives who had relied wholly on wages for income became unemployed and had to apply for government relief.

Daddy faced the grim times with Mama. They were exploring ways for more severe economy, and in their discussion, Mama said, "Jade Snow is old enough to take over my housework so that I can do as much sewing as possible. Perhaps you can go out and solicit odd work which I can do at home. It is time for our daughter to learn the meaning of money, the necessity for thrift, and how to keep house. I shall provide her with the money for groceries.

"But it is my desire not to apply for relief, even though we may need it. I do not want my children to experience getting anything without first working for it, for they may become selfish, and a selfish person can wander the world over and still starve for lack of food. Selfishness often starts with a spirit of dependency; therefore I want my children to learn to cope with the world, and to understand that they get what they want only after working for it."

Mama had spoken, and had spoken beyond her customary habit in both length and determination. When she gave her verdict on these rare occasions, Daddy silently accepted her judgment.

Almost overnight, the life of Jade Snow, heretofore characterized by gravity keyed to propriety, became weighted with the gravity which only anxiety over money can cause.

Now, every day after school she reported immediately to Mama, who gave her the usual fifty cents to purchase groceries for that evening's dinner and tomorrow's breakfast. Lunch was composed of leftovers. With prudent management, it was possible to get a small chicken for twenty cents, three bunches of Chinese greens for ten cents, three whole Rex soles or sand dabs for ten cents, and about a half pound of pork for the remaining ten cents. The household staples, such as rice, oil, salt, soy sauce, and soap were bought by Daddy.

The small chicken would be cut up, bone and all, into pieces which could be handled by chopsticks, marinated like beef or pork with a standard seasoning of a tablespoon each of flour, soy sauce, sugar, and oil and then placed in a bowl for steaming. This dish would be saved for breakfast. The sole to be served at night would be fried with a little chopped fresh ginger root, which was used more frequently than garlic in the Chinese kitchen.

Ginger root in this instance neutralized any fishy odor—no fish was ever cooked without it—but it was also indispensable as an herb for the relief of certain types of colds and stomach or intestinal upsets.

The pork was sliced thin and used to make soup stock in which the greens were cooked. The three bunches of greens made sufficient soup and vegetable for both dinner and breakfast. Together with generous bowls of rice this menu fed three adults and three children.

In shopping for groceries, Jade Snow soon learned which stores carried the best of a particular thing; and after scathing criticism from Mama, she learned how shiny a fresh fish should look and how firm it should feel; how solid a head of cabbage should be before it could be considered solid, how an old turnip looked as distinguished from a young one, how pink good pork was, how crisp a bean sprout should be, and how green a young onion. Jade Snow never tried to bargain, as Mama often did from Chinese habit, or to get more than her money's worth by begging or flattery, as she heard fellow shoppers do, but under Mama's watchful checking at home, she certainly had to get her money's worth. . . .

By four in the afternoon Jade Snow had usually completed her shopping and rushed home, where Mama would have started dinner preparations. The rice always received first attention. "Get your rice on the stove first," Mama said, "and if it is cooked well, the other accompaniments are secondary. But if the rice is underdone or improperly cooked, the most delicious meat or vegetables cannot make up for it. The reputation of a good cook begins with good rice."

They had only half an hour to prepare dinner, then only twenty minutes for the meal, before it was time for Jade Snow to grab her Chinese books and be off to the Chinese school with Jade Precious Stone. Returning home at eight o'clock, Jade Snow first washed the dinner dishes and then washed the rice for the next morning's breakfast. To wash rice correctly is the first step in cooking rice correctly, and it is considered one of the principal accomplishments or requirements of any Chinese female. When Jade Snow was six, Daddy had stood her on a stool at the kitchen sink in order to teach her himself this most important step, so that he could be personally satisfied that she had a sure foundation.

First, she dipped out the required amount of raw polished white rice from the rice barrel. In their household, the barrel held a hundred pounds of rice, and an abalone shell was the measure. This shell had been used in the family for years; Mama said it was older than Jade Snow. Its luster was dulled, but infallibly, one-and-one-half measurefuls would insure enough rice for one meal (a little more for dinner; a little less for breakfast; and two measures when there was company). The rice was scooped into a heavy aluminum pot with a tight cover, and was washed in the pot.

It was first dampened with a little water, then rubbed for a while with both hands (if you were a child like Jade Snow) or with one hand (if you were a grownup). White starch would come off the rice and bleed into the water. You rinsed after the thorough first rubbing of about a hundred strokes. Then rub, scrub, and rinse again. Rub, scrub, and rinse again. Then rinse, rinse, rinse. Three scrubbings; six rinsings; these were the minimum treatments. When the water came out clear, the rice had been thoroughly cleaned.

Now it was ready for cooking water. Cold water was added until it reached one of Daddy's first knuckle joints above the level of the rice. Jade Snow usually allowed on her fingers a knuckle and a half. Then she checked the quantity of water by tilting the pot gently so that the rice remained undisturbed on the bottom. In this position, the knuckle-or-so of water, if allowed to flow to the edge of the tilted pot, would reach to the diameter of the rice on the bottom of the pot.

The cooking of rice was not less important than the washing. The pot, with its lid tightly in place, was set over a burner with the flame turned high until the water began to bubble and boil over. Then the burner was turned very low, and the steaming rice water was gradually absorbed. Daddy said that this was a most delicate stage in the cooking and that one should never lift the cover of the pot to peer at its contents. Instead, one should give the rice the full benefit of its steam and only by observation of the escaping steam should one conclude how nearly done the rice was. At the first bubbling stage, the steam rose straight up, strongly. At the completion of cooking, the steam curled ever so gently around the edges of the lid. . . .

Working Women Organize

PROTEST TO A SHOP STEWARD —————————————

The great uprising of workers that culminated in organizing the militant CIO (Congress of Industrial Organizations) in the 1930s began with grassroots labor militance in the preceding decades. Women's participation in this activism often required first a challenge to existing union men, who so often disrespected, ignored, and even harassed women workers. The following open letter to a union shop steward was written by Sarah Rozner, a Jewish immigrant who came to Chicago from Hungary in 1908 and began immediately to work

in a garment shop. The letter was undated but comes from the early 1920s,
at a time when Rozner's written English was not yet polished—she never
had an opportunity for formal education—but her eloquence was nevertheless
impressive. She became one of the first female business agents in garment
work in Chicago. (Business agents are full-time union officers who handle
financial and administrative work.) Rozner was a union worker until her
retirement in 1959, when she established a leadership training scholarship for
women, especially Chicanas and blacks, in her Los Angeles union local.

In this letter, we can see how Rozner combined militant demands for
respect for women with rejection of organizing women as women ("not inter-
ested in creating a sex issue"). This complex attitude has sometimes been
called "labor feminism" and was prevalent in the labor movement well before
the revival of feminism in the 1960s.

We are grateful to Sherna Gluck for this selection.

Local 275, A.C.W. of A.

What is it that we want Br. Levin?

What do you think will become of our local, What is the need of it, does
it serve a necessary function, or is it a hinderance to our organization?

The committee is here to discuss this matter soriously with you. We have
promast you before you have gone on your tripp not to couse any disturbance
in the organization while you be away, but we have told you that we will
wait ontill your return and now we are here for honest a goodness business.

What we want!

Br. Levin you need not get frightent at our demands! Although you may not
approve of it as a whole at the first glance. But we are confidant that after
you have given it concidirable thought you will no doubt aggry with our
demnds fully. We are convincet that you will. You may wonder why we feel
so sure about it, we believe honestle that if you would have not approved of
our existance, that we would not have been here, for after all it was you that
helpt us almost entirly to bring this local into existance in 1920.

We want what ever is duly coming to us!

We feel that our local was created for the purpose of bringing our women
coat makers into its folds so that it will annable them to be in closer tuch
with the organization, to femiluarise themself with the different activities in
the organization, to participate more fully in the organization. For if you,
Br. Levin wouldn't have thought of the need of its functions and activities
you would'tof helpt us in bringing it to life. Now that you are largely respon-
siple for its creation, we expect you to help us in making it a real success. In
return we assure you that the organization as whole will benfit by it.

We want the women coat makers in our local not for the pupose of building a large treasure, and surely not for political reasons. As a matter of fact

for no selfish motives on our part. Our primary interst in bringing them into our folds is not prymarely for the purpose of immideately plcing women on paid jobs, not because we are not entitled to it, for their is no earthly reason why we shouldn't have it, but that does not happen to be our entire aim at present at least.

Our pupose, our aim and aspirations are for the real purpose of making our organization more firm, more inteligent and more progressive. We believe that our purpose is a good one and we feel that our aims and aspirations will meet with your approval as well as all sane thinking memmbers and officials in our organization. Moreover we believe that such activities as outlined by us for the benefits of women worker members will even travle considirably further than our own organization. The A. F. of L. at its last convention has given this matter considirable thought of working out ways and means of bringing the women into the folds of organized labor.

Br. Levin we want to assure you that we are not interested in creating a sex issue in our organition, if anything we want to do away with it as much as posible. The sex issue does not make for greater prog in our organization whereever it is prevelat. We have a life example of it in our eastern organiztion. We members are not in sympathy with their actions towards our women members, for the symple reason that the organiztion as a whole suffers byit. We want the same posibilities in promoting our members in industry as well as in the organization. We care not for special privilages, we want to be looket upon as part and parsel of our organization. As a worker of the "Discriminated Class", I take the privelege, an opportunity offered by the Chicago Wommen's Local, 275, in answering questions propounded by them. I say a *worker* and not a woman. For to me the sex question does not exist. To me it is a question of one group of workers undermining another. Although, in this instance, we cannot deny that the women workers are discriminated against.

It is true that the leaders in our organization tell this class of "Discriminated Workers", to elect their own officials. They have the full right to choose whom ever they please. But remember! the present exploiting capitalist calss gives us the same privelege. You workers! take for instance a business agent who goes in to make a price on a garment. He agrees with the manufacturer for so much and so much for the garment. Now let us see, how does our union representitive distribute the amount? Well, we will say that pocket makers, head operators and pressers should receive at least at the rate of $45.00 per week. Eighteen Dollars a week, accorded to women workers for the so called minor operations of finishing, button hole making and so forth is considered sufficient by our business agents.

Now let us see what our officials are doing to promote greater activities among women members. To my knowledge, as a member of the A. C. W.

of A. since 1914, the fraternal spirit has not been exercised. I know of a number of highly intelligent women who were discouraged from being active in the organization. Let us take as a specific case the late strike conducted against the International and J. L. Tailors. We all agree that the women did splendid work but when it came to acknowledging same all doors close. Not mentioning any names, a prominent official who has given a rather detailed account of their activities enjoyed the spirit shown by our Chicago fighting women members, but when it came to acknowledging same in our official organ he apoligized for not having mentioned some men who perhaps have not been on the picket line once. We want the immideate removel of such representatives that oppenly denounce women members and not only treatens to do away withem but actually does so at his convinient moments. We are able to annumirate cassess at hand. . . .

What have you to say about it Br. Levin and what can we expect from you?

LAUNDRY WORKERS ORGANIZE ——————————

The growing northern, urban black population participated actively in work-ers' movements in the period from 1920 to 1940. Urban black women often worked in commercial laundries, where the jobs were especially poorly paid and involved working in constant high heat. Laundry workers tried to union-ize in the 1920s but unfortunately received little support from white unions. So instead they turned to black unions and white and black middle-class women's reform organizations for support, such as those represented at the meeting described below in the Negro World, *a newspaper of the Garvey movement, the most prominent black organization of this period. We first met the Women's Trade Union League in the previous period, when it supported shirtwaist and textile strikes. Gertrude McDougald was a black settlement and educational leader.*

We are grateful to Barbara Bair for this selection.

WOMEN LAUNDRY WORKERS ORGANIZING TO DEMAND A LIVING WAGE

Twenty thousand Negro laundry workers are now engaged in an organiza-tion campaign with the determination to increase their wages and shorten their hours, as well as remedy the unsanitary conditions under which they work in the city.

This campaign is carried on under the leadership of a joint committee representing the Women's Trade Union League, the Trade Union Committee for organizing Negro workers, and the International Laundry Workers' Unions locals 280 and 290. This organization work has been going on quietly for months.

The first mass meeting will be held at 2 o'clock Sunday afternoon, March 14, at the West 137th Street branch for Colored Women of the Y.W.C.A. . . . Announcements of the meeting are being shown on the screens of Harlem theatres. . . .

It is estimated that 75 percent of the men and women employed in laundries in New York are colored. Most of the women are married and have children to support. Statistics show that 5,000 Negro babies die each year because the wages of their parents are too low to afford them proper food, proper living conditions and medical attention. . . .

Frank R. Crosswaith, one of the leaders in the organizing campaign in Harlem, said recently "the conditions under which these women labor are akin to slavery; so deplorable are these conditions that the majority of the ministers in Harlem as well as other public spirited men are now interested in the struggle of these girls, and many of them have pledged assistance in the fight."

Among the speakers for the meeting tomorrow are Mrs. Maud Swartz, president of the National Women's Trade Union League; Mrs. Gertrude E. McDougald, assistant principal of Public School 89; Roy Lancaster, secretary-treasurer of the Brotherhood of Sleeping Car Porters and John Mackay, organizer of the International Laundry Workers Union.

RANK AND FILE ORGANIZING

While the CIO as a whole did not excel at including women and women's workplaces in its organizing drives, the meatpacking industry was a notable exception. Meatpacking involved some of the worst working conditions in industrial production: heat, stench, dangerous machines, and a high-pressure assembly line. (It actually began as a disassembly line!) But meatpacking also produced militant worker leaders, such as Stella Nowicki. Interviewed first by Alice and Staughton Lynd over twenty years ago for a collection of CIO oral histories, Nowicki has since been featured in the fine women's history film Union Maids.

. . . The company didn't give a damn.

The meat would be so hot and steamy your fingers almost blistered but you just stayed on. In 1933–34 we worked six hour shifts at 37½ cents an hour. We would have to work at a high rate of speed. It was summer. It would be so hot that women used to pass out. The ladies' room was on the floor below and I would help carry these women down almost vertical stairs into the washroom.

We started talking union. The thing that precipitated it is that on the floor below they used to make hotdogs and one of the women, in putting the meat into the chopper, got her fingers caught. There were no safety guards. Her fingers got into the hotdogs and they were chopped off. It was just horrible.

Three of us "colonizers" had a meeting during our break and decided this was the time to have a stoppage and we did. (Colonizers were people sent by the YCL [Young Communist League] or CP [Communist Party] into points of industrial concentration that the CP had designated. These included mass basic industries: steel, mining, packing, and railroad. The colonizers were like red missionaries. They were expected to do everything possible to keep jobs and organize for many years.) All six floors went on strike. We said, "Sit, stop." And we had a sit-down. We just stopped working right inside the building, protesting the speed and the unsafe conditions. We thought that people's fingers shouldn't go into the machine, that it was an outrage. The women got interested in the union.

We got the company to put in safety devices. Soon after the work stoppage the supervisors were looking for the leaders because people were talking up the action. They found out who was involved and we were all fired. I was blacklisted.

I got a job doing housework again and it was just horrible. Here I was taking care of this family with a little spoiled brat and I had to pick up after them—only Thursday afternoon off and every other Sunday—and all for four dollars a week of which I sent two dollars home. I just couldn't stand it. I would rather go back and work in a factory, any day or night.

A friend of mine who had been laid off told me that she got called to go back to work. Meanwhile she had a job in an office and she didn't want to go back to the stockyards, so she asked me if I wanted to go in her place. She had used the name Helen Ellis. I went down to the stockyards and it was the same department, exactly the same job on the same floor where I had been fired. But it was the afternoon and Mrs. McCann wasn't there. Her assistant was there. Her assistant said, "Can you do this work," I said, "Oh yes, I can. I've done it." She told me that I would start work the following afternoon.

I came home and talked with Herb and Jane. We decided that I would have to go to the beauty shop. I got my hair cut really short and hennaed (similar to tinting today). I thinned my eyebrows and penciled them, wore a lot of lipstick and painted my nails. Because I hadn't been working, I had a suntan. I wore sandals and I had my toenails painted, which I would never have done before. I came in looking sharp and not like a country girl, so I passed right through and I was hired as Helen Ellis on the same job, the same forelady!

After several days the forelady, Mary, who was also Polish, came around and said, "OK, Helen, I know you're Stella. I won't say anything but just keep quiet" if I wanted to keep the job. I answered her in Polish that I knew that the job wouldn't last long and I thanked her. She knew I was pro-union and I guess she was too, so I kept the job as Helen Ellis until I got laid off. (Later on I was blacklisted under the name Ellis.) . . .

Swift's was in a different class than Armour's. Everyone who worked in Swift's was thought to be a higher class worker—they got more money. Swift's had a group bonus system called the Bedaux system. After you produced so much then each person in the gang got that much more money. It's diabolical. One worker slits the throat of another. They keep going so that the group production is great enough that they can all get a bonus.

Swift and Company had a strong entrenched company union with a paternalistic system to keep people sort of quiescent and controlled. The company actually selected the representatives from the different departments. They called it an "Independent Employees Organization." Anybody who spoke up about it was a troublemaker and they got rid of him.

I went to Swift's to get a job. The personnel director said they weren't hiring but what were my qualifications, where did I work last. I told her Independent Casing. "Well, why aren't you there now?" I told her that I got a scholarship to go to the University of Wisconsin through the Y that previous summer. And she said, "Well that's my Alma Mater!" So she hired me for the casing department.

Later I got sent to the sliced bacon department which is the elite department. It was the cleanest job and you made the most money. They had this visitors' ramp where people went by and would look down. We were freezing our asses off in this cooler of about forty degrees. I wore two pairs of wool socks and a couple of wool sweaters under my uniform and a cap. We'd have to go every two or three hours into the washroom to thaw out and spill out. . . .

The women themselves had gotten together and they would turn out a hundred and forty-four packages an hour of bacon. We were making $15 a week at 37½ cents an hour, but if we each produced 144 packages an hour we got $7 more in our pay. We made 50 per cent more than anybody else but we produced 90 per cent more than the set group rate. A new girl would come in and the oldtimers would train her. They would help her out so that gradually by the end of a certain period of time she was doing the 144. But they would never let anyone go beyond that 144 packages. They maintained that limit and they did it without a union. One smart-aleck girl came in there once and she was going to show them and go beyond that number because she wanted to earn more money: all the bacon that she got from the girls further up the line was messed up and scrappy and she'd have to straighten it up to put it in the package. She couldn't make a hundred packages an hour. (We took a loss just to show her.)

The checker would come around with the stop watch. You learned to wrap a package of bacon using a lot of extra motions because it was a time study thing. When he wasn't there we eliminated all those motions and did it simply. This was done everywhere—sausage, wrap and tie, bacon, everywhere. (It's all done by machine now.) There is always a faster way to do something, a simpler way where you save energy and time. The older women, in terms of experience, would show the new women. It was a tremendous relationship of solidarity. But they weren't about to join the union. They weren't about to put out a buck a month in union dues.

At first the women were afraid. It took quite a bit of courage to join. They were concerned about their jobs. Many of them were sole breadwinners. Also the Catholic Church said that the CIO was red: you join the CIO and you are joining a red organization. To talk about the CIO then was like talking about socialism to some people today. Even to talk union, you talked about it in whispers. You had to trust the person and know the person very well because he could be a stool pigeon. . . .

When I was at the University of Wisconsin, John Lewis made his speech that he was breaking away the coal miners union from the AFL and they were going to set up the CIO. We set up an organizing committee for the stockyards. There were seventeen of us that met, three women and fourteen men. One of them was an Irishman by the name of McCarthy who became the acting chairman of the Packinghouse Workers Organizing Committee. We met behind a tavern on Honore Street. The organizing of these seventeen people was on Communist Party initiative and we worked through contacts in the IWO, the International Workers Order. In this group of seventeen there were some Poles and some Slovaks who were indigenous to the community. . . .

We couldn't get the sliced bacon department at Swift's into the union because of the money they were earning. What could the union do that they weren't getting already, and they *were* organized! So I told them that it was the case that they had the money, but what about the conditions—it was colder than hell. What happens if you get sick? What happens if the foreman says that he doesn't like you and he wants somebody else to have your job? I said that the union could protect them on these real problems. But they wouldn't join. I think that I only got one or two out of that great big department.

They were all white, mostly Polish. There was one black woman who

worked on scrap bacon way in the back so that no one would see her when
visitors came through. The company could always say that they had one
black woman in this fancy department. I raised this matter of discrimination
but it didn't go over too well with white women.

One day the woman who worked in the coldest spot got sick. She didn't
come to work. We found out that she had become paralyzed. The door from
the cutting cooler opened as the men came back and forth. It was below
freezing there and every time the door opened she would get this tremendous
cold blast on her side. The whole right side of her body was paralyzed and
she died. Within a week we organized that whole department. She was a
young woman, probably around forty, and she died because of the freezing
conditions in which we all had to work. It was easier on the company to
have it this cold. There was less spoilage. But they didn't give a damn about
the workers. We showed that we could handle bacon and that it didn't have
to be that cold.

The National Labor Relations Act had been passed, giving workers the
right to organize. But this was not easy because people were laid off. I was
laid off, for instance, in the gut shanty and they tried to break my seniority.
We had departmental seniority and I would be shifted all around. Besides
casing and sliced bacon, I got to work in wrap and tie (hams), soap, glue,
fresh sausage, pork, ham, almost every department. By being shifted around
I became acquainted with many more women. I kept the names and
addresses of all the women because I knew that some day I would need them.
When we started organizing I knew women all over the whole plant. I would
call them and get information as to pro-labor union sentiment, problems
and issues, and so forth. We would print it up in the CIO news—the *Swift
Flashes* we called it.

The same woman who had hired me at Swift's approached me and asked
me if I'd like to work in personnel—they tried to buy me off. They offered
me better-paying jobs. . . .

You had to *earn* the respect of your fellow workers or you couldn't talk to
them about new ideas or unions, etc. You always had to be a good worker.

Women often did much harder work than men. For instance, in wrap and
tie department—where hams were handled, wrapped in paper and tied—it
is heavy lifting a twenty-pound ham. Then you'd have to put those great big
hams on a slip hook and hang them up so that they could be smoked in the
smoke shed. In the sausage department women used to link sausages by
hand; but the men would measure the meat and work with a pedal to shoot
the sausage into the casings.

The women worked much harder and much faster but they got less pay.
We were paid ten cents an hour less than men. There were jobs that men
had done that women took over and they'd still get the lesser pay. I worked
in a cooler cutting the fat from the lean with the guard on my thumb and

the sharp knife. Work with a knife is a butcher's job, but they had a pay differential. (The union corrected this inequity later.) There was also a differential between the southern rates and the northern rates.

Women had an awfully tough time in the union because the men brought their prejudices there. The fellows couldn't believe that women in the union were there for the union's sake. They thought that they were there to get a guy or something else. Some thought that we were frivolous. I would be approached by men for dates and they would ask me why I was in the union, so I would tell them that I was for socialism and I thought that this was the only way of bringing it about.

Some of my brothers, who believed in equality and that women should have rights, didn't crank the mimeograph, didn't type. I did the shit work, until all hours, as did the few other women who didn't have family obligations. And then when the union came around giving out jobs with pay, the guys got them. I and the other women didn't. It was the men who got the organizing jobs. Men who worked in plants got paid for their time loss—women didn't. I never did. But we were a dedicated group. We worked in coolers and from there I would go to the union hall and get out leaflets, write material for shop papers, turn in dues, etc., get home and make supper, get back. These guys had wives to do this but there was nobody to do mine. Sometimes I'd be up until eleven, twelve, or one o'clock and then have to get up early and be punched in by quarter to seven and be working on the job by seven. . . .

For a long time I fought dishonesty within my local. There were some guys who would pocket the dues money. I would debate them on the union floor. Many times I was the only female there.

The women felt the union was a man's thing because once they got through the day's work they had another job. When they got home they had to take care of their one to fifteen children and the meals and the house and all the rest, and the men went to the tavern and to the meetings and to the racetrack and so forth. The fellows were competing for positions and the women didn't feel that that was their role. They were brainwashed into thinking that this union was for men.

The union didn't encourage women to come to meetings. They didn't actually want to take up the problems that the women had. I did what I could to get the women to come to the meetings but very few came—only when there was a strike. I tried to make the meetings more interesting than just a bunch of guys talking all evening.

We organized women's groups, young women's groups. They liked to dance and I loved to dance so we went dancing together and I talked to them about the union. The women were interested after a while when they saw that the union could actually win things for them, bread and butter things.

We talked about nurseries. In World War II we finally did get some because women were needed in greater quantities than ever before in the factories. But the unions had so many things they had to work for—the shorter work day, improved conditions—so many things that they couldn't worry about these things in relation to women.

Later on, during the war, there was one department where I got the women but couldn't get the guys in. They hung out in the tavern and so I went there and started talking with them. I didn't like beer, but I'd drink ginger ale and told them to show me how to play pool. I learned to play pool and I got the men into the union. I did what they did. I went into the taverns. I became a bowler and I joined the league. The only thing I didn't do is rejoin the Catholic Church. . . .

Black Women against Racism

DOMESTICS ORGANIZE

The great majority of black women remained sharecroppers (see pp. 199–200, above) or domestic servants. Both situations were particularly hard hit by the Depression: sharecroppers were often evicted by their landlords, who could earn more from the New Deal's Agricultural Adjustment Administration by keeping land out of tillage, and domestics suffered drastic wage cuts—sometimes 100 percent—as middle-class housewives tightened their budgets. Despite the obvious difficulties of organizing workers who are isolated from each other, in many regions of the United States domestics tried to form unions during the Depression, frequently led by black women. Here we present two examples of such efforts. The first, from Texas, is a letter to Eleanor Roosevelt—who was extremely popular among blacks, having taken much stronger antiracist positions than her husband—asking that domestics be included in the protections offered by New Deal regulation of hours, wages, and working conditions (through the National Recovery Administration). The second, from a San Diego group, includes a proposal for union wage and work standards for domestics! The letters also illustrate the great differences in education among working-class black women between those in the south and those in the west.

We are grateful to Phyllis Palmer for this selection.

Fort Worth Tex.
Jan. 5 1937

Mrs. Franklin D. Roosevelt

I am asking you to please try help the cooks in private home's to have some kind of working schedule about our jobs we only get a small salary no one is paid over $8 per week that is when we keep the house, wash, iron the clothes. Cook the meals come to work 7.a.m. no limit to the hour we get off. No rest on the job not an hour to lie down or sit down to rest. but we poor Negro women have to work. Our husbands only get a small salary . . . And we must help and we dont mind the work but 18 hours out of 24 hours a day is killing our women If a party is to be given We get to work 7.a.m. off about 1.45 a.m. the next morning and look for us at 7.a.m., only 5 hours to sleep. Mrs. Rosevelt if you can help talk or organize something that will cause these dear house wives whom we work for [to] realize we are human even if we are a Black race . . . We get one evening out of a week, get off at 2.30 p.m. stores close at 5.30 P.M., a very short time to shop clean our own house cook that one decent meal at home . . . No time then to do Laundry at home . . . I ask the Lady whom I work for to grant me a few hours to care for some real business and bills that had to be seen after and I was sorry I spoke about it. I was answered with such grievious words. Will you please try to talk or write a coloum in the Southern Newspapers where the women can read it. the N.R.A. help the men but did not help we women. Mrs. Rosevelt please try some plan to help us. . . . hoping these few words will sink deep in your heart, that you may try help us get some justice about our labour. . . .

May god Bless you and our dear President of the. U.S.A,
yours, a Servant.

L. G. Huff, General Delivery, Ft. Worth, Texas.

p.s. afraid to sign my name. I put my initial would like to send my real name.

4584 Park Boulevard
San Diego, California
November 24, 1933.

Mrs. Franklin D. Roosevelt
The White House
Washinton D.C.
Dear Mrs. Roosevelt:

Your appeal for the Domestic Workers has stimulated those in San Diego into action. We have formed an organization now known as the Domestic

Employees Union and have affiliated with the American Federation of Labor.

We have formed a committee to work on a wage scale. However, because of opposition that developed while we were organizing, we realize that the employers are not in a receptive mood for such a step. The employees in this city are not vindictive toward the employer even though they have suffered many indignities and hardships at their hands. . . .

We are attempting to approach the employers through the P.T.A., womens clubs, and through women engaged in public work. . . .

You have recently announced your plan for reemploying women this winter I should like to explain our objects and how we may be of assistance to you, in this undertaking. . . . We want to raise the educational standards of the home employee. . . . There has been no means of direct training for employment in the home for the majority. A school for the home service workers would be the ideal plan but that is of course, a little too advanced just now. However, classes could be established in serving, laundering, second maid training and the care of children and similar subjects. Unemployed women who are expert in any one could be employed to teach these courses which would in turn help other women to become employable.

Would it not be possible that a portion of the funds allotted to women be used for this purpose in our city. The Adult Education Department of the Public Schools is willing to cooperate with us if these funds can be obtained.

One result from such training would be that the employer would recognize the advantage to be gained in engaging Organized Domestic Workers and would pave the way for acceptance of a wage scale. Also it would help improve the efficiency of the home.

We domestic workers realize our weaknesses and appreciate the advances made in the management of the home. We know that balanced diets, scientific preparation of food and the training of children and other improvements are due to the increase of general education. We ask to be given the opportunity to improve the quality of our services through a similar increase in vocational education.

. . . because you have expressed your interest in our cause we are asking your direct aid. Will you help us in whatever way appeals to you, by sanctioning such a program as ours and by publishing your idea of a fair scale of wages and conditions for Domestic Employee. . . .

Thank you for the interest and consideration that you have given us all along. It has been more than consoling to us to have the First Lady of the Land looking down into our hearts and finding the scars of this long seige becoming too numerous to disregard.

We are supporting you and the President in every way and have the utmost confidence in your ability to establish this new era of economic prosperity upon a solid foundation.

Respectfully,
(Miss) Gene Nicholson
Secretary and Organizer

Union Wage Scale for General Maids

Experienced

Living Out (Away from place of employment)

Maximum Hours	10 per day (must be broken)
" "	60 per week

Minimum pay $12.00 per week

2 meals per day (I of them hot)

½ hour out for each meal (included in the 10)   9 hrs. + 1 for meals

24 hours off duty per week

Pay not to be lower than 12 dollars per week whether full time of 60 hours' work furnished or not.

Living In

Maximum hours   10 per day (must be broken), must end no later than 8 p.m.
60 per week

Minimum pay   10 dollars per week and room and board. Board to be three meals per day. Room to be private (Not Shared)

At least one hour per day for meals (included in 10)

24 hours per week off duty (arranged as convenient) . . .

General Rules

No heavy laundry shall be done by any women doing domestic work, i.e. no bed linen, blankets, table linen, curtains, or similar articles.

Uniform to be furnished by employer if required.

All time over ten hours per day to be paid at the rate of 25¢ per hr.

All time after completion of regular shift to be considered as the domestic employees' own, with freedom to leave the premises if she so desires.

In the case of broken hours all time between shifts to be the employees' own, completely.

One week's notice to be given of discharge or resignation

Two weeks leave of absence with pay at the end of a year's service.

No woman engaged in this work shall do any outside work such as washing the automobile, cleaning the garage, sweeping the walks or yard or any such work. All work
to be confined within the four walls of the house. . . .

PROTESTING NEW DEAL DISCRIMINATION ———————

*Most New Deal programs discriminated against women and minority men.
Some of the bias occurred at the state or county levels, in programs in which
federal money was administered locally, such as work relief. In other cases,
discrimination was federal, imposed by statute, when programs specifically
excluded job categories occupied by minority men or white or minority women.
The following letters protest such discrimination. In the first, Serena Ashford,
a cook, is infuriated that the National Recovery Act, which gave workers the
right to organize and established minimum-wage codes, excluded domestic
service. In the next two letters, women protest local discrimination against
blacks by the Works Project Administration, the major source of federally
funded jobs.*

108 Post Road
Mamaroneck, N.Y.
March 9th 1934

President Franklin D. Roosevelt
Washington, D.C.
My dear Mr. President,
　　When you delivered your message to Congress in January, I was eager to
hear you and under almost unsurmoutable difficulties I did, but was sadly
disappointed to find that the large and unprotected class of Domestics were
not thought of. I keenly felt for my kind who you spoke of the robbery of the
Banker but never mentioned the robbery of the Housewives.
　　Today as never before we are being robbed, for now it is in three ways,
through our stomachs, our strength and health through long hours and last
our pocketbooks, which we are called upon to do three and sometimes four
Domestics work by one person for less than half of what they formerly paid
one. And it is a case of try and do it or starve.
　　When you mention a code for Domestics, they arrogantly tell you it will
and can never be done.
　　I wonder why it is that the same God made us made the rest of mankind
and yet when it comes to hours and wages there is such a difference.
　　I have appealed to President Green, Miss [Frances] Perkins, Father
Coughlin and asked them if they would not intercede for us, but up to present time to no avail. I also wrote to Senator Wagner and he turned it over to

the Chairman of the Committee you appointed on Crime, and he, the poor little fellow, didn't know that there was a racket going on, as it had not been reported to his office.

I would like to take him for a few days on some of the jobs I have been on and he would know it quick.

Now Mr. President, as you are the top of this Great American Body and possess more authority than any other President ever has, will you not use some of it for our cause and see that these intolerable conditions are changed.

Trusting that you will not become blind and deaf to our cause, I am.

Sincerely yours
Serena Elizabeth Ashford
(Cook)

Savannah,
Ga.
Jan. 13. 1939
Rec'd. 1/19/39

To the Presandent:

I am ritin of these few line to let you know the way they are doin in Savannah here between the white woman an the colord woman take all of the colard woman out of the sewing room and sent them on the fahm an in the worst field in all . . . to dig up skelton an dead body now Mr. Presendent I dont think it is rite for the people of Georgia to threat colored woman worst as they would threat mans the colored woman if they want to work they must go to the fahm or say we haven nothen for Fall for we are not goin to put no Negro in no sewing room there place is on the fahms cold an rain the colard woman haft to go no shelter for they to go out of the rain and till the trucks come from town for them sometime we get good an wet in the rain before a truck can get from town to get us. . . . these white men threat at these poor colord woman an have all the white woman in the house an we are in the wood cutting down three and digging them up by the roots with grub hoe an pick ax these thing ant fare if they are have fahm why dont white woman an the fahm too an have colord woman the sewing room too now if you want men to go to war the Negro mens haft go side by side with the white man an now the white man an now the colord woman can goin a sewing room like the white woman now some must be done with these hard tast Georgia white people. . . . Please for God sake send some one to see about us in Georgia we are under a hard tast master here haft to here from you soon for I am cold haven a piece of wood or cold in my home me an my one child I had to keep her out of school for haven clothes sufison to put on please look at this an fix some place for we as colord woman to have some way to work beside out in the bitter cold on frost too cold an wet.

From one who is out in the cold an rain an no where to go.

(Unsigned)

Raleigh, N.C.
Oct. 12, 1937

Mr. Harry L. Hopkins
Head Administrator of U.S. W.P.A.
Washington, D.C.
Dear Sir:

We the Workers Council of Colored People in Raleigh, N.C. do wish to state some facts to you about how the colored women, (mostly heads of the families) have been treated by W.P.A. heads here. Also wish you to make investigation about it at once for its pure injustice to us, the way it has been done.

We are blamed for private service scarcity of servants and farmers not being able to get workers etc is not our fault.

We can say truly that all women with families and dependent husbands. Cannot get along on such poor wages because wages will not or is not sufficient etc. responsibilities. Some and most of these women have never in their lives worked on farms and some left farms 20 & 25 years ago. We are sure that prices paid are the whole cause & such long work days beginning 6 to 6:30 A.M. till 7:30 & 8:30 P.M. this we know is whole cause of this scarcity. We answer want adds & meet white people that want such help, prices paid not even the rent let lone food and up keep, (rent here is high and one better gett enough to pay it or he's put out sure). Mr. Hopkins, colored women have been turned out in streets to starve & children go to rack, for these prices paid are not enough for a poor willing working mother to care for her children, there by much more distress & trouble is in for as one question is this; Does the government provide money for white people only a certain class of colored people to get help. As you know we all donot like to work in tobacco for good reasons, We are settled women mostly & different troubles that prevent us from riding in open trucks, standing up 20 odd miles twice a day, stand & work all all day long, we're given no notice but to quit work here and work no where not regarding nothing. We also wish you to investigate why that so many teachers unemployed & elegible to teach have not been employed by the Adult Education here, that these teachers can have classes as they once had & help the illiterate colored people. One time it was many grown & old people going to the classes learning & proud of the opportunities etc. Mr. Hopkins colored women have been turned out of different jobs projects to make us take other jobs we mentioned and white women were hired & sent for & given places that colored women was made to leave or quit.

Let us say that if we cannot work on W.P.A. Projects & be compel to take these poor paying jobs; that food, clothes & rent money be provided for us at once because we are suffering. We the Workers Council understood that no colored women cannot be hired this winter on any of the W.P.A. projects. We wish you to tell us why.

We shall be glad to have a reply from you at your earliest convenience.

Respt.

Workers Council for Col. Raleigh, N.C.

Reply to: Mrs. Mary O Kelly Abright
            8 N. Swain St., Raleigh, N.C.

DON'T SHOP WHERE YOU CAN'T WORK

As blacks migrated to northern cities, they often moved into neighborhoods once occupied by white immigrants, and many of the businesses in these neighborhoods remained in white hands. Stores in poor neighborhoods frequently charged more for shoddier goods than in prosperous neighborhoods, since the poor were unable to find alternative outlets. Adding insult to injury, even large chain stores usually refused to hire blacks. As the Depression deepened the sufferings of an already poor people, Harlem women sparked one of the first modern, northern civil rights actions: a boycott of white stores that would not hire blacks.

The first newspaper article reprinted below gives a flavor of the demonstration that inaugurated this campaign. The second articulates one strategic approach being developed at the time—a kind of black economic nationalism.

We are grateful to Barbara Bair for these selections.

WOMEN STAGE PROTEST PARADE; URGE BOYCOTT OF WHITE STORE

April 15th, 1931, will go down in history as the beginning of the end of economic injustice in Harlem!

It was on that date that a small band of courageous Negro women, about sixty in all, without any sustaining cheers from the crowd, marched. . . .

The signs they carried were significant of the rising tide of indignation that is rising in the heart of every one in Harlem against those who boycott our labor and still ask us to patronize them. They expect you to buy from them, yet they literally spit in our faces if we ask to be given employment.

"Don't Buy Where You Can't Work!"

"We are Protesting Against The Boycotting of Colored Labor in Harlem."

"CHICAGO DID IT—WE CAN TOO!"

"WE ARE FIGHTING FOR THE RIGHT TO LIVE."

"BUY FROM NEGRO-OWNED STORES."

"WE PAY THE SALARIES OF 6,880 WHITE CLERKS IN HARLEM." . . .

These were some of the many signs carried and they reflected the sentiment of thousands who stood and looked on, yet didn't have nerve enough to join.

Slowly but surely, Negroes are beginning to realize that the solution to their economic problem is in their own hands. The immense buying power of 250,000 people is a more powerful weapon, needing only the guidance and direction of a leader with courage.

Get yourself into the habit spending every nickle you can in store owned by a Negro. . . .

THE HARLEM HOUSEWIVES BAND TOGETHER TO EMANCIPATE RACE

The New York Urban League in the fall of 1930 in its effort to find employment for its many applicants turned to the buying power of the Negro himself to help solve his own economic problem. Where employers are requested to consider salesgirls and clerks in chain stores on a basis of racial patronage the response is almost negligible. Realizing that a concerted effort on the part of Negroes was necessary to open the industrial world, the Harlem Housewives League was formed. Its purpose is to throw its trade where openings can be made for employment in business patronized by the Negro—and to develop its own business.

Fortunately, the National Negro Business League organized the Colored Merchants Association in Harlem during the year and stood behind the stores, urging new business methods, courtesy, sanitation, fresh stock of the best grade and low prices through organization. The soundness of the program of the National Negro Business League was clear to all and its success depended upon the support of the public. The larger the organization the greater the purchasing power, and thus the lower prices, which would compete favorably with the other chain stores so numerous in all neighborhoods.

The stores taken into the C. M. A. improved greatly and the Harlem Model Grocery at 144th and 7th Avenue set a high standard not excelled by any store of its size in Harlem.

The Harlem Housewives League has the opportunity of pointing out the need of patronizing the C. M. A. stores and other colored business. The first duty is the patronage of its members to these stores. Women of the League believe and are willing to do this even at a sacrifice. If the prices have not obtained in all articles the low level of other stores, they are willing to pay the difference in price, knowing that they are speeding the day for Negro business to succeed and thus give the Negro the economic background which he now lacks.

Business acumen can only be secured through experience. If the Negro continues to return his pay at the end of each week to his white butcher, baker and candle stick and cabinet maker he gives them the opportunity for experimenting in and developing business sagacity. This experience and sagacity he must develop for himself and he can only do it when the income and salaries of his fellowmen come into his hands.

The League recognizes that the churches, lodges, colored insurance companies, schools and all business built up among Negroes have been developed because the prejudices in these fields have given the Negro a chance for training and development.

In mentioning outstanding clergymen of America, Professor Mordecai Johnson of Howard University was named as one of five (by Rabbi Wise of New York). If business men of the country were named, a much longer list would not include a Negro. We have an example of concentration of the race on Madam Walker and Madam Malone's beauty products and methods and we have a fortune in each case and thousands of women throughout the country independently and gainfully employed. This is just one industry. Other industries can be equally developed in our race and give employment to thousands of our boys and girls leaving high school and college each year.

This effort in self-support in no way is a drawback to the Negro in his contact with other races and business. The chain stores have their organization personnel and employees. They do not readily open up to the Negro clerk and as for managership it was impossible to secure an opening. After the Harlem Housewives League was formed and the C. M. A. stores were patronized by former customers of chain stores, colored help has been put in chain stores.

The more the Negro knows about business the more he will be sought in white business concerns. Training is what our race needs and he will not be in demand until he has something to offer, and he cannot offer any contribution until he gets the chance to learn.

The Housewives League pledges its support to the promotion of this program. It has also other civic duties in the community in which it is vitally interested, but at present the economic problem far excells any other in its demands. The housewives have the power to make any business in their neighborhood succeed or fail.

Using the State

UNIONS OPPOSE THE ERA

An Equal Rights Amendment (ERA) was first proposed in 1923 and became the focus of a major split in the women's movement. Feminist ERA advocates, centered in the National Woman's Party, argued that anything other than strictly identical treatment of men and women was bound to be discriminatory; any use of the law to support gender distinctions would continue to deprive women of access to jobs, property, education, and more. By contrast, the majority of women reformers opposed the ERA. "Social feminists," reformers who worked in groups like the Women's Trade Union League and the National Consumers' League, and more mainstream groups like the League of Women Voters, believed that some gender distinctions in law were necessary to protect women's health and safety in a most unequal world. For example, they feared that the ERA would be used by the courts to invalidate the protective labor legislation for which they had fought so hard—laws preventing employers from hiring women for heavy labor or night jobs, for example. Some of these ERA opponents believed that men and women were biologically and psychologically different while others emphasized women's different social roles—for example, motherhood—as the basis of a need for distinctions. (The same controversy, at root, continues in today's feminist movement.)

The ERA also divided women along class lines. The pro-ERA faction usually had privileged women in mind, women who sought access to universities and professions. Trade unionists, the U.S. Women's Bureau, and many working women believed, by contrast, that poor women benefited more from the protective labor legislation than they would from an ERA. They believed that achieving substantive equality between men and women required recognizing and compensating for considerable social and economic inequalities.

They were convinced that equal legal treatment on an unequal playing field would only create more inequality.

WHAT DO WORKING WOMEN SAY?

The Woman's Party Amendment Would Endanger Labor Laws Now Affecting 4,000,000 of Them

Would you say that, in order to give women in Ohio the right to be taxi-drivers or open a shoe-shining parlor, you ought to take away the 48-hour law for women in Massachusetts and the hour laws of 42 other states?

Would you say that in order to give the right to jury service to women in twenty states, you ought to throw into court the mother's pension laws of 39 states?

Would you go so far as to say that you would be justified in even taking the risk of such consequences to the millions of wage earning women and mothers, for the sake of a few prospective women taxi-drivers, bootblacks, and jurors?

Especially when you could get what you want without taking such risk?

Yet it is just exactly those risks—and many more—that the National Woman's Party proposes to take in its constitutional amendment which reads:

"Men and women shall have equal rights throughout the United States and every place subject to its jurisdiction."

The risk is due to the fact, first, that this is an amendment to the United States Constitution and would invalidate automatically all laws in conflict with it, without automatically replacing most of them.

It is due, second, to the fact that blanket provisions in law, whether in the constitution or in statutes, require court interpretation in each case, and the term "rights" and "equal rights" are subject to diverse construction.

And, last but not least, the risk is due to the fact that legal rights and other rights are not by any means identical. Legal equality is not necessarily the same as economic equality. It may actually defeat economic equality.

For instance, a state may give the wife a right to sue her husband for non-support. The husband has not the same right to sue her. The proposed amendment would probably, lawyers say, give this man and this woman equal rights by taking away, automatically, the woman's right to sue.

Having thus achieved legal equality, however, the wife, whose best years have been spent caring for her home and children, now finds herself confronted with the necessity of earning her living and also of contributing to the support of her children. Untrained for business or industry, her life's experience totally different from her husband's, she is now faced with identi-

237

cal responsibilities and a handicap which only a superhuman could overcome.

Legal equality it may be.

Economic equality it is not.

Or consider the woman in industry. She is working, say, in a state with an 8-hour law for women, passed because women had been working much longer hours. The man-employing industries of that state, however, are probably on an 8-hour schedule established by their unions. The 8-hour law and the 8-hour trade agreement both limit the worker's freedom of contract. But the law would probably be destroyed by the so-called "equal rights" amendment, because the legal rights of women are restricted thereunder but not the legal rights of men. In other words, to give the women legal equality with the men, the amendment would take away the 8-hour day from the women but not from the men.

This may be legal equality.

Economic equality, decidedly not.

The risk involved in the National Woman's Party amendment is, moreover, a wholly gratuitous risk. The amendment is altogether unnecessary, because the things it purports to do can all be done, right now, exactly as most of them would have to be done in any case by Acts of Congress and the states, which already have the power the amendment would confer.

Not only can those things all be done, but they are actually being done— 86 new laws or amendments to laws in 30 states since the federal woman suffrage amendment was passed.

Why take a gratuitous risk?

SHALL MARRIED WOMEN WORK?

Americans were growing accustomed to "working women" as their numbers increased, but they were supposed to be single. Married women's employment was still seen by the white majority as a misfortune or, worse, as a sinful and unwomanly state of affairs. In fact, married women's wage labor was more plentiful than was widely recognized, because it was so often temporary, part-time, and / or done at home. Nevertheless, even the underestimated official counts were growing: in 1940, 17 percent of married women were listed as employed, up from 12 percent in 1930 (and the proportion would grow to 25 percent by 1950). That increase was causing controversy because it threatened so directly the ideal of maternal domesticity and the family-wage myth. Depression unemployment intensified the feeling that married working women were stealing jobs that belonged by rights to men. And indeed a number of states and the federal government enacted limitations on married women's right to work.

. . . The Gallup poll found, in 1936, that 82 percent of the people were opposed to married women's working. In 1939 Gallup found that 78 percent were opposed. The Vox Pop poll in 1939 likewise showed that the majority were opposed to the idea. In 1936 *Fortune* made a survey of public opinion and found that 85 percent of the men and 79 percent of the women interviewed thought married women should not work outside the home. None of these polls tested the *degree* of opposition. It would seem that it was mild because so far few laws have been passed against the employment of married women in spite of the many attempts.

Within the last few years, bills have been introduced in the legislatures of twenty-six states against married women workers. Only one of these passed. This was in Louisiana, and it was later repealed. Six other states have either joint resolutions or governors' orders restricting married women's right to work. Three other states have made a general practice of prohibiting married women from working in public employment. . . .

The National Federation of Business and Professional Women's Clubs made a survey early in 1940 of local employment policies. This was part of a general study which assembled all materials relating to the employment of married women. The survey shows that married women are most likely to find bars against them if they seek jobs as school teachers, or as office workers in public utilities or large manufacturing concerns. Only a very small number of department stores refuse jobs to married women. However, in 1939, the *Department Store Economist* reported that the sentiment against married women "is growing stronger." Opposition, it was found, came from customers, labor organizations, women's clubs, and miscellaneous groups of the unemployed. Despite this opposition, "nearly all stores are either doubtful whether it would be a wise plan to announce publicly a policy against hiring or retaining married women, or believe it would not be helpful to public relations." This attitude may reflect the fact that married women's employment has been advantageous to department stores because the necessary part-time arrangements suited both parties well. Single women usually want full-time employment, but many married women prefer to work only a few hours each day. . . .

The bars against married women are of different kinds—all of which exist for some school teachers. They may take the form of refusal to hire married women (the most frequent), of dismissal upon marriage, delay in granting promotion, or actual demotion, and either permanent or temporary dismissal when pregnant. Discrimination is often difficult to detect; a married woman may assume that her marriage is the cause of her inability to hold a job, or to get a new one, when the real reason may lie in her lack of ability, personality, or training.

The National Education Association has from time to time made surveys of employment policies in local communities with respect to married women teachers. Its material is more complete than any other. Its survey, made in 1931, revealed that 77 percent of the cities reporting made a practice of not employing married women as new teachers and 63 percent dismissed women teachers upon marriage. Tenure acts protect married teachers from being dismissed in some states. But although tenure acts may protect teachers who marry after being employed, they do not assure a new teacher that marriage will not be a bar to getting a job. The National Education Association reported in 1939 that teachers in at least thirteen states are legally protected by court decisions from being dismissed for being married. Kentucky seems to be the only state where the contract of marriage is deemed "the very basis of the whole fabric of society" and hence is not an obstacle to employment. . . .

Studies show that men have been affected by unemployment to a much greater extent than have women, because unemployment has been most acute in the heavy industries (steel, oil, mining, etc.) where men are mostly employed. . . . The administrative and clerical jobs connected with these industries, which are partially filled by women, have not been eliminated to anything like the same degree as production jobs.

Consumer and service industries (textiles, food, beauty parlors, telephone service, to name only a few), where women are mostly to be found, were not affected so seriously as heavy industries by the depression. The government's recovery measures, based on artificially increasing purchasing power, chiefly stimulated the consumer and service industries, thus opening up relatively more opportunities for women than for men. As a result, women have fared better than men in getting new jobs. . . .

State and federal employment offices also give evidence of the relative ease with which women have obtained jobs compared with men and indicate that men have been unemployed for longer periods of time than have women. One study of a community of 14,000 people in the West makes this point specific. Women's work in the town increased during the early years of the depression in the needle trades and textiles as well as in the service occupations, while men's work in glass declined sharply. Another study in a steel town showed much the same thing. Few of the people who oppose married women's employment seem to realize that a coal miner or steel worker cannot very well fill the jobs of nursemaids, cleaning women, or the factory and clerical occupations now filled by women. Unhappily, men accustomed to work in the heavy industries have not been able to fill the jobs in consumer and service industries. Retraining of these men has been practically negligible, and could not have been done in time to benefit them immediately. Expenditures for defense are now once more increasing opportunities in the heavy industries, so we may expect to see a fundamental change in the situation in coming months. . . .

ABOVE. In the 1909–10 shirtwaist strike, women demonstrated their militance and persever-
ance. This photograph, although probably posed, illustrates their genuine enthusiasm as
they volunteer for picket duty at strike headquarters. *(Courtesy Cornell University Library)*
BELOW. Women sometimes physically fought armed guards, as in the important Gastonia,
North Carolina, textile strike of 1929. *(Archives of Labor and Urban Affairs, Wayne State
University)*

ABOVE. The Depression stimulated many different groups into political action. This photograph illustrates that militance among the handicapped has roots in earlier periods. *(Schomburg Center for Research in Black Culture) BELOW.* Political activity is also social activity and brings its own rewards, as these jitterbugging packinghouse strikers show during the CIO organizing drive of the 1930s.

ABOVE. Many agricultural workers were forced to "follow the crops" as migrants, particularly Mexican Americans. The New Deal established some farm labor camps for them, providing healthier living conditions, education, and better wages. These women are harvesting spinach in such a camp in 1942. *(Library of Congress)*

LEFT. Although World War II produced a decline in the number of domestics working for individuals, many women did the same kinds of work for business and government. This famous photo by Gordon Parks shows Mrs. Ella Watson, who supported an adopted daughter and three grandchildren as a government charwoman. *(Library of Congress)*

LEFT. The drive to draw women into production for World War II simultaneously insisted that women would remain responsible for housework and child care—that they would still be traditional wives to their husbands. *(John Rawlings. Courtesy* House & Gardens. *Copyright 1943 [Renewed 1971] by The Condé Nast Publications, Inc.)*

BELOW. The war brought women unprecedented access to skilled, unionized, and racially integrated employment, as these 1943 defense-industry welders. *(Library of Congress)*

Above. Despite the fact that the great majority of women are now employed, they still continue to do almost all the housework and child care and they still sometimes find ways of doing it together with other women as in this 1962 photo from the Midwest. *(State Historical Society of Wisconsin, WHi [x3]49245)*

Below. Although prostitution declined in the early twentieth century as sexual mores relaxed, there is still a demand for prostitutes, as this 1985 photo shows, and it remains an extremely dangerous occupation, especially for streetwalkers like these. *(Ethan Hoffman Archive)*

LEFT. Women in traditionally female occupations have been renewing struggles for unionization in the last few decades. These saleswomen were striking against Gimbel's in Milwaukee in 1955. *(State Historical Society of Wisconsin, WHi [x3]11249)*

BELOW. Even stewardesses, once stereotyped as the most conventional of women workers, have built unions, inspired by the women's liberation movement. The victories of flight attendants' unions in the 1990s grew out of two decades of struggle, as illustrated by these Northwest Orient Airlines picketers in 1970. *(State Historical Society of Wisconsin, WHi [x3]49286)*

1940–1955

1940–1955: INTRODUCTION

WARS have always had a significant impact on women and none more so than World War II. While its effects were mainly short-lived and did not fundamentally alter long-term employment patterns, its challenges to women's consciousness of themselves as wage-earners probably did have a far-reaching impact, contributing to the revival of the women's movement in the 1960s.

The proportion of women working increased during the war from 25 percent to 36 percent, a jump greater than that of the preceding four decades. Wages rose during the war and unionization of women quadrupled. Most employers remained skeptical about hiring women, but since women were the only available labor force reserve, they had no choice.

The war gave women access to skilled, higher-paying industrial jobs for the first time. Many women taking these jobs had always been employed, but had been previously restricted to lower-paying, unskilled, service jobs. Women responded to these new opportunities with skill, ingenuity, patriotism, and resourcefulness, as they became switchwomen, precision toolmakers, overhead crane operators, lumberjacks, drill press operators, and stevedores, demonstrating that women could fill any job, no matter how difficult or arduous. War plants paid wages often 40 percent higher than in the traditional women's industries. Twenty-nine thousand women joined the Women's Land Army, helping to replace the farmers who had been shipped overseas. Three hundred thousand enlisted in the military service, although none were trained in the use of weapons.

Not only were more women working, but different kinds of women were drawn into the labor force. Despite employer resistance, many minority women found jobs in the manufacturing sector for the first time. The proportion of married women and mothers in the labor force increased greatly; as the fighting ceased, wives for the first time composed the majority of women workers. Previous bans on the employment of married women were discarded, and the average age of employed women increased. Housewives planted victory gardens, rationed scarce resources, and volunteered in droves to help the war effort.

The war did not, however, make a lasting or profound difference in the public attitude toward employed women nor did it redefine sex roles. During the war, women continued to receive less pay than men (65 percent less in manufacturing), to be denied opportunities for training and advancement, and to work in separate job categories. Unions fought for equal pay when women took jobs left by men, usually out of concern for preserving a high wage for the returning veterans; but they rarely objected to the separate seniority lists for women and the continuation of job segregation which reserved the best jobs for men. Often, collective-bargaining contracts created separate job classifications and granted women union membership and seniority only for the duration of the war.

The war even made discrimination against women more profitable for many companies. The government encouraged companies to hire women with grants, special tax reductions, and other incentives for installing women's restrooms, lighter fixtures, and conveyors to slide parts from one machine to another. In many cases, whole new factories were built with the government footing most of the bills. Yet industrialists argued that women should receive lower wages because of these special adjustments.

At the end of the war, the U.S.-Soviet alliance disintegrated and a new "Cold War" emerged, with the United States dedicated above all to the destruction of communism at home and abroad. This period of virulent anticommunism from 1947 through 1954 is usually called the McCarthy period, after the senator from Wisconsin who spearheaded the congressional investigations of "unAmericans" in government, media, unions, schools, and even the armed forces. In this hysteria, thousands of radicals and progressives were persecuted and fired, hundreds were jailed, and Ethel and Julius Rosenberg were executed on charges of giving atomic secrets to the Russians—the only case in U.S. history of an execution in peacetime for espionage.

The Cold War influenced working women in several ways. Despite increases in membership and control, unions lost some of their prewar power when (with the single exception of the United Mine Workers) they took a no-strike pledge for the duration of the war. Furthermore, workers were pressured by unions, management, and government to make sacrifices because of the war and accept less beneficial working conditions: the average work week was extended to forty-eight hours, time-and-a-half pay for overtime was suspended, and piece work (being paid on the basis of the number of items produced) was reinstated.

After the war, between 1945 and 1947, workers responded to high inflation with the largest strike wave in U.S. history, usually led by the rank and file rather than union leadership. Government and corporations countered with an attack on communists in the unions, hoping to break the power of the New Deal/Labor/Democratic Party alliance. The majority of unions cooperated and conducted anticommunist purges themselves. In a further attempt to break labor's power, the Taft-Hartley Law of 1947 allowed injunctions against strikes, gave courts the power to fine alleged violators, established a sixty-day cooling-off period during which strikes could not be declared, outlawed mass picketing, denied trade unions the right to contribute to political campaigns, abolished the closed shop, prohibited secondary boycotts, and authorized employers to interfere with employee attempts to join unions.

McCarthyism also stopped the progress toward a welfare state that the New Deal had promised. A hoped-for public medical insurance program never materialized. Indeed, McCarthy's first victory was in defeating a public housing bill in the Truman administration.

The Cold War terror also expressed itself culturally. McCarthyism, with its insistence on conformity, had a chilling impact on experimentation in the arts and education and enforced conventional gender relations. The witchhunt included a major repression of homosexuals and a reassertion of traditional femininity and marital relations sometimes known as the "feminine mystique." Educators, social workers, psychologists, and journalists were among those who tried to convince women that their place was in the home, rearing children. The emphasis on homemaking also served, conveniently, to drive women out of the labor force as employment contracted, and to encourage consumption just as new markets were needed to prevent a postwar depression. In many ways, the feminine mystique was the gendered face of McCarthyism.

In fact, it is not clear how successful this propaganda campaign was. Throughout the 1950s, the participation of women in the labor force climbed. Many women displaced from heavy industries did not in fact return to the kitchen but found work in "traditional" low-paying women's jobs. In spite of the conservative cultural turn, many women continued to participate in peace, housing, integration, child welfare, and educational activism, thus planting the seeds for the liberation movements of the 1960s and 1970s.

The War

MOTHERS IN OVERALLS ————————————————

The War Manpower Commission undertook campaigns to encourage women to take jobs in 1943. Newspaper ads, radio spots, even ten-minute films for local movie theaters were used. The following is a sample of an outdoor billboard.

> "What Job is mine on the Victory Line?"
> If you've sewed on buttons, or made buttonholes, on a machine,
> you can learn to do spot welding on airplane parts.
> If you've used an electric mixer in your kitchen,
> you can learn to run a drill press.
> If you've followed recipes exactly in making cakes,
> you can learn to load shell.

BLACK WOMEN IN WAR PRODUCTION ————————————

At the beginning of the war, black people found it difficult to obtain jobs and housing despite the increased demand for labor power. In January 1941, A. Philip Randolph, leader of the Brotherhood of Sleeping Car Porters, proposed a March on Washington to demand that the government take remedial action. To head off the demonstration, President Roosevelt promised Randolph that the government would act against discrimination and in June 1941 issued Executive Order 8802 banning discrimination in defense industries or in government "because of race, creed, color, or national origin." A Fair Employment Practices Commission was set up to carry out the order. This government intervention plus increased labor shortages brought more blacks into the labor force. Black women entered steel foundries, munition and aircraft plants, the army, canneries, and hospitals. The number of blacks in civilian jobs increased by a million between April 1940 and April 1944; but only six thousand of these were women. The most significant change for black women in these war years was a movement from the farms to the factories; the proportion of black women on farms halved in four years. Some upgrading took place, but most blacks remained in unskilled jobs. For many black women the war nevertheless provided a first opportunity to demonstrate ability in factory work.

The following excerpt from an Urban League publication describes the situation in St. Louis and is reasonably typical of the problems faced by black women in other industrial centers.

In July 1942, the Curtiss-Wright Company and the U.S. Cartridge Company announced that they would accept Negro applicants for training for skilled and semiskilled operators. By August the Curtiss-Wright Company had approximately 500 Negro workers in a segregated building on a variety of skilled jobs including welders, riveters, assemblers and inspectors.

Simultaneously, the U.S. Cartridge Company provided a segregated plant identical with other production units and employed a complete force of Negro production workers. . . .

At peak production the company employed a total of 4,500 Negroes, many of whom held jobs as machine operators, millwrights, inspectors, and adjusters.

If this form of segregation in industry can be looked upon with favor, it might be said that these firms made a reasonable effort to use the available Negro labor supply. However, other large industries attempted to restrict the number of Negroes to the population ratio of one to ten. Further, they made little or no effort to upgrade Negroes according to seniority or skills. This flat refusal to comply with the spirit and letter of the Executive Order has precipitated a very unsatisfactory situation and has caused numerous strikes and work stoppages among dissatisfied Negro workers. The prejudices of white workers in the area is usually blamed for the failure to upgrade Negroes. In at least 100 important war production plants no Negro workers have been employed.

The employment of Negro women in St. Louis industries presents a more discouraging picture as might be expected. Stronger resistance to their use except as maids and cleaners, or in segregated workshops, has been encountered in almost every instance. With the exception of the Curtiss-Wright Company which employs about 200 women as riveters, assemblers, and inspectors, and the U.S. Cartridge Company which used almost 1,000 women as operators and inspectors, few plants in the area have attempted to use them. The lack of separate toilet facilities and the prejudices of white women workers are the main barriers to the wider use of Negro women, according to officials of many of 200 plants that refuse to employ them.

Perhaps the one bright spot in this picture is the development in the garment industry, although the policy of segregation has been followed even in this field despite our efforts to eliminate it. Since 1930 the Urban League of St. Louis has worked to secure employment opportunities for Negro women in some of the numerous textile plants. In the Spring of 1941 the Acme Manufacturing Company opened an all-Negro plant employing 28 operators, a packer and a foreman. . . .

Until March, 1943, no other manufacturer would consider the employment of Negro women. With depleted labor reserves and mounting war orders, several plants were forced to look elsewhere for workers and the Portnoy Garment Company was one of the first to consider the use of Negroes. While not willing to integrate Negroes in the plant, the Portnoy Company agreed to open an all-Negro plant if a suitable building could be obtained and qualified workers were available. Because of the exclusion of Negroes from the trade, there were few if any experienced operators except those employed by the Acme Co. However, the St. Louis and East St. Louis N.Y.A. projects had given training to approximately 300 girls and a few had been trained at the Washington Technical School. From these groups, it was possible to recruit a sufficient number of operators to open the new plant on May 10, 1943. By the end of the year 60 women were employed and by May 1, 1944 the factory had 90 workers and was planning an expansion to accommodate an additional 40 operators. . . .

Negro workers in the St. Louis area have not accepted the discrimination against them without protest. Through mass meetings and petitions they have expressed their disapproval of the situation even after they secured employment. No less than a half dozen all-Negro strikes have occurred in protest to discriminatory hiring or working policies. In June, 1943, Negroes employed in the segregated plan of the U.S. Cartridge Company struck because the company would not upgrade qualified Negroes to jobs as foremen. The company finally agreed to comply with their demands. A few weeks later the workers in the segregated Curtiss-Wright staged a sit-down strike protesting the lack of adequate cooling equipment. In August, 1943, 600 Negro workers in the General Steel Castings plant in Madison, Illinois, struck because of a number of grievances including differentials in pay rates and discrimination against Negro women workers. After several weeks of negotiations in which the Urban League took an active part, 61 of the 62 grievance cases were satisfactorily adjusted.

In November, 1943 and March, 1944, 380 Negro employees of the Monsanto Chemical Company staged a series of work stoppages, one of which lasted 10 days. Long-standing grievances against both the company and the union were responsible for the difficulties, but the refusal to upgrade Negro workers was the major complaint. The League was instrumental in placing their grievances before company and union officials and an acceptable settlement was finally negotiated. Minor incidents involving the introduction and integration of Negro workers in the industries in this area have been too frequent to enumerate, and they have served to further confuse a very tense and unsettled war production center. . . .

SHIPYARD DIARY OF A WOMAN WELDER ————————

Augusta Clawson was a federal government worker who went to work in a shipyard in Oregon in order to write up her experiences and encourage other women to enlist in war production. Her employers were not aware of her patriotic purpose.

Until World War II women were not accepted in shipbuilding, even as office secretaries. By January 1944 women were 9.5 percent of all the workers in the industry. The problems of physical, administrative, and psychological adjustment in an industry totally unprepared for women workers were formidable, but women adjusted far better than the industry expected, as Clawson's memoir illustrates.

Back to work and more welding. I "dis-improved" as rapidly after lunch as I had improved during the morning. One girl stopped to ask, "How you doin'?" and watched me critically. "Here, let me show you, you're holding it too far away." So she took over, but she couldn't maintain the arc at all. She got up disgusted, said, "I can't do it—my hand shakes so since I been sick," and I took over again. But she was right. I held it closer and welded on and on and on. . . .

The redheaded mother of seven was terribly upset. Her boy got his papers yesterday, and she hadn't slept all night. First thing this morning she had to take her test and was as jittery as could be. I wonder if this is the sort of thing that people glibly call "the emotional instability of women" without investigating first to find its cause! A mother has a right to be at less than her calmest when her eldest son is leaving to join the Army. But this woman, in the midst of all her worry, had room for concern about me. She came running up. "Say, my eldest boy leaves tomorrow. You can come and live with us if you like." I hesitated, reflecting that it would be difficult to record my daily impressions without risking her suspicion that I might have an ulterior motive for taking this job. So I temporized. "You're a brick to suggest it, but you can't spare a room for me when you still have six children in the house." She looked puzzled. "A room?" she said. "Why, I don't know—maybe I could fix you up a room." Then she shrugged her bewilderment away. "No, I mean just come and live with us." That's what I call hospitality. . . .

We were called to another safety lecture—good sound advice on Eye Safety. . . . Only Chile has a higher accident rate than the United States. Last year the shipyard had fairly heavy absenteeism, but this year they hope to build an extra ship on the decrease in absenteeism. He cautioned us about creating hazards by wearing the wrong kind of clothing, and told us not to wear watches or rings. After it was over, Missouri was bothered about her wedding ring. It hadn't been off in fourteen years. She was willing to take it off, but only if necessary.

The lecturer brought up the rumor that arc welding causes sterility among women. He said that this was untrue, and quoted an authoritative source to prove its falsity. . . . Actually, welders had *more* children than other people. "No, thanks," said the first girl; "I don't like that either!"

The Big Swede is a real pal. She had not forgotten the patch for my overall trouser leg. She had cut a piece from an old pair of her husband's, scrubbed it to get the oil out, and brought it to me with a needle stuck in the center and a coil of black thread ready for action. "Here," she said, "I knew you wouldn't have things handy in a hotel room. Now you mend that hole before you catch your foot in it and fall." . . .

I, who hates heights, climbed stair after stair after stair till I thought I must be close to the sun. I stopped on the top deck. I, who hate confined spaces, went through narrow corridors, stumbling my way over rubber-coated leads—dozens of them, scores of them, even hundreds of them. I went into a room about four feet by ten where two shipfitters, a shipfitter's helper, a chipper, and I all worked. I welded in the poop deck lying on the floor while another welder spattered sparks from the ceiling and chippers like giant woodpeckers shattered our eardrums. I, who've taken welding, and have sat at a bench welding flat and vertical plates, was told to weld braces along a baseboard below a door opening. On these a heavy steel door was braced while it was hung to a fine degree of accuracy. I welded more braces along the side, and along the top. I did overhead welding, horizontal, flat, vertical. I welded around curved hinges which were placed so close to the side wall that I had to bend my rod in a curve to get it in. I made some good welds and some frightful ones. But now a door in the poop deck of an oil tanker is hanging, four feet by six of solid steel, by *my* welds. Pretty exciting! . . .

Poor Texas had to work all afternoon in double bottom. She said she couldn't stand; she couldn't even sit up straight. She rested somewhat on a narrow pipe and did production. She was not very happy about it. It's funny the way we all dodge production. There isn't such a great difference between the techniques of tacking and doing production welding, but there is in the responsibility. When we tack we know a production welder will weld over the tack, and any gaps will be filled by him (or her). But when we do production we know ours is the final responsibility. . . .

I talked with Joanne, a very attractive brunette who had previously been a waitress in Atlantic City. She came West when her husband came on for a job. She, like the other waitresses, preferred welding because you "don't have to take so much from the public." . . .

I had a good taste of summer today, and I am convinced that it is going to take backbone for welders to stick to their jobs through the summer months. It is harder on them than on any of the other workers—their leathers are so hot and heavy, they get more of the fumes, and their hoods become instruments of torture. There were times today when I'd have to stop in the middle of a tack and push my hood back just to get a breath of fresh air. It grows unbearably hot under the hood, my glasses fog and blur my vision, and the only thing to do is to stop.

For almost an hour I tacked on in spite of the fact that there was no blower in the room. Then I took Texas's advice and decided "no blower, no welder." . . . My work was in the poop deck where the last crew had put brackets in place *upside down*. The burner had to burn off six of them completely. For me, this meant climbing halfway up the wall and tacking them in place with horizontal, vertical, and overhead tacks. One's position is often so precarious at such an angle that it is hard to maintain a steady arc. Add to this that often I could not stand straight nor kneel. The result was that trying to hold a position halfway between would start some contrary nerve quivering so that my hand would carry out the "jiggle" and affect the weld. Yet the job confirmed my strong conviction—I have stated it before—what exhausts the woman welder is not the work, nor the heat, nor the demands upon physical strength. It is the apprehension that arises from inadequate skill and consequent lack of confidence; and this *can* be overcome by the right kind of training. I've mastered tacking now, so that no kind bothers me. I know I can do it if my machine is correctly set, and I have learned enough of the vagaries of machines to be able to set them. And so, in spite of the discomforts of climbing, heavy equipment, and heat, I enjoyed the work today because I *could do it*. . . .

The drinking fountains are a godsend in such weather as this. The water is always cold. Often I hesitate to leave work long enough for a drink, since if a tack is needed the shipfitters have to stop work until it is done. But I think we are all getting to be more sensible about realizing that once in a while we have to stop, even if work waits for a moment. So midway in the morning I told my men, "Guess I have to have a drink," and off I went. All the time that I was tacking, three or four shipfitters would be sitting down waiting for me to finish. Several weeks ago this would have given me a hurried feeling; I'd have rushed the work, done it less well, and been more tired. I've learned now to work a steady pace and to ignore the fact that anyone is waiting. It relieves the strain and the work really gets done faster. There is a lot in this game in learning to relax *on* the job as well as *between* jobs. . . .

MILITARY SEGREGATION

Women had first been admitted to the armed forces as nurses during World War I. However, in World War II the number of women in uniform jumped dramatically to over 350,000: 140,000 served in the Women's Army Corps, 100,000 in the Navy, 23,000 in the Marines, 1,000 in the Air Force, 13,000 in the Coast Guard, and another 74,000 in the Army and Navy Nurse Corps. (Indeed, one-third of all active professional nurses were in the armed services.) Most of these military women were segregated into traditionally female jobs, such as typing, filing, keeping records, and cleaning, and many military men expected the women to function as their servants and, not infrequently, as sexual partners upon demand. Minority women were even further discriminated against. African Americans were only integrated into the armed forces by President Truman's executive order in 1948, and not fully integrated until the Korean War. Before this, blacks served in segregated units, where they were often relegated to menial labor, as the following letter shows.

We thank Leisa Meyer for this selection.

4844 Indiana Avenue
Chicago, Illinois
Feb. 26th, 1944

Dear Sir:

I am a Wac stationed at Florence Army Air Field in Florence, South Car. at present I am AWOL and will really kill myself before I'll return to that, excuse the expression, "hell's hole." . . . I was placed in a white outfit, then I asked to be transferred to a colored training unit because I am very much a negro despite my make-up. I was told by the commanding officer there that the social standing of the negro was so low that I would not want to be associated with them and once I was with the white she would not have me transferred. . . . I took a discharge and stayed out about a year, but it is more or less a tradition in my family for some member to be associated with the armed forces. I reenlisted at the recruiting station in Chicago. I stated my problem and received assurance that I would be with a colored outfit. I had a picture published in the Chicago defender [a Chicago black newspaper] and also enlisted as far as I could at the 47th St. station. Yet I was shipped to a white outfit. I was treated royal, a swell job and what have you, but its more than I can take. The cracks [crackers, a derogatory term for southern rural whites], being associated with people who's only thought is to keep the negro back. I can not have my boy friend who has been overseas almost three years return to me wherever I am. I can't have my mother and father visit me. Yet I can't get a transfer. My problem is too much for me. I am not hiding out. I'm staying at the same address I enlisted from and am asking you to offer me your aid. I do not wish to return to S. C. but I do want to return to the WAC *with a colored outfit* where I *belong heart* and *soul.*

Please lend me your advice and aid. I'll be waiting for your answer at the above address.

Sincerely,

/s/ Pvt. Nellie R. Holliday
A.S.N., A-204102
4844 Indiana Ave.
Chicago, Ill.

ACCOMMODATING THE WORKING WOMAN

When the government and private industry needed women in the work force, they managed to furnish women with day care and other services to lighten the triple burden of managing a home, children, and job. Some of these services have become commercially available today due to the growth of women's employment. Others, like housing and day care, are still scarce.

To correct conditions such as Mrs. War Worker often faces, local industries are cooperating in many places to provide night shopping hours for industrial workers. In one case a grocery store, meat market, and barber and beauty shop have been established at the plant. At another factory the local department store brings out a display of articles for selection and order placement at the plant during the lunch and off hours. Banking services also are available at this plant on pay days for deposit of checks.

In many cities, stores are readjusting shopping hours for the benefit of war workers. Some stores are staying open one or two nights a week. Various other methods have been adopted in an effort to solve the problem.

In Philadelphia some butchers hold back part of their meat supply until 6 P.M. to accommodate housewives who must do their shopping late. St. Louis volunteers collect last-minute information on the "best buys" at stores and markets, and get it to the warplant workers before they leave their jobs, eliminating unnecessary shopping.

Several plants in New York and New Jersey have plans worked out by management and unions that are helping to solve the food problem. A representative from a grocery store comes to the plant every morning, takes food orders from the women workers, and brings the food at the end of the shift.

A plant manufacturing electrical equipment has arranged with a local department store to open a branch in the plant. The items sold are selected to cover essentials, and a special extension service has been set up which will help workers solve their shopping problems without having to miss work.

When women war workers in the Niagara Frontier Area were not getting a fair shopping break, the Labor-Management Council decided to do something about it. Mrs. Stay-At-Home was buying up all the bargains; Mrs. War Worker found the stocks depleted. The council, composed of representatives of management, of the AFL, the CIO, and the International Association of Machinists from 28 war plants in this area, and representing more than 200,000 potential shoppers, sought the cooperation of the merchants in the Buffalo area. Merchants promised to keep back a certain part of their bargains until evening for women war workers.

In an attempt to ease the shopping problem for its thousands of employees who work in the Pentagon, world's largest office building, in Arlington, Va., just across the Potomac from Washington, the War Department has set up various shopping facilities within the building. Among the most popular of these services is a shoe-repair shop, which reports a flourishing business. Many hundreds of pairs of shoes a week are rejuvenated here. Employees may also order articles from the Washington stores through personal shoppers stationed in the building.

In four big war plants, the personnel workers accept lists of wanted articles culled from the advertisements in a nearby city's newspapers. Department-store representatives call at the plants with samples, from which the employees may order. Deliveries are made to the workers at the plants.

Even the most ideal shopping conditions, however, will not solve the food problem. Consider the case of Jean Smith, who is all too typical. She works in a west coast aircraft factory and likes her job. But she's not getting enough to eat. In order to make the 8 A.M. shift she must leave her home at 6 o'clock, which means that she very often eats no breakfast. (In another west coast plant it was found that of 293 workers interviewed 84 percent of the women factory workers were eating poor breakfasts and 40 percent of the men had insufficient breakfasts.) The company provides a good hot lunch, but dinner is a problem. Mrs. Smith, tired, hot, and dirty after a day in the plant, must either stand in line at some restaurant or shop for food when she finishes work. Then the chances are that the butcher and the grocer are out of nearly everything. As a result she is suffering from malnutrition.

It is for people like Mrs. Smith that a Detroit food company has begun a prepared-food service for carry-out orders in its 21 stores. The carry-out line thus far worked out includes such items as macaroni and cheese, spaghetti, chile con carne, codfish balls, chicken à la king, chicken pies, potato salad, and creamed spinach.

Mrs. Dorothy Roosevelt, specialist on women's problems in war industries for the War Production Board in the Detroit area, in urging that such a program be set up on a mass basis said, "Through such a set-up we figure we could save a woman three hours a day—a minimum for shopping and preparing and cooking food."

Since the early days of the war the Women's Bureau has recommended that community kitchens be established where women war workers might purchase hot, nutritious food at prices within the means of working people, which they could take home.

"British restaurants" are serving daily over ten million nourishing meals in some 2,000 restaurants and canteens. These meals are priced at about 23 cents. . . .

In recruiting women, one large firm told them among other things that there was a nice housing project near the plant. The recruiters failed to add that the nice housing project was already filled. Needless to say, such tactics worked havoc with the morale of the company's new employees. Fortunately for war production such false promises are rare.

Women looking for rooms face problems just as difficult, for all too often only men are wanted by the renters. Landladies report that women are "more bother," "more trouble around the house," "always under foot," "always using the one bathroom in the house to do personal laundry," "women want to wash and iron and cook, and they think the telephone is their private property."

In a small North Carolina town a survey showed that only six percent of the housing listed was available to women. . . .

In one city a Mrs. A. turned her small grocery store and most of her house, which is attached, into a dormitory and several large sleeping rooms. At first she had men roomers, but she changed to women roomers after a girl who was unable to find lodgings came to her one night and pleaded for a place to stay. She is now furnishing accommodations for industrial women who work at an airfield and the two shipyards. . . .

JAPANESE INTERNMENT

The forced relocation and confinement in concentration camps of Japanese and Japanese Americans completely disrupted people's work and daily lives. Many lost farms and businesses that they had painstakingly built up for decades, and others lost jobs. Work in these miserable, often desert, camps was mainly tedious, unskilled, and unfulfilling, and the breakdown of the traditional age and sexual division of labor offended many older people. How-

ever, some women and youth benefited from new opportunities and the loosening of old boundaries.

Before the war, we were very quiet about our heritage, and if we wanted to do anything about it, we were doing it almost under cover because it wasn't popular and it felt dangerous. We were criticized for being unassimilated, and hanging onto Japanese ways was another proof we were unassimilated.

. . . on a Sunday morning on December 7, 1941, we heard over the radio the news of Pearl Harbor. Because we knew of the long, ugly background of anti-Oriental sentiment in which we grew up, it was a frightening thing to realize that Japan was at war with the United States. We sensed something very, very foreboding and frightening. And immediately that night, the FBI was already at the doors of the Isseis [Japanese immigrants] and arrested many, many, and the rumors and news of all of this was frightening. Then one Issei committed suicide and real fear and terror and a great sense of helplessness came over us. . . .

There were people who wanted us out of the way for economic reasons and found the war was a good opportunity to do what they had been wanting to do for the last fifty years. They were upset because of our farming success. But many of the farms would never have produced as much if it hadn't been for the Isseis. They were willing to work hard, and where other people would never have thought of farming, the Japanese reclaimed the lands and changed them into productive estates. But, with the war, many were anxious to get our land and our flowers, fruit, vegetables, and fishing industry. . . .

The military people had said, "Well, we are going to try to keep the families together." But when we went to sign up it was terrible. Already families had been sitting there and lining up who thought they were going to go together, but then they found out that there weren't enough seats all together so they were going to send certain ones to another place, to Manzanar. Families were split up at the moment of departure and there was such anguish. But our family of six remained together, and we left Florin on May 29 and went to the Fresno Assembly Center.

And when we arrived there all the ugliness came out. We were herded in together in terrible heat, and tar was dripping in from our barracks. So many feelings were hurt and some of us blamed us, and people were running around trying to come and tell me that it was my fault that families were split up. That I had betrayed them by helping with the evacuation. We were tearing at each other; when you get frightened, you do that. The ugliest part of us came out, and we were surprised that we were doing that to each other. We had been friends. [Cries.]

And the floor was asphalt and the beds were sinking, and they had a pile of straw and gave us a mattress to fill with the straw for our own mattresses.

The first night that we got there, we got separated and we couldn't find our parents. We were supposed to stay together, as one family; we had our family number. But for some reason, they had put Grandpa and Grandma and Al's sister in another room way on the other end of the camp. Finally Al found them. We asked the military, "Please, we're one family. Put us together." So eventually they got us together. They had another family in with us in a small room for the first night. There were six of us and four more. It was Al's cousin and his wife and two little babies and the babies cried all night. So I never will forget that first night. We were hot and dusty and taken from our own homes, from our own lives, from our own security of farming, and we were thrown into that.

My daughter was five and I remember her crying for a whole week. You really never understood why the children were crying. They were just upset about the whole thing. They had left all they knew. I suppose when you're reporting to the federal government, little things like the disruptions we faced were unimportant, but they were very big things for human beings because we were a family. We each had our human lives. Each of us 110,000 have a different story to tell.

When we went to camp, I was in real pain from my arthritis, having gone through trying to get 2,500 people ready for evacuation and having wept so much all along the way. Then, when I arrived in Fresno Assembly Center, I was so much in pain that I went to the hospital to see a doctor, and he decided that maybe if I kept my arm immobile it would get better, and he put it in a plaster cast. Well, that's the way it stayed. So that was the wrong thing to have done. I've never been able to move my arm since.

Then we were slowly sent from the Fresno Assembly Center in California to Jerome, Arkansas, by train. We had to sleep sitting up, and life was going on on the train; babies were born and people died; and there was chicken pox and measles. We had to quarantine the people with chicken pox, and there was no place to quarantine but the women's restroom so the family had to sit in there. And some children who were very nervous were on the verge of nervous breakdowns; it was very hard for them because it was so confusing. I'm just surprised some of the children came out as well as they did. When we finally got to Jerome, Arkansas, the camp was crowded and in a hot, swampy lowland with water moccasins all around. But that's where we stayed.

It was such a hard time for all of us. We were surrounded by barbed wire fences and military guards, and people were confused about how to deal with all of it. Some family members turned against each other, and the government blundered in so many ways.

But, still, more than 2,500 boys volunteered from these camps to go into the Nisei [Japanese Americans born in the United States] combat unit and prove the Japanese American's loyalty, and they were sent to Camp Shelby and went overseas. They became the most decorated unit of that size in the history of the American military forces, the 442d of the Hundredth Infantry. But the boys came out to our camp, a concentration camp, on their furloughs because their parents were far away in Hawaii or they were in Manzanar or Tule Lake, and the soldiers weren't allowed to go to California to see their parents! So they just went to any one of the relocation centers where they could see other Japanese people because they were so lonely and so worried about their families. We realized that we needed to provide dances for them, to have the girls organized for when they came. I was the director of the camp YWCA and opened up a USO and organized the girls and tried to help the boys when they came. We ended up being invited to Camp Shelby before they shipped overseas. We took a bus load of girls over there for a dance and had our worship service with them the Sunday morning before they left. And many of the boys never came through the war experience. So many of them got hurt and died.

Many people lost their farms or stores or homes. Many of us still had mortgages on the land when we went into the camps, and the government said they were going to freeze the mortgages, but they didn't. So the banks wrote to the farmers and asked what they were going to do with the debt they owed when they couldn't pay it. Then the banks said, "Somebody wants to buy your property." Well, in the headlines at that time, the spring and summer of 1943, the American Legion was demanding that we be deported. All these headlines were sounding like we'd never get to come back to California, and so people decided maybe they should sell and they sold their property. They got very little money for it since they owed the money to the banks. So the banks made the money. During the war, grape prices were high, and people made a lot of money who stayed here. They just sent us away at the right time, so some people who drove us out must have surely known. . . .

So we Japanese Americans must fight to make it right. We don't want to be pointed out as a model minority group so people can say, "Oh, they made it so it's OK. Let's forget the wrong we did to them and the wrong we do to others." That's not the way it should be. If they wronged us and others, we all need to clean it up. If the Constitution is going to be interpreted the way it was with the evacuation, another group might be mistreated. . . .

So seeking redress is a very difficult thing for me to do because I'm breaking through a cultural background that is different and that taught me to be meek. But I'm finally learning that as an American I need to speak out. And I'm finally beginning to realize, after I'm sixty-six years old and maybe don't have that many years ahead, I'm suddenly realizing that I've wasted a lot of my time just being afraid and just being polite and just holding back and just letting people do just what they want with us. And that's what happened. We let them do everything.

Feminine Mystique and Feminine Reality

POSTWAR PLANS

In 1944–45 field agents for the Women's Bureau conducted a study of more than thirteen thousand women employed in ten war-manufacturing areas, about their reasons for working and whether they wanted to continue to work after the war. Popular mythology has implied that women happily left the work force and returned to housewifery after World War II. Recent feminist scholarship, union grievances, and government reports like that excerpted here tell another story. Although most women wanted to keep their wartime jobs, they expected to be laid off at the end of the war. What they did not expect, and what made them angry, was that they were not rehired in accordance with their seniority when plants were converted to postwar production. The majority of the grievances show that most unions either collaborated to keep women out of well-paid work or refused to support their grievances.

Besides filing individual grievances, women protested collectively. Several conferences to discuss discrimination in reemployment were called by a wide range of organizations, from the YWCA to ad hoc union committees to government agencies. At the Ford Highland Park Motor Plant, for example, in December 1945, two hundred women picketed over discriminatory practices.

That very large numbers of wartime women workers intend to work after the war is evidenced by their statements to interviewers. On the average, about 75 percent of the wartime-employed women in the 10 areas expected to be part of the postwar labor force. . . .

These prospective postwar women workers did not, for the most part, contemplate out-migration from their areas of wartime employment. Over 90 percent of them, in most areas, looked forward to continued employment after the war in the same areas where they had worked during the war period. . . .

In each area, the number of wartime-employed women who intended to work in the same area after the war greatly exceeded the number of women employed in the area in 1940. In the Detroit area, for example, for every 100 women who were working in 1940, excluding household employees, 155 women will want postwar jobs. About two and one-half times as many women wanted to continue working in the Mobile area as were employed in 1940. . . .

The highest percentage of prospective postwar workers in most areas came from the group of women who had been employed before Pearl Harbor, rather than from those who had been in school or engaged in their own housework at that time. On the average over four-fifths of the women who had been employed both before Pearl Harbor and in the war period intended to keep on working after the war. Among the war-employed women who had not been in the labor force the week before Pearl Harbor, over three-fourths of the former students expected to continue working, while over half of those formerly engaged in their own housework had such plans. . . .

The nature of postwar employment problems is influenced not only by the number of wartime workers who expect to remain in the labor force but also by their expressed desires for work in particular industries and occupations. Postwar job openings as cafeteria bus girls, for example, are not apt to prove attractive to women who are seeking work as screw-machine operators.

The bulk of the prospective postwar workers interviewed in this survey, or 86 percent, wanted their postwar jobs in the same industrial group as their wartime employment, and about the same proportion wanted to remain in the same occupational group. Postwar shifts to other industries were contemplated on a somewhat larger scale, however, among the wartime employees in restaurants, cafeterias, and similar establishments, as well as in the personal service industries in certain areas. In the Dayton area, for example, among the war-employed women who expected to remain in the labor force, fully 36 percent of those in eating and drinking places and 30 percent of those in personal service industries said they wanted jobs in other industries after the war. . . .

In the Mobile area almost a third of the women employed in the war period were Negro. In four other areas between 10 and 19 percent, inclusive, were non-white (including some oriental in San Francisco). In the remaining five areas less than 10 percent of the war-employed women were Negro or of other non-white races.

In each of the nine areas where there were enough non-white employed women in the war period to make comparison valid, a much higher proportion of the Negro women planned to continue work than of the white women. In six areas 94 percent or more of the Negro or other non-white women who were employed in the war period planned to continue after the war. . . .

Responsibility for the support of themselves or themselves and others was the outstanding reason given by war-employed women for planning to continue work after the war. As already pointed out, about three-fourths of the wartime-employed women in the 10 areas (excluding household employees) planned to keep on working after the war. Fully 84 percent of them had no other alternative, as this was the proportion among them who based their decision on their need to support themselves and often, other persons as well. Eight percent offered special reasons for continuing at work, such as buying a home or sending children to school; and only 8 percent reported they would remain in the labor force because they liked working, or liked having their own money.

Virtually all of the single women and of those who were widowed or divorced (96 and 98 percent, respectively) who intended to remain in gainful employment after the war stated they would do so in order to support themselves or themselves and others, whereas 57 percent of the married wartime workers who expected to remain at work gave this reason. The remaining married prospective postwar workers interviewed offered reasons of the special purpose type, such as buying a home, about as often as those of the "like-to-work" type. . . .

That the need to work is just as pressing among some married women as among some single women was highlighted by the replies from the war-employed women on the number of wage earners in the family group. Out of every 100 married women who were living in family groups of two or more persons, 11 said they were the only wage earner supporting the family group. This was almost identical to the proportion of sole supporting wage earners among single women living with their families. The state of marriage, therefore, does not, in itself, always mean there is a male provider for the family. . . .

I DENIED MY SEX

The "feminine mystique" is a concept derived from the title of a book published in 1963 by Betty Friedan, a founder of the second wave of feminism. It referred to the post-World War II ideology that women belonged at home as full-time wives and mothers. In many ways, the feminine mystique was an updated version of the nineteenth-century cult of domesticity. It was promoted by a propaganda campaign aimed at women of all classes, flooding not only the popular media but also scholarship and professional expertise. There was nothing subtle about it, as the following selection illustrates. It not only argued that women ought to stay home but warned that if women ventured outside or defied conventional gender codes, they would be damaging themselves, their children, and the whole society.

From the first moment I can remember I wanted to be a boy. With three roughneck brothers, and a father who was football coach at the high school, I suppose it was natural. Besides, my mother had died in giving birth to me and, as a child, I shuddered at the whispered tales of her childbed agony. As

I grew up, there was never any woman in our house to talk to, so I never learned to appreciate my own sex. . . .

"Don't call me a girl!" I'd scream. "I'm just as good as my brothers! Just as strong and tough!" . . .

So Dad began to pretend he had four sons—Michael, John, Harry, and "Al." He let me take all the bumps and bruises that came my way. . . .

One night at dinner Harry said to Dad, "I can lick any kid in this block except Al. And personally I think it's about time she began washing her face and doing girl-things."

"Oh, shut up!" I yelled. "I'll never do that sissy stuff!"

Mike and Johnny laughed, but Dad said thoughtfully, "Harry has a point. It won't be long now before you'll have to settle down and be a girl whether you like it or not." . . .

I listened with anger and resentment welling up inside of me. "It isn't fair!" I stormed finally. "I didn't ask to be a girl!" . . .

That summer Butch [a boyfriend] and I went to dances, or to the movies, or just sat in the old swing on our front porch talking. But there was no thought of love in my mind. Even after we started going steady. Everyone admired Butch and trusted him, and I was proud to be his girl—that was all.

Outwardly I was changing, though, becoming less and less of a tomboy and looking and acting more like a girl. I found myself trying hard to win nice compliments from Butch on my appearance. But inwardly, I hid my real feelings from myself. And then strange things kept happening between Butch and me.

There were those tennis games, for instance. I used to try so hard to beat him, and when I couldn't, it filled me with a fury Butch couldn't understand.

"But, honey," he'd say, "I should think you'd want me to win. After all, I'm the man in this outfit."

I'd turn on him almost hysterically. "I'm as good as any boy. I've beaten every other boy I've known at tennis."

Why I didn't know. I just *had* to. Butch might not like me if I couldn't keep up with him. Fear struck me.

It struck me again that first night he kissed me. When I felt his arms tighten around me and his lips searching for mine, my body responded with such fire and excitement that I was filled with terror. I pushed away from him furiously. "Don't!" I cried. "Don't ever do that again."

His face was white and angry. "Are you trying to make me feel like a heel just because I kiss my girl good night. What's the matter, Alice?"

"And don't call me Alice!"

"I *will* call you Alice. 'Al' is a boy's name." He turned and left me. I could hear the angry sound of his heels clicking against the pavement. . . .

Then after graduation Butch was called into the service and became an aviation pilot. He looked handsomer than ever in his Army Air Force uniform the few times I saw him on leave. I admired him, but secretly I was consumed with envy. Even when he was sent into the danger zone in Korea, and I knew I would spend years of anxiety and loneliness during his absence, I resented the adventures and opportunities for glory he'd have. . . .

I dreamed of being the first woman to climb Mount Everest, of breaking the men's speed record of flying, of being a champion on the Olympics pole vaulting team. But these were only dreams. I decided finally to be a newspaper reporter. I'd go dashing out to murders, fires, and exciting events.

Because the editor of the local newspaper was a friend of Dad's I got a job all right—pasting typed notices of sports events on a large wall calendar. I was never so bored.

Then Butch came home a Major! Covered with medals! The war was over! But not my private civil war! . . .

He seemed changed, older somehow, willing to settle down. Sometimes there was a sad, tired expression in his eyes as if he had seen too much, and never wanted to see anything more beyond our humdrum little town.

For the first time, I was disappointed in him. Besides, after our first joyful reunion, he had little time for me. I sat and kicked my heels while he spent evenings and Sundays making business calls and going to club meetings. I had sat out the war waiting for him, and now it was the insurance business!

"Every contact I make is important," he had to explain. "I'm not making much money now, but there's a chance to build a good, steady future. Just be patient. After all, in your little job you can work nine to five and forget it afterward. I can't."

My little job! Again that masculine superiority! All right, I decided, I was going to go out and get the toughest job in town! I'd show him.

An idea had been brewing in my mind for some time, and as soon as I was twenty-one, I acted on it. Without saying a word to anyone, I marched down to the Police Department and had a long conference with Captain Clarke, Director of the Policewoman's Bureau. . . .

I gave notice at the newspaper office and went through the preliminaries of physical examinations and signing papers at Police Headquarters. Afraid there might be some slip-up, I kept it all a secret.

But at the most unexpected moment I had to reveal my plans. Butch had a free evening and we drove to the Look Out Point above Sylvan Lake and parked. It was one of those heavenly nights when the moon is clear and close and all the stars have a personal intimacy as if they're shining just for you.

Suddenly Butch pulled me to him with a little aching cry. He held me so tightly that I could hardly breathe. He kissed my eyes and my hair and finally my mouth. One strong gentle hand caressed me.

My first instinctive reaction was one of complete surrender. I wanted to be loved, to forget myself and be possessed by him.

And then, suddenly, something exploded in my mind. I was consumed by the same unreasoning terror I had experienced the first time he had kissed me with passion. I struggled away from him and he released me almost instantly.

"Darling, don't be frightened. We've known each other such a long time. I don't feel ashamed or guilty because I love you like this. I want to marry you as soon as possible. Why do you suppose I've been working so hard?"

"Marriage!" I blurted. "But I don't want to get married!"

He sat stiffly and stared at me as if he could not believe what he had heard. "But why not?"

"I've got a job to do. . . .

"I'm going to be a policewoman!" I announced grandly.

"A—what?" He laughed. "Have you lost your mind? Do you have any idea what you're getting into?"

"Sure I have. It's a real he-man job. That's why I'm doing it." . . .

"So that's what's behind it. Competition again! Why do you always have to start the battle of the sexes? Couldn't we be a team with you doing your part and me doing mine?"

"By that I suppose you mean I should give up all my opportunities and get stuck in a tiny apartment cooking your cabbage and washing diapers while you spend all your spare time making good contacts," I jeered.

Butch lost his temper then.

"No!" He said furiously. "I don't expect *you* to do that, but I would expect my wife to."

"What do you mean by that?"

"I mean you'll have to make a choice. Either you want me, or a career as a policewoman. You can't have both."

"You're a selfish, domineering—*male!*" I cried. "You can have any kind of job you want, and still get married! Why can't I? It isn't fair!"

"I can't help that. Which do you choose? I'm ready to get married now and settle down."

"Well, I'm not! I'm going to be a policewoman!" I said angrily. All the years of suppressed resentment and anger at Butch for beating me at everything had finally come to a head. . . .

"Okay! This is it!" he said finally through clenched teeth as he started the car. He drove me home in icy silence. His profile in the moonlight was hard and unrelenting. . . .

I went into training as a policewoman. It was rugged. I spent long hours at the rifle range learning to shoot. I would have to carry a revolver in my handbag at all times, as a policewoman is on twenty-four hour duty. To be honest, the gun frightened me and I hoped I'd never have to use it. I took gymnastics and judo until I was almost muscle bound. I studied law and first aid. . . .

As a rookie, I was first assigned to direct traffic at a school crossing. . . . It was a busy corner, a shopping center where mothers parked baby carriages outside the stores while they bought groceries and gossiped.

And while I was worrying about an accident, a baby was kidnapped practically under my nose!

I didn't realize what had happened until the mother started screaming. I knew her by sight. I had often helped her cross the street with her baby carriage, packages, and two other small children. Skipper, the baby, was a blue-eyed boy with sandy hair who looked like Butch must have looked as a baby . . . showing the dimples in his fat cheeks and holding out his arms lovingly to strangers. Everyone adored him.

The police did not find Skipper. The newspapers published a story and his picture, offering a reward for any information about him. The story began: "In broad daylight at one of our busiest corners and under the very eyes of rookie Policewoman O'Hara, six-months-old Daniel, son of Mr. and Mrs. Howard Slocum, was snatched in one of the most daring kidnappings—"

It stung! I decided I would find Skipper if it took the rest of my life. . . .

[Alice interviews the distraught mother.]

"Was it terrible, having a baby?"

"Terrible?" she replied, as if trying to remember something from a dim past. "Oh, it was no picnic! I nearly died. But that's the price a mother pays for the privilege of having a baby. I think Nature must make mothers suffer so their children will be more precious to them. I'd take the pain again any time to have Skipper back. . . .

"Poor Howard, he's close to a breakdown," she sobbed, "but men can never know the closeness to babies that mothers do. Poor men! They miss so much."

"Poor *men!*" I exclaimed. "I always thought they were so lucky."

"Oh, they go around showing off their muscles and playing lord and master, but they can't have babies. I doubt if they would if they could. It takes real courage to have a baby. Fathers just become slaves working to support their wives and children."

"I never thought of it in that way," I said slowly, mulling her words over and over in my mind. . . .

[After much searching, Alice finally locates the couple who have kidnapped Skipper.]

"Skipper!" I cried out excitedly. "Where did you get him, Mrs. Gorell?"

"I don't know what you're talking about," she said, backing away from me. "His name is Bill, after my husband. He's our baby." . . .

As I moved toward the crib, she pounced on me with maniacal strength, a knife gleaming in her hand. I felt it slashing my left shoulder and arm again and again. I stared in horror at my gashed sweater which was rapidly turning crimson. As we struggled, Skipper cried louder and louder. The sound seemed to drive Mrs. Gorell into a frenzy. She kicked and stabbed wildly. But finally, with the help of my judo lessons I threw her to the floor where she lay limply.

In my pain I hardly knew what I was doing. There was only one thought in my mind—to get Skipper out of here and back to his mother. I picked him up with my good arm and started out of the room. The door was blocked by a burly man in shirt sleeves. . . .

"I'm a policewoman. You're—you're under arrest," I stammered weakly. It sounded ridiculous even to my ears.

The man actually laughed. "Put that baby down! You're not making any arrest, youngster." . . .

But Skipper put his arms around my neck and hid his face against me, crying. It did something to me. . . . Skipper, who went lovingly to any stranger, was afraid of this man and was clinging to me for protection!

My rigid limbs came to life. My bag suddenly sailed through the air and struck Mr. Gorell in the face. A shot rang out and I felt the hot singe of a bullet grazing my head, but the revolver clattered to the floor. As Mr. Gorell bent over, I tripped him expertly and sent him sprawling.

I ran, faster than I ever knew I could, zigzagging through the basement to the rear exit. I heard Mr. Gorell shouting and cursing at me, but somehow I found myself in the alleyway and then out in the street. Then I knew I couldn't go any farther. I was shaking violently all over and my knees were buckling. Skipper was slipping down out of my good arm. That's when I saw the two policemen hurrying toward me with an excited Sally showing them the way.

Thank God, I thought, a man! Someone to take charge and know what to do. I dumped the baby into the first officer's surprised arms just as blackness closed all around me.

When I came to, I was lying in a hospital bed. Harry and Dad were looking down at me, grinning with relief. My shoulder and arm were bandaged.

"What happened?" I asked. "Is the baby all right?"

"The baby's okay," Dad said.

"Did I conk out?" I asked.

"Yeah, just like a girl. When you should have been dragging in the kidnappers," Harry answered gruffly, "you fainted."

"I was wounded! Dying from loss of blood!"

"Just scratched! You took one look at your own blood and fainted." . . .

"You might have been killed!" Harry growled. "What do you carry a gun for, I'd like to know, if you're not going to use it to defend yourself? What do you think it is—a lipstick?" . . .

"All right, I bungled everything! So I'm not meant to be a tough cop," I sobbed. "I'm a girl and I don't care. I want Butch." . . .

My words tumbled over each other in my eagerness to explain to Butch. "Mrs. Slocum nearly died having Skipper and she was ready to do anything to get him back. And poor Mrs. Gorell would have murdered anyone to keep Skipper. Butch, you should have seen the tender expression in her eyes when she cuddled him. They weren't afraid. They were real women! But all this time I've been afraid. I resented being a girl. I fought against it—denied it. Why, it's a privilege!"

"I never *could* see what you had against being a girl," Butch admitted. "I always thought it must be pretty nice to let the men do the fighting and grubbing for you."

"I give up, Butch. I'm not tough enough to take it. I never want to see another fight!"

WORKING MOTHERS AND DELINQUENCY ————————

By 1955 the increasing number of employed mothers of young children began to attract the attention of social scientists, politicians, newspaper commentators, and the general public. "Experts" with feminine-mystique values argued that it was a dangerous trend and that pressure should be applied to force women back into their homes. One of the linchpins in their argument was that if the mother worked, her children would become juvenile delinquents.

In this selection, Joyce Cowley comments on "evidence" used against women. Cowley was a trade unionist for over forty years, working as a waitress, textile worker, shoe worker, machinist, clerk.

Ex-president Truman has a cure for juvenile delinquency. He's joined the judges and politicians and police officials who, with monotonous regularity, tell mothers to stay at home.

Several working mothers interviewed by the *New York Post* said they would be glad to stay home if someone would take care of their bills. . . .

Statistics don't back up . . . attacks on working mothers. . . . A recent article in *McCall's*, "Is A Working Mother a Threat to the Home?" tells about a study of 20,000 Detroit delinquents made over a period of eight years by social scientists at Wayne University in cooperation with the Detroit Police Dept.

This study indicates that children of working mothers have a delinquency rate 10% lower than that of children whose mothers stayed at home.

"Delinquency," *McCall's* explains, "is most prevalent in very low-income families . . . if the woman in such a situation has enough gumption and self-respect to go out to work—on top of her regular housework—it means she is still struggling. Her children have something to cling to. There is some hope in their lives. 'There are plenty of things that are worse for children,' says Judge Polier of the N.Y. Children's Court, 'than finding mother at work when you come home from school. Perhaps the worst is finding her resigned to hopelessness.' " . . .

The real question for the experts is: "Why are so many of our children not delinquent?"

I'm glad a great many young people have the physical and emotional fortitude to overcome what look like insurmountable difficulties, but instead of just wondering how they do it, I think we should give them some help. . . .

Of course, a police chief may urge that we get more cops but there is a possibility of self-interest involved here. You don't hear much from these people about over-crowded schools, slum clearance, playgrounds, clinics or guidance bureaus in the schools.

Right now in New York City there are 100 vacancies in the Bureau of Attendance which attempts to handle truancy problems and might be of some help in the earliest stages of delinquency. Salaries are so low that no one applies for the jobs.

The Bureau asked if a small increase in funds could be included in the new city budget. Of course, their request was brushed aside but I don't remember any judge or police official denouncing the Board of Estimate. A working mother, struggling to provide for her children, is a much easier target.

There is one thing wrong with this mother. She's working alone, and it will take the combined efforts of all parents to bring a real change in the conditions in which our young people grow up. The first step parents should take is to turn the heat on these politicians who are really responsible for the present mess and who condemn "working mothers" and "bad parents" so they won't have to admit their own failure and guilt.

MILITARY HARASSMENT OF LESBIANS ───────────

Opportunities for women in the armed forces appear to have attracted many lesbians. The military experience had both positive and negative aspects for them. Homosexuals were persecuted and discriminated against, but they also gained the space in which to come together with other lesbians and create a collective identity, as this personal story shows.

When I graduated, the Korean conflict was going on, and although I had a good job at Kimberly-Clark Corporation, the big paper manufacturer, it was not a job that would guarantee a great future. Since I was very career-oriented, [but] nobody in our family had ever gone to college, and we were really very poor, on relief and that whole thing, I thought perhaps the service could offer me that elusive opportunity. It would take care of me, so I thought, and give me a lifelong career. The bottom line was that I really went into the service to be a career woman. And I'd have stayed there. I loved it! . . .

You know, I never entered the military with the idea of finding other lesbians or having any sort of affairs or anything. I entered the military *knowing* that I was a lesbian, but also knowing that I wanted to do what was right by military standards and stay there! But, by God, when I got into basic, I thought I had been transferred to hog heaven! No damn kidding! Lordy! But I was smart enough to know that doing anything would be my downfall. And like I said, I really wanted to stay in. There was no doubt in my mind, from the time I raised my hand and was sworn in until the day I was discharged, that that's where I wanted to be. I liked everything about it. I loved the parades, I loved the uniform, I loved . . . I even liked taking orders. I liked standing at attention. I liked getting out there on the field, standing there at parade rest for an hour and a half waiting for a parade. I liked everything about it. I even *liked* KP. I liked everything about it. You would have thought they would have been smarter than to have kicked someone out who liked KP!

I did very well. I did *very* well. I was up at two o'clock ironing my uniforms, and when the whistle blew at 4:30 to get up, man, I was out there and loved it. The challenge was great, and I went for it with gusto. Yeah, I was made squad leader. I remember our trainer was a corporal by the name of Tater, and everybody called her Spud. I have pictures of her and her lover, Powers, who was also there, and Corporal Nichols, who was a dyke, just like they were. They were all affiliated with our flight. Even though there was never anything mentioned, you know, there was that bond that exists that is never acted upon or never mentioned. But the rapport—that was there, and I had that. Actually, once we recognized the bond, believe it or not, we pretty much *stayed away* from each other. In retrospect, I'm sure, it was the survival instinct. I guess we all seem to have it.

After basic, I went to McClellan Air Force Base in Texas, where I spent the rest of my time. They were cross-training me. Then it all came to a stop because I discovered sports, and more women! I was on this basketball team, of course . . . I mean, why not utilize my height to my advantage? I'm about five ten, five eleven. And through some of the women on this civilian team I met this gal. As I said, I discovered women. The teams are an avenue. I don't think it's the only one, but I think it's one of the better avenues, just as it is in everyday life. You know, God, we used to go to other games and the stands were just filled with lesbians of all shapes and sizes! But overshadowing it all was the fear of discovery. I still had that caution button going, you know, don't do anything . . . and I never did anything on base.

I would stay with this gal over the weekend, and I figured, now, when I put on my civilian clothes and go into Sacramento, that's my weekend and what I do has no bearing on what's going on at the base. So I had this relationship with Marie and there were never any problems, until right around the spring of 1953, when basketball season had ended . . . and the OSI started stalking me. My theory is that periodically they'd go through the bases and go on these purges. They would start first with all the women who were involved in athletics and then move from there with any info they had gotten, to snare other women.

They opened my mail. They'd get me up in the middle of the night and take me over to the OSI office for questioning. They'd look under my mattress for anything that I might have hidden, any material, letters, notes, valentines, just anything that I might have hidden that could be incriminating. They'd call me from work or they'd come down and personally escort me back to the OSI office. I was embarrassed being called away from work. I'd just say, "I have to see the OSI," and off I'd go and come back whenever I was released. Sometimes I'd be there ten minutes. Sometimes I'd be there two hours. Most of the time, I would say if I had to make an average, probably forty to forty-five minutes, but their short times were in the middle of the night, just enough time to get me up, awake, out of bed, and disturb my whole night. They asked me things like when was the last date I had with a man, what did I do about my sexual desires, did I know any women who saw other women in a physical kind of sense, did my Catholic upbringing forbid me to masturbate? Hell, my own *mother* forbade me to masturbate!

This whole psychological warfare went on and on. It happened countless times. I mean, we're not talking just once or twice a week; we're talking one or two times a day for about four months! Finally, I went to my commanding officer, who my instincts told me was a lesbian, and as I look back on it, she tried so hard to help me, but couldn't—her hands were tied. Anyway, I went to her and said, "I can't handle this anymore." I had reached the point of breaking, and I knew that if this went on any longer, I was going to end up in a psych ward—I just could not handle it emotionally. I couldn't do my job, you know. . . . They'd come to the mess hall and get me right in the middle of a meal. I mean, they knew no bounds! It was awful.

There was one gal whom they would call in periodically, and she would go over there when she was drunk. She'd volunteer all this information, but never sign anything. When they'd call her back in, she'd be sober and deny it all! They really got pissed off at her. As for me, I just totally denied everything. Well, about the last month that I was being called in, they brought Marie into it, the civilian gal, and said that they knew that I was having this affair with this girl in Sacramento. They knew where she lived, what her parents' names were, what her brothers' and sisters' names were. They also knew about her sister and *her lover*, they knew the times I was there, the buses that I took, how long I stayed, my mode of transportation home, what I wore, for Christ's sake, they knew every damn move I made. It was mind-shattering, it boggled the imagination to believe that they were so concerned about what I did in my spare time, that they would go to such lengths!

So then they started propositioning me. If I would agree to say that I was having an affair with this woman in Sacramento and mention her name, they would give me a *general discharge*. Now, nothing would be done as far as Marie or her family were concerned because they were civilians and the military's not interested in civilians. However, I was threatened with a court-martial if I didn't agree to mention Marie and sign the statement. I could sign and get a general, or not sign, get court-martialed and be dishonorably discharged, which meant I would pay for it for the rest of my life. So I stopped seeing her, for one thing.

When I stopped seeing Marie, it was bad enough, but the whole thing was just terrible.

First of all, you didn't have any outlet. I had no outlet. When you were under investigation, you were pretty much by yourself, so except for Carol, who was also being intensely investigated, neither of us had another friend, because you were just not nice to be around during that time. Besides, no one wanted to be found associating with us for fear of their own careers. Birds of a feather kind of thing, you know, so the people that you had to talk to about it were minimal. Carol and I would commiserate, and that was the extent of it. I was thwarted in that respect, frustrated and angry. There was no way I could tell Marie what was happening and explain to her that my whole relationship with her *was* something of value, not some tawdry affair. And I was angry and feeling paranoid because I didn't even feel safe going off base anymore. So I locked myself onto the base knowing full well that no matter where I went, they would follow me somehow or know where I was going. I also had a fear of incriminating other people and I didn't want to do that.

During their interrogation sessions, they would produce a whole list of names. They must have had a whole goddamn squadron of names. But I denied . . . I really did. I said, "I don't even know them," you know, that was my answer all the time. They told me more than once that I would get a general discharge, which was the same thing as an honorable and carried with it all the same benefits. Of course, the main thing was that there were no negative aspects attributed to it. It was the only way I would be able to get out of there and still be able to hold my head up. All they wanted me to do was sign that statement, and I remember them saying that "Marie's family will not be a part of it." I was worried about my mental and emotional health. I felt I was beginning to crack. I knew myself well enough to realize that I was at a saturation point, and didn't want to end up in any sort of psychiatric unit someplace. But I guess my ego said that I wanted to handle this.

I went to my commanding officer again and said, "I don't think I can take any more of this bullshit, it's just too much, so I'm considering signing that paper, getting a general discharge, and getting released." I was sitting with my hands on her desk, and she reached across, put hers on top of mine, and said, "Well, Ret, (that was my nickname), I think you really need to think about this. Before you do anything, think real hard about the effect it's going to have on your future," and she drew her hands back. I simply said, "I can't think about the future right now, you know, I'm trying to make it day by day."

The next time they called me in, I said, "Well, what do I have to sign?" They surprised me by saying, "Tell us about your relationship with Marie." I wasn't sure what that had to do with my own discharge, particularly since she was a civilian, but I did. I told them all about my relationship with Marie. A day or two passed and they never bothered me. Then they called me in again and said, "Okay, now we need to hear this story again," so I had to tell them again. I left, and the very next day, the major called me in again and said, "I've been contacted by the OSI, and you're going to have a hearing in about a week." I was shocked, and said, "A hearing, what for?" "Well, yes, in order for them to do the paperwork on this and get your discharge, you have to go through a hearing." And I said, "Is that the same as a court-martial?" And she said, "Yes." To protect herself, she was quite detached and official-acting. It was a pretty sad scenario as I recall.

Once the "court-martial" was in session, nobody read me any rights, told me I could have a defense counsel, or that it was my right to have somebody on that board representing me. I was like a lamb to slaughter. They asked me things like: Did I think that my homosexuality had an adverse effect on my Air Force performance and my military performance? Did I think that being a homosexual in the AF influenced other people? Did I realize that I was a security risk being a homosexual? Those were the kinds of questions, but never anything at all as far as "Is there anything you want to say?" until the end, the very end.

The entire process took about fifteen minutes, including my comments. And when I was allowed to speak, I said, "Well, about the only thing I want to say in my defense is that I don't think I deserve this, to be released, to be discharged from the service, because I feel that my record speaks for itself, that I have never done anything injurious or harmful to anybody else." You know, I was totally career-oriented, and I reiterated to them the fact that I had planned on being a thirty-year Waf and was exceptionally gung ho as far as the AF was concerned. Obviously, all my words fell on deaf ears. I was asked to leave the room for a few minutes while they "deliberated." After about five minutes, they called me back and said, "Well, we've reviewed your case (what could they do in three or four minutes? I ask), and we find that under the circumstances, you should be generally discharged."

Case closed. I was dismissed to get my things in order and get off the base.

It took me that day and the morning of the next day to check out, and about two o'clock the next afternoon, two MPs escorted me off the base. I had fifty-nine dollars in my pocket and bus fare back to my hometown in Wisconsin. However, the corker was that I got an *undesirable discharge*, not a general, as had been expected! *And*, on top of that, the military, the OSI, went to Marie's house in Sacramento, two of them, questioned her parents, questioned her sister, her brothers, questioned Marie, questioned the neighbors . . . and if there's anything in my life that I regret, it's that. I wish I had never mentioned that girl's name, because that family didn't understand what was going on. They were Portuguese and had little understanding of the language, let alone what these guys were doing. Those two assholes questioned the neighbors and said awful things about Marie that her parents didn't understand, and because of that, Marie has *never* spoken to me since. And me with this undesirable discharge in my pocket with no explanation from anybody. Just what I needed.

I was pretty devastated. I was pretty numb, but, honestly, I think what I felt was relief that I wasn't going to go through that anymore. However, the down side was that the impact of an undesirable discharge had never occurred to me, *never* occurred to me. I knew it wasn't an honorable, I knew it wasn't the general that I was promised, but the force of it never dawned on me. But I was grateful to be out from under all that pressure and all that investigation. It wasn't until two weeks or so after I was discharged that I realized the impact of *this* discharge. Two pieces of paper arrived in this envelope telling me all the things that I couldn't do because of my undesirable discharge. I could no longer vote. I didn't have any benefits. I could never work for any government-affiliated agency or company. I could not do anything with any state-run organization or state supported agencies like education or any civil service that had to do with prisons. I couldn't be involved in anything that had to do with security because I could never get a security clearance. I couldn't even work for the post office! You know, all these places where I could never work, the list went on and on . . .

I learned too late that had I the money, time, and the intelligence, I probably could have fought that discharge. It was illegal, totally illegal. With no defense, no reading of my rights, and the fact that I had been lied to all the way down the line, I could have won! But alas, I didn't know all of that at the time. When I got my upgrade, I didn't feel like I had gotten *them*, because after they've *had you* for forty years, it's hard to feel you've *gotten them*. I pay my taxes because I don't want to go to jail, but I'd never do anything service-oriented for this country, and I'm not a patriot. You know, I figure that I gave them all I had so very long ago and they just fucked me over. So fuck them now! I would hope that what I gave *after* I was kicked out of the military proves the value of my contributions as a lesbian. I still see absolutely no reason for that regulation that discriminates against people like me.

ANTI-UNION VIOLENCE

Runaway shops and plant closings are nothing new. Employers have often moved in the search for cheap labor. The textile industry began in New England in part because it could take advantage, first, of female labor, then, of immigrant labor. As these workers organized for higher wages in the late nineteenth century, the factories began moving to the South seeking a cheaper, divided, nonunion labor force.

Neither is violence against union organizers new, although the fact that it has been directed against women as well as men has not always been recognized.

The southern textile industry was hard to unionize because employers took advantage of southern racism and white workers resisted making common cause with blacks. Because southern workers were largely unorganized and as a result worked for very low wages and in often hazardous conditions, in 1946–48 the AFL and the CIO launched organizing drives in the South in the textile, chemical, oil, and lumber industries. Over $1 million and one hundred organizers were poured into the campaign, which nevertheless failed because of employers' violence, intimidation, and legal harassment. The violence was so great that the U.S. Senate was forced to investigate it even in the midst of the McCarthy period, in 1950. Following is an excerpt from those hearings.

Statement of Mrs. Edna Martin Concerning Her Abduction From Mrs. Pounds' Rooming House in Tallapoosa, Ga., on Monday, November 17, 1947

My name is Edna Martin and my home is in Athens, Ga. I was born in Madison County, Ga., and have lived in the State all my life. I am a widow and have raised six children. My oldest son was in the Army for 4 years, fighting in Italy and Africa.

I have worked in cotton mills all my life and have been a member of the Textile Workers Union of America, CIO, for 4 years.

Because I know what the union can do for cotton-mill people, I have been putting in all the time I could in the last 3 months as a volunteer CIO organizer.

One of the places I have been helping on has been the American Thread Mill at Tallapoosa. Kenneth Douty, State director of the union, assigned one of the organizers to Tallapoosa after a list of workers there who were interested in a union was sent in to the Atlanta office. There are about 300 workers in the mill and about half of them were on this list.

I have been going into Tallapoosa about 2 days a week for the last 2 months with one of the organizers, working especially with the women workers. I would return to Atlanta at night. . . .

I decided that if I could spend at least a week in there, full time, we could really help the people get their union started. . . .

One of the union members at the mill found a room for me in the rooming house of Mrs. George Pounds, 73 Meadow Street. I moved into this house on November 17 at noon. I paid Mrs. Pounds a week's rent in advance and told her that I was a CIO representative. . . .

While I was taking my things into the room, Mr. McGill, American Thread Mill superintendent, drove by the house, went down to the corner of the block, turned around and came back the second time, and eyed me very closely. . . .

After lunch I came back to my room and went to Mrs. Pounds' room and asked her if she would telephone and ask someone to send me some coal.

There were two ladies in Mrs. Pounds' living room. She introduced them to me as Mrs. H. O. McGill, wife of the American Thread Co. superintendent, and Mrs. Grimes, wife of the overseer of the card room. Mrs. Grimes and Mrs. Pounds were making a patchwork quilt and I sat down with them in Mrs. Pounds' living room and helped them quilt for a little while.

Soon after I joined these women Mrs. McGill left. Just before she left Mrs. Pounds took Mrs. McGill back into the kitchen. I imagine they were gone about 10 minutes, leaving Mrs. Grimes and me in the living room. Mrs. McGill went away from the back of the house and I did not see her again. . . .

At 4 o'clock I left my needle and thimble on the quilt and went down to Cliff's place to meet a group of our union people, because I had an appointment with them there.

When I went out the door to go down to Cliff's, there was a 1939 Ford sitting down below the house, and it turned around when I walked out on the porch, and when I got on the sidewalk it passed on. I walked on about half a block and the car passed me again. A man was driving the car. He went down about half a block and turned and came back and passed me the third time right at Cliff's place where I was supposed to meet the people.

The people were there, sitting outside Cliff's in a car, waiting for me. I walked up to them and said: "This car has been following me, do you know the man who is driving it?" One of them said "Yes, it is Mr. Davis, he is a deacon of the Baptist Church here in Tallapoosa, and Mr. McGill is a member of this same church." That was Mr. McGill, the thread plant superintendent.

I got in the car with this group of people and we visited all over the mill village. I guess we stopped at 8 or 10 houses, and I went in all of them, except one, and all were very friendly but that one. At this house, which was a Mr. Davis' home, the people were very cold and did not ask me in. They said they were not interested in unions and did not think they could better themselves by signing a union card.

After this last visit, the people I was with drove me back to the rooming house. I still did not have any coal to make a fire in my room and the people I was with went to their home and brought me some coal and kindling.

When I got in my room and looked around, it was approximately 8 o'clock and it was dark and I was by myself and wanted to fasten my room up. It was on the first floor (it was a one-story house). . . .

In my room there were four big, long windows that opened clear down to the veranda. . . .

There were no locks of any description on those windows. There were marks where locks had been, but there were no locks on the windows that night. I tried all four of them, and they opened very smoothly, a shove would push them all the way up.

There were no shades to pull down over the windows. There were little cheese cloth curtains that anybody on the porch could see through and see over. I had no privacy in my room at all.

There was no lock on my door, and Mrs. Pound had not at any time offered me a key or any means of locking my door.

After I had examined my room to see if I could fasten the door and windows, I took a pitcher that was on the washstand and went down to the back porch to the bathroom to get water. The bathroom had another door that opened into the kitchen. That door was open and Mrs. Pounds was in the kitchen cooking and Mrs. Grimes was still sitting in the room. I saw her when I walked to the kitchen door and asked Mrs. Pound for a glass to drink out of.

Mrs. Pounds said in a very unfriendly voice: "There is a hydrant in the front yard where you are supposed to get water." Then I asked her about the water she had promised me earlier in the day that she would heat for me to take a bath. She made no reply at all, just turned back into the kitchen.

I carried the pitcher of water back to my room and poured half of it in an old wash pan that was sitting in my room and put it on the heater to heat it for a bath. I had paid Mrs. Pounds 50 cents extra to heat water for me.

I began to wonder how I was going to take a bath in this room with no way to keep people from seeing through the windows. When the water got hot I put the light out and took a bath in the dark. The floor was so dirty I took towels from my suitcase and spread them on the floor. I then put on my gown, turned the light back on and sat down in a chair to read a *Saturday Evening Post*.

While sitting in that chair I had a sensation of being watched. I felt like there were eyes watching my every move. There was a big old timey wardrobe in the corner of the room—my clothes were hanging in this wardrobe. I got up and opened both those wardrobe doors and pulled my chair back in between those doors and sat there and read maybe 30 minutes.

Then I got up and got a notebook and made some notes of the happenings during the day, and wrote a card to my baby in Athens, and laid these on a table. I put this table against the door, because it did not have any lock.

Over by the front window I set one of the chairs, and at another window I put the only other chair in the room. At the third window I set the pan of water I had bathed in. The fourth window, at the foot of my bed, I did not have anything to put by it at all. I turned out the light and went to bed about 9. . . .

About midnight there was a knock on my door and a woman's voice called out: "Mrs. Martin," and I answered. She said: "I would like to talk to you." I got out of bed, turned on my flashlight and turned on the light in the middle of the room.

I said to the woman: "Are you by yourself?" She said: "No, I am not." I asked her: "Who are you?" and she did not answer. Then I said, "Well, you will have to excuse me." At this time, while I was talking to the women outside the door, four men came in at the windows as I was facing the door expecting somebody to turn the knob and come in, as there was no lock on the door.

One of the men crossed the room and opened the door and pushed the table in front of it back, and five women came in—three of them came on in the room and the other two stood in the door.

Each of the four men had a long shotgun. I remember I was looking in the hole in a single-barrel gun as it was pointed at me. At this moment I said: "I would like to put on a dress." The man who seemed to be leader of the mob said: "You don't need no God damn dress where you are going." . . .

Then an outspoken woman in the mob began talking. She said: "Mrs. Martin, you represent the CIO." I said "Yes." She said: "Well, we don't want no God damn CIO here, and we don't want no CIO representatives here."

She said: "In fact we are not going to have a union here and you have got to leave."

I said: "It is your privilege if you don't want a union, but I am not going anywhere. My son went across the water to fight for freedom that I go where I want and stay where I please. I am not going to bother you."

The woman said: "Well you are not going to stay here in Tallapoosa." I said: "Well, if you want me to leave why don't you give me a fighting chance and go get a policeman and tell him I say come down here and carry me to Atlanta. I have no way out of here except walking."

Then the old man who was the mob leader said: "We are not bringing the God damn law in this—we are the law here." Then he said: "Where is that CIO man?" I said: "I don't know." He said: "Didn't a CIO man bring you here?" I said: "Yes." He said: "Where is he now?" I said: "Gone back to Atlanta." He said: "Are you sure he has gone back to Atlanta or Cedartown?" I said: "I don't know."

The old man asked me, "What is the man's name?" I said I did not know. He said: "You mean to tell me you don't know the name of the man that brought you out here?" I said: "I don't know." He said: "Lady, where are you from?" I said: "I am not from this part of the country." He said: "We are going to take you across the Alabama line." I said: "You might as well take me that way as any way because you will not carry me toward my home anyway you take me."

Just about this time the old man said: "Ain't you that damn CIO woman that was in Bremen about 3 weeks ago?" The outspoken woman said: "No, she ain't. I thought she was at first, she is about her size." The old man said: "It is a good thing you are not that damn CIO woman, or a man, or you would not even take a ride from here."

About this time the old man said: "There has been enough damn arguing. Go get the hemp rope from the truck." A man in the mob who had a crooked mouth went and got the rope. . . .

I asked them again to let me put on my dress; I did not have on anything but my gown, and the old man turned around and said: "Put on her God damn dress." I asked the men to get out while I put on my dress and they refused to get out. The woman put my dress on before all those that were present. I did not have on any underclothes.

Then one of the men tied my hands in front of me with the rope. . . .

As we left the room one of the men stuffed a piece of cloth in my mouth. I took it to be a man's dirty handkerchief. It made me gag and nauseated me.

All the time the argument in my room was going on, Mrs. Pound's living-room door was open and the light was on. As they took me out the outspoken woman said: "Thank you, Mrs. Pound." . . .

They took me out to the truck and pulled me into the back. It was an old truck with a built-on body of wood which brought the sides up to shoulder height. They kept the lights off when they started and the truck did not turn around. I don't know which way we went out of Tallapoosa. The whole mob went along, with most of them in back with me. One of the women was half sitting on me.

Before we left the room the people went through all my things and then pitched them together, carried them out and put them in the back of the truck. They threw my shoes in the truck, too, and I went out barefoot. They pulled me up into the truck. I was half lying down and could not see anything.

They did not turn on the truck's light and it was very dark. I don't know how they went out of Tallapoosa, but they did go in such a direction they did not hit a street light. I could have seen that, or the light from it. They went out on a dirt road. I don't know when and how they hit the highway. I didn't know where I was—I only knew they told me they were going to take me across the Alabama line. After while they put on the lights.

After we had gone a considerable time, and I know at a very fast rate, the lights were turned off and the truck turned into another road or a field—the place was rough and it was very dark.

I thought my time had come then. The truck stopped and a man in the back part where I was went to the driver and talked with him. I don't know what was said because I could not hear them and no one made any comment after the man got back in the truck.

Still without the light on the truck they turned back to the road. Then they put their lights on and rode what seemed a long time. I was very cold, in fact shaking all over with cold. I had nothing on but my dress and my coat thrown around me, no underclothes and barefoot.

Once I saw lights and that could have been a town; I don't know. The truck made a great many turns and I don't know in which direction we were going at any time. Part of the time I know we were on dirt roads.

After a considerable time they turned the lights off and made a very sharp turn. It seemed it was about 2 miles they drove down a dirt road, because I had to walk back over that same road.

When they stopped on that dirt road the driver, who was the watery-eyed old man, said: "This is about as good a place as any." Then I was pulled out of the truck and my things pitched out, including my radio. . . .

The truck started rolling and the man on the road had to run after it. Before he left he said: "Don't come back to Tallapoosa or you will be shot on sight." . . .

A PUERTO RICAN FIGHTS FOR A GARMENT JOB ——

By 1960, close to a million Puerto Ricans had migrated to New York, forced off their island in part by the economic plan for industrialization and modernization of Puerto Rico known as "Operation Bootstrap." Outmigration and population control through female sterilization, often coercive, were integral to this plan. Direct and relatively inexpensive flights between San Juan and New York made Puerto Rico accessible, and additional large Puerto Rican communities arose in Connecticut, Massachusetts, New Jersey, and the Midwest.

Entering the United States as citizens, Puerto Ricans nevertheless encountered discrimination. Barred from most craft unions, excluded from many neighborhoods, Puerto Ricans on average have the lowest income of all the Hispanic groups in the United States.

The following oral history comes from a project of the Center for Puerto Rican Studies at Hunter College, which is attempting to document the history of the pioneering mainland Puerto Ricans.

We would like to thank Geraldine Casey for bringing this piece to our attention.

. . . María is a 55-year-old garment worker and mother of seven children who migrated to New York from rural Puerto Rico in 1948. Married at fifteen, she had two daughters when she and her husband decided they could not raise a family on the land and also "get ahead." First her husband, then María, and finally her two daughters migrated to New York between 1948 and 1950. . . . María explains how she learned to sew on a machine:

> Well, I continued working with the intention of looking for something better but every time I went out to find a job all the jobs available were for sewing machine operators and I said to myself, "My God, I have to learn to sew." I told [my husband] that we had to find a school so I could learn to sew. Then I went to a school on 14th Street and Union Square and I signed up for three classes. They charged $25 and the only thing they really taught us was to sew a straight seam.
>
> But I took the classes, and I went to look for work as an operator. I didn't really know how to sew. I only knew how to start the machine although I had some knowledge of the machine because my mother had a small manual one in Puerto Rico. I used to watch my grandmother sew on that machine and I thought I could do it.
>
> Well, I went to look for work, and oh, my God, wherever I went, whenever I sat down at the machine and touched the pedal the machine seemed to run by itself! I was thrown out of a number of factories but five minutes here, fifteen minutes there, I kept getting more and more practice.

Then, I said to myself, "I'm going to see what kind of machines they have and if I see a Singer machine I'm going to say that I don't know how to sew on that particular machine." I went to a factory at 380 Broome Street and I noticed that they had Merrow machines and no Singer machines. Now, since I had failed so many times I told the man that I knew how to sew but not on the machine they had. I told him I knew how to sew on a Singer. Blanca, because of that lie they showed me how to sew on the Merrow. The man said to me, "If you can sew on a Singer, this one is easier." Then I said to him, "How is that possible with all those spools of thread?" He said, "Well, I'll show you." He sat me down and calmly showed me how to thread the machine, how to tie up the thread when a spool ran low, not to let it run out, and that's where I started working on chenille robes. . . .

The second story María tells takes place a few years later. . . .

I went to another place making panties. Then I learned another machine, the zig zag machine. At that time I was earning about $40 a week. Only two people know how to work on that machine, an American guy and I. We used to start the garment and then we would give it to the other operators. So that meant that any day that we missed these other people doesn't have no work to do and they had to send them home. So I was very important on the job.

Every time that a garment was new and it took me longer I had to fight for the price. So at one point [a new garment] came in and this work was very hard. I cannot make enough money for the hours, and I said, "No, I am not doing this." He gave me a little more money but I said, "No, no, I can't do this job at this price," and so he fired me. I never was fired in my life from no job. He told me if you don't want to do the work just go home but at this time I had the protection of the union. So I said, "OK, I go home." I get up, took my pocketbook, then my coat and left but I don't come here, I went to the union place and I report him. [The agent] said, "Don't worry about it. I'll be there tomorrow." I'll never forget, it was a Friday. On Monday he came up with me and he talked to the boss and said, "You're going to time her with a clock and you are going to see how long she takes with the garment and you're going to pay her accordingly."

He did that and it come out to be more money. So he paid me but inside of me I was mad because he had fired me, embarrassed me in front of fifty people. And I say, you are going to pay me one of these days. I was very rebellious in that.

And I waited. That particular day, the work was piled up to the ceiling, work that only I and this man, we have to work first. I wait for that moment [when] this fellow was sick. I worked two days, I'll never forget. I worked Monday and Tuesday and on Wednesday I didn't report to work. I went next door and I find another job, this time in bathing suits. They paid me about 75 cents a garment which at that time, this was in 1956, was good money.

So on Friday when I was supposed to collect my money for the days I worked, the secretary told me that Al want to talk to me. So he came over and he told me, "María, you can't do this to me. You know that we don't have nobody to operate that machine. How much you want?" I said, "I don't want nothing. I don't want to work for you no more." He said, "You can't do that to me, you know I was paying good money." I said, "I don't care for your money." He said, "You don't find no job." I said, "I already have another job and I'll give you the address. I now work in Julia Sportswear." He knew that place paid good money.

1955–
Present

1955–PRESENT: INTRODUCTION

THE period since 1955 has been characterized by two connected cycles: from the ascendancy of widespread, vibrant progressive social movements to a revitalized conservatism that has put those movements on the defensive; and from apparent prosperity and economic optimism to recession and doubts, even despair about the future of the U.S. economy. These changes have deeply affected working women.

The social movements of the late 1950s, 1960s, and 1970s involved more Americans than in any other equivalent period in U.S. history. For the first time, a civil rights movement gripped the attention of the entire U.S. population; it not only generated major reforms but also stimulated other movements. Movements against the war in Vietnam, for educational reform, and for Hispanic and American Indian rights directly derived from civil rights. These came together to form a New Left, a largely decentralized but nevertheless loosely connected mass mobilization and political culture critical of established institutions and policies. Although short-lived, the New Left created an enduring transformation in political, personal, sexual, and artistic consciousness.

Out of this general ferment grew the women's liberation movement, which had the greatest impact on working women. An illustration comes from a 1994 *Esquire* poll of women eighteen to twenty-five years old:

> Would you rather be thought of as:
> Brilliant but plain   73.7%
> Sexy but dumb   25.0% *

This factoid, however unscientific, captures extensive changes in women's consciousness: their awareness that they will have to support themselves virtually all their lives, their increasing concern with self-esteem rather than the approval of men, and their rejection of stereotypes about women. Part of the power of the women's liberation movement was that it questioned every aspect of life, not limiting itself as had some previous women's movements to

---

* "Would One Thousand Young American Women. . . ," *Esquire*, February 1994, p. 66.

campaigning for political, economic, and legal reform. The new feminism challenged the division of domestic labor, romanticism about motherhood, conventional ideas about sex and relationships, family structure, and standards of femininity. Feminists dared to question male behaviors and to suggest that masculinity deformed not only personal relationships but domestic and international policy as well.

In educational institutions, which were expanding rapidly in the early decades of this period, the women's movement had particular successes. More and more women, notably working-class and other poor women, gained access to higher education for the first time. Women challenged male-centered instruction, curricula, research, personnel, financing, and extracurricular activities. Particularly dramatic has been the spectacular growth of women's studies programs and scholarship, without which this book would not have been conceived, let alone written.

The women's movement never cohered into a single unified national organization. Though it remained primarily a local and fragmented movement, this decentralization had advantages. It allowed a variety of female social and political groupings to articulate their own feminisms, although some do not choose that label. Black and lesbian feminism have had great impact, and more recently other racial/ethnic feminists have come together and offered unique perspectives.

The New Left movements—in which we include civil rights, women's and gay movements, environmental movements, and many other radical challenges to existing power structures—naturally produced a backlash of substantial proportions. Powerful social movements have always produced reactions, as in the 1920s and in the McCarthy period. Many of the causes included in the New Right and neoconservatism, such as anti-abortion, anti-ERA, anti-gay, and anti-welfare, have hostility to feminism and to women's new assertiveness and public prominence at their core. The conservative revival was associated with the strongest revival of religious fundamentalism in 150 years. Just as the New Left movements were nourished by economic prosperity, the right-wing ones have been fed by economic decline.

This conservative wave has imposed some significant losses on women. It slowed the enforcement of affirmative action, limited access to abortion, and stimulated homophobic and racist violence, for example. Perhaps most significant is that conservative victories have narrowed the range of what seems possible and pushed the mainstream of political thinking to the right; the result is a national mood more hostile to women, gays and lesbians, minorities and the poor. This reaction has forced organizations concerned with working women onto the defensive. But as innumerable polls show, conservatives still confront widespread national support for feminist policies such as equal pay, abortion rights, gay rights, and women in government. And 1980s conservatism has stimulated a new wave of feminist struggle, particularly among younger women; the fastest growing NOW chapters are among high school students.

A particular source of resistance to the conservative agenda for women arises from basic economic and social changes which continue to draw more women into the labor force while depressing working conditions for those at the bottom. With hindsight we can now see that the relative prosperity of the 1950s and 1960s was based on increasing inequality, an enlarging gap between those workers with stable jobs and benefits and those with low-wage, uncertain, and marginal jobs. This inequality divided women as well as men. While professional women have in some cases made substantial gains from feminist pressure against sex discrimination, poor women, particularly minority poor women, did not always share in those gains. Moreover, as globalization of the big corporations began to deindustrialize the United States, even privileged white men with skilled jobs were laid off, and as they began to seek lower-paying service sector jobs, the relatively disadvantaged position of poor women increased. The increasing numbers of mothers relying on welfare reflect the fact that so many women cannot earn a wage large enough to support their children.

If there is a positive side to these developments, it is that steady employment for women is now accepted as a norm throughout the society, for the middle-class as well as the poor, by conservatives as well as progressives. Even those women who benefit from a male wage, through marriage or other male support, rarely have the choice to remain unemployed. Since women must enter the workplace, they will have no choice but to continue to struggle for equality there as well as in politics and at home.

Continuing Patterns

MOTHERING OTHERS' CHILDREN ─────────────────────

Women have always taken care of children other than their own, sometimes for long periods of time as foster or adoptive parents. This kind of labor has tended to be invisible, as if child care was not work; especially if the woman had her own children, observers sometimes imagine that a few more make no difference. In fact, child care is not only difficult but also skilled labor. The need for it has expanded directly in proportion to increases in the number of

*women in the labor force, and the supply is never adequate. But, in a vivid
example of how the market does not work—how increased demand for labor
does not raise wages—the earnings of child-care givers remain at the absolute
bottom of the wage scale, often even below the minimum wage. This is both
because their customers, working mothers, simply cannot afford higher wages
and because the workers are usually those without access to better jobs.*

*Day care for working women is highly stratified. The most privileged
employed women use not-for-profit day care centers or individual in-home
babysitters. Most women workers rely on friends and relatives. Those who
can't are likely to use family day care, which usually means women taking
children into their own homes for low fees, or commercial day care centers.
Here scholar Margaret Nelson discusses the pleasures and problems of that
kind of work.*

As they give the children the security of a home, five days a week, for
eight or nine hours each day, sometimes over a period of several years, family
day care providers "learn to love" the children and they genuinely become
attached to their charges. . . . Family day care providers speak about being
relied on and loved by the children in their care, and they present this as a
positive feature of their work: "Cassie left the other day and told me she loved
me. Things like that are the reward. What can you have more than a child
who loves you?"

. . . Family day care providers talk about the skills on which they draw in
ways that make little or no distinction between being a caregiver to others'
children and caring for one's own children. A woman can begin offering her
services as a family day care provider without receiving any specialized training. Indeed, many providers think training is irrelevant. Because they see
the work as an extension of mothering, they feel equipped to handle the job
by drawing on their personal childrearing experiences:

> I've been told—and I feel—that [my own children] are great kids. . . . The way I
> raised them is what I do with the kids I baby-sit for . . . and [my children] are
> doing fine so far.

> Some of the new mothers, so many of them, go by the book. And I just threw the
> book out. . . . I threw the book away. You don't need to go by the book. Just let
> your child grow, and out of common sense you should know what to do.

But for many women, locating the source of skills in the experience of
mothering is tantamount to a denial of expertise. Perhaps because in our
culture mothering is trivialized, providers denigrate their own (often considerable) abilities: "I don't have any skills," said one woman. "Anyone who has
been a mother can do this," added another. . . .

A contradiction is present. Mothering is also something a family day care
provider cannot achieve and something she does not want to achieve. Moth-

erhood confers rights to claim, to mold, to keep—other people's children cannot be claimed, molded, and kept. To think that one can do so with other people's children creates a situation where one can only be hurt. Motherhood denies a financial calculus and limits: as a day care provider, to refuse reimbursement or to fail to establish limits to the care one will give creates a situation where one will be exploited. The family day care provider cannot answer a question about feeling easily because there is no simple answer for threading one's way between a stance that is both an ideal and a threat.

Family day care providers expect that they will become close to these children, and they see the development of love as appropriate; they are also expected by others to achieve a strong bond. But they have to face certain realities. . . . For day care providers, the limits of protection are narrowed. The day care provider can ensure a loving and safe environment for specified hours; she cannot ensure that the child is being adequately clothed, fed, and nurtured during the hours that the child is with his or her parents. . . .

The women find enormous satisfaction in exercising their managerial abilities, but they are often thwarted in their attempts to do so. . . . Parents give explicit instructions pertaining to the care of their own children. These instructions can undermine a provider's confidence; they can also serve to remind the provider that her authority is limited: "[I don't like it when] they're saying, well, I'm still in charge even though I'm not here; therefore, I'm going to tell her like I would tell a teen-aged baby-sitter the rules."

. . . Providers are aware of a "public" which judges their actions. As one woman said, "You don't yell out the back door to the children because someone might hear you." . . .

The final and most painful emotional reality is that of loss. Mothers go in and out of the work force, parents change jobs, children outgrow the need for daily care. The constant awareness of potential loss makes becoming too attached to the children a risky proposition.

There is an economic reality as well. Family day care providers do this work because they need the money. If they become too attached to the children in their care, that is, if they identify too strongly with the model of mothering, they cannot ask for money at the end of the week, nor can they impose restrictions on the hours of care they provide.

The resolution to the dilemmas I have identified is found in the creation of a feeling rule, which I call *detached attachment*. It is characterized by a less claiming, less self-confident, and less intense affection for the children. This differentiated feeling is necessary if providers are going to draw limits around and charge fees for the care they provide. It is not, however, the emotional detachment professional caregivers strive to achieve. Attachment persists. But the particular attachment they develop relies on the ongoing work of creating a space, a distance which "saves" them from an overwhelming emotional engagement and allows them to ask for money.

Providers refer to this detachment they created and the emotional labor involved frequently (and perhaps unconsciously): "I reserve something, knowing that they're not mine"; "I hold back a little." . . .

Many providers can also speak about a time when they allowed intense involvement to interfere with establishing limits and claiming reimbursement:

> I had one parent who owed me money when she left. It was as much my fault as it was hers because I just let it go on and on for six months. But she was in the process of a divorce. It was really affecting the child I had. I just could not put that child through one more trauma of having to go to a new sitter on top of everything else he was going through. He was three years old, and I could just see what this divorce was doing to this little boy. . . . It was really my fault. I should have given him up. I just couldn't because I wouldn't put him through not knowing where he was going to go.

Of course, some relief exists in the limits that providers create. As one woman said, "I have the pleasures of caring for them without the full responsibility." But this relief is contingent on a perception that the children are receiving competent care from their own parents. No such relief is possible when parents are seen as being inadequate. . . .

RUNNING A SAFE HOUSE

Women have often had to do illegal work in order to support themselves, their families, and their communities. For example, both urban and rural women traditionally distilled and brewed alcoholic beverages and continued to do so during Prohibition. Much of this illegal work was indistinguishable from and disguised by conventional women's domestic labor. Lidia Sanchez, like her mother, harbors illegal immigrants, in the tradition of the underground railroad that helped runaway slaves escape to freedom. Her safe house is a kind of boarding house, such as women have operated for centuries, simultaneously bringing in a bit of income for themselves and providing a necessary service for their community. The recent increased policing of illegal immigration makes work like hers more risky. Nevertheless, in the current economy, women are turning to all sorts of informal arrangements to earn money.

CHULA VISTA, CALIFORNIA

It's an insignificant little stucco house, beige with white trim, in the middle of an older neighborhood. A well-maintained square patch of green lawn, roses lining the driveway, and a bicycle and scooter on the front porch; an "average American family" must live here. Inside it's the same. The living room–dining room combination is neat and orderly, furnished with the standard couch, easy chair, rocking chair, TV, coffee table, dining table, and six chairs, all in an early American style. From the books and games on the shelf and pictures on the wall children obviously live here, but at ten in the morning they are in school and Lidia's day is well underway. She has already been to the grocery store and has a load of wash in the machine.

So where are all the illegal aliens? Four who stayed last night left with rides early this morning. A pretty young woman in an old-fashioned print dress with pink roses and a white collar is washing dishes. The conversation is about children: getting them to eat, high fevers and ear infections. Obviously comfortable in Lidia's kitchen, she must be a friend or relative, certainly not the skulking fugitive from the Border Patrol—but she is. Her husband, who has resident papers, and her baby boy, who was born in the United States, passed yesterday. But with only four years here, she always has to pass with a *coyote* [guide to get immigrants across the border]. Her sister-in-law will pick her up this afternoon. She is one of Lidia's clients.

Lidia has coffee and is putting groceries away. Her warm and easygoing manner makes people comfortable.

When I graduated from high school I got a job in food service at Mercy Hospital. I was thinking I'd like to be a nurse, but I met my husband there and we got married. When my son was born I left my job, and before you know I had three children. I really never had time to go back to school. At that time I was busy with the children, and my husband supported us, so I didn't think about working.

Then in 1979 he left us. He left me with a five-year-old, a two-year-old, and the baby was just six months. That's when I moved here with my mom. This was her house. At first I thought my husband would come back, but I'm sure he's got another family in Mexico by now. I get aid for dependent children, and for the first few years I babysat my neighbor's children. She has three too, so I was taking care of six little kids.

But the thing is, my oldest son, from the time he was a baby he was sick. He learned to walk and all, but by the time he was eight he couldn't walk anymore, and I had to spend every day going to the hospital, or to the doctor, or therapy, so I couldn't babysit anymore. But by that time all the kids were in school, except my daughter.

Of course I would like to go out and work, but what would I do with my son? He's in eighth grade and goes to a special school. The bus picks him up at nine o'clock, but they bring him home at one and I have to help him do everything. That's why I can't just go out and get a job. They pay his medical bills and that, but to feed and clothe three kids, it isn't enough. We can't get by on what I get from welfare.

My mom, she died in 1985, but she always helped people coming across. So she always had someone here. Then when I wasn't babysitting, I would help her. Around that time more people started coming, so I've just kept it up.

It's quiet today, but it gets hectic around here sometimes. I don't mind. Really, it's the only thing I can do and stay home with my son. My other boy is in sixth grade and my daughter is in fourth grade, so they still need me too. I think of it as a job, but it's not bad. Most of the people are real nice, and it's good for my son. There's always different people to talk to. He likes that. He's in a wheelchair now.

The men begin bringing people from ten o'clock at night on. Oh, sometimes we have someone come during the day, but most people cross at night. But they have the key, so I don't have to get up for them. I have couches and cots set up back there in the garage so they can sleep. As it is, most of them leave early in the morning between five and six, so I get coffee for them. Some people have to stay. They have other arrangements, or they have to fly to other places, or relatives have to come pick them up. But they can stay here and I let them bathe or wash their clothes. They eat their meals with us. They can sit here and watch TV, whatever they want.

I get to know the people who stay over. I've had people stay for a week or more. Sometimes they're waiting for their money to arrive. They mostly come from Mexico. I've never been there myself, except to Tijuana. But we always spoke Spanish at home, so I can speak with them. Some of them are from other places in South America. When you talk to them it makes you realize how much we have here, because they come from areas that are very poor. I'll often have to show them how to use the shower or washing machine because they have never seen one. Some of them don't even have toilets and indoor plumbing where they come from.

When they get to where they are going they will call and thank us, or they'll recommend us to a relative. You'd be surprised, we often hear from them again. You get some that go back and forth so you see them. One lady, who went to Chicago a couple of weeks ago, sent a postcard to my son. They come here with hardly anything, but they always want to leave us something.

They pay me $10 for each person. If they stay and eat meals and all, it's $20 a day. It's not like a fancy hotel, but I always have a pot of beans and tortillas. They can have eggs, fruit, bread, milk, whatever they want. For dinner I make some meat or fish. Whatever we eat is what I serve. When I have women here they always help me. I don't ask them to, but they're nervous and always want to clean, wash, or do dishes.

I've had up to forty people here in one night. But that doesn't happen very often. Usually there are three or four, and I almost always have someone eating with us. Every once in a while I'll get a day off with no one here.

I always try to treat the people who come here fair. I think about the hard times they're going through and all. I always think, we're the first family they meet in the United States. I feel sorry for those poor people. Sometimes they're left off at a motel. You know they don't come here with that kind of money. Then the *coyote* tells them someone will pick them up and no one comes. There are *coyotes* that leave people in the back of trucks, for days, without food. You wouldn't believe the stories. I feel sorry for them. I only deal with a couple of people I know. They were friends of my mother's, so I know them pretty well.

You know these people just went to a lot of trouble to get here, so they're not going to do something stupid now. No, really they never cause me any problems: drugs, fights, nothing. Oh, sometimes you have someone who is very nervous, or upset, maybe crying and like that, but I just talk to them.

Really, I never think about this being illegal. I know it is, but I don't have time to stop and think about that. In my mind, this is my house, and I'm not endangering anyone. I think I'm helping people and doing what I have to, to make a life for my kids. At the same time, I am careful. I have rules. They always bring people around the back alley, and they are picked up out in back. The people have to be quiet. My neighbors know what I do, they understand, but I don't have a lot of noise and people back there bothering them. I know they would never report me. I grew up in this house and I've known them since I was a little girl.

PROSITUTION

Part of the "service sector" is the sale of sex. Some women sell sex itself; some sell titillation through words, images, dancing, posing or stripping; some sell their beauty and stylishness through ads. Recently, feminists have begun to see the connections among all these types of sexualized services and have labeled them "sex work." The sex trade is a multimillion-dollar growth industry in spite of the fact that much of it is illegal and dangerous, even before the AIDS epidemic. Because so much of it is underground, it is hard to measure; estimates of the number of working prostitutes range from eighty-four thousand to 1 million. In the mid-1980s, men spent $40 million a day on prostitutes, and police forces in big cities average $7.5 million a year enforcing antiprostitution laws. The women's liberation movement gave rise to prostitutes' unions, which campaigned for decriminalization, as in some European *countries, but feminists are by no means unanimous on this or any other approach to sex work.*

The following is excerpted from a 1980 radio discussion among prostitutes and an extended interview with one of them; the names are pseudonyms.

WENDY: I live in a whole lot less fear of a lot of things. Little fears like can I afford milk this week, or can I come up with the twenty-two bucks for my son to go to school? Can I pay the phone bill? I'm a single woman and a mother, too. If I were living on what I could make as a waitress I'd be frightened a lot of the time. I'd feel a great deal more pressure because I remember what it was like to live from one paycheck to the next.

LOU: I'm not advocating that women should be prostitutes, but we want alternatives. Unfortunately, more women are going into prostitution because the economic situation is getting worse. You got two little kids. Welfare isn't really enough to survive, and it's humiliating besides. . . .

LISA: Why work so hard that when you come home, you just fall out because you're so tired? All right, for a woman to bring home $200 a week—and that's a good-paying job for a woman—it's nothing for a woman in a bathhouse or on the street to make $200 in an hour.

SALLY JO: What is prostitution? Selling of the body? To me, every woman is a prostitute in one way or another. I've been a housewife for fifteen years. If I would be good to my husband during the week, like extra sex, I'd get extra money at the end of the week to buy a pair of shoes or a blouse. . . .

ANNIE: I worked at Steak 'N Eggs for a while, and there's a lot of guys come up there regularly, just to sit and drink coffee. And when they want to pinch you on the ass, I thought, "Hey now. Wait a minute. I'm not getting paid for somebody to pinch me on the ass up here. You leave me a $50 tip for that cup of coffee or you keep your hands off. . . .

LISA: Sex gets to be just like working in a factory or being in an assembly plant. It's just something you do. You close your eyes and do it. It gets to be an everyday thing that doesn't bother you anymore. And if it does, after you look at the money it doesn't bother you anymore.

GINA: I never thought I'd do it. I'd always been a prude. You had to go with me two months before you could touch me. But finally I did. I started working in the hotels at first, but I got barred from all of them. I thought it was cheap to walk the streets. But there's a way to do things. You can have some class about yourself no matter where you work. So from the hotels I went to the bathhouses, and then I finally went to the street. I work from my car. But even now, I have to get high to go to work cause I don't like to deal with the fact of giving my body to everybody. I don't mind blow jobs that much. I'm very good at it. But I can't stand to have somebody jumping up and down on top of me all the time.

MARY: They're buying your time. They're not really buying you. Most of the women I met were fairly proud. They felt like they were doing a job, and they knew what they were doing. . . .

MAE: If you get a case [arrested], you say I'm just going to go straight after this. But by the time you get the money to pay the lawyer you get another case. It's a vicious circle. So you can't stop. They fine you so much money—working in a straight job, you could never pay it. A $300 fine *today*. A $500 fine *today*. Or thirty, sixty, ninety days in the stockade. And the judge isn't going to believe you instead of an officer. There is no such thing as innocent until proven guilty when you go before the judge that first day. It's whatever he says you did, that's what you did. . . .

MAE: Do you think I could get any protection? *Hell no!* We're streetwalkers. We don't have no rights. We shouldn't be out there. I met a man last night, driving a Mercedes-Benz, money all over the place. He almost killed me. I blacked out three times—he strangled me. He kept screaming, "I have so much money, what could anybody do to me? I could buy my way out of anything. The headlines would read: 'Another Prostitute Killed by Wealthy Man. Good Riddance.' " . . .

MARY: It consisted of an apartment where a bunch of girls would sit around the telephone. And there were a couple of guys who backed the thing with money. The people I worked for did certainly make a lot of money. They had the income of maybe five or ten girls, maybe more, coming into them every night. Even after their expenses they made enough to make it worthwhile to them. Definitely more than any of us made.

It's safer working for the escort service. And it's better money. And it's probably more socially acceptable in the eyes of the person who is picking you up. Which means it's safer and more money.

LISA: A lot of the girls on the street would love to work in the bathhouses. There just wasn't ever any room for them. Then you're out of the cold in the winter, you have showers, all of the comforts of home. Plus you don't have to run from the cops on the street. You don't have to worry about being taken in for loitering. True enough, the man that owns the place, he did make a lot of money. But the girls took a lot less chance of being hurt. . . .

Q: What about decriminalization?

We need it decriminalized, not legalized like it is in Nevada. The situation in Nevada is good for the capitalists, the person that owns the business and the customer, but not good for the women. . . . We're working for jobs to be upgraded all the way around, for all women, including prostitutes. If you decriminalize prostitution and raise women's economic status in legitimate work, you will see less prostitution. If women continue to earn 59¢ for every dollar, you will not see a diminution of prostitution.

Q: Why do you do it?

This is not no easy business. It's not like people think. A lot of men say, "Oh boy! If I could be a woman, I'd be rich!" It's not easy at all. It's not easy on your psyche. It's not easy on your self-esteem. It's not easy with being arrested. It's not easy getting bad customers. It's not the kind of money people think it is. Maybe you'll see one person a night, that's fifty bucks. What the hell.

I'll tell you this, when you're losing your home and you're about to lose your child and your child don't have shoes or you're hungry, you learn you can do anything. You'll learn that you can do anything, even if it had to be robbery. You'd do anything to eat. People have to survive and that's the way it is.

In my hometown, there was no kind of work there. I worked in soap plants, chemical camps, textile mills, shoe factories. That's the type of work. I've worked hard in my life. I've worked real hard. . . .

I remember the first time I did it [went with a man as a prostitute]. . . . This man offered me $300 and I needed the money so bad. We went over to this building and he was undecided whether I should do it, too. We got there and I said, "I can't do it. I can't do it!" We drove away and he said, "I don't want you to do anything that you don't want to do." I said, "$300 . . . take me back." Then I said, "No, I can't do it." We must have drove around four times before I got the guts to even go up there. And it was very simple. Here I had been with the man. I'd massaged him. I had seen him nude and everything. It just seemed . . . well, you know how society makes it seem.

It's hard to put a line on what is prostitution, you know? Everybody prostitutes theirself. Now, this is what I say to the men that say, "I never paid for sex in my life." I say, "Oh, yes you have. You take a girl to dinner. You take her to movies, and you buy her drinks. You've spent $40, $50 on her. You take her home and then you still don't know. Maybe she still won't jump in the sack with you anyway. You're just playing on the odds." I say, "I don't want you to pay for my dinner. I don't want you to pay for the drinks. Give me the money, let me spend it the way I need to. I don't *need* dinner and drinks. I need to pay my bills." In the long shot it's the same way. A man is paying for it. But they got a phobia about paying for it as putting cash in a woman's hand for sex. They'd rather do it the underground way.

My prices are more expensive than the other girls. One night maybe I'll make $200 and some nights . . . I won't sell myself short. I don't know, something about that, I just won't do it. I guess it's keeping up my self-esteem, like I'm worth it. If I've got to do this, I've at least got to prove I'm worth something. . . .

If they're nice guys, if I've known them for a long time and we get along good, talk, you know, talk and friendship, it isn't offensive to me. Sometimes it's very offensive to me. Sometimes I'll get somebody who I wouldn't even speak to normally. I don't mean to sound like a snob, but I wouldn't give them the time of day, and yet I got to give them my *body*. It's something you got to really steel your mind to.

. . . Then, you always have to get your money first hand. You always, you *always* have to be in control. *Never* let them get in control because then you're in trouble.

Never go without getting the money first. They try to steal the money back. . . .

We're all okay to each other [on the street]. It's a code just like anything else. If I stand there and offer $50, the girl next to me would never, *should* never say, "Well, I'll take you for $40." She won't be on the street long. Somebody will do something to her.

We also look out for each other. Let's say I see a customer in a car eyeing me, a girl will come up, poke me, "He ain't got no money." Or they'll come up and say, "He's trouble. Don't mess with him." Same way with me, if I see one of the girls looking at a customer I've been with that's been trouble. You give warnings to each other. If you feel like it's gonna get trouble, you tell a girl to take the license number down, "If I'm not back in an hour, yeah, call the police." But we very seldom do that. We just try to let the person know ahead of time that we got the other girls looking out for us. If one of the girls don't show back up and something might be wrong . . . you know. It's a system of lookout. It's sisterhood.

IMPRESSIONS FROM AN OFFICE

Most educated women work in offices of some sort. The majority work in highly sex-segregated situations, like most clerical workers, and for them lower wages and lack of advancement results from the fact that female jobs are not valued as highly as male jobs. Occasionally, women and men work side by side, but even then, they are often judged by different standards. We found this poem, "Impressions from an Office," in the Wall Street Journal, *a sign that feminists have begun to have their say even in conservative locations.*

The family picture is on HIS desk.
Ah, a solid, responsible family
   man.
The family picture is on HER desk.
Umm, her family will come before
   her career.

HIS desk is cluttered.
He's obviously a hard worker and a
   busy man.
HER desk is cluttered.
She's obviously a disorganized scat-
   terbrain.

HE is talking with his co-workers.
HE must be discussing the latest deal.
SHE is talking with her co-workers.
She must be gossiping.
HE's not at his desk.
He must be at a meeting.
SHE's not at her desk.
She must be in the ladies' room.
HE's not in the office.
He's meeting customers.
SHE's not in the office.
She must be out shopping.
HE's having lunch with the boss.
He's on his way up.
SHE's having lunch with the boss.
They must be having an affair.
The boss criticized HIM.
He'll improve his performance.
The boss criticized HER.
She'll be very upset.

HE got an unfair deal.
Did he get angry?
SHE got an unfair deal.
Did she cry?
HE's getting married.
He'll get more settled.
SHE's getting married.
She'll get pregnant and leave.
HE's having a baby.
He'll need a raise.
SHE's having a baby.
She'll cost the company money in maternity benefits.
HE's going on a business trip.
It's good for his career.
SHE's going on a business trip.
What does her husband say?
HE's leaving for a better job.
He knows how to recognize a good opportunity.
SHE's leaving for a better job.
Women are not dependable.

WORKING WOMEN WITH DISABILITIES

Women have been prominent in a revitalized disabled rights movement and have won significant victories in guaranteed equal access to education, jobs, public space, and sports. The movement also insists on valuing each individual's contribution and challenges society's competitive values. Still, disabled women as a social group remain disproportionately poorly paid and discriminated against, as the following excerpts from a U.S. Woman's Bureau publication show.

Women with work disabilities represented 8.4 percent of all women 16 to 64 years of age in the United States in 1988, down one-tenth of 1 percent from 1981. Of the 79.8 million working women in the U.S. in 1988, 6.7 million had a work disability. More than half of those (3.7 million) had a severe disability.

Women with work disabilities are nearly three times as likely as nondisabled women to be unemployed. The unemployment rate of women with work disabilities was 14.2 percent in 1988 (the same as for disabled men) compared with 5.2 percent for nondisabled women—an improvement from 1981 when the rate was 15.5 percent.

Disabled working women have poorer educational backgrounds. One nondisabled woman in five in the 25 to 64 age range has a college degree— a sharp contrast to the 3.8 percent of disabled women in the same age range who have similar degrees. On the lower end of educational attainment, 22 percent of women with a work disability have less than a high school education.

Black women workers are much more likely to be disabled than white women workers. Nearly 1 black woman in every 7 (13.8 percent) has a work disability, compared with 1 in 13 (only 7.7 percent) of white women.

Only 7.9 percent of Hispanic-origin women have work disabilities. However, since the size of that population is increasing at five times the rate of other ethnic minority groups, this group saw a 31 percent increase in disabled women between 1981 and 1988.

The incidence of work disability increases with age. More than 22 percent of women 55 to 64 years of age had a work disability compared with 3.6 percent of the women aged 16 to 24.

Disabled women workers earned 38 percent less than nondisabled women workers in 1987. This compares to a 30 percent difference in 1980. Disabled women had mean earnings of $8,075 in 1987, while women workers with no work disabilities had mean earnings of $13,000. Men with work disabilities had mean earnings of $15,497.

. . . The Americans with Disabilities Act (ADA), signed into law in July 1990, provides the means to narrow the gaps in employment statistics between disabled and nondisabled working women.

. . . The ADA . . . requires covered Federal contractors to . . . employ and advance qualified individuals with handicaps; . . . forbids discrimination against handicapped individuals in programs receiving Federal financial assistance and in programs conducted by the Government itself. The ADA also builds on the experience of the Civil Rights Act of 1964, as amended, extending to individuals with disabilities, similar civil rights protections provided by the Civil Rights Act to persons on the bases of race, color, sex, national origin, and religion.

The employment title of the ADA becomes effective for employers of 25 or more employees on July 26, 1992, and for employers of 15 or more on July 26, 1994. The ADA prohibits discrimination in all terms and conditions of employment against qualified disabled persons who can perform the essential functions of the job with or without reasonable accommodation. An employer would have to make any reasonable accommodation which would not cause undue hardship to the business.

Education and disability are related. . . . Disabilities may make it difficult to attend and complete school—a situation especially true for the current disabled population. As late as the 1960s, an estimated one in every eight disabled children received no education at all. . . . More than half did not receive special instructional services. The same factors that lead to low educational attainment also may lead to the increased likelihood of becoming disabled; for example, lack of access to preventive health care. It may be that less well-educated people and poorer people tend to obtain jobs involving physical labor. Such jobs may have higher risk for physical injury. Physical limitations, whether or not their origin is job related, may be more disabling in physically demanding work environments. For example, impaired mobility may not effect the work status of a psychotherapist, but it may be a major work disability for a waitress or a nurse. Whichever causal relationship is assumed, it can be argued that increasing educational opportunities is an important strategy for preventing work disability.

This strategy is especially important for women. Work-disabled women are five times as likely as other women to have less than an elementary level of education (17.4 percent versus 3.5 percent). Age is positively associated with work disability and negatively associated

Employment, poverty, and disability also are related . . . people who would not be economically disadvantaged may become so when they are ill. Poor people are less likely to be educated, lack prenatal and postnatal care, are malnourished, and have inadequate access to preventive health services—all of which contribute to risk of chronic illness, physical and mental disability, and the inability to participate in the labor force. . . .

Disabled women are much less likely to be covered by pension and health plans than are disabled men; 24 percent of disabled females, compared with 41.6 percent of disabled males, were covered by both pension and health plans in 1981. Forty-six percent of disabled females, compared with 33.9 percent of disabled males, were not covered by either type of plan. For nondisabled women, 34.6 percent had both health and pension coverage, while 36.3 percent had none.

DROP THE MOP, BLESS THE MESS ———————

Although more women are employed out of their homes, there has not been a commensurate change in who does the work in the home. Men are doing more housework and child care, but on average their contribution is nowhere near equal. Women still take by far the greater share of the responsibility not only for housework but also for the less visible emotional and social work of main-

taining daily life. As a result, they have sometimes been forced to lower their standards, often with some guilt.

Dust bunnies under the couch. Cobwebs in the corners. A grimy shellac over the contents of kitchen cupboards. In a culture where cleanliness has long been equated with godliness, these telltale signs should be anathema. But rather than repenting with a vigorous spring cleaning, many Americans are changing creeds.

. . . "I'd prefer to say that modern homemakers are reprioritizing," said Carolyn Forte, associate director of the Good Housekeeping Institute in New York, the magazine's research group. . . .

Housekeeping standards have dipped strikingly in the last five years, in the opinion of executives with moving companies, maid services and extermination businesses in New York, Atlanta, Boston, Chicago, Cincinnati and San Francisco. The professionals who regularly enter private homes say the change cuts across socioeconomic lines but is most evident in households with young children and two working parents. . . .

Lack of time, more than a slothful nature, accounts for the decline in spotlessness, said Dr. Juliet Schorr, a professor of economics at Harvard University and the author of "The Overworked American: The Unexpected Decline of Leisure." Studying time-use diaries of 1,000 Americans, she found that for every hour a woman works outside the home, she cuts back 30 minutes of housekeeping time.

. . . In 1985, women spent about an hour and a half less cleaning house each week than they did in 1965. In the same period, men devoted about an hour more to cleaning, which left a 30-minute void for dust to grow.

According to a telephone survey of 500 adults, . . . the discrepancy—and the dust—have grown. Forty-three percent of the women surveyed said they were doing less housecleaning than they had done five years ago, but only 21 percent felt their husbands were contributing more than they had in 1987.

"It's easier to cut back on scrubbing the floor than it is to cut back on child care, laundry or meal preparation," Dr. Schorr said. . . .

Deindustrialization

PLANT CLOSINGS

For at least several decades, the United States has been exporting industrial jobs to low-wage regions of the world. Virtually all the clothing, shoes, and accessories we wear are made in less-developed countries by workers earning a small percentage of what U.S. workers would have to be paid, working longer hours under worse conditions. Within the United States this deindustrialization means that many former unionized industrial workers have been forced into service and often part-time jobs with much lower wages and no benefits. Many others are unemployed. Although the popular image of the unemployed is usually male, in fact women are often particularly vulnerable to layoffs and plant closings, and the consequences may be just as serious because so many women support dependents, as we see in this 1992 newspaper article. But there is less public sympathy for unemployed women because of a lingering sense that men have an entitlement to jobs that women do not.

Ypsilanti, Mich.—After everything they have been through, after all the victories won so slowly over the years, there is one more test for the women of General Motors. Sometime next year, the company's Willow Run assembly plant here will shut forever. Seniority is everything when it comes to jobs at other plants, and the women have less of it than their male co-workers. . . .

The women of Willow Run have done it all—welding raw metal in the body shop (the hell hole, it is called), loading 70-pound seats, fighting the deadening monotony of the neverending line, just like the men. But the women, many of them, were often the ones who went home and cooked dinner for their families. They found baby sitters who would cover for them on the 3:30 to midnight shift. . . .

. . . They have less seniority because they did not get in the door at Willow Run until 1968, 12 years after G.M. acquired the plant. And many more of them have the added burden of being single parents. . . .

At 36, now recently divorced, she has such a severe case of carpal tunnel syndrome—an affliction caused by performing repetitive motions—that she wakes up at night with her hands throbbing. Two weeks ago, she was hospitalized with bleeding ulcers. But what Ms. Pittman talks about is her 17-year-old daughter, LaToya, who will graduate from high school next spring.

LaToya wants to be a television broadcaster, and Ms. Pittman intends to put her through college.

As a black woman, Ms. Pittman would have faced even tougher job prospects beyond the auto plant. Her responsibilities keep getting bigger. A few weeks ago, after her sister-in-law's house burned in Detroit, Ms. Pittman invited her and her three small children into her two-bedroom apartment. Ms. Pittman is now sleeping on the sofa.

"My mother says, 'Carla, you're always trying to help somebody,' " Ms. Pittman said the other day. "I said: 'Mama, I'm sorry, but this could be me. I have a job now, but I might not tomorrow.' "

For many women, the money from the auto plant was a ticket out of bad relationships. Tammy Killingbeck, who has worked on the line for 14 of her 33 years, said she and many others live by this credo: Never depend on a man.

"Men always leave," said Ms. Killingbeck, whose parents were divorced when she was small. She married at 15, was a mother at 16 and is now divorced.

Ms. Killingbeck was talking the other day over lunch with three friends from the plant. "The thing that scares me the most," said one of them, Velinda Asam, known as Sam, "is losing my independence."

That, said her friends, is also what they fear. Ms. Asam is 32, divorced and raising an 18-month-old daughter, Sara. "I'm afraid I'll end up on welfare," she said. . . .

She is hoping for a transfer to a plant nearby. In Ypsilanti, she counts on relatives and her best friend, Willie Smith, for moral support and emergency baby sitting. But her backup team cannot follow her to Texas or Tennessee, where there are G.M. plants that will have openings for Willow Run workers.

Ms. Pittman says she has another reason for being nervous about moving to the South: racism. "I feel comfortable at Willow Run," she said.

While most of Willow Run's workers are expected to get transfers, it is too soon to know who will go where, or when. And, with 21 G.M. plants scheduled for closing by 1995 and additional closings predicted, there are no guarantees that some people will not end up unemployed. . . .

Ms. Kaye-Sennett, who is 38 and is married to an iron worker, has worked at Willow Run since 1986. Before that, she was the only woman pouring hot metal at a steel mill until she was laid off.

"I'm going to have to prove myself all over again," she said. "I know what they're going to say: 'Have you seen the woman? There's a woman carpenter. Did you see her yet? Geez, I wonder if she puts out. If not, she's going to be a bitch.' "

She says she is just glad to be working. In 1988, a co-worker accidentally ran over her left foot with a 12-ton vehicle. "The doctors were saying 'beyond repair,' " she said.

She took off her left running shoe. "I still can't bend it," she said, demonstrating. She laughed ruefully. "I'll never wear high heels again. I love high heels." . . .

When a lot of people recall the day General Motors announced that Willow Run would close, they talk about Mrs. Arter sobbing. Her rule had always been: Never whine, never cry.

"I just fell apart," Mrs. Arter said. "I was in this big despair. Finally, I got mad. I said, 'I'm not going to just walk out of here without fighting.' "

Along with her husband, she has thrown herself into organizing union protest rallies and phone banks to help elect Bill Clinton President. She recently completed a Dale Carnegie course. At the graduation party at the union hall, the teacher, Bob Stackpool, announced that her 35 classmates—most of them men—had unanimously voted Mrs. Arter the winner of the leadership award.

As they prepare for uncertain futures, Mrs. Arter and many other Willow Run women are emboldened by their past. "I used to be intimidated by office women," Ms. Killingbeck said. "They were all pretty, and they got to wear nice clothes."

Ms. Killingbeck has long blonde hair and calluses on her hands from building cars. "Now I'm proud," she said. "I think, 'We've worked in a factory. We're strong.' "

HOME WORK REVISITED

In the Progressive era, one of the reformers' victories was the abolition of home work, which then meant manufacturing labor done at home. Because it was impossible to regulate, home work was maximally exploitive, particularly oppressive to women and children, and potentially dangerous to consumers. In recent decades, home work has increased in several areas: some are traditional, like garment manufacture, while others are new, such as computer data entry and word processing. The growth of home work comes from several interrelated factors: deindustrialization has reduced unions' power and encouraged employers to cut back on labor costs and overhead, while more women who want to stay at home with children need to supplement their husbands' incomes. In addition, women who do low-wage labor often prefer to escape factory conditions and prefer the comfort, flexibility, and autonomy that they can have in a home setting while saving time by not having to travel. Home work remains problematic, however. While it frees some women, it also can lower wages, worsen working conditions, and further weaken unions. The following letters offer some of the reasons women choose home work.

We are grateful to Eileen Boris for these selections.

April 18, 1984

William M. Otter
U.S. Department of Labor
Washington, D.C. 20210

Dear Sir:

I have been a homeworker sewing sweaters for Blueberry Woolens in North Anson, Maine for the last four years. . . . I have earned well over the minimum wage at all times. My family have recently been participating in a study by a Ph.D. candidate in early childhood education who is studying children of parents who work at home. In connection with this study I have had to keep a log of my daily activities and have been amazed to see how infrequently I work for a whole hour at a time for Blueberry Woolens. It is one of the great advantages of working at home that I can look after my daughter, keep the wood stove going, bake bread, and hold a well-paying job at the same time. But punching a time card is not really possible in these circumstances.

I have worked for minimum wage in mills and factories in Maine and Massachusetts in the woolen, paper, plastic and shoe industries. I know what the conditions in factories like those are and what the workers have to tolerate in the way of noise pollution, air pollution and other poor working conditions. I know what working seven to three is like; getting to work when the sun is just rising in the morning, getting home just as it is going down, not seeing the sunshine for five days a week. I know mothers and fathers who only see their babies when they are asleep in their cribs. Believe me, "minimum wage" doesn't begin to cover it.

The advantages of working at home are such that even if I could make more money "working out", which I'm afraid isn't a possibility here in central Maine, it would have to be a great deal more to tempt me away from home work. The first and foremost advantage, as I mentioned before, is being able to look after my daughter myself and not have to put her in day care especially as there is little quality care available in this rural area. I am also able to look after our home and keep the woodfire burning in the winter. I have only one trip a week to make to pick up and deliver work. This is a great saving on gas and wear and tear on our car. Not having to go out in all weather especially in the winters we have here in central Maine is another consideration.

Needless to say, I think the ban on homework in the knitted outerwear industry should be removed. It strikes me that some form of licensing would be a good solution to the overseeing of industries which employ home workers. The licensing agency should be on the state or even county level. If there was an agency close to home with a local phone to whom a home-worker could complain or go to to discuss problems, then abuses could be dealt with on an individual basis with single industries rather than affecting all homeworkers, most of whom are more than happy with their jobs. . . .

Sincerely,
Linda Clutterbuck

William Otter, Administrator
Wage & Hour Division
Employment Standards, Room 53502
U.S. Dept. of Labor
200 California Ave., NW
Washington, DC 20210

Dear Mr. Otter,

I feel strongly on the issue of the Ban on Homework in the Knitted out-erwear industry.

Not every woman is inclined to march for equal rights. Many of us prefer to stay at home with husband and children and *work* for equal rights. We believe in FREEDOM OF CHOICE.

I can knit, be at home when my two teenagers need me, bake a chocolate cake, collect my neighbors UPS packages and deliveries, keep an eye on the neighborhood for vandals and burglars (a common occurrence in the city). *And* provide city & state with taxes all at the same time. This makes me something of a Wonder Woman compared to my "sister" marches.

As long as the income is reported, and taxes paid on this income, I feel the Government should collect the taxes, applaud my efforts, and give me credit for having the common sense to accept nothing less than minimum wage for my work.

Yours most sincerely,
In Stitches!

(Owner of a Denver home-knitting enterprise)

FAST FOOD ──────────────────────────────

Nothing exemplifies the kind of work that has replaced industrial employment better than the fast-food industry. One of the few growth sectors in the U.S. economy, these jobs are usually part-time, poorly paid, and supervised to the extent of demeaning workers. This study of Burger King in Canada is equally applicable to a wide range of similar chains in the United States.

. . . Burger King's profits rest on the availability of a shifting labour force, one that Burger King can call upon and dismiss as the need arises. By simplifying the work tasks and cross-training at all stations, Burger King has attempted to create a work situation that allows any worker to do any job in the restaurant. Just as almost all discretion is removed from the job, workers are told how important each of them is to the restaurant's success. Thus we see some of the contradictions involved in grafting a human relations approach to labour management onto a division of labour determined by the principles of scientific management. The organization of production at Burger King is geared to treating human labour as an undifferentiated, quantifiable input. At the same time, workers must be convinced of their individual importance in order to elicit their maximal output.

. . . The single greatest challenge facing managers is dealing with the workforce that meet Burger King's criteria for availability—teenagers and married women. While young people are fast workers, they need to be impressed with certain basic job skills such as punctuality. . . .

The adult women workers, normally hired to work daytime during the weekdays, are slower, but generally more reliable. The women are there strictly for the money and have few options. As the ex-Burger King manager said,

> Let's face it—what other kinds of jobs are available? Where else can they go—to a variety store? They have responsibilities to their kids, want to see them off to school and be there for them when they get home in the afternoon. They have demanding husbands who come home from work at night and want to be looked after. The job at Burger King gives them a bit of extra money. They live nearby and even if the job isn't too pleasant, well it'll do.

. . . "Keeping crew in the know" is seen as very important in maintaining good communication. To this end, crew meetings are held regularly to keep crew informed about company policy and to enlist their support. One meeting I attended asked for suggestions about how to solve the ever-present problem of keeping the crew room clean. The enthusiastic suggestions elicited from workers involved docking pay and taking away the "privilege" of a free meal. Interestingly, no one suggested including crew room maintenance along with other tasks of running the restaurant, like keeping the dining room and the customers' bathroom clean. It was assumed that crew room maintenance should be a voluntary activity.

The crew meeting also included a skit given by the managers acting out what "bad" crew members do and concluding with a discussion of how a "good" crew member should look and act. The bad crew member had mustard on his uniform, and made hamburgers with too many condiments. Everyone enjoyed the managers' antics. . . .

Burger King social activities are planned to help foster an identification with the company and keep morale high. During my fieldwork a group of teenagers, most of whom were production leaders, "volunteered," with a bit of managerial prodding, to form a "social committee." It was their job to organize and sign up workers for various Burger King events—skating parties, dances, bowling, baseball. These activities were presented as entirely for the benefit of Burger King crew and as such, it was accepted that they would be funded by crew members.

The social committee had some difficulties. The first problem was lack of sufficient interest from other crew members. Helen, the second assistant manager, made it clear that it was up to the production leaders on the committee to whip up the necessary enthusiasm. Various ways of raising money were suggested, such as a car wash, wiping windows, mowing lawns. All of these were vetoed by the first assistant manager. Burger King will sponsor community activities to improve community relations and encourage more business, but funding crew events does not fit into that category.

The social committee finally decided to organize a garage sale. Eileen, a production leader, generously offered her parents' garage, but the parents vetoed the idea. Finally, Maria, an older Italian woman who was vociferous in her criticisms of Burger King, volunteered the use of her lawn, since she lived close by. She felt that she was helping out the youngsters. Signs were put in the crew room to encourage people to bring things in for the big day, but the sale never happened because not enough workers brought in things to sell. Some money was raised through fines levied for renting uniforms when people either forgot theirs or came in to work with dirty ones. For the most part, individual crew members paid their own way to the social events. Thus those who signed up for the Burger King baseball team were charged $12.52 each for their Burger King team jersey. . . .

Because the labour scheduling system assigns different groups of workers to work together each day, workplace social relations can only develop from shared commonalities based on other aspects of workers' lives. These common ties based on gender and age influence the way in which workers relate to each other; they are used by Burger King to promote activities geared to its particular labour force. . . .

As in other industries characterized by high turnover and absence of unionization, women, visible minorities, and young people are overrepresented. I also noted how once this cheap labour is recruited, it is interchangeability rather than gender, age, or race which becomes the major consideration in assigning people to work stations. Interchangeability of workers is desirable for a fluid production team where all workers can do all the jobs. Another current, however, runs counter to the first goal; local management places the prettier younger female workers at the cash register, the adult women in the back, and the young men at jobs where slightly more strength is required.

The overriding determinant is to keep replacement costs as low as possible. Some young men and adult women do work up front, women do the heavier jobs when young men are not around, and teenaged women are sometimes assigned to the fry station. Management policy from Burger King headquarters actively encourages this versatility because if any worker can do any job, then the cheapest workers can be used.

I heard accounts of overt racism at Burger King. One of the young black women who was fed up with the job and was quitting told me that one of the managers had called her a "nigger." I was shocked, and asked another young black fellow in the crew room if he could confirm what she said. "Sure," he said, "Big Ira and Donny routinely refer to Ben as 'nigger.' " I asked my informant why no one had complained to management. He said that if they wanted the job, the best course of action was to do nothing and not "make waves." . . .

In early 1990, a coalition of fifty church, labour, and community groups in Philadelphia banded together to launch a boycott of McDonald's because of discriminatory wage policies practised in McDonald's outlets. The coalition, called the Campaign for Fair Wages, was acting on documentation that the starting pay of fast food workers in the inner city averaged almost one dollar less than that of suburban workers. Seventy-five percent of the inner city fast food workforce is black, compared to only 37 percent in the suburbs. . . .

Age and gender considerations sometimes affected the way in which workers did their jobs, and how they felt about them. Management's observations were that adult women workers were generally steadier and more reliable. In the dining room, in particular, there seemed to be a battle that had generational overtones. The two women who were assigned to the dining room during the weekdays complained that the part-time teenagers from the night before left the place in a mess. The day workers then had to rush around emptying garbage bags left from the night before and cleaning the tables and trays when they began their shifts. One of these women resented this so much that she insisted that the manager station her in the kitchen, or she would quit. Nevertheless, neither of these two women seemed to mind the dining room station as much as the young people did.

The women who prepared the condiments for the lunch rush also felt that loose ketchup bottle tops from the night before reflected the poor work habits of young people. There seemed to be shades of "mom looking after the kids" in the women daytime workers' views of the high school evening workers. . . .

"LIVES UPSIDE DOWN"

Another new trend in employment is working around the clock. Some shift work arises from necessity—such as hospital jobs—and some from employers' desire to increase productivity by twenty-four-hour operation. Shift work is often especially stressful for women because they bear the major responsibility for children and domestic labor.

At 11 P.M., or 1 A.M., on the many nights she must work overtime, Allison McClure stops at her mother's house to retrieve her 3-year-old daughter, Mia, take her home and put her back to bed. Then she packs Mia's bag for nursery school, does the ironing, cleans house and takes a shower. "I'm in bed by 3 or 4," she said during her 9–9:30 P.M. "lunch" break at a mail processing center.

Then she gets up at 6:45 A.M. "I get her up, I fix her breakfast, I feed her and I take her to school. I'll lie down for about an hour and a half, and then I'm up. Any business I have to do, I try to fit in between then and the time I have to be at work at 3."

Ms. McClure is a shift worker. Thirty years old, paid around $30,000 a year, she is hard at work for the United States Postal Service when most people take it easy or sleep. Because of her personal obligations, she said: "I'll never sleep eight hours. Sometimes you get tired, so you have to push yourself." She has jet lag without the jet, and she has it all the time. . . .

Millions who work unconventional hours have become objects of concern to psychologists and occupational-health specialists. While some people, like police officers, nurses and factory workers, have always worked unconventional hours, more and more do now. And among them new strains have developed as two-earner families and single working mothers have displaced one-earner, married-couple families.

Typically, statisticians define shift workers as people who spend less than half of the daylight hours on the job or who work some hours in the morning and some at night. Others put in long, dawn-to-dawn shifts or rotating schedules—days one week, nights the next. Growth in shift work, like the growth in part-time temporary jobs, is a part of a sea change in the labor force that has to accommodate a global economy that runs around the clock.

Shift work accounts for a quarter to nearly half the jobs in the fastest growing occupations. It is built into 8 of 10 occupations that the Bureau of Labor Statistics predicts will add the most workers in the next decade: sales clerk and cashier in stores, nurse, nursing aide, truck driver, janitor, waiter and fast-food worker. Shift work, of course, also breeds shift workers. They work in convenience stores, supermarkets and gas stations that stay open long after dark to serve other people who work long after dark.

No one knows just how many shift workers there are. The last time it looked, in 1985, the Census Bureau found 20 million, or a fifth of the work force. It counted them again last year, but the results will not be reported until later this year. . . .

Occupational-health experts find that shift work exacts a toll beyond just losing sleep. Years of research, assembled in a recent study of shift work and health by the Congressional Office of Technology Assessment, show that shift workers typically suffer from insomnia and chronic fatigue. They have more trouble with their health and dispositions than other workers, more marital problems, more strains rearing children. Night workers, the study says, complain inordinately of gastrointestinal disorders, including peptic ulcers. It says that pregnant shift workers, according to some limited research, suffer more miscarriages, premature births and lower birth weights than women who work regular hours. . . .

Many foreign governments regulate shift work, but in the United States, neither the government nor the institutions that support workplace regulation, like labor unions and advocacy groups, have fully addressed the issue. In the interest of public safety, Federal agencies regulate shift work in public transportation and in a few other areas, like operating nuclear power plants, where a groggy employee can endanger a community. But no one protects the community when a groggy employee hits the road for home. . . .

For [women] workers, the greatest stress occurs in trying to meet the daytime demands of their families—caring for children or preparing meals that they often cannot be home to eat. Ms. Sanders, 32, usually works from 5 P.M. to 1:30 A.M. During her 9–9:30 break she was having lunch—popcorn. She has two boys, 4 and 1. Her husband is a road manager for entertainment groups, so he is away a lot. "I have kind of dozed off at the wheel going home, but only when I have to work until 3:30," she said. "I like the hours because they're convenient for getting my kid to school and picking him up. But I don't get to spend any time with him other than on the weekend." . . .

Ms. Jones said her marriage was solid until she started working nights. Her husband worked for the Postal Service, too, from 4:30 A.M. to noon. She was getting home then about 7 A.M. He would want to talk as soon as he got home, she said, and she would want to sleep. "He still wanted me to be like I was before, making meals, taking the kids to school. It was hard."

No one monitors changes in family relationships here, but clearly the work is murder on marriages. "When young women come here to work," said Mr. Beasley, a steward for the postal workers' union, "you know what the older women say? They say, 'Honey if you've got a man, you're not going to have him long.' " . . .

The workers' health problems are serious. Alana Farino, who works from 10 P.M. to 6:30 A.M. on the letter-sorting machine, said her eyesight is beginning to fail. Sarah Peterson, who works with her, says she is getting asthma. . . . Linda Brown, the nurse at the center from 2 P.M. to 10:30 P.M., said: "They're throwing their bodies completely out of kilter. I see a lot of people walking around in a fog." Lancy Rocker, the nurse who follows Linda Brown on what the workers call the "zombie shift," said she sees a lot of workers with stomach problems. "They have real short patience," she said.

The Movements

WELFARE IS A WOMEN'S ISSUE

Today more than half of all children will spend some time in single-mother families. Single-mother families are disproportionately poor, because of high unemployment, the low wages of women's jobs, and the difficulties of finding reliable and affordable child care. The problems of "welfare mothers" are inseparable from the problems of working women and of all poor mothers.

When Aid to Families with Dependent Children (AFDC) was first established as part of the Social Security Act of 1935, the program was essential to women precisely because most women were excluded from the more generous and honorable Social Security programs such as old-age insurance and unemployment compensation. But even AFDC at first excluded most needy single mothers: virtually all southern blacks, most Hispanics, and American Indians were left out, and even in northern areas with less racially discriminatory policies, the funding was never enough to meet the need. In the 1950s and 1960s, influenced particularly by the civil rights movement, many poor minority single mothers were able to get themselves covered by AFDC, staking out a claim to an equal citizenship entitlement to welfare similar to the claim for the right to vote. As a result, welfare rolls grew substantially.

One of the social movements of the 1960s was a welfare rights movement, which harked back in some ways to the relief recipients' agitation of the Depression of the 1930s. The National Welfare Rights Organization (NWRO), established out of a local group in 1963, developed into an influential national network by the end of that decade. It stimulated victorious legal challenges that ended some humiliating and unconstitutional welfare practices such as unannounced midnight searches of clients' homes, residency requirements, and cutoffs of welfare without prior hearings. Some historians have perceived that the issue of welfare rights was part of civil rights. But few have understood that welfare rights was also part of the women's liberation movement, a connection often missed because the women's movement is so often pictured as exclusively white. The following selection from 1973, by Johnnie Tillmon, first chairwoman of the NWRO, elucidates this connection.

I'm a woman. I'm a black woman. I'm a poor woman. I'm a fat woman. I'm a middle-aged woman. And I'm on welfare.

In this country, if you're any one of those things—poor, black, fat, female, middle-aged, on welfare—you count less as a human being. If you're all those things, you don't count at all. Except as a statistic.

I am a statistic.

I am 45 years old. I have raised six children.

I grew up in Arkansas, and I worked there for fifteen years in a laundry, making about $20 or $30 a week, picking cotton on the side for carfare. I moved to California in 1959 and worked in a laundry there for nearly four years. In 1963 I got too sick to work anymore. Friends helped me to go on welfare.

They didn't call it welfare. They called it A.F.D.C.—Aid to Families with Dependent Children. Each month I get $363 for my kids and me. I pay $128 a month rent; $30 for utilities, which include gas, electricity, and water; $120 for food and non-edible household essentials; $50 for school lunches for the three children in junior and senior high school who are not eligible for reduced-cost meal programs.

There are millions of statistics like me. Some on welfare. Some not. And some, really poor, who don't even know they're entitled to welfare. Not all of them are black. Not at all. In fact, the majority—about two-thirds—of all the poor families in the country are white.

Welfare's like a traffic accident. It can happen to anybody, but especially it happens to women.

And that is why welfare is a women's issue. For a lot of middle-class women in this country, Women's Liberation is a matter of concern. For women on welfare it's a matter of survival.

The truth is that A.F.D.C. is like a supersexist marriage. You trade in *a* man for *the* man. But you can't divorce him if he treats you bad. He can divorce you, of course, cut you off anytime he wants. But in that case, *he* keeps the kids, not you.

The man runs everything. In ordinary marriage, sex is supposed to be for your husband. On A.F.D.C. you're not supposed to have any sex at all. You give up control of your own body. It's a condition of aid. You may even have to agree to get your tubes tied so you can never have more children just to avoid being cut off welfare.

The man, the welfare system, controls your money. He tells you what to buy, what not to buy, where to buy it, and how much things cost. If things—rent, for instance—really cost more than he says they do, it's just too bad for you.

There are other welfare programs, other kinds of people on welfare—the blind, the disabled, the aged. (Many of them are women, too, especially the aged.)

But when the politicians talk about the "welfare cancer eating at our vitals," they're not talking about the aged, blind, and disabled. Nobody minds them. They're the "deserving poor." Politicians are talking about A.F.D.C. Politicians are talking about us—the women who head up 99 per cent of the A.F.D.C. families—and our kids. We're the "cancer," the "undeserving poor." Mothers and children.

In this country we believe in something called the "work ethic." That means that your work is what gives you human worth. But the work ethic itself is a double standard. It applies to men and to women on welfare. It doesn't apply to all women. If you're a society lady from Scarsdale and you spend all your time sitting on your prosperity paring your nails, well, that's okay.

The truth is a job doesn't necessarily mean an adequate income. A woman with three kids—not twelve kids, mind you, just three kids—that woman earning the full federal minimum wage of $2.00 an hour, is still stuck in poverty. She is below the Government's own official poverty line. There are some ten million jobs that now pay less than the minimum wage, and if you're a woman, you've got the best chance of getting one.

The President keeps repeating the "dignity of work" idea. What dignity? Wages are the measure of dignity that society puts on a job. Wages and nothing else. There is no dignity in starvation. Nobody denies, least of all poor women, that there is dignity and satisfaction in being able to support your kids through honest labor.

We wish we could do it.

The problem is that our country's economic policies deny the dignity and satisfaction of self-sufficiency to millions of people—the millions who suffer everyday in underpaid dirty jobs—and still don't have enough to survive.

People still believe that old lie that A.F.D.C. mothers keep on having kids just to get a bigger welfare check. On the average, another baby means another $35 a month—barely enough for food and clothing. Having babies for profit is a lie that only men could make up, and only men could believe. Men, who never have to bear the babies or have to raise them and maybe send them to war.

There are a lot of other lies that male society tells about welfare mothers; that A.F.D.C. mothers are immoral, that A.F.D.C. mothers are lazy, misuse their welfare checks, spend it all on booze and are stupid and incompetent.

If people are willing to believe these lies, it's partly because they're just special versions of the lies that society tells about *all* women.

For instance, the notion that all A.F.D.C. mothers are lazy: that's just a negative version of the idea that women don't work and don't want to. It's a way of rationalizing the male policy of keeping women as domestic slaves.

The notion that A.F.D.C. mothers are immoral is another way of saying that all women are likely to become whores unless they're kept under control by men and marriage. Even many of my own sisters on welfare believe these things about themselves.

On TV, a woman learns that human worth means beauty and that beauty means being thin, white, young and rich.

She learns that her body is really disgusting the way it is, and that she needs all kinds of expensive cosmetics to cover it up.

She learns that a "real woman" spends her time worrying about how her bathroom bowl smells; that being important means being middle class, having two cars, a house in the suburbs, and a minidress under your maxicoat. In other words, an A.F.D.C. mother learns that being a "real woman" means being all the things she isn't and having all the things she can't have.

Either it breaks you, and you start hating yourself, or you break it.

There's one good thing about welfare. It kills your illusions about yourself, and about where this society is really at. It's laid out for you straight. You have to learn to fight, to be aggressive, or you just don't make it. If you can survive being on welfare, you can survive anything. It gives you a kind of freedom, a sense of your own power and togetherness with other women.

Maybe it is we poor welfare women who will really liberate women in this country. We've already started on our welfare plan.

Along with other welfare recipients, we have organized together so we can have some voice. Our group is called the National Welfare Rights Organization (N.W.R.O.). We put together our own welfare plan, called Guaranteed Adequate Income (G.A.I.), which would eliminate sexism from welfare.

There would be no "categories"—men, women, children, single, married, kids, no kids—just poor people who need aid. You'd get paid according to need and family size only—$6,500 for a family of four (which is the Department of Labor's estimate of what's adequate), and that would be upped as the cost of living goes up.

If I were president, I would solve this so-called welfare crisis in a minute and go a long way toward liberating every woman. I'd just issue a proclamation that "women's" work is *real* work.

In other words, I'd start paying women a living wage for doing the work we are already doing—child-raising and housekeeping. And the welfare crisis would be over, just like that. Housewives would be getting wages, too—a legally determined percentage of their husband's salary—instead of having to ask for and account for money they've already earned.

For me, Women's Liberation is simple. No woman in this country can feel dignified, no woman can be liberated, until all women get off their knees. That's what N.W.R.O. is all about—women standing together, on their feet.

"YOUR CLERICAL WORKERS ARE RIPE FOR UNIONISM"

Despite some campaigns to organize office workers in the 1930s, most clericals were not unionized at the beginning of this period. Renewed organizing drives among women office workers were part of the second wave of feminism in the 1970s. They addressed grievances such as dress codes, requirements for nonprofessional tasks (such as making coffee, cutting the boss's hair, shopping), and general disrespectful treatment and sexual harassment in addition to traditional union wages, hours, and benefits demands. Out of a variety of local organizations one national group—9-to-5—gained great prominence (it was eventually featured in a hit movie by the same name). A key to 9-to-5's success has been its retention of its independent identity as a women's movement organization at the same time that it affiliated with a national union. In 1993, President Clinton appointed 9-to-5 founder Karen Nussbaum as head of the U.S. Women's Bureau, the Department of Labor agency that women fought for and established in 1918. (Mary Van Kleeck, author of one of our selections in the 1890–1920 period [see pp. 156–58], was the first head of the Women's Bureau.)

Employers understood the dangers of their clerical workers becoming more demanding very early on in the new women's movement, as this 1971 article from a business journal shows.

Numerous observers have pointed out the difficulties that face unions attempting to organize clerical employees. Some of the reasons are structural (e.g., the physical problem of reaching this group with the union message). But the majority of reasons for clerical workers' resistance are sociological:

(a) the widespread feeling that unions are beneath their dignity and that they can bargain for themselves, (b) the belief that they, as members of the middle class, are identified with management and therefore should reject unions, and (c) the tendency to think of unions as unseemly, rabble-rousing organizations. Consider what clerical workers themselves have often said about unions:

"Unions are for the birds—for people without much education who can't stand on their own." (Oil company secretary)

"Unions are undesirable and distasteful to people like me. I just can't imagine myself out on a picket line." (Young bank clerk)

"I don't need a union. I can handle myself. If I want a raise, I go see my boss." (Household-products company stenographer)

"What do I know about unions? No one has ever talked to me about them." (Insurance company clerk)

During the past decade, unions have had only modest success at best in organizing clerical workers and other white-collar employees. For example, while over one million nonmanagerial white-collar workers were recruited by unions from 1958 to 1968, the yearly level of this group's union membership has remained at about 11%. . . .

But beneath the surface there are signs that attitudes are changing, the clerical employees are becoming sufficiently provoked by management to take a second look at unions. Comments like the following are now commonplace:

"In my opinion, unions aren't desirable for my kind of employee, but they may come if companies don't treat us right." (Chemical company secretary)

"Unions kill all incentive, they help create mediocre people. But at the same time they furnish a much-needed bargaining power." (Electronics company clerk)

"Unions may be a necessary evil, despite the strikes and all. If companies recognized individual worth, unions would not be needed." (Electric utility telephone operator)

Clerical workers indeed *have* become much less satisfied on most key employee relations issues in recent years (1966 to the present) than in past years (1955 to 1965). . . .

Note too that clerical employees feel increasingly remote and shut off from management. . . . Clerical employees are beginning to feel like mere cogs in a great impersonal bureaucracy, and there is a growing tendency to see management as a nameless, faceless mask of authority and indifference. . . .

The [critical] attitudes of clerical employees [toward management] have declined more sharply than those of any group for which we have similar comparative information. They have, for instance, sloped down considerably more than those of the heavily unionized blue-collar employees who have historically viewed management far less enthusiastically on a comparative basis. . . . It is important to point out that I am talking about relative declines in favorable ratings. Clerical employees currently have more favorable opinions of their employers and, on balance, still express less criticism than do blue-collar workers. But the gap is closing . . . and there are actually some issues where clerical attitudes are already less favorable than those of blue-collar employees. These include:

- Applying policies consistently.
- Letting employees speak up to higher authority.
- Telling employees what is going on in the company.

While the attitudes of clerical employees in the companies studied have moved, overall, in a more negative direction since 1966 than have the attitudes of hourly workers, this trend has not yet caused an en masse movement to unionization. For most companies, there is still time to act—time to find out how much discontent exists among clerical employees and what their major problems are.

Of course, it is possible that many companies will be lucky (we are presuming that most would prefer not to have their office employees unionized) and will avoid unionization of their clerical work force by ignoring the problem and doing business as usual. The traditional reluctance of office employees to join unions, for whatever reasons, may be a sufficient deterrent.

However, teachers, nurses, and other middle-class groups have already begun to turn toward unions, and, in view of what is happening to employee attitudes, it would be a bad bet, I think, for companies to depend on the historical reluctance of clerical workers to sign up.

WOMEN INVADE MALE PRESERVES ———————

Occupational sex segregation has been firmly entrenched in well-paying male blue-collar jobs. But even here, the energy and daring of the women's liberation movement, and the promise of much higher wages, inspired some particularly courageous women to break these gender barriers. Women have fought for jobs in the skilled trades (e.g., carpentry, plumbing), in construction work, and in the farming and forestry industries. Some received help from government-funded training programs and from government-imposed affirmative action requirements. Lesbians have often been in the forefront of opening these jobs to women. In this oral history, a Latina describes her experiences as a police officer.

I was recruited by a Latino officer. I was working in the Mission (a predominantly Latin neighborhood [in San Francisco]) as a youth employment counselor and he said to me, "Someone like you would be great. You speak Spanish and English, you're young, you have the energy. Come on, you can do it." Finally I just showed up at one of the training programs. My interest was aroused, and also my determination was strengthened by the Department saying, "You can't do it."

The first two classes of sixty recruits, in July and November of 1975, included about thirty women each. The instructors let us know right away they didn't want us, saying, "We'd like to welcome you all here, even though we know a lot of you shouldn't be here." They weren't prepared for women. There were no locker room facilities. They put us in men's uniforms. At one point they tried making us shower with the men, then they split us up because it was worse for the men—they were shyer than we were.

The training techniques were developed more to set us up to fail than to train us for the job. In the physical training they set a standard that had never existed before. You had to complete a certain number of critical tasks to graduate from the academy. It was brutal. I remember people coming out of there with broken collar bones from being whacked, necks all twisted—men and women. Some of the takedowns and techniques they used were not properly developed or explained. You were told to just pick someone up and wham 'em down on the ground. All kinds of injuries resulted. I think in the backs of their minds they wanted us to get hurt so we'd quit. A lot of guys were fresh out of Vietnam, and some—not all of them—thought they were in a war zone. When the instructor said, "You grab her and throw her down NOW"—boom, there you were. It was like an order from the commander-in-chief. Eventually, many of the guys sensed that they were being used to get the women out, and they started working with us. But it was the sense of unity and the support of the other women that got us through those seventeen weeks in the academy. . . .

For the first year after my training, I worked the night shift at Potrero Station. None of the men would talk to me. That was the worst. If they had said something negative, I could have dealt with it, but when people just ignore you like you're not there. . . . We'd be driving around, midnight till eight in the morning, and my partner wouldn't talk to me all night long. Or we'd respond to a call and my partner—it was always a man then—would handle everything, and I'd feel like a little shadow, asking myself, "Why am I here?"

That was a question I asked myself seriously when I was assigned to work with an officer who had problems getting along with partners. That's what would happen to rookies—they'd make you work with the guys everybody else hated. One night he drove us to a secluded area and stopped the patrol car. When I asked why we were stopping, he said he wanted to shoot rats.

Then he opened his shirt, pulled out a small handgun and pointed it directly at me. "I just want to see how fast you women cops can run," he said.

. . . I couldn't believe what was happening, but I put my left hand up to get his attention and at the same time I reached for my gun with my right hand. In the most forceful voice I could muster I said, "Take me back to the station *now.*" He protested that he was just kidding, but we drove directly back to the station, and I let him get out of the car first so I could keep an eye on him. When I reported the incident to the sergeant, he just laughed it off. But I stuck up for myself and refused to work with that officer again. He's no longer in the Department. . . .

We'd go to a domestic dispute, husband and wife going at it, and we were able to relate to both people. He would deal with the man and I would deal with the woman. Two male officers might have just said, "Come on buddy, why don't you just take a walk and cool down." Instead, I would say to the woman, "Are you hurt? Has this happened before?" She'd be amazed that someone was talking to her. So the communication seemed to be better. . . . In an arrest situation sometimes men would say to me, "Well, what are *you* going to do with me." Then I'd have to come on strong and say "Hey, buddy, just cool it. Don't mess with me." I've always been able to take care of myself but now I had to develop a body language and presence that said: "No, no no, you're not hitting me; you might hit your wife, but you are not going to hit *me.*" It took time, but soon I could walk in and gear my communication to the particular circumstances. . . .

The reality is that ninety percent of my job is communication. You have the five percent where you're in a critical life-and-death situation, and then another five percent when you have to be physical. But the majority is communication and you learn how to express yourself. Questioning a rape victim, for example, I have to be sensitive to what he or she has gone through. . . .

Since 1977, my partner has been a woman. . . . [After working only with men, I said to a friend,] "I've been thinking about this. I'd really like to work with you as a partner. Why don't we approach the lieutenant and tell him we want to work together." When we walked into his office and told him, he started laughing. Well, my attitude came out right away. I said, "What's so funny?" We convinced him to give us a try, and he put us in the felony car. Now, Northern Station at that time was very busy, and the felonies there are likely to be homicides, knifings, shootings or bank robberies. They figured we'd botch up and probably leave. Well, of course, we loved it.

We made fantastic arrests. I remember one midnight shift while patrolling Union Street, we routinely cruised down an alley. We saw a disturbance, but couldn't really tell what was going on. It looked like three or four guys fighting. Poor visibility is a problem that goes with night work. As we got close, we heard one of them shout, "It's the cops!" and two of them took off running. Pam jumped out of the car, and the other two took off. That's when I saw one of them had a gun. This all happened in a matter of seconds. Pam was on foot, I was driving, and at the same time working the radio putting out information and calling for help. Just as I turned the corner, I saw the guy pull his gun and point it at Pam. I didn't have time to get out, so I ran over the curb and hit him with the car, pinning him against the wall. When he saw me coming, he panicked and dropped the gun. We made an arrest and he was convicted.

When Pam and I first started working together, it was very new to see two women officers. We would respond to some calls from women who just wanted to have men around. I'm serious—you know, women who live in hotels by themselves and want to have the guys over for a drink or whatever. We'd knock on the door, "Police," and she'd answer the door, "Police! I called for a man!"

Men were not used to being arrested by women, so at times we'd have to fight. Our academy was real hard; I mean, we learned to fight. So whenever anybody challenged us on the street just because we were women, it was like we were back at home base. Here was somebody telling us we couldn't do it. The poor individuals would be laid out in a matter of seconds. The public learned quickly, but there were always some individuals who still wanted to talk to men; they didn't think women could handle it. I found that Third World people were much more accepting of women with guns. We had the most problems with white, middle-class men. They were rude, and we'd just have to be really blunt.

Feminists were not necessarily supportive of women in the police force. In the beginning, my women friends said, "Why do you want to be in police work? That's sick. You're arresting people and putting them in jail." But I'm also helping people. . . .

The negative attitude toward police did cause problems within the women's community. When we first started, women had no support in the Department. So we set up a women's support group where we could meet and talk about our problems and how to approach the administration with some ideas to better our working conditions. We didn't want to meet at . . . one of the police stations because we wouldn't have any privacy. The San Francisco Women's Building . . . would be an ideal place to meet once a month. When we approached them about renting a room, I was flabbergasted by the response. They said, "No way, because you're representing a segment of society we don't approve of." "But," I said, "we also represent women—Third World women—all kinds of women who are in a non-traditional job." . . .

We finally found a church where we could meet. But the incident split the women's community down the middle. Some were very against us meeting at the Women's Building, and others said, "Hey, that's not fair. We're women, we're the ones who fought to get them in the police department, and now you're not even giving them space to meet in our building?" Then the whole thing got in the papers, and I got called into the chief's office; he was worried it would reflect on the Department. Finally, the Women's Building told us they would give us free space, but we declined—we were fine in our church. . . . There are thirty to forty women participating. We have single women, married women, lesbians, single mothers, every kind of woman. We deal with getting the Department to provide better facilities, medical care for women, pregnancy care, and many other issues.

Another group of us got together to address the sexual harassment that was causing life-threatening situations on the street. For example, when you're calling in for help or you need backup and somebody cuts you off, or starts talking so you can't get through, or they don't show up when you call for help. Some of the men got tired of this too; they were getting cut off on the radio just because they were friends with or worked with one of the women. Until recently, harassment had been tolerated. But the chief took it seriously when we approached it as an officers' safety issue. Our point is that we should be able to do our jobs with mutual respect, and work in a safe environment where we can all get along.

We developed a professionalism panel—men and women—who had experienced sexual harassment, and now we're providing awareness training. We discuss different types of harassment that occur subtly: the ignoring, the obnoxious comments that aren't meant to be heard by anybody except you. The training is working; it's changing attitudes. It's opened up communication and allowed us to confront the issue. You can say, "Hey, Joe, cool it. I don't like that," and he knows what you mean.

"WE ARE EVERYWHERE"

Lesbians have been, although often unnoticed, disproportionately prominent among women labor activists, not only in recent decades but throughout modern labor history. They have, for example, been overrepresented among female shop stewards. But working women's debt to lesbians has often been hidden because lesbians were forced to stay "in the closet"—to hide their sexual preference—in the union movement as elsewhere. As a result of the gay liberation movement, in the last few years, lesbians and gays have been able to "come out" in the union movement, not only to identify themselves but to organize caucuses and to press for union support on issues of special concern, such as harassment and discrimination.

We are grateful to Tess Ewing for this selection.

How (and Why) to Organize Lesbian/Gay Union Committees

It has not been easy for lesbian and gay union committees to get started. Most have been active for less than three years. They have had to contend with considerable prejudice and bureaucracy. Still, their successes have inspired the formation of more such groups and have changed a lot of people's lives for the better.

. . . In many unions, we have formed rank and file committees and negotiated contracts that include domestic partner benefits. We have organized care for union members with AIDS and proposed strong resolutions on gay and lesbian rights at international conventions.

Through these activities, we have been joining our community's issues to the cause of labor in general, and we have found a unique way to "put the movement back in the labor movement." In the process, we have been mobilizing the energies of a number of union members who, even though their labor movement experience may be limited, are talented and seasoned gay rights organizers.

WHERE IT CAN HAPPEN

While forming a union gay and lesbian caucus will certainly encourage union members to be less fearful, it might not be the best strategy for every industry or every town. Often if we are "out" on the job at all, it is only to a few select friends. The closet is a fact of gay life. It isolates us all, yet may be the only protection we have from homophobic hostilities.

But having come out and gotten active in the community, we want to make union halls places where it's "okay to be gay." As a first step we look for the union's tradition of support on civil rights issues, and we check constitutions for language barring discrimination on the basis of sexual orientation. SEIU, AFT, NEA, AFSCME, CWA, APWU, UAW, and UFCW [unions] have all taken a stand on this question.

Strong gay and lesbian union committees have taken hold in communities where there is a large gay population and a thriving gay culture. There, our co-workers and union leaders have been receptive to our issues because they already know "out" gay people from their neighborhoods, families, and churches.

At workplaces where there are more gay men and lesbians than the average one-out-of-ten (for example, libraries, restaurants, schools, theaters, or hospitals), our committees have also organized successfully.

REACHING OUT, COMING OUT

There is a paradox for lesbians and gays organizing at the workplace: We may be there in numbers even larger than one-out-of-ten, but we may also want the protection of our invisibility. Yet, if we don't make our presence known, we'll never meet our allies. So, while we're reaching out, it's very important to respect individuals' needs for discretion.

We can assess our co-workers' openness by asking them as individuals to donate to a community AIDS fundraiser. We can raise gay and lesbian political issues during social conversations. . . .

To test the waters among the other gays and lesbians at our workplaces, we can set up a social evening to see if people are willing to do union work. Placing an announcement on the gay community bulletin board or in the local lesbian newsletter might draw in some new folks who have had little to do with union politics till now.

Only when there is a dependable core of people should the group come out and request the resources of the union to support an official committee. Even when the union has sanctioned the group, some of its work should remain located in the gay community. Typically, the first meetings are held elsewhere than the union office.

To keep harassment at a minimum, mailing lists must be kept confidential. While individuals may provide their home phone numbers for initial contacts, as soon as possible the union should provide a contact number with a phone machine. And clearance must be obtained if photos or names are published in the union newspaper.

Stewards and local officers have an important role to play in the success of the committee. They can provide a line of defense when members complain, by reminding them of anti-discrimination resolutions of the AFL-CIO or in their union's constitution. They can caution members that union solidarity doesn't always come easy: it means overcoming personal prejudices for the sake of all the workers. Members who continue to oppose gay and lesbian rights should consider that many who agree with them also oppose workers' rights.

WHAT COMMITTEES CAN DO

Here are a few examples of what gay and lesbian committees can do:

- Work on contract goals: Some activists have focused on winning benefits for domestic partners and have organized for representation in bargaining. The cities of Santa Cruz, West Hollywood, and Berkeley now provide health insurance for workers' domestic partners and children.

- Survival in a hostile work environment: In New York City, the Lesbian and Gay Teachers Association was established as a support group in 1977, and in 1989 negotiated official relations with the United Federation of Teachers (AFT). During a recent wave of bigotry in Queens, two longtime elementary school teachers came out to the press. Their press conference

was held at union headquarters; standing by them throughout their statement was Sandra Feldman, president of the UFT.

• Workplace campaigns: On some issues, union members can work with
non-union gay and lesbian employees. At New York University, gay fac-
ulty, administrators, and AFT Local 3882 clericals are working together
on a drive to gain health insurance and tuition benefits for domestic partners and children.

• Long-term standing committees can establish policies and develop major
gay and lesbian projects. At AFSCME's 1992 convention, the union's
official national advisory committee on lesbian and gay issues sponsored
an exhibit of AIDS quilt panels created by local unions to memorialize
members. The Lesbian and Gay Issues Committee of AFSCME District
Council 37 in New York has sponsored district-wide educational conferences, as well as performances by gay African American and Latino cultural groups at Black History and Hispanic Heritage celebrations.

New Initiatives

COMPARABLE WORTH

*One sign of the strength of the civil rights and women's movements of the
1950s through 1970s was winning government programs to promote race and
gender equity. These have included voting rights, affirmative action rules in
hiring and education, and requirements for equitable resources in education
and sports. But one problem that women workers always confronted was that
equal pay for equal work was not an adequate demand, even if it had been
implemented, because the jobs themselves were sex segregated and women did
not have access to equal work. In response to this problem came the proposal
for payment on the basis of "comparable worth." Never adopted by the federal
government, several state and local governments and some private employers
accepted comparable worth guidelines and tried to put them into effect with
varying degrees of seriousness.*

*Comparable worth is a limited strategy at best, because what is at issue is
not just paying people with equal training and responsibility equally, but also
increasing the opportunities for women and minorities to enter the most highly*

paid professional and managerial sectors—something that comparable worth does not address. Moreover, comparable worth and similar government programs are only as successful as the social-movement pressure behind them forces them to be.

We are grateful to Sara Evans and Barbara Nelson for this selection.

Wendy Robinson worked as an entry-level secretary at the University of Minnesota at a time some years ago when there was a severe shortage of clerical workers. Interested in other opportunities, she would wander by the employment bulletin board in the basement of Morrill Hall to look at the jobs posted there. In the section labeled "clericals" there were "scads" of jobs, each of which had a lengthy description including requirements of from three to five years of post-high-school education or experience, typing skills, shorthand, excellent command of grammar, and basic writing skills. The pay rate for such jobs, like her own, was $756 per month. One day she glanced over at the section of the bulletin board marked "technical," where there was only one job posted. "Custodian," it read, "job requirements: eighth grade education, the ability to read and write, no experience." The starting salary, however, was $200 a month more than Wendy was making. . . .

Comparable worth, or pay equity as it is often called, is the concept of providing equal pay for different jobs of equal value (i.e., jobs with similar scores along measures of skill, effort, responsibility, and working conditions). . . .

This type of analysis also takes into account race and ethnicity, looking to see if jobs held disproportionately by racial or ethnic minorities are paid less than equivalently valued jobs held primarily by whites. What is important to remember about comparable worth is that *only* equivalently evaluated jobs within a specific workplace are compared. Clerk typists' salaries are not compared to doctors' salaries, and clerk typists working for the state of Minnesota are not compared with clerk typists working elsewhere. Comparable worth is an *internal* wage policy.

Why do mostly male jobs like delivery van driver consistently get better pay than mostly female jobs like clerk typist? Among full-time workers, why do white women make 64 cents, Black women make 58 cents, Hispanic women make 54 cents, Black men make 74 cents, and Hispanic men make 71 cents compared to every dollar made by white men? There are no easy answers. The National Academy of Sciences, commissioned to address this question, reported in 1981 that although education, number of years worked, interruptions in work life, and extra hours worked per week explain part of the wage difference, they do not explain it all. The National Academy found that "in many instances jobs held mainly by women and minorities pay less at least in part *because* they are held mainly by women and minorities." In other words, the usual people to hold a job affect the rate of pay for that job. More recent work by the Census Bureau suggests that about half, or 18 cents, of the difference between the 65 cents earned by all women to a man's dollar is explained by education, length of time worked, interruptions, extra hours worked, and similar factors. The Census Bureau suggests that the other 17 cents in wage difference is caused by historically based, structural wage discrimination. . . .

The problem of low wages for women and minorities is indeed broad and systemic. Opponents of public policies addressing wage rates cite the market system as the best mechanism for adjusting wages. Proponents point out that until the early 1960s it was perfectly legal and customary to pay women and men, and whites and minorities, differently for exactly the same work, and market or no market, that is precisely what was done. When women entered the teaching profession and factory work in the nineteenth century, wages dropped. Employers argued that men had to support families, and that women's income was secondary. The primacy of women's responsibilities for home and family meant that few considered them seriously as wage earners.

Not only did women and minorities receive lower pay, however. In addition they generally found jobs in separate sectors of the economy, jobs specifically for women or minorities. This was true in the 1820s when young white women entered newly opened textile mills, in the 1880s when white women dominated teaching in public schools, in the 1920s when they flocked into the new pink-collar ghetto of clerical work, and it is still true today.

Minority women often did not have these opportunities. All minority workers faced both legal and customary controls on what jobs they would be offered. For instance, in 1920, 408,000 women and girls were employed in textile production. But less than 1 percent of this labor force was comprised of Black women and girls. These jobs were not available to Black women and girls until well after World War II, when other employees [won these demands] through the collective bargaining process. . . .

Implementing a comparable worth policy raises a number of questions. Economists opposing comparable worth predict severe economic dislocation resulting from this intrusion into the market and reallocation of government resources. Economists supporting comparable worth suggest that governments which implement comparable worth show a "taste" for more equity, and are willing to value employee wage equity more highly when making tradeoffs about what goods and services government will provide. At the state level it appears that the economic cost is quite manageable and local jurisdiction reports indicate a similar range of costs to make the required pay adjustments (between 1 and 4 percent of payroll, usually spread over several years). . . .

HEALTH HAZARDS AND EXCLUSIONARY POLICIES ——

Workers have long been aware of occupational dangers, but increasingly many of these hazards have been invisible to the workers, because they arise from new and often unlabeled chemicals and processes. Industrial health reformers in the Progressive era, such as Crystal Eastman and Alice Hamilton, pioneered the scientific work of detecting connections between workplace exposure and workers' health, and the movement of which they were a part won some reforms such as mandatory health inspections and rest periods.

In recent decades, occupational health hazards have accelerated dramatically, invading not only the traditionally dangerous workplaces but now also clerical offices, homes, armed services, and agricultural fields. Now as in the past some of these toxins particularly threaten reproduction, producing miscarriages and/or fetal deformities. As a result, some employers tried to avoid having to protect their workers simply by excluding those workers who could become pregnant—women. In this selection, political scientist Sally Jane Kenney evaluates these exclusionary policies.

. . . Many questionable assumptions underlie exclusionary policies. The first assumption is that the fetus is at risk from women's exposure, even nonpregnant women's exposure, but not at risk from men's exposure. Some employers have approached the scientific evidence differently depending on whether it revealed that maternal exposure or paternal exposure is risky—adopting a gendered posture toward risk. American Cyanamid maintained that exposing men to lead did not endanger their offspring but exposing women to lead did. They presumed that women were always endangering a fetus until conclusive evidence emerged to the contrary, but presumed that men were not similarly endangering a fetus until conclusive evidence showed otherwise. Several prominent scientists, whose research Johnson Controls relied on to support its exclusionary policy, argued strongly that the scientific evidence on lead did not justify "protecting" fetuses by preventing only women's exposure.

A double standard on the evidence of risk is even more problematic when one considers the lopsided nature of scientific evidence on reproductive hazards. Scientists have focused largely on the risk to offspring from women's exposure, despite the National Institute for Occupational Safety and Health's acknowledgement that, in situations of scientific uncertainty, the only safe assumption is that men are also at risk. Johnson Controls argued that without hard evidence about the effect of lead on the fetus at different levels of maternal exposure, one could extrapolate from evidence about children's exposure to lead. Yet the company vociferously denounced attempts to speculate about the risk of lead exposure to men, denying such a risk existed. The company assumed a different posture toward scientific evidence according to whether the evidence supported or undermined its policy of excluding women.

The second assumption is that no risk to the fetus is acceptable, however minimal. After firing a pregnant X-ray technician, Shelby Memorial Hospital's administrator said that a pregnant woman's sunbathing in a bikini posed an unacceptable risk to the fetus. Yet the hospital let male X-ray technicians assume a low-level risk that their exposure to radiation would affect their fertility or cause mutations in their genes. When *UAW v. Johnson Controls* reached the court of appeals, the dissenting judges questioned the "zero-risk" strategy for pregnant or even nonsterilized women. Judge Easterbrook preferred to think of the risks to the fetus in the context of women's lives, questioning whether the fetus was more at risk from low-level exposure to lead or from having an unemployed mother who may lose not only her ability to secure such health benefits as prenatal care, but even the ability to maintain proper nutrition. Judge Easterbrook recognized that no life choices for pregnant women, or anyone else, are without effect. Pregnant women drive cars, drink coffee and alcohol, smoke, and eat sugar. Those who live in Los Angeles breathe; those who live in New York take the subway. The differences between the magnitude of risk to which Johnson Controls would refuse to subject fetuses and that women assume outside of the workplace become more stark when one considers that many of the women working in the plant would not become pregnant. Judge Easterbrook demanded that Johnson Controls quantify the net risk, concluding that "surely Title VII does not allow an employer to adopt a policy that makes both women and their children worse off."

The third assumption underlying exclusionary policies is that reproductive hazards affecting women are different and more serious than other occupational hazards. . . . The danger is that by focusing on the risks of reproductive hazards—hazards that attract a lot of media attention, such as the alleged higher incidence of miscarriage among workers using video display terminals—other occupational health issues will be eclipsed. . . .

Many workers are exposed to carcinogens and assume an increased risk of developing cancer. . . . Is an increased risk of miscarriage, particularly for a woman who is not and does not want to be pregnant, more serious than an increased risk of developing cancer? . . . We must embed any policy on reproductive hazards in a sound health and safety policy. Removing women workers is a simpler and less expensive alternative to lowering exposures to all hazardous substances, but it should not be employers' chief way of minimizing reproductive hazards or, more likely, insulating themselves from an exaggerated risk of tort liability.

The fourth assumption underlying exclusionary policies is that women are always pregnant. By adopting exclusionary policies, employers treat women as if they are incapable of making choices about or controlling their reproductive capacities. Most women, however, plan their pregnancies. Very few are pregnant for their entire working lives. . . .

The fifth assumption . . . is that women's childbearing role takes priority over their role as a breadwinner. A corollary assumption is that it is only appropriate for women to hold certain kinds of jobs (usually low-paid, dead-end jobs). . . . Companies' concern about reproductive hazards only in male-dominated, well-paid jobs, when they lack concern for reproductive hazards in job categories dominated by women, raises questions about the partiality of the "protection" of women workers. In the past, these same inconsistencies led many to question protective legislation that, for example, banned women from tending bar but not from serving as cocktail waitresses.

Sixth, some employers have assumed that excluding women should be the first option considered rather than the last. The policies in this study reveal that employers have been too hasty in excluding women rather than exploring such alternatives as lowering exposure, substituting another product, using protective clothing, removing workers registering high levels of the substance in their bodies, or more carefully determining who is likely to conceive. Although practicing good industrial hygiene can often minimize exposure, employers assume that women, or pregnant women, cannot be relied upon to act in their own interests and in the interests of their offspring. . . .

. . . When ICI ordered Freight Hire to ban women from merely driving trucks filled with hazardous substances, when Shelby Memorial fired a pregnant X-ray technician without reference to the medical literature or the level of exposure, when Johnson Controls refused to transfer a man wanting to start a family, when American Cyanamid required women to be sterilized on the basis of "an educated guess," we begin to have serious questions about exclusionary policies. *Cyanamid* brought all exclusionary policies into question. Women were sterilized but lost their jobs anyway. Cyanamid's policy, like Olin's and Shelby Memorial Hospital's, arose in a male-dominated workplace. In all three examples, the hazard posed potential reproductive risks to men as well as women. Freight Hire did not consider the possibility of doing something to lessen exposure or even to determine the level of exposure. Although the company considered the risk to be to fetuses, not adult men and women, and Jacky Page was not and did not plan to be pregnant, she could not drive a truck because the company treated her as if she were pregnant. The company ignored the potential health risks, reproductive and nonreproductive, to men. . . .

A WORKING WOMEN'S CENTER —————————————

*In this interview, Chicana garment worker and union activist Cecilia Rodri-
guez explains why her group in El Paso, Texas, established a women's center
rather than a union. In doing so, they were continuing a long tradition of
alternative forms of organizing among women workers, a pattern we have
seen in several earlier selections.*

I became involved in this work because of my own background as a second
generation Mexican in El Paso. Most of my family were involved in the
garment industry, and as a student I had supported the two-year Fada strike
in the mid-1960s, and had seen how the women workers centrally involved
in it had ended up totally burnt out and cynical, while the men took the
credit. In 1981 some of us started a Workers Centre, and our first struggle
was over the role of women within it. We argued that the centre should have
a special focus on women as they formed 85 per cent of the workforce; but
the men accused us of taking up the ideology of white 'women's liberation'
and felt this was inappropriate for Mexican women (Chicanas).

The process of identifying goals took about three years. We eventually set
up as a workers' information centre. Being a non-profit-making structure
allowed us to receive funding from the church and the state but prohibited
us from labour organising or lobbying. These rules did not limit our aims as
the workers themselves had become very anti-union, both because of their
negative experience of the Fada strike and because of their experience of
yellow unions in Mexico, who worked in collusion with the employers and
often used violence to achieve their ends. Also in 1983, many of the largest
garment factories were closing down and the women were increasingly having to work in sweatshops. Lastly, the US labour laws are so difficult for
workers to use that it is easier to operate outside them. For all these reasons,
we were clear that we did not want to establish a union. The long-term aim
we identified in 1981–2 was to build up committees of five or six women in
each factory to address the problems of that particular factory.

We knew that if we were to win the trust of the workers and achieve these
goals, we had to develop a strong leadership who were themselves textile
workers. However, there was a lot of strife between staff over this issue:
between middle-class Chicanas and factory workers. The middle-class
women often felt that garment workers did not have skills, education or
understanding to organise. This struggle was important in establishing the
principle that the workers in the Centre could not see themselves as superior
or different from the textile workers; the middle-class workers had to learn to
live, eat and breathe conditions in the garment factories, to appreciate the
workers' point of view. If you have a commitment to develop leadership,

then you must understand that women have to go through stages of development; it is your responsibility to provide the information they need in order to make more strategic decisions. It was this understanding that finally determined the success of the group.

We undertook two activities in the factories that helped establish our image as a new group. In 1984 we undertook a 'factory gate' questionnaire survey about workers' needs: we asked about income, benefits, transport, etc., but nothing about employment conditions or unions. Then in 1985 we organised a health screening programme for 800 women in twelve factories. The contacts we made through these activities were followed up by home visits and a monthly newsletter. Our message was that we were 'women helping women' to develop alternatives, for ourselves and our daughters. It was not until 1985 that women finally began to bring their work problems to the Centre, and then we could in all honesty say, 'we have to organise, you cannot negotiate on your own'. We waited until the women themselves raised the questions.

We developed a leadership training programme over a number of years of trial and error. This includes the study of capitalism and political economy—concepts of wages, profit, use value, exchange value—concepts that workers need to understand in order to negotiate with employers. We also study labour history. Employers in El Paso try to make workers think that they are outsiders, privileged to be 'allowed' in. Studying labour history shows these workers that immigrant workers have always been at the forefront of the labour movement in the US. We provide as many opportunities as possible for women to learn about women's struggles in other parts of the world; through films, exchanges and visits. Paulo Freire's methods are used a lot: getting workers to draw and talk about their experiences in the factory.

However, much of the learning comes from the time spent in developing the organisation itself. We have five women on the Board of Directors of the Centre, and it is this group who are involved in the training programme, and in the policy making for six hours a week. They are learning all the time through the process of decision making: setting up factory committees, recruiting new members, and developing activities and services for members. They have full responsibility for the membership fund, part of which is used for a revolving emergency loan fund. They have developed a food-buying club for cheaper food, an advocacy service, English classes and immigration advice. They are also involved in the development of factory committees and work with women in the factories to document conditions.

This group of women share the information learnt in the training programme with the members who come into the Centre by setting up an exhibition or wall newspaper each week. The role of the women both domestically and in the workplace is a frequent theme in these; and they are around to explain it, so that every woman who comes into the Centre for food or services, also gets a political message. So all the local organisation is now done by local organisers; they are very strong women and it will be difficult to defeat them.

WOMEN PUT SEXUAL HARASSMENT ON THE AGENDA

When the first edition of this book was published in 1976, the behaviors we today label sexual harassment were considered standard male behavior, and women who did not want to go along were considered "uptight" and humorless. The women's movement has not only problematized this ancient practice of keeping women down, but has succeeded in criminalizing it.

Sexual harassment is a fact of life in the American workplace; 21 percent of women polled by *Newsweek* said they had been harassed at work and 42 percent said they knew someone who had been harassed. Other surveys indicate that more than half of working women have faced the problem at some point in their careers. The situation tends to be worst in male-dominated workplaces; in a 1990 Defense Department study, 64 percent of military women said they had endured such abuse. Although the severity may vary—from a pattern of obscene joking to outright assault—the emotional damage is often profound and long-lasting. Men "don't understand that caged feeling," says University of Texas sociologist Susan Marshall. "But women know what sexual harassment is. It's when your neck hairs stand up, when you feel like you're being stalked."

Defining sexual harassment is one of the law's newest frontiers. While some of the boundaries have been set by recent decisions, there is still considerable debate over just what constitutes actionable behavior. Most people understand that when a supervisor demands that a woman sleep with him in order to keep her job, he's stepped over the legal line. But what about aggressive flirting? Or off-color conversation? Often, it's a matter of perception. Some women may find such activities offensive; others may just shrug. And men and women may see things very differently. University of Arizona professor Barbara Gutek surveyed 1,200 men and women for a study on harassment. She asked her subjects whether they considered a sexual proposition flattering. About 67 percent of the men said they would, while only 17 percent of the women agreed. In contrast, 63 percent of women would be insulted by a proposition, compared with 15 percent of men.

Even when their cases seem clear-cut, women say they feel ashamed—as though they were to blame for what happened to them. . . .

Until just a few years ago, women had no recourse when confronted with unwanted advances or offensive comments by a boss or co-worker. In offices where they were the minority, women thought they had to go along to get along. Palma Formica, a family practitioner in New Jersey, recalls that when she was a medical student more than 30 years ago, it was "standard procedure" for professors to make "male-female jokes, usually genital oriented, with the woman bearing the brunt." Women never objected. "What are you going to do, get up and walk out of class? You want to be a doctor? You want to be in a man's field? Then you swallow hard and pretend you don't hear."

But in the past decade, as women have grown to represent nearly half the work force, the courts have begun to strike down what was once "standard procedure." In 1980, the Equal Employment Opportunity Commission (the federal agency that investigates bias in the workplace) said that making sexual activity a condition of employment or promotion was a violation of the 1964 Civil Rights Act. Also forbidden: the creation of "an intimidating, hostile or offensive working environment."

The EEOC rules had little effect on most women's lives until 1986, when the Supreme Court agreed that sexual harassment did indeed violate civil rights. In the landmark case of *Meritor Savings Bank v. Vinson*, Washington, D.C., bank employee Mechelle Vinson claimed that her supervisor fondled her in front of other employees, followed her into the ladies' room, exposed himself and, on several occasions, raped her. The supervisor and the bank denied her claims, but the court sided with Vinson.

Two other major federal court decisions in January of this year refined the legal definition. In a Florida case involving a female shipyard worker, the court ruled that nude pinups in the workplace constitute illegal harassment. A week later a three-judge panel in San Francisco stated that in cases where men and women might see a pattern of behavior differently, the deciding factor should be whether a "reasonable woman" might feel threatened. In that case, a female IRS worker turned down a request for a date by a co-worker. He responded by writing unwelcome love letters to her. "Men, who are rarely victims of sexual assault, may view sexual conduct in a vacuum without a full appreciation of the underlying threat of violence that a woman may perceive," wrote Judge Robert R. Beezer. . . .

Even if they work for a company with a well-established harassment policy, many women still keep their mouths shut. They don't want to be seen as troublemakers—and they worry about the long-term consequences of complaining. . . .

Women who take their accusations to court face even more formidable obstacles than public disapproval. The legal process is long and cumbersome—it can be years from first complaint to final verdict—and in the interim, the woman is in a legal, professional and often financial limbo. "A woman will complain and then becomes a pariah," says Judith Vladeck, a

New York lawyer who has argued anti-bias cases for 20 years. "If the male is in any way sanctioned, his male cohorts come to his defense, and the woman becomes the wrong-doer, and she's frozen out." . . .

Whatever happens on the street or in the courts, the publicity surrounding Anita Hill's allegations has brought the issue into the open. . . . It shows that charges of sexual harassment can be taken seriously—even in an almost all-male institution like the Senate. In fact, Congress could be the first test of how well the public has been educated by the week's proceedings. Congressional employees are not covered by the Civil Rights Act, and therefore have no protection against harassment. To correct this oversight, the Women's Political Caucus sent a written policy in April to all 535 members of Congress. Those who agreed to run harassment-free offices joined the caucus's "Honor Roll." At the start . . . there were 200 members. By the end of the week, 12 more had signed up. After listening to Anita Hill, a lot of women voters would like to see Congress put its own House—and Senate—in order.

A NEW HERO FOR WORKING WOMEN

Professor Anita Hill had no intention of becoming a hero for working women. Nevertheless, her integrity and courage led her to speak out against sexual harassment at great risk to her career, personal reputation, and even safety. She had to face down the U.S. Senate and speak against another African American with the media broadcasting her statement throughout the world. Through this action, she joined a tradition of those who have stood up for working women, along with Joanna Draper, Leonora Barry, Rose Schneiderman, Elizabeth Gurley Flynn, Suzanne La Flesche Picotte, Fannie Barrier Williams, Stella Nowicki, and Johnnie Tillmon, to mention just a few of those represented in this book. Anita Hill became a symbol of women's aspirations for respect and equality in the workplace.

STATEMENT OF PROFESSOR ANITA F. HILL TO THE SENATE JUDICIARY COMMITTEE, OCTOBER 11, 1991

Mr. Chairman, Senator Thurmond, members of the committee:

My name is Anita F. Hill, and I am a professor of law at the University of Oklahoma. I was born on a farm in Okmulgee County, Oklahoma, in 1956. I am the youngest of thirteen children.

I had my early education in Okmulgee County. My mother's name is Irma Hill. She is also a farmer and a housewife.

My childhood was one of a lot of hard work and not much money, but it was one of solid family affection as represented by my parents. I was reared in a religious atmosphere in the Baptist faith, and I have been a member of the Antioch Baptist church in Tulsa, Oklahoma, since 1983. It is a very warm part of my life at the present time.

For my undergraduate work, I went to Oklahoma State University and graduated from there in 1977. I am attaching to this statement a copy of my resume for further details of my education.

Senator Joseph R. Biden, Jr.: It will be included in the record.

Professor Hill: Thank you.

I graduated from the university with academic honors, and proceeded to the Yale Law School, where I received my J.D. degree in 1980.

Upon graduation from law school, I became a practicing lawyer with the Washington, D.C., firm of Wald, Hardraker & Ross. In 1981 I was introduced to now Judge Thomas by a mutual friend.

Judge Thomas told me that he was anticipating a political appointment, and he asked if I would be interested in working with him.

He was in fact appointed as assistant secretary of education for civil rights. After he was—after he had taken that post, he asked if I would become his assistant, and I accepted that position.

In my early period there, I had two major projects. The first was an article I wrote for Judge Thomas's signature on the education of minority students. The second was the organization of a seminar on high-risk students, which was abandoned because Judge Thomas transferred to the E.E.O.C., where he became the chairman of that office.

During this period at the Department of Education my working relationship with Judge Thomas was positive. I had a good deal of responsibility and independence. I thought he respected my work, and that he trusted my judgment.

After approximately three months of working there, he asked me to go out socially with him. What happened next, and telling the world about it, are the two most difficult things—experiences of my life.

It is only after a great deal of agonizing consideration, and . . . great number of sleepless nights, that I am able to talk of these unpleasant matters to anyone but my close friends.

I declined the invitation to go out socially with him, and explained to him that I thought it would jeopardize at—what at the time I considered to be a very good working relationship. I had a normal social life with other men outside the office. I believe then, as now, that having a social relationship with a person who was supervising my work would be ill advised. I was very uncomfortable with the idea and told him so.

I thought that by saying no and explaining my reasons, my employer would abandon his social suggestions. However, to my regret, in the following few weeks, he continued to ask me out on several occasions.

He pressed me to justify my reasons for saying no to him. These incidents took place in his office, or mine. They were in the form of private conversations, which not—would not have been overheard by anyone else.

My working relationship became even more strained when Judge Thomas began to use work situations to discuss sex. On these occasions he would call me into his office for a course on education issues and projects, or he might suggest that because of the time pressures of his schedule we go to lunch to a government cafeteria.

After a brief discussion of work, he would turn the conversation to a discussion of sexual matters. His conversations were very vivid. He spoke about acts that he had seen in pornographic films involving such matters as women having sex with animals, and films showing group sex or rape scenes.

He talked about pornographic materials depicting individuals with large penises or large breasts involving various sex acts.

On several occasions, Thomas told me graphically of his own sexual prowess.

Because I was extremely uncomfortable talking about sex with him at all, and particularly in such a graphic way, I told him that I did not want to talk about this subject. I would also try to change the subject to education matters or to nonsexual personal matters, such as his background or his beliefs.

My efforts to change the subject were rarely successful.

Throughout the period of these conversations, he also from time to time asked me for social engagements. My reaction to these conversations was to avoid them by eliminating opportunities for us to engage in extended conversations.

This was difficult because, at the time, I was his only assistant at the office of education—or office for civil rights. During the latter part of my time at the Department of Education, the social pressures, and any conversation of his offensive behavior, ended. I began both to believe and hope that our working relationship could be a proper, cordial, and professional one.

When Judge Thomas was made chair of the EEOC, I needed to face the question of whether to go with him. I was asked to do so, and I did.

The work itself was interesting, and at that time it appeared that the sexual overtures which had so troubled me had ended.

I also faced the realistic fact that I had no alternative job. While I might have gone back to private practice, perhaps in my old firm or at another, I was dedicated to civil rights work and my first choice was to be in that field. Moreover, at that time, the Department of Education itself was a dubious venture. President Reagan was seeking to abolish the entire department.

For my first months at the EEOC where I continued to be an assistant to

Judge Thomas, there were no sexual conversations or overtures. However, during the fall and winter of 1982 these began again. The comments were random and ranged from pressing me about why I didn't go out with him to remarks about my personal appearance. I remember his saying that some day I would have to tell him the real reason that I wouldn't go out with him.

He began to show displeasure in his tone and voice and his demeanor and his continued pressure for an explanation. He commented on what I was wearing in terms of whether it made me more or less sexually attractive. The incidents occurred in his inner office at the EEOC.

One of the oddest episodes I remember was an occasion in which Thomas was drinking a Coke in his office. He got up from the table at which we were working, went over to his desk to get the Coke, looked at the can and asked, "Who has put pubic hair on my Coke?"

On other occasions, he referred to the size of his own penis as being larger than normal and he also spoke on some occasions of the pleasures he had given to women with oral sex. At this point, late 1982, I began to be concerned that Clarence Thomas might take out his anger with me by degrading me or not giving me important assignments. I also thought that he might find an excuse for dismissing me.

In January of 1983, I began looking for another job. I was handicapped because I feared that if he found out, he might make it difficult for me to find other employment and I might be dismissed from the job I had. Another factor that made my search more difficult was that there was a period—this was during a period—of a hiring freeze in the government. . . .

In the spring of 1983, an opportunity to teach at Oral Roberts University opened up. I participated in a seminar, taught an afternoon session in a seminar at Oral Roberts University. The dean of the university saw me teaching and inquired as to whether I would be interested in further pursuing a career in teaching beginning at Oral Roberts University.

I agreed to take the job, in large part because of my desire to escape the pressures I felt at the EEOC due to Judge Thomas.

When I informed him that I was leaving in July, I recall that his response was that now I would no longer have an excuse for not going out with him. I told him that I still preferred not to do so. At some time after that meeting, he asked if he could take me to dinner at the end of the term. When I declined, he assured me that the dinner was a professional courtesy only and not a social invitation. I reluctantly agreed to accept that invitation but only if it was at the very end of a working day.

On, as I recall, the last day of my employment at the EEOC in the summer of 1983, I did have dinner with Clarence Thomas. We went directly from work to a restaurant near the office. We talked about the work I had done, both at Education and at the EEOC. He told me that he was pleased with all of it except for an article and speech that I had done for him while we were at the Office for Civil Rights. Finally he made a comment that I will vividly remember. He said that if I ever told anyone of his behavior that it would ruin his career. This was not an apology; nor was it an explanation. That was his last remark about the possibility of our going out or reference to his behavior.

In July of 1983 I left the Washington, D.C., area and I've had minimal contacts with Judge Clarence Thomas since. I am of course aware from the press that some questions have been raised about conversations I had with Judge Clarence Thomas after I left the EEOC. From 1983 until today, I have seen Judge Thomas only twice. On one occasion, I needed to get a reference from him and on another he made a public appearance in Tulsa. On one occasion he called me at home and we had an inconsequential conversation. On one occasion he called me without reaching me and I returned the call without reaching him and nothing came of it. . . .

It is only after a great deal of agonizing consideration that I am able to talk of these unpleasant matters to anyone except my closest friends. As I've said before, these last few days have been very trying and very hard for me and it hasn't just been the last few days this week.

It has actually been over a month now that I have been under the strain of this issue.

Telling the world is the most difficult experience of my life, but it is very close to having to live through the experience that occasioned this meeting.

I may have used poor judgment early on in my relationship with this issue. I was aware, however, that telling at any point in my career could adversely affect my future career, and I did not want, early on, to burn all the bridges to the EEOC.

As I said, I may have used poor judgment. Perhaps I should have taken angry or even militant steps, both when I was in the agency or after I left it. But I must confess to the world that the course that I took seemed the better as well as the easier approach.

I declined any comment to newspapers, but later, when Senate staff asked me about these matters, I felt I had a duty to report.

I have no personal vendetta against Clarence Thomas. I seek only to provide the committee with information which it may regard as relevant.

It would have been more comfortable to remain silent. I took no initiative to inform anyone. But when I was asked by a representative of this committee to report my experience, I felt that I had to tell the truth. I could not keep silent.

Credits and Sources

Before 1820

PAID AND UNPAID LABOR

Bartlett, Katharine. "Pueblo Grinding Tools." In *With These Hands: Women Working the Land*, ed. Joan M. Jensen. New York: Feminist Press, 1981. Copyright © 1981 by Joan Jensen. Reprinted by permission. Originally published in Katharine Bartlett, *Pueblo Milling Stones of the Flagstaff Region and Their Relation to Others in the Southwest*. Flagstaff, AZ: Museum of Northern Arizona.

A Narrative of the Life of Mrs. Mary Jemison, ed. James E. Seaver. Canandaigua, New York, 1824.

Ulrich, Laurel Thatcher. *A Midwife's Tale: The Life of Martha Ballard, Based on Her Diary, 1785–1812*. New York: Knopf, 1990. Copyright © 1990 by Laurel Ulrich. Reprinted by permission of Alfred A. Knopf, Inc.

Mackenzie's Five Thousand Receipts in All the Useful and Domestic Arts, by an American Physician. Pittsburgh: C. H. Kay & Co., 1829.

Earle, Alice Morse. *Colonial Dames and Good Wives*. Boston: Houghton Mifflin, 1896.

———. *Home Life in Colonial Days*. New York: Grosset and Dunlap, 1898.

Abbott, Edith. *Women in Industry*. New York: D. Appleton and Co., 1913.

McKee, Samuel. *Labor in Colonial New York, 1664–1776*. New York: Columbia University Press, 1935. Earle, Alice Morse. *Home Life in Colonial Days*. New York: Grosset and Dunlap, 1898.

The Reports of Alexander Hamilton, ed. Jacob E. Cooke. New York: Harper and Row, 1964.

SERVITUDE

"The Trappan'd Maiden: Or, The Distressed Damsel," traditional.

Advertisements, Williamsburg, Virginia *Gazette*, 1767. Rep. in *A Documentary History of American Industrial Society*, ed. John R. Commons, et al. Cleveland: Arthur H. Clark Co., 1910.

Salmon, Lucy. *Domestic Service*. New York: Macmillan, 1897.

Morris, Richard B. *Government and Labor in Early America*. New York: Columbia University Press, 1946; rep. New York: Octagon Books, 1965. Copyright © 1946 by Richard Morris. Reprinted by permission of Octagon Books.

Petition of Anttonia Lusgardia Ernandes, August 9, 1735. Bexar Archives, Barker History Center, University of Texas, Austin, Texas.

CREDIT AND SOURCES

Carr, Lois Green, and Lorena S. Walsh. "Economic Diversification and Labor Organization in the Chesapeake, 1650–1820." In *Work and Labor in Early America*, ed. Stephen Innes. Chapel Hill: University of North Carolina Press, 1988. Published for the Institute of Early American History and Culture, Williamsburg, Virginia. Copyright 1988 by The University of North Carolina Press. Used by permission of the University of North Carolina Press.

1820–1865

SLAVES AND FREE BLACKS

Advertisements, Charleston, South Carolina *City Gazette*, February 21, 1825.

Botkin, B. A., ed. *Lay My Burden Down*. Chicago: University of Chicago Press, 1945. We have made diligent efforts to contact the copyright holder to obtain permission to reprint this selection. If you have information that would help us, please write W. W. Norton & Company, 500 Fifth Avenue, New York, NY 10110.

Yetman, Norman R. *Life under the "Peculiar Institution."* New York: Holt, Rinehart and Winston, 1970.

The American Slave: A Composite Biography, vol. 11, ed. George P. Rawick. Westport, Conn.: Greenwood Press, 1972.

Kemble, Frances Anne. *Journal of a Residence on a Georgia Plantation in 1836–1839*. New York: Harper and Bros., 1863.

Louis Manigault Papers, 1776–1883. Special Collections Library, Duke University, Durham, North Carolina.

Phebe Jackson Account Book, 1849. Microfilm Collection No. 2120, Ante Bellum South Plantations, Series F, Reel 5, Petersburg, Virginia.

THE CONTESTED LAND

Kesselman, Amy. "Diaries and Reminiscences of Women on the Oregon Trail: A Study in Consciousness." Unpublished essay.

"Random Recollections of Harriet Taylor Upton." Typescript in Schlesinger Library, Radcliffe College, Cambridge, Massachusetts.

"The Memoirs of Mariano Vallejo." Qtd. in David J. Weber, *Foreigners in Their Native Land: Historical Roots of Mexican-Americans*. Albuquerque: University of New Mexico Press, 1973.

"The Journal of William Brewer" (ca. 1860s, California). Qtd. in Gloria E. Miranda, "Hispano-Mexican Childrearing Practices in Pre-American Santa Barbara." *Southern California Historical Quarterly* 65 (Winter 1983).

Godfrey, Kenneth W., Audrey M. Godfrey, and Jill Mulvay Derr. *Women's Voices: An Untold Story of the Latter-day Saints, 1830–1900*. Salt Lake City: Deseret Book Company, 1982.

Guerin, E. J. *Mountain Charley, or the Adventures of Mrs. E. J. Guerin Who Was 13 Years in Male Attire*. Norman: University of Oklahoma Press, 1986.

FACTORY LIFE

Abbott, Edith. *Women in Industry*. New York: D. Appleton and Co., 1913.

Ware, Norman. *The Industrial Worker, 1840–1860*. New York: Quadrangle, 1964.

Commons, John R., et al. *Documentary History of American Industrial Society*. Cleveland: A. H. Clark Co., 1911.

Sumner, Helen. *History of Women in Industry in the United States*, vol. IX of *Report on the Condition of Woman and Child Wage-Earners in the United States*. U.S. Congress, 61st Congress, 2nd. Session, Senate Document 645. Washington, D.C.: Government Printing Office, 1910.

Andrews, John B., and W. D. P. Bliss. *History of Women in Trade Unions*, vol. X of *Report on the Condition of Woman and Child Wage-Earners in the United States*. U.S. Congress, 61st Congress, 2nd. Session, Senate Document 645. Washington, D.C.: U.S. Government Printing Office, 1911.

Ernst, Robert. *Immigrant Life in New York City*. New York: Columbia University Press, 1949.

Petition to Edwin M. Stanton, July 1864. In *The Collected Works of Abraham Lincoln*, vol. 2, 1848–1865, eds. Roy P. Basler and Christian O. Basler. New Brunswick, N.J.: Rutgers University Press, 1990.

CONTROVERSY ABOUT WOMEN'S WORK

American Medical Times, July 18, 1861. Qtd. in Anne L. Austin, *History of Nursing Source Book*. New York: Putnam, 1957.

Letter to the Editor, *Philadelphia Daily News*, 1854.

Caroline Dall. *Women's Right to Labor*. Boston: Walker, Wise and Co., 1860.

1865–1890

INDUSTRY

Papers of Dwight Manufacturing Company, Chicopee, Massachusetts, Labor file, Baker Library, Harvard University, Cambridge, Massachusetts.

Abbott, Edith. "Employment of Women in Industries: Cigarmaking—Its History and Present Tendencies." *Journal of Political Economy* 15 (January 1907): 1–25.

Levine, Louis. *The Women Garment Workers*. New York: B. W. Huebsch, Inc., 1924.

Letters to the Editor, *Lynn Record*, 1879. In *We Will Rise in Our Might: Workingwomen's Voices from Nineteenth-Century New England*, ed. Mary H. Blewett. Ithaca: Cornell University Press, 1991.

Papers of Dwight Manufacturing Company, Chicopee, Massachusetts, Miscellaneous file, Baker Library, Harvard University, Cambridge, Massachusetts.

"Report of the General Investigator." *Proceedings of the General Assembly of the Knights of Labor*, 1887 and 1888. "Report of the General Investigator and Director of Women's Work." *Proceedings of the General Assembly of the Knights of Labor*, 1889.

Terence V. Powderly to R. Glocking, Esq., Toronto, Ontario, Letterbook 48, April 10, 1890. Papers of Terence K. Powderly, Catholic University, Washington, D.C.

"The Girls' Co-operative Collar Co." *Revolution* 5.17 (April 28, 1870): 267.

COPING WITH NEW CONDITIONS

Fletcher, Alice B. "The Indian Woman and Her Problems." *Southern Workman* 28 (May 1899): 172–76, and "Among the Omahas," *The Woman's Journal* 13 (February 11, 1882): 46–47.

G. G. Batchelder to Major General R. Saxton, October 10, 1865. Reel 20, M869: Records of the Assistant Commissioner for the State of South Carolina, Bureau of Refugees, Freedmen, and Abandoned Lands, 1865–1870, National Archives Microfilm Publication.

Green, Mrs. Amy. *16 Days on the Great American Desert, or Triumphs of a Frontier Life.* Titusville, Penn.: Frank Truedell Printer, 1887.

Likins, Mrs. J. W. "It was a great trial for me to know just how to approach them." In *So Much to Be Done: Women Settlers on the Mining and Ranching Frontier,* ed. Ruth B. Moynihan, Susan Armitage, and Christiane Fischer Dichamp. Lincoln: University of Nebraska Press, 1990.

Sanger, William. *A History of Prostitution.* New York: The Medical Publishing Company, 1858.

The Social, Moral and Political Effect of Chinese Immigration. Testimony taken before a Committee of the Senate of the State of California, April 1876. Sacramento: State Printing Office, 1876.

Letters to the Editor, *Chicago Daily Tribune,* 1873.

"The Working Women: White Slavery in New England. Twenty Cents a Day. The Right Kind of Talk by the Right Kind of Folks, etc." *Workingman's Advocate* 5.41 (May 8, 1869): 3.

1890–1920

MIGRANTS AND IMMIGRANTS

Scott, Emmett J., collector. "Letters from Negro Migrants, 1916–1918." *Journal of Negro History* 4.3 (July 1919): 296–319.

Breckinridge, Sophonisba. *New Homes for Old.* New York: Harper Bros., 1921.

RURAL LABOR

Wilson, Gilbert Livingstone. *Agriculture of the Hidatsa Indians: An Indian Interpretation.* 1917; rep. New York: AMS Press, 1979.

Interview with Rosalia Salazar Whelan. In *Songs My Mother Sang to Me: An Oral History of Mexican American Women,* ed. Patricia Preciado Martin. Tucson: University of Arizona Press, 1992. Copyright © 1992 Patricia Preciado Martin. Reprinted by permission of University of Arizona Press.

Picotte, Suzanne La Flesche. Journal, 1910–1911. Nebraska State Historical Society, Lincoln, Nebraska.

Social and Labor Needs of Farm Women. Washington, D.C.: U.S. Department of Agriculture Report No. 103, 1914.

Abel, Emily K. *Who Cares for the Elderly? Public Policy and the Experiences of Adult Daughters.* Philadelphia: Temple University Press, 1991. Copyright © 1991 by Temple University Press. Reprinted by permission of Temple University Press.

INDUSTRIAL LABOR

Byington, Margaret F. *Homestead, the Households of a Mill Town.* New York: Charities, 1910; rep. New York: Arno and the New York Times, 1969.

"Women on the Night Shift." *Life and Labor* 6 (December 1914).

Van Kleeck, Mary. *Artificial Flower Makers.* New York: Survey Associates, 1913.

"Case No. 45, Sadie G." *Preliminary Report of the New York State Factory Investigating Commission.* Albany, N.Y., 1912.

THE TRADITION OF STRUGGLE

McCormick, Fannie. "A Kansas Farm." *Farmer's Wife* 1.3 (September 1891). Garside, Frances L. "A Frontier Farmer's Wife." *Farmer's Wife* 11.6 (January 1893).

O'Donnell, Edward. "Women as Bread Winners—the Error of the Age." *American Federationist* 4.8 (October 1897).

Henry, Alice. "The Woman Organizer." *The Trade Union Woman.* New York: D. Appleton and Co., 1915.

Williams, Fannie Barrier. "The Problem of Employment for Negro Women." An address delivered at the Hampton Conference in July 1903. Rep. in *Southern Workman* 32.9 (September 1903): 432–37.

"Brooklyn Mob Loots Butcher Shops." *New York Times*, May 23, 1902. "Butchers Appeal to Police for Protection." *New York Times*, May 26, 1902.

Marot, Helen. "A Woman's Strike—An Appreciation of the Shirtwaist Makers of New York." *Proceedings of the Academy of Political Science of the City of New York* 1.4 (October 1910).

Schneiderman, Rose. "Triangle Memorial Speech." In *All for One*, Rose Schneiderman and Lucy Goldthwaite. New York: Paul S. Erikson, Inc., 1967. Reprinted by permission of Paul S. Erikson, Inc.

Flynn, Elizabeth Gurley. "The Lawrence Textile Strike." Flynn Papers, Tamiment Library, New York University, New York, New York.

Abbott, Mabel. "The Waitresses of Seattle." *Life and Labor* vol 4.2 (February 1914).

Conger-Kaneko, Josephine. "Does a Woman Support Her Husband's Employer?" *Progressive Woman* 7.74 (August 1913).

Sanger, Margaret. *Motherhood in Bondage.* New York: Brentano's, 1928.

Senators vs. Working Women, pamphlet, Wage Earners' Suffrage League of New York. Manuscripts of Leonora O'Reilly, Schlesinger Library, Radcliffe College, Cambridge, Massachusetts.

1920–1940

NONINDUSTRIAL WORK

Lynd, Robert and Helen. *Middletown.* New York: Harcourt Brace, 1929, 1956. Copyright © 1929, 1956. Reprinted by permission of Harcourt Brace.

Interview with Naomi Williams, from Leah Wise and Sue Thrasher, "The Southern Tenant Farmers' Union." Reprinted by permission of *Southern Exposure*, published quarterly by the Institute for Southern Studies, P.O. Box 531, Durham, N.C. 27702.

Interview with Mrs. Taniguchi, conducted and translated by Evelyn Nakano Glenn, 1975. Reprinted by permission of the interviewer.

Case of Alma N. Z., c. 1926. Paul Cressey Notes, Ernest Burgess Papers 129:6, University of Chicago Manuscript Collections, Chicago, Illinois.

Bratton, Augusta C. "Men and Bank Work." *Coast Banker* 20.5 (May 1918): 440–41.

Davies, Margery. "Woman's Place Is at the Typewriter: The Feminization of the Clerical Labor Force." *Radical America* 3.4 (July–August 1974). Reprinted by permission of *Radical America*.

CREDIT AND SOURCES

THE DEPRESSION

Bakke, C. Wight. *Citizens Without Work*. New Haven, Conn.: Yale University Press, 1940. Copyright © 1940 by C. Wight Bakke. Reprinted by permission of Yale University Press.

Wong, Jade Snow. *Fifth Chinese Daughter*. New York: Harper and Row, 1950; Seattle: University of Washington Press. Reprinted by permission of University of Washington Press.

WOMEN WORKERS ORGANIZE

Rozner, Sarah. "What Is It That We Want Brother Levin?" Rozner Papers, collected by Sherna Berger Gluck, Feminist History Research Project.

"Women Laundry Workers Organizing to Demand a Living Wage." *Negro World* 24 (April 1926).

Lynd, Alice and Staughton, eds. *Rank and File: Personal Histories by Working Class Organizers*. Boston: Beacon Press, 1973. Reprinted by permission of the authors.

BLACK WOMEN AGAINST RACISM

Unsigned to Eleanor Roosevelt, January 5, 1937. Gene Nicholson, Domestic Employees Union, to Mrs. Roosevelt, November 24, 1933. Domestic Employees Union, "Union Wage Scale for General Maids," U.S. Women's Bureau, National Archives. Washington, D.C.

Ashford, Serena, to President Roosevelt, March 9, 1934. National Recovery Administration Files, Library of Congress, Washington, D.C.

Unsigned to President Roosevelt, January 13, 1939; Workers Council of Colored People to Harry Hopkins, October 12, 1937, both from Works Project Administration Files, W89, Box 11, Moorland–Spingarn Research Collection, Howard University, Washington, D.C.

"Women Stage Protest Parade: Urge Boycott of White Store." *Negro World*, May 2, 1931. "The Harlem Housewives Band Together to Emancipate Race." *Negro World*, May 16, 1931.

USING THE STATE

Christman, Elisabeth. "What Do Working Women Say?" National Women's Trade Union League Files, Tamiment Library, New York University, New York, New York.

Shallcross, Ruth. "Shall Married Women Work?" National Federation of Business and Professional Women's Clubs, Public Affairs Pamphlet No. 40, New York.

1940–1955

THE WAR

Lapin, Eve. *Mothers in Overalls*. New York: Workers Library Publ., 1943.

Jefferson, Richard R. "Negro Employment in St. Louis War Production." *Opportunity* 22.3 (July–September 1944).

Clawson, Augusta. *Shipyard Diary of a Woman Welder*. New York: Penguin, 1944. Copyright © 1944 by Penguin Books Inc. Reprinted by permission of Viking Penguin, a division of Penguin Books USA Inc.

Holliday, Pvt. Nellie R., to Truman K. Gibson, February 26, 1944. Army G-1 Women's Army Corps Decimal File, 1942–1946, File H, National Archives.

Blood, Kathryn. *Community Services for Women War Workers*. Washington, D.C.: Women's Bureau Publication No. 5, February 1944.

Interview with Mary Tsukamoto. Reprinted by permission from *Dignity: Lower Income Women Tell of Their Lives and Struggles: Oral Histories*, comp. Fran Leeper Buss. Ann Arbor: University of Michigan Press, 1985. Copyright © 1985 by Fran Leeper Buss. Reprinted by permission of The University of Michigan Press.

THE FEMININE MYSTIQUE AND THE REALITY

Women Workers in Ten War Production Areas and Their Postwar Employment Plans. Washington, D.C.: Women's Bureau Bulletin No. 209, 1946.

"I Denied My Sex." *True Romance*, April 1954. Reprinted by permission of Sterling/Macfadden.

Cowley, Joyce. "Working Mothers and Delinquency." *The Militant* 12 Sept. 1955.

Interview with Loretta "Ret" Coller. In *My Country, My Right to Serve: Experiences of Gay Men and Women in the Military, World War II to the Present*, ed. MaryAnn Humphrey. New York: HarperCollins, 1990. Copyright © 1990 by MaryAnn Humphrey. Reprinted by permission of HarperCollins Publishers Inc.

U.S. Congress, Senate. Committee on Labor and Public Welfare. *Labor Management Relations in the Southern Textile Manufacturing Industry. Hearings before the Subcommittee on Labor-Management Relations of the Committee on Labor and Public Welfare*, 81st. Congress, 2nd. Session, August 21–24, 1950.

Erazo, Blanca Vazquez. "The Stories Our Mothers Tell: Projections-of-Self in the Stories of Puerto Rican Garment Workers." *Oral History Review* 16.2 (Fall 1988): 23–28. Originally from Centro de Estudios Puertorriquenos Working Papers Series. Reprinted by permission of Blanca Vasquez Erazo and *Oral History Review*.

1955—Present

CONTINUING PATTERNS

Abel, Emily K., and Margaret K. Nelson. "Mothering Others' Children." In *Signs* 15.3 (1990): 586–605. Copyright © 1990. Reprinted by permission of The University of Chicago Press.

Interview with Lidia Sanchez. In *Mexican Voices/American Dreams: An Oral History of Mexican Immigration to the United States*, ed. Marilyn P. Davis. New York: Holt and Co., 1990. Copyright © 1990 by Marilyn P. Davis. Reprinted by permission of Henry Holt and Company, Inc.

"Prostitution I: Trying to Make a Living," adapted by Phaye Poliakoff. In *Speaking for Ourselves: Women of the South*, ed. Maxine Alexander. New York: Pantheon, 1984. Copyright © 1984 by Maxine Alexander. Reprinted by permission of Pantheon Books, a division of Random House, Inc.

Josefowitz, Natasha. "Impressions from an Office." In *Is This Where I Was Going?* copyright © 1983 by Natasha Josefowitz. Reprinted by permission of Warner Books/New York.

"Facts on Working Women: Women With Work Disabilities." Washington, D.C.: U.S. Women's Bureau Publication No. 92.2, March 1992.

Russo, Nancy Felipe, and Mary Jansen. "Women Work and Disability: Opportunities and Challenges." In *Women with Disabilities: Essays in Psychology, Culture, and Politics*, eds. Michelle Fine and Adrienne Asch. Philadelphia: Temple University Press, 1988. Copyright © 1988 by Temple University Press. Reprinted by permission of Temple University Press.

O'Neill, Molly. "Drop the Mop, Bless the Mess: The Decline of Housekeeping." *The New York Times*, April 11, 1993: 1, 18. Copyright © 1993 by The New York Times Company. Reprinted by permission.

DEINDUSTRIALIZATION

Rimer, Sara. "A Test for Women Who Build Cars." *The New York Times*, October 12, 1992: D1,3. Copyright © 1992 by The New York Times Company. Reprinted by permission.

Letters on Home Work, 1984. Wage and Hour Division, Department of Labor, National Archives, Washington, D.C.

Reiter, Ester. *Making Fast Food: From the Frying Pan into the Fryer.* Montreal: McGill University Press, 1991. Copyright © 1991 by Ester Reiter. Reprinted by permission of McGill University Press.

Kilborn, Peter T. "Lives Upside Down to Help a World Go Round." *The New York Times*, May 16, 1992: 1, 8–9. Copyright © 1992 by The New York Times Company. Reprinted by permission.

THE MOVEMENTS

Tillmon, Johnnie. "Welfare Is a Women's Issue." *Liberation News Service*, no. 415, February 26, 1972.

Vogel, Alfred. "Your Clerical Workers Are Ripe for Unionism." *Harvard Business Review* 49 (March–April 1971). Reprinted by permission.

Interview with Rose Melendez, police officer. In *Hard-Hatted Women: Stories of Struggle and Success in the Trades*, ed. Molly Martin. Seattle: Seal Press, 1988. Reprinted by permission of Seal Press.

Frank, Miriam. "How (and Why) to Organize Lesbian/Gay Union Committees." *Labor Notes*, March 1993. Reprinted by permission of Miriam Frank.

NEW INITIATIVES IN WORKERS' ORGANIZATION

Evans, Sara M., and Barbara J. Nelson. "Comparable Worth in Minnesota: Implementing an Innovative Wage Policy." *Northwest Report* (Fall 1986): 18–21. Reprinted by permission of the authors.

Kenney, Sally Jane. *Reproductive Hazards and Exclusionary Policies in the United States and Britain.* Ann Arbor: University of Michigan Press, 1992. Copyright © 1992 by Sally Jane Kenney. Reprinted by permission of The University of Michigan Press.

Interview with Cecilia Rodriquez. In *Dignity and Daily Bread: New Forms of Economic Organizing among Poor Women in the Third World and in the First*, ed. Sheila Rowbotham and Swasti Mitter. London, New York: Routledge, 1994, p. 44. Reprinted by permission of the authors.

Kantrowitz, Barbara, et al. "Striking a Nerve," from *Newsweek*, October 21, 1991: 34–40. Copyright © 1991, Newsweek, Inc. All rights reserved. Reprinted by permission.

"Statement of Professor Anita F. Hill to the Senate Judiciary Committee, October 11, 1991," S. Hrg. 102–1084, part 4. Washington, D.C.: GPO, 1993.

Index

INDEX

INDEX